HEATH AND THE HEATHMEN

HEATH
and the Heathmen
Andrew Roth

Routledge & Kegan Paul
London

First published 1972
by Routledge & Kegan Paul Ltd
Broadway House, 68–74 Carter Lane,
London EC4V 5EL
Printed in Great Britain by
The Camelot Press Ltd, London and Southampton
© Andrew Roth 1972

ISBN 0 7100 7428 x (c)
ISBN 0 7100 7429 8 (p)

CONTENTS

ACKNOWLEDGMENTS   viii

INTRODUCTION: HEATH AND THE HEATHMEN   ix
MAN AND OPPORTUNITY   CARRY-OVER OF 'HEATHMEN'
NO IDEOLOGUE

1 **THE BUTTONED-UP PRIME MINISTER**   1
COMMANDER'S CONFRONTATION

2 **MOTHER'S PRIDE**   18
THE SCHOOLBOY SHAPE   TARGET: BALLIOL

3 **THE OPEN DOORS OF BALLIOL**   28
ORGAN SCHOLAR   POLITICAL COMPARTMENT   UNION
ACTIVIST   TUTORS' VIEWS   ESTABLISHED VOICE
NUREMBERG AWAKENING   CROSSING SWORDS WITH DALTON
THE EDEN TRAGEDY   HOMAGE TO SPAIN   OVERHANGING
CLOUD   AMERICAN TOUR

4 **THE RUNGS TO MASTER GUNNER**   43
WAITING FOR INVASION DAY   LEAVE WITH ATTLEE
THE SHOCK OF TORY DEFEAT   BECOMING HONOURABLE

5 **THE PURSUITS OF PEACE**   56
TIME OFF FOR WEDDINGS   BEXLEY BECKONS   NO KISS FOR
THE BRIDE   SECRET CHURCH JOURNALIST   MAMMON AFTER
GOD   THE PHENOMENAL CANDIDATE   ECONOMIC RIGHTIST
THOUGHTFUL ABROAD   APPROACHING ELECTION   TIGHT
COUNT

6 **BEING NOTICED IN THE CLASS OF '50**   71
THE CONSTITUENCY CONNECTION   REG THE 'RIGHT-HAND MAN'
ONE NATION/ONE NOTION   A BACHELOR'S FOREIGN 'MAIDEN'
HEADING SOUTH   BELATED CHRISTMAS PRESENT
TIME OFF FOR TERRITORIALS   MOTHER'S SHOCK
NO RECOUNT DOWN HERE

7 **PRAETORIAN MONK**   85
SUEZ ON THE HORIZON   CHURCHILL'S SECRET STROKE
AMERICAN EMBARRASSMENT   INVALUABLE DEPUTY   FAMILY
COMPARTMENT   OFF TO AFRICA   PRIMA DONNA HOLDS BACK
ANOTHER WAIT

8 **EDEN'S SCOURGE**   98
EDEN'S ABLE SERVANT   MIDDLE EASTERN FURY   ASWAN
CLASH   THE FAÇADE CRUMBLES   CRISIS NIGHT

9 **ON MACMILLAN'S CHAMPAGNE TRAIL**   112
FAILURE IN EUROPE   BANK RATE 'SCANDAL'   HEATH'S
NUCLEAR ADVICE   REVOLT OF THE TREASURY TRIO   HEATH
FALLS FLAT   THE UNEXPECTED BREAKTHROUGH   UPSETS IN
FRANCE AND JORDAN   ELECTION PREPARATIONS   LUCIFER
FALLS   OUT OF ACTION   CABINET FORMING
HAMMER AND TONGS

10 **BRIEFLY IN LABOUR**   133
NO DOUBT ABOUT COMPETENCE   PUBLIC RELATIONS
IN CABINET COMMITTEE   HAPPENINGS AND MISHAPS
THE SUDDEN CALL

11 **THE DOUBLE-HOBBLED 'Mr EUROPE'**   146
AFTER-CHRISTMAS INTERLUDES   MORE EUROPEAN 'MUSCLE'
ORDEAL OF THE TRAVELLING SALESMAN   GETTING UP COURAGE
THE GREEN LIGHT   CONGO HEADACHES   BETWEEN TWO
NARROW WALLS   MACMILLAN SLIPS   SEPTEMBER EFFORT
BACON AND EGGS

12 **OVERTAKING FROM BEHIND**   169
FIRST HEATH BOOM   CHARLEMAGNE PRIZE   SECRET
ISLAND VISIT   LONGEST LABEL   THE ANTI-RPM WAR
CAMPAIGNING TO SURVIVE   SIR ALEC REDISPOSES
THE DROP-ALEC CAMPAIGN

13 **THE 'SICILIAN VENDETTA'**   187
UNUSUAL VACATION   OVERHANGING ELECTION   ABANDONED
BY COLLEAGUES   WELL-COVERED VACATION
COLD DOUCHE RETURN   RHODESIAN SUSPICIONS   THE CALL
FOR HOPELESS BATTLE   SAVED FROM THE COUNT-OUT
THE RUNNING FIGHT WITH POWELL   BATTLES OVER RACE
THE ROAD TO SELSDON PARK   THE SUDDEN DROP

14 **ATTACKING ON THE RIGHT FLANK** 210
MISLEADING PICTURE   OVERSHADOWING ECONOMICS
REVERSING WITH ROLLS-ROYCE

15 **TACKING TOWARDS THE TARGET** 223
VOLTE FACE   DOWN FROM THE MUSICAL SUMMIT   CLOSER
TO FRANCE, COOLER TO USA   MINTOFF STANDOFF   FOCUS ON
BRUSSELS   BACK TO 'REALITIES'   RECOIL FROM
LONDONDERRY   EATING HUMBLE REGIONAL PIE

NOTES 235

INDEX 243

ACKNOWLEDGMENTS

The author would like to express his grateful thanks to those of Mr Heath's family, friends, brother officers, Cabinet and party colleagues who have helped him to discover how much more there is to the Prime Minister than has been allowed to meet the public eye.

I much appreciate the generosity of the Editor of the *Bexleyheath Observer* and the staff of the cuttings library at Conservative Central Office who have amplified the resources available at Parliamentary Profiles.

As usual, my colleagues in the Lobby and Parliamentary Press Gallery have been helpful with their recollections and assessments on top of what they had previously committed to print.

I must also express my appreciation to my wife for allowing her toleration to be stretched to the utmost during my prolonged communion with the typewriter.

INTRODUCTION
HEATH AND THE HEATHMEN –
THE LONELINESS OF THE
LONG-DISTANCE CLIMBERS

Had Edward Heath submitted his qualifications to the tender ministra-
tions of a computer on returning to civilian life in 1946, among the
last jobs it would have considered him suitable for was the one he came
to hold twenty-four years later. A chair at an Army music school,
perhaps. But the Tory Prime Minister of Britain?

Despite Balliol and his Presidency of the Oxford Union, his other
disabilities would have ruled him out. How could the son of a carpenter
and a housemaid hope to shine in a party then led by the son of Lord
Randolph Churchill and the grandson of the Duke of Marlborough?
How could a grammar school boy rise past the class-conscious sons
of Eton and Harrow? (Even after Heath became leader of the Tories
in 1965, Old Etonian Lord Hailsham was fond of confiding, 'Heath
envies me two things. First, I am a *gentleman*. Second, I have a *first*-
class degree.')

Snobbish regrets over his 'over-promotion' have surfaced whenever
he has threatened to fail to produce the results demanded. 'The trouble
is that Ted is not really a politician, 'complained his longtime sponsor
Lord Swinton. 'He doesn't see the situation as it really is, but as he
would *like* it to be.' After Heath lost in 1966 and then turned out to be
the least popular Opposition Leader in three decades of Gallup polling,
only the sharp drop in Labour's support silenced those trying to drop
him. When Labour again seemed headed for victory early in June 1970,
his closest friends were resigned to seeing jettisoned the man who had
seemed almost computer-selected to oust Harold Wilson.

Computers, of course, are only as good as those who program
them. And in politics in Britain, the pretence has long been that the
main talent required is ability for verbal jousting, for conducting
a parliamentary pillow fight modelled on the proceedings at the Oxford
Union. There Heath could have pointed to the competence he showed
as President of the Union, although he could not compare with, say,
Michael Foot or Christopher Mayhew at the Union debates. Although
often a competent speaker, Heath has more often been tedious, seldom
brilliant or capable of moving an audience which has not already put

on its roller skates. He cannot show in words the emotion he can show in music. And he is normally too 'buttoned-up' to convey his real feelings to his audience.

What proved our imaginary computer so wrong? What produced the first Tory Prime Minister of proletarian origins? What enabled him to bring into his Cabinet four other Ministers – Anthony Barber, Geoffrey Rippon, Peter Walker and Margaret Thatcher – from the same sort of lower middle-class and upper working-class background? What has changed since the fifties, when it was so much more slippery for Ernest Marples and Reginald Bevins to climb the 'greasy pole' of advance?

Part, but not the whole, of the explanation is due to the greater number of 'ladders' that have been put in place, making it easier for the ambitious to climb the social pyramid. Heath was lucky that a good grammar school – the pre-war ladder for the talented sons of modest families – was on hand near his Broadstairs home. He was again lucky that Balliol, which has long considered itself a training ground for an intellectual élite, had so broadened its social catchment area under its famous Master, A. D. Lindsay.

The Second World War, of course, was more like an escalator than a ladder. A nation fighting for survival has to lower its class barriers and try to promote the more able instead of the better-connected, as is normal in peacetime. Without fighting a glamorous war in the heavy anti-aircraft, Heath wound up in the prestigious Honourable Artillery Company, in which he later became a Lieutenant-Colonel. To have had a 'good war' was for his generation and its elders a better passport to advancement than a first-class Honours degree.

All these factors help to explain how Heath entered the House with the vintage Class of '50. That intake in the Commons was exceptional in the large proportion of its new Tory entrants who were ex-officers – and who were professionally competent and had made their way without benefit of family wealth and connections.

Yet Heath's extreme competence in the Whips' Office – even his outstanding achievements during the Suez crisis – hardly suggested any peak beyond that of a middle-rank Minister. When the swash-buckling journalist, Henry Fairlie, first predicted in 1959 that Heath not only *intended* to be Prime Minister but *could achieve it*, he later felt it necessary to backpedal for some time.

MAN AND OPPORTUNITY

Heath was able to surprise his detractors and even some of his friends because of the conjunction of two factors: the historical opportunity and the daring man of destiny.

By the fifties, when Britain was emerging from the immediate post-war crises, a sharp dilemma confronted its governing class. The bleeding of the Second World War had accelerated Britain's relative decline and the emergence of the two super-Powers. At the same time it had accelerated the growth of nationalist movements which were taking control of the Asian and African members of the old Empire, as well as semi-colonies in the oil-rich Arab world, as elsewhere. This inevitably meant the relative decline of protected markets in the Empire, now renamed the Commonwealth.

As early as 1946, Tory leaders realized that they had an historic choice. On the one hand they could preside over a slow relative decline of Britain's economy and international influence. On the other hand they could daringly create a new 'super-Power' in Western Europe. Their recognition of the potentialities of Europe were reflected in Churchill's Zurich speech in 1946. Churchill was supported in this European crusade by Duncan Sandys and Harold Macmillan, who helped godfather the Council of Europe and its Consultative Assembly which took shape in 1949.

The problem of the traditional Tory governing class – as illustrated in the sprawling memoirs of Harold Macmillan – was its languid indecisiveness. Once back in office in 1951 it was easier to sit on the well-upholstered 'stool' preferred by Sir Anthony Eden, with its three 'legs': the Commonwealth, the Anglo-American alliance and Western Europe. The Anglo-American leg could split over Suez; Dr Adenauer and President de Gaulle could make the West European leg unpredictable; and revolting nationalists had the bad habit of pulling bits of the Commonwealth out from under Britain. But the three-legged stool nevertheless helped preserve the illusion of world-wide influence.

Although a far-sighted statesman like Harold Macmillan could be as misleading as any other politician, he was fairly realistic in what he confided to his diary – and to his Chief Whip and confidant, Edward Heath. Macmillan was unscrupulously cynical in exploiting his wartime relations with Eisenhower and de Gaulle to exert a bit more leverage on world affairs. But he himself was fairly clear – and Heath even more so in his detached position – that he was using cleverness as an inadequate substitute for waning power.

As the EEC began to succeed as both an economic and a quasi-political grouping in the sixties, a conviction grew in the City, among senior civil servants and in the upper reaches of the Conservative Party, that the 1947–9 pro-European orientation of Churchill, Macmillan and Sandys had been correct and its subsequent abandonment an error.

The major problem, however, was to overcome the enormous inertia of traditionalism. It was not until 1960 that the top mandarins in the Treasury and the Foreign Office went 'European'. The balance in the Cabinet was not tipped towards EEC entry until 1961, with R. A. Butler, who chaired the Cabinet Committee on the subject, slipping back frequently thereafter.

It is only under conditions of indecisive, long-drawn-out warfare that one can comprehend the emergence of so single-minded and hard-cutting a politician as Heath. The Conservative Party, having slowed itself into immobility as a result of its indecisiveness over EEC entry, wanted a 'Ted the Knife' to cut its Gordian Knot.

Although Heath was not from within the 'magic circle', he was given his opportunity by those who were. In the Whips' Office he had long been an understudy but he had befriended each successive casting director as well as those who whispered in their ears. It was no accident that Lord Swinton, one of the Tory Establishment's most skilled intriguers, was in Heath's corner from the earliest days.

'The rise of Mr Heath . . . tells us much not only about the man himself but about the Conservative Party,' wrote David Wood in *The Times* of 29 July 1965, when Heath became its Leader. 'It is a party that has chosen Mr Heath at least in part because he will do rough things roughly that they will sometimes not like to have done.

'Yet the picture would be incomplete without making one point about Mr Heath. For all his contemporary, Wilsonian classlessness, he has always had a knack of commanding the confidence of any "magic circle" with which he has had to deal, or wanted to influence.

'You do not become President of the Oxford Union without knowing how to manage men and make yourself useful and agreeable to them. You do not serve succeeding Conservative Prime Ministers as Chief Whip without knowing how to play the smoking-room as well as the political game. You do not stand very close to three Prime Ministers in succession – Sir Anthony Eden, Mr Macmillan and Sir Alec Douglas-Home – without having adaptable qualities that go far beyond intellectual or ministerial ability, or political ambition.

'The truth is that of all the outstanding new men who entered the Commons in 1950 and 1951 to refurbish the tarnished Tory image, Mr Heath is pre-eminently the one who had the best rapport with the

Conservative Party's ruling inner group, through one change after another. His is the kind of classlessness that takes on the protective colouring of the company he keeps, and the Tory Praetorian Guard now see him put on the Leaders' mantle with no special trauma. His energy and his pace will disturb them on occasion, but the orientation of his Conservatism will not.'

The Tory gentlemen accepted Heath as captain knowing him a highly professional player, and knowing the risks as well. He had shown, in fighting James Callaghan's 1965 Budget, that he rather despised the gentlemanly dilettantes of Eton and Harrow. There were no public school boys in his 'task force', made up of Anthony Barber, Peter Walker, Peter Emery, William Clark and John Hall. But it was wholly professional and extremely combative in its operations.

CARRY-OVER OF 'HEATHMEN'

One of the signs of Heath's dynamism was the naming of four 'Heathmen' to his Cabinet, the first time so many non-Establishment Tories had risen so high. There were doubts about his judgment when, on the death of Iain Macleod, he named Anthony Barber to succeed him as Chancellor. Few suspected that the pleasant and slight-looking Mr Barber could make the Treasury mandarins and Inland Revenue jump through hoops. No such doubts, of course, had been expressed about the dynamism of the coldly efficient grocer's daughter, Mrs Margaret Thatcher. There was some amusement that Peter Walker, the son of an engineer turned grocer, was leaving to Old Etonian Julian Amery the difficult job of pushing through the increase in council house rents for workers on average pay. But it was undeniable that the dynamism of the 'Heathmen' was producing sharper confrontations with the militant working class. There were no doubts, only second thoughts.

The Conservative Establishment has long feared the lack of objectivity of the 'back-street Tories'. The third of the working class that votes Conservative, and the lower middle-class Tories as well, tend to be bitter about the 'privileges' of council-house tenants, partly paid for by the rates of the semi-detached Tories. They were willing to give Mr Heath his head only because of the new spectre which haunted them: that of the giant trade unions now under leftwing leadership. The staunchly anti-Communist moderates Ernest Bevin and William Carron had been replaced by Frank Cousins and Hugh Scanlon at the head of transport and engineering workers. The days of agreement on foreign affairs and appeasement through small wage concessions were over. The need for tougher resistance to more militant trade union leadership was accepted.

Some of the older members of the Tory Establishment fear that Heath risks too much on his confrontations. At the time of the miners' strike early in 1972, Harold Macmillan was privately critical of the tough tactics of the man he had done so much to sponsor. After Heath had had to capitulate, Macmillan tended to rub it in by telling him that Stanley Baldwin had advised: 'There are three groups that no British Prime Minister should provoke: the Vatican, the Treasury and the miners. . . .' It was not a mistake that Heath was likely to make again, because he had shown the miners their real strength more effectively than any revolutionary handbook. Having made a wrong decision he immediately jettisoned it and tried to work out a new route to his familiar targets: a highly efficient and socially mobile new Britain at the head of a new West European super-Power.

NO IDEOLOGUE

Some observers, including Robert Rhodes James, appear to be under the illusion that Heath is an 'ideologue', a man long committed to pre-fixed theories. It is easy to see how this error has gained currency. Heath made a 'let's divide and rule Western Europe' maiden speech in 1950. He proclaimed himself an enthusiast for entry in the midst of his 1961–3 negotiations and thereafter. Therefore, it is widely (and incorrectly) assumed he has always been an enthusiastic European.

In fact this is wrong. Although he was effectively silenced in the House by his entry into the Whips' Office in 1951, this did not inhibit his speaking in his constituency. He gave talks almost every month on foreign affairs during the fifties. These showed that he was a serious and perceptive student of world developments; but they did not portray him as a European. Nor was this the impression of the liberal-internationalist Tories who became enthusiastic Europeans in the fifties. They would have been delighted to consider the Chief Whip one of them, but they had no reason to think he was. In fact, when Heath was selected as Lord Privy Seal and 'Mr Europe' in 1960, one of the main reasons given for his selection over, say, Peter Thorneycroft was that he was *not* a 'Eurofanatic'.

Heath cannot be accused of being an 'ideologue', partly because he does not understand even the ideology he claims to hold. He keeps telling people how much he admires Disraeli, but that is largely because Disraeli too was an 'outsider' who reached the top without the background of wealth or a public school. Heath fails entirely to understand what Disraeli's 'One Nation' concept was about. At its essence the idea was that the Conservative gentry would protect the working class against the rapacious industrialists, then in control of the Liberal Party.

It is difficult to understand how Heath can be regarded as an ideologue after comparing his second year in No. 10 with his first year there. Initially he gave the *impression* of being wholly committed to a classic prewar capitalist ideology: let government disengage from industry; let industrial 'lame ducks' go to the wall; no regional subsidies. This did form a cohesive ideology suitable for a pre-war Tory or the son of a small entrepreneur.

But one after another these notions were jettisoned like soiled garments as their execution threatened Heath's continuation in power and Britain's entry into the EEC. Heath rediscovered Keynes, turned reflationist, turned 'lame ducks' into golden geese and gave industrial subsidies to the regions. He even began donning, slightly dyed, the industrial-aid garments of the hated Harold Wilson.

Heath is easily mistaken for an ideologue, because, as Alan Watkins has put it, 'he has a gift, if that is the phrase, for dressing up his decisions in the language of dogma'.[1] He has decided that the way to rebuild Britain as a world Power is to make it the leader of Western Europe over the next decade. This is not ideology, it is a risky strategy for replacing the lost Empire with the new 'Empire of the white Wogs' as one Tory humorist has it.

What Heath has is the special quality of the grown-up school prefect who feels that he is fulfilling his destiny and the nation's at the same time. This provides the self-confidence, the drive, which his less obsessional colleagues think are needed to shake up Britain's lethargic society.

Heath's Establishment colleagues put up with his vices – his egocentric silences, his arrogance – because of his dynamic virtues. They regard Heath as Abraham Lincoln regarded his best general, Ulysses S. Grant. When abstainers complained that General Grant drank very heartily, Lincoln asked them to find out the brand so that he could send the same whisky to his other generals. When you ask Cabinet Ministers close to Heath how they can stand his single-mindedness, even when wrong-headed, they come back with 'It's better than the indecisiveness from which we suffered before!'

Heath is regarded by his knowledgeable colleagues as a 'political Montgomery', a military-style commanding officer who produces results despite his idiosyncrasies. There is no doubt that he is in complete control, and that he is supremely confident. For that, they are willing to put up with Heath's peculiarities, his wooden-soldier gestures, his speeches like wartime communiqués.

It is because Heath has a military decisiveness that he has been able to knit together in the Cabinet a curious coalition of the grammar school 'Heathmen' and those members of the traditional Establishment who feel that his type of 'political Montgomery' is what the Tories need today. People outside may think it scandalous that a government should jettison in its second year the very principles thought essential and distinctive in the first year. But the target has always been the same: entering the EEC with the economy at full stretch. To enter the Market with a stagnant economy afflicted with a million unemployed and galloping inflation was a sure recipe for disaster. So the Cabinet wheeled about and went smartly in the reverse direction, with Heath still very much in command and boasting that his government had pumped more into the economy than any previous one. This may have been an ideological U-turn, but when the total of unemployed dropped by 100,000 below the million mark in May 1972, Heath's colleagues were happy. 'What did they want us to do?' asked one Minister, 'go over the cliff with flags flying?'

Heath did not see himself as the hero of a suicide mission. Like Montgomery, he sees himself as the hero of a success story: a 'greater Britain in a greater Europe', as he puts it. Heath's hero-image of himself is revealed in various ways. One was the way in which he was able to sit at his Steinway in the Albany facing a large, almost overbearing oil painting of himself. Another is his exaggeration of his successes and the dangers attending them. Thus, the *only* vote for entry to the Common Market which he quotes is the largest: the majority of 112 on 28 October 1971. Similarly, he tends to recall only the narrowest majority on the repeal of RPM in 1964 – the margin of one vote on a single clause. This, he feels, entitles him to say, 'I got through the repeal of RPM on a majority of one!'[2]

Heath's difficulty is that his hero-image of himself is shared by a small group of people around him in his Cabinet and a larger number in the House and in the Tory party in the country. The much larger number of Tories and supporters of EEC entry who would *like* to cheer him on have great difficulty because they do not really know who he is or where precisely he is trying to take them.

It is comparatively easy for a military leader to inspire confidence in his troops, if he has military competence and tries to establish communication with his men. In North Africa, it was win with Monty or be driven into the Nile by Rommel. Persuading a tradition-ridden country to make a clean break with its past in a whole series of areas requires a much more exceptional talent. It requires the talent to reach the *whole* nation in peacetime in a way that Churchill was able to do in wartime. To do this you have to have at least two qualities. One is the quality of detachment, of being 'above it all' and being widely accepted as being interested in the welfare of all equally. This has been recognized by Heath in his increasingly frequent references to 'the national interest'. His difficulty is in having *his* interpretation of 'the national interest' accepted as impartial. He clearly believes in encouraging efficient business and helping the helpless while resisting the demands of well-organized trade unionists as 'inflationary'. One does not see this son of a carpenter persuading, say, the woodworkers' union that his view is as 'impartial' as, for example, that of the late Sir Walter Monckton.

Heath's is one of the tragedies of long-distance climbers. There is wide recognition at the end, which makes up for the loneliness en route. But once you have been accepted as a sharp tool by those among whom you have climbed, you are no longer acceptable among the people from whom you come. Heath was born and brought up only a few miles from the Kent coalfield. But in the winter of 1972 it was apparent that it could have been light-years away.

1 THE BUTTONED-UP PRIME MINISTER

Does *anyone* know Heath?

> Conservative MPs and Ministers,
> almost in chorus

It was a revealing incident on the fringe of Edward Heath's ink-bespattered signature of the Treaty of Accession to the EEC, on 22 January 1972. His closest friend, Madron Seligman – whom he shares with Roy Jenkins – approached him: 'A lot of people, particularly pressmen, have been asking me when you became a "European". Just when was it?' 'It happened when I was twelve,' joked the Prime Minister in reply. 'I looked out from Broadstairs across the Channel to the cliffs of France. . . .'

The fact that his oldest friend, with whom he has been travelling to the Continent for over thirty years, could not answer or secure an answer to this question is symptomatic of Heath's curiously 'buttoned-up' approach. It is even more difficult to pin down accurately what *kind* of 'European' he is, after a dozen years in the spotlight on this issue. There are all sorts, from liberal internationalists to reformed imperialists, anxious to create an 'Empire of the white Wogs'.

Although Heath has been a publicly committed 'European' since his maiden speech in 1950 and the Tory 'crusader in chief' since 1961, even those closest to him in the Conservative hierarchy and outside on this issue have difficulty in defining his commitment precisely. All that one can conclude is that he is convinced that Western Europe can only pull its potential weight in the world if it is drawn by a three-horse 'Troika' of Britain, France and Germany, with Britain as the lead horse. Although he has spoken often of the economic benefits of West European unity, those closest to his thinking are sure he is preoccupied above all with peace and the politico-military problem of enhancing Western Europe's ability to play a role on the world stage comparable to the Americans and Russians. But whenever one tries to put flesh on this skeleton of Heath's thinking one runs up against a thick, rubbery wall. A pro-European peer, asked what sort of 'European' the Prime Minister is, answered with some asperity: 'People assume that, just because we are on the same side, I know something about him. . . .'

All of this is a reflection of the Prime Minister's long-standing barriers. Penetrating the enigma of his character is no new parliamentary or press game. 'What do you make of Ted?' was a constant refrain among the Heaths and Pantonys in his family. His young friends were struck by his long silences and his early talent for closing down conversational openers. Even at Oxford, where he was at his happiest and most relaxed, many of his contemporaries noticed a fence of restraint. In the wartime anti-aircraft battery he commanded, his gunners were puzzled by him, according to an admiring fellow-officer: 'They knew his good qualities, utter honesty and candour, coupled with undoubted ability, but I don't really think they ever got on the same wavelength. He was something of an enigma to them, in the same way as he does not get across to the ordinary man in the street.'

Right across the years and in all activities, the overwhelming majority of those who have tried to puzzle out the enigma of Edward Heath have bounced off. 'I've worked for him for years,' was one reaction, 'but I knew him no better at the end of three years than I did after three hours.' 'Heath is one of the most impenetrable people in public life,' remarked one TV interviewer. 'I had to see him a dozen times for a programme. Instead of beginning from where we left off – as is normal with most people you interview – each time I had to begin from square one.' 'It's as if he had a moat around him,' added another.

Heath protects his personality and his inner thoughts by two types of defence. One is the deep moat of silence. The other is the high wall of trite and stereotyped phrases. Like many who barricade themselves in, Heath has become the prisoner of his own defences. Normally, when he appears on TV, he can resemble a rubbery glove-puppet. The tight mouth moves, the heavy jowls sag, the sharp nose points. But all that emerges is a string of trite politicians' phrases which neither explain nor move. It is only on the exceptional occasion, where he is relaxed and speaking off the cuff on, say, Europe or music, that the public can see that there is 'another Heath', a warmer and more attractive man than he allows himself to appear.

For Heath, as for most insecure people, his failure to communicate is part of his defence mechanism. In a hostile world – particularly the political world full of hostile opponents – the less you say, the less can be used against you. The politician's equivalent of silence is responding to questions with a well-constructed statement full of open-ended clichés. Heath has found himself less vulnerable when speaking from behind a barrier of stereotyped phrases than when speaking from the heart. When, in 1961, he spoke of 'when' Britain joined the Common Market, instead of 'when and if', he was attacked for long weeks. The 'at a stroke' phrase in the 1970 election – which was not even his – gave his Labour opponents a target for months, if not years.

Elaborate defence mechanisms are normally a result of insecurity, and tend to be dismantled with the growth of self-assurance. Since becoming the first Tory of proletarian origins to make it to No. 10 Downing Street, Heath has begun to relax in the warmth of power. He has become more expansive and natural in the Commons, more willing to use humour against his detested adversary, Harold Wilson. People who used to know him in the Whips' Office – where he was far from matey – were surprised at the extent to which he had relaxed when they entertained him at Boodles' in 1970. One of the signs has been the lengthening of his sideboards into a hair-style a far cry from the short-back-and-sides Heath of yesteryear. He is also much less cautious about his drinking. He no longer limits himself to one drink. And it no longer has to be *malt* whisky.

Heath would be relatively easy to understand if he were simply shy and impenetrable. In fact, he *does* unbutton, to a limited number of persons and under a limited number of circumstances. He has long been able to unwind with old Balliol friends. With wartime brother officers. With his agent, Reg Pye, and his wife. With Lord Aldington and his wife. With Madron Seligman and his wife. With Teddy Denman and his wife. He can laugh with them and – quite typically – once he relaxes he falls asleep on them. The description 'Edward Heath slept here' is the rare privilege of a handful of people in whose company he is so much at ease that the removal of tensions puts him to sleep, sometimes for days.

Heath is a great believer in specialized relationships. In No. 10 he will talk about one sort of problem to one member of his staff, about another to a different one, without overlapping. He will talk politics to political professionals. He will talk music to professional musicians, or music critics or a handful of knowledgeable or talented amateurs like himself or Lord Boyle. He will talk about army days to wartime buddies or fellow Territorials in the Honourable Artillery Company. But he will very seldom violate his watertight compartments. It is only the rare politician, such as Lord Boyle, who is encouraged to discuss music as well as politics. For the most part the Prime Minister likes to surround himself with capable and loyal satellites, while remaining at the core of his solar system. His style owes much to his wartime experience as Adjutant and Commanding Officer of Honourable Artillery Company regiments, postwar. 'Ted functions army-style,' says an old friend. 'He concentrates on the problems to be solved.'

A commanding officer can be friendly with some of the officers he has come to rely on, but not *too* friendly. He can take their advice when they persuade him – as he did in having the vote on Europe in October 1971, instead of July. But they must not be allowed to get 'too big for their boots'. Thus, when someone close to Heath 'leaked' the fact that Nicholas Ridley and Sir John Eden had to be sacked, in what looked like an attempt to force Heath's hand, he gave the two threatened Ministers another seven months in their offices. It is probably no accident that his style – as well as his 'buttoned-up' character – has a similarity to another middle-rank officer: Major Attlee.

Heath's relationship with his closest lieutenants is symbolized by his ban on smoking in the Cabinet. The first postwar ban on smoking in the Cabinet Room was imposed by Attlee in 1947, at the suggestion of the Chancellor of the Exchequer, Hugh Dalton, who wanted to emphasize the need to save on dollar imports. Winston Churchill reintroduced smoking in 1951. Pipe-smoker Harold Wilson consulted his colleagues in 1964; they voted to allow smoking.[1] Heath, a lifelong non-smoker, decided in 1970 not to permit smoking during Cabinet meetings, despite the barely concealed cravings of his Cabinet colleagues.

Sometimes Heath's lifelong tendency to organize people along lines that appeal to *him* can be enlightening as well as hilarious. There was a businessmen's luncheon at Chequers. After brandy and cigars Heath suggested, 'Would you like to listen to some Bruckner ?' Without finding out whether one of his favourite composers was everybody's choice, he marched them in to sample the delights of his hi-fi. It was like a regimental 'church parade', for the good of their musical souls.

COMMANDER'S CONFRONTATION

As a contrast to the gimmicky styles of Macmillan and Wilson, Heath's army-style command posture has brought him both the warmest support and the most bitter criticism. It has thrilled those who have longed for a simpler order to be restored to an increasingly complex society with fudged and overlapping lines of authority. It has frightened those who have become convinced that such confrontations – as in the postmen's, miners' and railwaymen's strikes of 1971 and 1972 – can tear apart a country that can only be run on the basis of substantial consensus. The latter have been puzzled that the most dramatic eyeball-to-eyeball confrontations have been encouraged by a Prime Minister who has often expressed his admiration for Disraeli and was a member of the 'One Nation Group'.

From the moment Edward Heath entered 10 Downing Street, he was determined to follow a policy of confrontation. Where the controversy has raged is over his *intentions*. Because most of his public confrontations have been with the unions, it has been fairly easy for his opponents to tag his Government as 'the most reactionary since the war'. On the other hand, his close political friends, none of them reactionary, are convinced that he will emerge as the most *radical* Prime Minister since the war. It is symptomatic of his preference for decisive action rather than clear words that both views can be held by equally intelligent and perceptive people.

Heath *is* a radical in the sense that he wants to replace the old, comfortable class-ridden Britain by a tougher, more competitive society with better rewards for the able. This means he is as hostile to managerial incompetents as to lazy, tea-drinking workers. He almost tore the Tory Party apart in 1964 by his zealous effort to force price competition by abolishing Resale Price Maintenance. His initial resistance to providing crutches for 'lame ducks' was part of that effort. Part of his enthusiasm for entry into the Common Market derives from his belief that intensified competition will stimulate those worthy of survival and purge the incompetents. It is not, however, something which he would be likely to say, even if he were naturally more expansive. He is the Leader of the Conservative Party, largely financed and supported by a governing class containing a high proportion of hereditary incompetents. 'I can tell you he has no time for hereditary aristocrats,' said one peer, 'except for Lord Carrington.'

Heath has been compelled to be silent about his explosive plans to bring efficiency to the Establishment because, in the words of one aide, he has played the role of the 'classic infiltrator who looks perfectly at home in the best houses'. As a Tory of modest background, he has long enjoyed the backing of leading members of the Conservative Establishment: Lord Swinton, Harold Macmillan, the Churchills. An 'infiltrator' risks all if he explains where he plans to place the explosives.

It is partly because he lacks a solid social base that he has tended to use internally a confrontation technique more suitable to diplomacy. There is a striking resemblance between Heath's domestic 'brinkmanship' and the sharp alternatives posed by President Kennedy to the Soviet Union over Laos in 1961 and the Cuban missile crisis of 1962. Kennedy offered the alternatives of expanded conflict or graceful withdrawal. In both cases the Russians settled for what Kennedy wanted: a neutralized Laos and the withdrawal of Soviet missiles from Cuba. Heath clearly admired Kennedy's willingness to take risks to achieve what he deemed desirable. Unfortunately for Heath, his intelligence on the toughness of the miners and the extent of their support among the general public was not as good as Kennedy's intelligence about Russian intentions.

THE DRIVE OF A POLITICAL MONTGOMERY

Heath has attracted support, often unexpected support, within his own party because he has been seen as 'Ted the Knife', able to cut Gordian knots, and carve a clear path for EEC entry. He was chosen as Leader in 1965 not for his charm or public appeal but for his capacity for total commitment and for his 'drive'. He was to be the Tories' political equivalent of Field-Marshal Montgomery in wartime: a commander who got things done. Heath showed his drive in 1964 by getting the end of RPM through the Cabinet and on the lawbooks, when a previous Minister had failed to get it through the Cabinet.

Heath's 'drive' is composed of two interactive qualities. One is his complete confidence in his own ability to identify objectives and then, by asking the best qualified, to work out methods of achieving them. His self-confidence is such that it can very easily seem like arrogance, both to his opponents on any argument and to his friends. When old Tory peers go around complaining, 'But he's so *arrogant*!', they often mean that he has not accepted the views of his elders and 'betters'. But his friends can complain too. 'He's trying to teach *me* about music,' Lord Boyle has been known to mutter.

Because politics permits of so few objective tests apart from winning elections, Heath had to prove his ability in another field: yachting. For most yachtsmen, his transformation into a world-beater in this field is little short of miraculous. Skilled sailors who saw him moving from dinghies to racing yachts in the late sixties winced in anticipated embarrassment because they knew *they* had learned their skills from a lifetime of 'messing around in boats'. Some took turns to participate in races where they lagged behind to avoid the 'humiliation' of having their upstart Leader come in last! Yet Heath had begun studying racing when he was already almost fifty. When he was elected Leader in 1965, at forty-nine, a TV company had put him on a boat to show him as a sportsman. But even at that late date he had difficulty bringing the dinghy about. Yet within four years he was able to win the 640-mile Sydney-to-Hobart ocean race. He showed the ability to select a brilliant racing crew and both learn from them and command their confidence.

Heath showed in yachting competition his ability to combine self-confidence with total commitment. He has shown this before in politics: in his dedication to keeping the Tories united despite the strains of Suez, in his pushing through of the end of Resale Price Maintenance over enormous internal opposition in 1964, in his drive to secure entry into the EEC in 1961–3 and again in 1970–2.

So total is his commitment, so dynamic his drive, that most of his enemies and some of his friends thought that he might 'explode' under the pressure of frustration. During the most frustrating years, 1966–70, he could get furious and 'snap people's heads off' but the widely-predicted 'breakdown' never occurred. One of the very important reasons for this was his special quality of relaxation. Although one of the most full-time politicians in the business, he always had one, and latterly two, 'safety valves'. He could always lose himself totally in music. And recently he has been able to immerse himself completely in competitive racing.

Heath is not the sort of person who 'enjoys' good music but whose mind wanders away to compose his next political speech while listening. He enters fully into the deeply emotional music to which he is committed. His musical centre of gravity is 'late romantic': Elgar, Richard Strauss, Mahler. This is music that emerged at the end of the nineteenth century when a long period of musical repression ended and emotional outpourings and self-revelation became the order of the musical day. Originally he could not indulge this preference because it was written for large orchestras. On the piano he tended to prefer Beethoven. On the organ he usually opted for Bach. He also loves Bruckner. But it is indicative of his musical character that the first time he had a chance to conduct a full orchestra, he chose Elgar's 'Cockaigne Overture'. Originally he was prejudiced against Richard Wagner. Like many anti-Fascists of his era, he conceived what he now considers to be an 'absurd prejudice' against Hitler's favourite composer; no Wagner operas were performed in Britain during the war. But of late he has become interested in Wagner's moving and dramatic music.

Music is one of the few things sure to unbutton Heath. This was illustrated in July 1970 when his two closest friends, Lord Aldington and Madron Seligman, threw a birthday party for him aboard a ship in the Thames. Care was taken to include only his closest friends among the thirty on board: only William Whitelaw and Lord Carrington from the Cabinet, only Ian Trethowan from the media. The party was rather stiff until Heath sat down at the organ that had been specially installed. An old Balliol friend of his, ex-diplomat Phil Kaiser, joked about this: 'You'll have to install an organ on the *Morning Star*!' 'You mean *Morning Cloud*!' corrected the Prime Minister's father, Will Heath.

Particularly since he fell seriously ill with jaundice in 1968, after a prolonged period of overwork, Heath has watched his health. He fought the 1959 election on half-bottles of champagne – on doctor's orders, of course – and when he was permitted to return to something stronger drank only malt whisky for a while.

He understands that he needs to 'switch off' completely with something like music or yachting. When you fish, he has explained to friends, you have time to think about your normal preoccupations. But when you are engaged in competitive boat racing – particularly on ocean-going yachts – you cannot think about anything else if you are out to win. And Heath has never been interested in anything but winning in competition. He has never taken his expensive yacht out for a day's cruise. He has only sailed it between ports – for a race – on one occasion; on that occasion the ship went aground, to the delight of his persistent critic, the Beaverbrook press. Since then the *Morning Cloud* has moved from race to race by a crew different from the one which races it.

Although he soon established his command over his first-rate racing crew, it took a lot longer for Heath to become friendly. Initially there was a gap like that between a talented amateur and a group of paid professionals. TV cameramen and producers who went to film Heath's achievements were struck by the fact that at the end of the race the crew went one way to drink and Heath was left on his own. On board ship, too, there was a gap initially. It was symbolized by the fact that, while the rugged crew slept in their underwear, originally Heath would prepare for bed in dressy pyjamas. 'All that's changed now,' says one of his crewmen. 'Heath now beds down in his Y-fronts like the rest of us!'

Although their husbands have been able to applaud Heath's yachting achievements as a demonstration of Tory and national virility, this has not been true of the traditional Tory matrons. There is, of course, a type of middle-aged, middle-class woman to whom any unencumbered bachelor is a standing affront. Curiously, they seem to think that even an unsuitable marriage is better than no marriage at all. Tory matrons wrote to their MPs, particularly on the South Coast when Heath was learning the ropes as a racing yachtsman, to complain about having to look at pictures of their Leader always surrounded by his male crew. One rightwing Tory on the South Coast used to take malicious joy in passing such letters over to William Whitelaw, Heath's friend, then Chief Whip. This may well be the explanation for the sudden appearance on Heath's yacht of an attractive young lady who later turned out to be a public-relations plant. But this sort of public relations 'gimmick' tends to wear thin if not based on an essential reality. Far more truthful was the revealing photograph of Heath on a yacht in Singapore harbour staring past the scantily-clad figure of a young woman as if she were part of the deck furniture.

Nobody has been as direct as the American woman who bearded him on the subject during a private lunch in the South of France just after he was elected Leader in 1965. 'You'll *have* to get married now, won't you, if you want to become Prime Minister ?' she asked. 'A man who married to become Prime Minister,' replied Heath, 'would be neither a good Prime Minister nor a good husband.' His oldest friend, Madron Seligman, observed to his table companion, pianist Moura Lympany: 'I'm sure that if Ted marries it will be *after* he is Prime Minister.' 'Why is that ?' asked Miss Lympany, who had been going to concerts with Heath for several years. 'It's because he wants to make it to 10 Downing Street on his own,' replied Seligman, 'and he couldn't stand the idea that he had made it only because he had married.'

Although most of the wives of Tory MPs seem to think him an 'unsociable' 'cold fish', this is not the view of a small group of women. He enjoys concert-going with a number of attractive women, including Moura Lympany. He takes pleasure in the badinage of actress Joan Fontaine. He notices what his women companions wear, although his comments can be brutal to close friends: 'What are you wearing that antimacassar for,' he said of a Nina Ricci creation, 'don't you know they went out of fashion years ago ?' He is a favourite of the wives of some of his few close friends. A number of Tory *grandes dames*, led by Lady Spencer Churchill, have befriended the talented bachelor. And there is the famous remark of Dame Irene Ward, the back-bench Brunhilde: 'Oh, Ted! You handled me beautifully!'

To safeguard the reputation of Dame Irene, twenty years his senior, it is necessary to suggest that Heath has never regarded women as instruments of sexual gratification; as political colleagues, as fellow concert-goers, as friends, but nothing more. One Tory lady music-lover used to dine out on stories about how she got him as far as putting his arm around her shoulder, 'And then he must have begun thinking about VAT. . . .'

Talking to women who have been friends of Heath over a stretch of forty years, one gets the impression he has gone through two phases, at least, with women. During the war, which for him stretched between the ages of twenty-four and thirty, he tended to keep them at a distance. This was the reverse of most young men who abandoned sexual restraint while away from the ties of home and family, particularly when welcomed with open arms in liberated towns and cities. Heath was among the first liberators of Antwerp, but this did not liberate him.

After the age of forty, Heath appeared to find it easier to establish a friendlier, if brotherly, relationship with women. He has obviously enjoyed the company of attractive, well-dressed, intelligent and talented women like Joan Fontaine and Moura Lympany. With them he could exchange badinage or argue about music or the arts. But these relationships have not appeared to progress beyond the 'just good friends' stage.

Here, Teddy's apparent difficulty in establishing more intimate relationship with women bothered his late mother. Her wistful remark, 'You can't imagine Teddy kissing a girl,' reflected this. She tried her best to overcome this failing. She kept inviting the prettiest and most likely local girls to the house to talk to them about Teddy. She was not above playing them off against one another, as if to whet their appetites and, consequently, Teddy's. But without success, as one after another of her candidates tired of waiting and married others.

Although she bemoaned Teddy's unmarried state, Mrs Heath unwittingly and unconsciously contributed to his disinterested attitude towards women, if we are to believe psychoanalysts.[2] A youngster's emotional attitudes are a product and reflection of family emotions. He can reflect family tensions that are invisible to the outside world and uncomprehended even by members of the family itself. Where there is a rivalry for leadership between mother and father, the one parent can tend to deprive a child of the disliked attributes of the other parent.

On the surface, the Heaths were a close, warm and hard-working family, the envy of their neighbours. Below the surface there was an unseen rivalry in life-styles, reflected in William Heath's sad confession, 'In the end we had nothing to talk about except the children.' Having been 'in service', Mrs Heath had taken over Edwardian middle-class manners and their preoccupation with respectability and appearances. She was more socially ambitious, genteel, churchy and puritanical. She even disliked the idea of her Teddy swimming with his sister-in-law. Although Will Heath was ambitious enough to convert himself from a carpenter into a master builder, he was not so anxious to be genteel in speech and behaviour where it interfered with enjoying life. He was not a regular churchgoer and liked a drink with the boys, and other similar masculine pursuits. He was not as determined as his wife to struggle to pay the fees at Balliol – before Teddy won the organ scholarship. When Edward Heath told a Tory MP friend, 'I owe it all to my mother!', he spoke more truthfully than he knew. Ironically, it was his father who lived to bathe in the reflected glory of having sired the first Tory Prime Minister of working-class origins.

Although he once showed an interest in Jung's ideas, there is no evidence to show that Edward Heath discussed the problems resulting from these below-the-surface tensions with psychoanalysts or even friends. The fact that he did not appear to share the girl-chasing appetites of his Oxford contemporaries did not even emerge because there the opportunities abounded to mix with girls as members of choirs or as concert-goers. Some of his friends hint at an unsettling experience in the trying period in 1939–40, when he was waiting end-lessly to be called up. Certainly, by the time he reached the 107th Heavy Anti-Aircraft Regiment in 1941 he was already very 'buttoned up'. He seldom drank with fellow officers and appeared to avoid the company of women. This was certainly not what his mother had in mind. She kept encouraging him to get married. During the war and afterward she kept pushing at him two nice local girls: Joan Stuart and Kay Raven. But both gave up. When he was adopted for Bexley in 1947 he reassured his constituency association that he had nothing against matrimony, but thought that it should not be 'rushed'!

Edward Heath's personality has also been distorted by his social repres-sions. He was born a carpenter's son in the class-conscious town of Broadstairs. His own preoccupation with the higher status of his 'betters' was unconsciously sharpened by the anxiety of his ambitious parents to 'get on', in their differing ways. This meant that he could never 'be himself', but must always pretend to a middle-class status not really his. This type of conflict has been dramatized frequently when the subject is a miner's son from Wales or Durham. But very slight attention has been focused on the tensions imposed on the man climbing from a Kentish working-class Tory background. In fact, in some ways it is as tearing as the efforts of very pale Negroes in the north of the United States to 'cross over' into white society, with its need to hide one's family and background. It is astonishing to discover how few of Heath's closest friends knew that his father had started life as a car-penter. 'His life began at Balliol,' smiled one of those close to him in the Whips' Office. Heath has observed the silences of the long-distance climber.

The most obvious example of Heath's desire to climb is his curious speech pattern, frequently the Englishman's indicator of class back-ground or aspiration. It is neither the normal speech of educated people on the Kent coast nor is it 'BBC English' – the *lingua franca* of the middle class. It is curious that someone with so sensitive an ear does not hear that he speaks the 'poshed-up' English of someone who, as a young man, attempted to adopt the speech patterns of his 'betters' without really getting it right.

Heath's curious status – neither working-class Tory nor middle-class Tory – has presented him with 'image' problems. People like to identify with their politicians. But since Heath has seemed neither classless nor having any clear class identity, it has been difficult for voters to identify with him. This was recognized as a problem at Conservative Central

Office when he became Leader of the Tories in Opposition in 1965. At a time when an election threat overhung Tories, it was put to the new Leader that he could be 'put across' either as a working-class boy who had made good on his own, or as a classless meritocrat. When Heath avoided a decision on this, one of his slightly malicious senior colleagues joked that this demonstrated Heath's 'crisis of identity'.

Heath was chosen in 1965 because he was thought better able to fight fellow grammar-school boy Harold Wilson than Old Etonian Sir Alec Douglas-Home. His similarity to Wilson was enormously exaggerated. 'We needed someone with drive and incisiveness,' explained an Old Etonian, 'a real professional – an infighter equipped to deal with an all-in wrestler like Wilson.'

On the surface, this seemed reasonable. Heath and Wilson were the same age, both from modest but ambitious homes, both went from grammar school to Oxford, which was the open sesame to the big Establishment world. Both have quick and retentive minds, enormous physical vitality and resilience, analytical rather than original minds and a natural secretiveness. It was understandable that the Tories should have thought that they had selected a sharp-witted technocrat from the same classless mould as the then Labour occupant of 10 Downing Street.

In fact, the difference of identification has been crucial. Wilson has kept his roots in Yorkshire with his still discernible accent, which he sometimes exaggerates. He has retained his identification with the industrial and nonconformist North, rejecting the idea of an Establishment élite with which he must conform. He has remained more at ease with trade unionists and businessmen and Liverpool comedians than with intellectuals. Although he did not bring the pottery ducks from Hampstead Garden Suburb to 10 Downing Street, the Prime Minister's residence then took on a distinctly lower middle-class air.

Although Wilson can recall precisely how many times he has seen 'Swan Lake', when it is not at Russian invitation, he prefers watching Huddersfield Town play football. If Heath prefers Glyndebourne to Wembley it is not because it is more 'highbrow'. For him music gives complete satisfaction, both emotional and intellectual. He enjoys being carried away by his favourite composers and artists as others let themselves go when their favourite teams and stars are scoring. He can also 'let himself go' in his musical analysis. Although knowledgeable enough to keep up with the professionals, he is not judged as a professional musician. Therefore, while he watches every word in the political world, he can let fly uninhibitedly in the musical world. On one occasion everyone at Glyndebourne was looking with astonishment at the loud and prolonged laughter of Heath and Moura Lympany and another couple.

Heath enjoys Covent Garden and Glyndebourne, not only for their fine music, but also because he does not think that the best things in life should be limited to the hereditary governing class. He is an English version of the American or German 'meritocrat' who believes, not only that the world is best run by the most able, but also that they are entitled to the 'spoils' of good eating, first-rate pianos and hi-fi sets and frequent visits to concerts and opera. When he was elected Leader in 1965, among his congratulatory telegrams was one from 'Comme Chez Soi', Brussels' best and priciest restaurant. He brought with him into 10 Downing Street old prints of the Honourable Artillery Company, the 'City's military club' with which he has identified himself since 1945. His yacht, *Morning Cloud*, is among the world's best, and not cheap. Heath has been able to enjoy 10 Downing Street as 'his' town house, and Chequers as 'his' country house much more wholeheartedly than his puritanical predecessor, Harold Wilson. In fact, Heath has enjoyed Chequers more than Sir Alec Douglas-Home and Harold Macmillan, who had their own *inherited* country houses.

Like most men who have succeeded on their own merits in a class-conscious society, Heath was originally very reticent about his origins and later discomfited when too much attention was paid to his background. Like most socially insecure types, the original preoccupation was with glossing over the modest background. When, in 1939, the *Daily Express* commented on the fact that the new President of the Oxford Union had a father who was a 'jobbing builder', a correction was sent in to point out that William Heath was a '*master* builder'. It was only after he had become Leader of the Conservatives that Ted Heath admitted publicly that he was born a carpenter's son.

Although you can take an able young man out of a bourgeois seaside town, you cannot always take the middle-class mentality out of the man, even when mature. Heath has retained the 'prefect's mentality', developed in Broadstairs and Ramsgate, with ideals out of *Boy's Own Paper*, according to one close friend. He remains tremendously preoccupied with the *forms* of behaviour. Associates insist he was more upset by the 'un-parliamentary' behaviour of the truculent young Labour MP, Dennis Skinner, in waving his fist under the Prime Minister's nose in the Chamber, than by the ink-throwing incident in Brussels which received so much more publicity.

His preoccupation with form can also be observed in the character of his politeness. He is, in the formal sense, one of the most polite people in politics. He answers personal letters of congratulation, sends gifts to his relatives or the wives of his staff or his godchildren in the best text-book manner. And for a small, inner circle of family and friends there is genuine warmth. But he can be incredibly rude in snapping people's heads off in press conferences, crushing conversational gambits or in retreating into prolonged silences. Although he appears to have swallowed the middle-class rulebook about formal behaviour, he has never absorbed its talent for small-talk as a lubricant of social intercourse. Even in Broadstairs he surprised his family and friends by his capacity for long silences. In the army a brother officer recalls travelling on leave in the same car to Brussels with Heath for six hours without exchanging more than a few words. In his constituency his agent warns Young Conservatives about to travel with Heath not to worry if their MP happens to lapse into a prolonged silence.

Heath probably realizes that, for him, silence is safer than being tempted into the small talk he detests. Around 1965 he went to Balliol with Moura Lympany for a concert she was giving at his old college. A faculty wife said casually, 'I hope you like my new curtains.' 'No!' was Heath's brutal reply. Whatever his other acquired attributes, his conversational manners are not those of an English middle-class gentleman.

Heath feels that this preoccupation with background rather than achievement is part of the 'English disease'. His satisfaction lies in achievement in competition. He takes satisfaction in identifying targets. He enjoys working out the strategy of achieving the targets set. But he is much less interested in short-range tactics, or presentation. This is one of the reasons why he impresses fellow Ministers but bores the Commons with speeches which are seldom moving or attractive. To him a speech often seems a chore whose main object is to avoid giving the Opposition a damaging handhold, or offering hostages to fortune. He seldom sees the point of moving people, or of showing the sort of love of words that he shows for music. The result is that he allows too many of his speeches to be written for him, some of them by several contrasting hands. It is rarely – one occasion was at the end of the October 1971 Conservative Conference – that a speech shows the 'inner' Heath rather than the rubbery exterior of a 'buttoned-up' Heath.

This does not mean that he has not 'put over' very effectively conference-rousing speeches written mostly by others. He is even willing to carry the can for those he has not written or delivered – such as the 1970 'at a stroke' statement, so often attacked since. Although this statement *was* used in the election, none of the newsmen covering the campaign attribute it to him. But, during the long months in which the Labour Opposition prodded and poked at him over this, he remained silent, accepting responsibility for it.

Heath has been an exceptional politician in that he has remained 'buttoned up' even where explanations might have won him wider understanding. Without ever explaining in Bexley he has refused to dine in the homes of the officers of his association. This was to avoid favouring those who had the social background to invite an MP, as against those who had not. He was similarly silent in avoiding explaining his policies when Chief Whip. Only after he left that office did he disclose that he had tried to strengthen the role of back-bench Tory MPs' committees to avoid having decisions reached at the town houses of top Tories.

Heath has also been odd as an ambitious politician in tending to expose his least attractive side while keeping his real talents concealed. In the House or in press briefings he can bore people to tears by the stereotyped way in which he suppresses information. But in smaller, more private meetings he can scintillate. Tory MPs who came up through the Young Conservative movement still speak of the brilliance of an unscripted talk on 'Leadership' he gave at Swinton College in the early fifties. A few years later he spoke to a seminar at the London School of Economics, enormously impressing Professor Michael Oakshott with the perceptiveness of his analysis of the nature of political decision.

Throughout his army and political life Heath has been preoccupied with the problem of leadership. Not only how to attain it but once acquired, how to deploy the tools at hand to achieve the ends desired. He has studied the examples to hand with considerable care, interest and ruthless objectivity: Attlee, Churchill, Eden, Macmillan, Douglas-Home, Wilson. He has never been modest about his own ability to do at least as well. One of his friends was startled to hear him explode, on the edge of a Macmillan–Kennedy meeting: 'You can't leave those two alone for more than a few minutes without their getting things fouled up!'

This enormous self-confidence certainly paid off in his victory at the polls in June 1970. Any candidate with less assurance would have faltered with the polls so much against him, when almost all around him had lost faith and were speculating about how to replace him for the next try. Heath retained his conviction that concentrating on the Wilson Government's economic inadequacies during a period of inflation would bring them home and dry. When, a week before the election, his colleague and friend William Whitelaw told him that he believed a Tory victory just possible, Heath welcomed his conversion with: 'Well, so you've decided to climb on the bandwagon at last!'

His 1969 yachting victory and his 1970 victory over Wilson tremendously enhanced Heath's confidence in his style of leadership. But he

C

surprised many by the quality and character of his political decisions. Before his election – and certainly before his Selsdon Park policy conference – Heath had had the reputation of being a Centre Tory, hated particularly by imperial rightwing Conservatives. But, soon after the election, he had persuaded more than his opponents that he was leading the most rightwing Tory Government since prewar days. He seemed prepared to kill off industrial 'lame ducks', sell arms to South Africa happily, engage in union-bashing, force Post Office strikers to their knees. Outsiders tended to neglect the lesson Heath had learned at Macmillan's bony knee: of starting out unpopularly as a deflationist so that you could end popularly as a reflationist.

Heath's preoccupation with radically reforming Britain as part of preparing it for Europe appeared to make him curiously insensitive to changes in popular thinking. He underestimated the extent to which public opinion would allow regions, industries or groups of workers to go to the wall. He also underestimated the amount of reflation required to bring down unemployment. The amount of reflation which enabled Macmillan to win the 1959 election hardly made a dent in 1971–2 unemployment.

One of the things which surprised even close observers was the ease with which Heath made a complete U-turn between his first rightwing or Mark I phase of 1970–1, and his second, leftwing or Mark II phase of 1971–2. The contrast was startling. The 'lame ducks' which seemed destined for the freezer in 1970–1 were converted into 'golden geese' as Glasgow's UCS shipyard and Rolls-Royce were saved from extinction. To reduce unemployment in Wales, Scotland and the North-east, a modified version of Labour's much-attacked investment grants was reintroduced. He went further than the Wilson Government in reforming Northern Ireland: disbanding Stormont and promising regular plebiscites on Irish unity. Heath even jettisoned the need to maintain the fixed parity of the pound, a god at whose shrine he had earlier worshipped publicly with great fervour.

This illustrated a striking aspect of Heath's style of leadership. Once he has established *targets*, such as European entry or the improvement of British industrial efficiency, he is virtually immoveable. But he is usually somewhat easier to persuade that the strategy originally adopted to attain the objective is faulty. Like any driving racing-captain or regimental commander, he will jettison the failed strategy and adopt a new course of action.

This does not explain, however, why, having been defeated by the miners earlier in 1972, he seemed willing to tangle with the moderate railwaymen. Was it a hangover from the time when his father made the transition from carpenter to builder and had to be somewhat 'tough' with his former workmates to survive? Could it be explained by his desire to show that the 'softness' of Sir Walter (later Lord) Monckton and John Hare (later Lord Blakenham) was part of the easy-going quality of the old Establishment he was trying to modernize? Was it the conviction that he had to 'treat 'em mean, keep 'em keen' to survive in the EEC he wanted so much to enter? Or was it something he had to prove to himself: that he could be as virile a leader at No. 10 as he had proved on the *Morning Cloud*?

2 MOTHER'S PRIDE

I owe it all to my mother.

Edward Heath

A man who has been the indisputable favourite of his mother keeps for life the feeling of a conqueror, that confidence of success that often induces real success.

Ernest Jones, *The Work and Life of Sigmund Freud*

It was one of the last great joys of Mrs Edith Heath to visit her former employer, Mrs Taylor, in the apartment she had rented over 'The Copper Kettle' in Broadstairs. It was no small satisfaction for the former parlourmaid to accept the congratulations of her formidable former mistress that Mrs Heath's boy, Teddy, had done so well. By this time Edward Heath had been for eighteen months the Conservative MP for Bexley. Moreover, he had been appointed by Winston Churchill as the Assistant Whip for the South-east: Kent, Surrey and Sussex.

Her son's initial successes gave Mrs Heath particular satisfaction because of the special character of Broadstairs. Although most widely known as the place where Charles Dickens vacationed and wrote, among other works, *Bleak House*, it is a quiet, middle-class seaside town on the Kent coast. It is on 'the Isle of Thanet, this tiny sand-girt isle where I was born'[1] as Heath once described it. On a clear day you can see the cliffs of France.

As in most places, the social pyramid in Broadstairs was thicker about the middle and bottom – the merchants and boarding house keepers and those who worked for them. But the social spotlight was always focused towards the top – towards the wealthy meat-packing Vesteys and McAlpines on the north shore and the London professional families who had their summer or weekend homes here on the Kent coast.

Almost half a century before that final meeting in 1951, Edith Annie Pantony, the pretty daughter of 'Old Stump' Pantony, a poor and illiterate farmworker, had gone into domestic service with the Taylors on leaving school at fourteen. The Taylors were a middle-class family who lived during the year in Hampstead but spent their summers in Broadstairs. Edith's mother, a determined, ambitious woman, was proud that her bright daughter had found such a good position, but she was less pleased when, on her summers back in Broadstairs, she began 'going steady' with an energetic young local carpenter, Will Heath, known to his friends as 'Darkie'. Will's father, Stephen, the son of a merchant seaman, had run a small dairy business which had failed. Although Stephen Heath remained a 'rank Tory' according to his son, he had then become a porter at the Broadstairs station of Southern Railways, carting holidaymakers' bags to their boarding houses and hotels. His son, Will, was not considered a good enough 'catch' by the ambitious Mrs Pantony. 'With her looks,' she told neighbours, 'she could do a lot better.'[2]

By 1913, when they were both twenty-five, the pair had saved enough to get married and settle down in the ground-floor flat at No. 1 Holmwood Villas, in Albion Road. The outbreak of war in 1914 hardly disturbed the drowsy tenor of life in Broadstairs, although its sons were often shipped across the Channel to their deaths in French trenches from Dover further down the coast. There was great excitement however on 9 July 1916, with policemen cycling down the street warning of a Zeppelin raid on nearby Ramsgate. It was during this hullabaloo that a son was born to the Heaths, a son named Edward Richard George, partly after his mother's brother who had died in the war.

When young Teddy was only five months old, the Heaths were uprooted. Will Heath found a good job building airframes in the Vickers aircraft factory in Crayford, in north Kent, enabling the young couple to rent a whole house. From time to time they interrupted their north Kent 'exile' to travel back to Broadstairs. Sometimes young Teddy travelled down on his own to visit his grandparents in Broadstairs. 'My sister,' Aunt Emily later recalled, 'used to put him on the train with a label tied to him. He first came down like that when he was five. . . .'[3] Young Teddy's grandmother, Mrs Pantony, died during the war of three strokes – 'from fear of Zeppelins' according to her daughter Emily.

By that time Teddy was no longer an only child. Just after his fourth birthday, his mother gave birth again. She had longed for and prepared for a girl – even to the extent of naming it Mary. 'I'm sorry it's not a girl,' were her first words to her husband.[4] They called their second son John, but Teddy called his little brother 'Bubbles' after the Millais painting then widely used as a soap advertisement. Teddy never had to worry about his brother's competition. From the outset he was his mother's favourite, the focus of her affection and ambition. 'She worshipped him,' recalled a family friend. Teddy very seldom had to throw a tantrum to get his way.

'I still have a sense of everything beginning when I came back to Broadstairs at the age of seven,' Heath later recalled.[5] He went to the flintstone church school. Although drab by modern standards – despite the white cupid over its entrance – the school was a big advance on Crayford's wartime temporary school of galvanized iron – the 'little tin school' as his family called it. 'Young Teddy arrived with a glowing introduction from his Crayford headmistress,' remembered James Bird, then an Assistant Master. 'Teddy . . . was better academically, especially in history and maths, than in practical subjects, though he tried hard to do things with his hands. He was bigger than other boys of his age and his bones were well-covered. This and the fact that his mother always sent him to school impeccably dressed, a condition which he managed to maintain all day, made him a model pupil.' He added: 'Ted the schoolboy was not a good mixer. He was inclined to be aloof.'[6]

Teddy's tendency to be an unusually neat but lonely 'teacher's pet' was spotlighted as soon as his brother, John, followed him to school. John was not so good at his studies. Nor did he keep himself as neat to win his mother's approval. John often returned home to be scolded for a 'ragamuffin' by his mother, because he enjoyed joining in rough games with his schoolmates.[7] From the outset he seemed in revolt against the path and pattern set by his adored older brother. 'His brother, John, was much more the average tearabout youngster,' Mr Bird recalls.

John's appearance bothered his mother because she had 'all copybook standards to excess', as one family friend put it: 'cleanliness, Godliness, good manners – the lot'. She was calm, quiet and dignified, but her beloved family soon learned when they were falling below the standards she set for them. She was enormously impressed with the need to appear respectable, working hard to attain the middle-class standards she had learnt 'in service'. Her husband then brought home a good, steady wage of about five pounds a week from his employer, a local builder.[8] She saved as much as she could from this and, after three years back in Broadstairs, they decided to buy a house, a semi-detached named 'Helmdon' at 4 King Edward Avenue.

Will Heath also had his upward-looking aspirations. He liked to do 'top class work' for the 'better element', not only as a craftsman, but because he enjoyed mixing with his 'betters'. He liked his wife to be well-dressed because he liked good-looking women well turned-out. 'He's a ladies' man' thought at least one neighbour.

Will Heath prided himself that he would not allow his wife to go out to work. But he did not object to her taking summer visitors, locally regarded as a respectable occupation for lower middle-class as well as working-class wives. It was not easy, in their little house, to find room for summer visitors. The boys had to bunk together and furniture had to be shifted, including the newly-acquired piano.

The piano was one of the middle-class extras much emulated by the upward-striving working class. '. . . my parents were very keen that I should learn,' Heath later recalled. 'They gave me great encouragement. We weren't very well off but they bought a piano for me, by instalments . . . in the village of St Peter's, where I lived, which is part of Broadstairs, there was a charming teacher of the piano who used to come and teach me . . .'[9]

His teacher was Miss Grace Locke. Only seventeen when she started giving Teddy a lesson a week, she was impressed by the diligence of the little boy in the modest home. 'He was a serious, unsmiling little boy who never had to be reprimanded for not knowing his lessons. He was full of questions and one would have had to be an encyclopaedia to answer them all. . . . He . . . was always anxious to learn, and at one lesson I found he had taught himself Grieg's "Wedding day". He just sat down and played it for me as a surprise.

'His mother was full of encouragement for him and would sit in the same room with him and knit while he practised so that he wouldn't feel shut away from the family.'

Teddy's parents worked very hard during the summer, the only time when Broadstairs hummed with life. They never took a vacation themselves those days, even when the summer was over. The bathing tent they owned was used largely by the summer boarders, hardly ever by themselves. Teddy learned to swim – although his brother never did – and to cycle. He liked to walk. But he was hardly an outdoor type. He didn't 'mess about with boats' as did so many of his school-mates. More surprisingly, he never joined the Scouts, as one would expect from the son of a churchy, rather conformist mother. This was largely because his father thought the Scouts killed a boy's initiative.[10]

Will Heath was more relaxed than his quietly determined wife, but he tried to support her in her ambitions for their sons, particularly Teddy. This was partly because he too was ambitious for them, partly because this was his main point of contact with his wife, who veered away from his more relaxed, manly pursuits.

The Heath family probably 'crossed the line' between the skilled working class and the lower middle class about 1930. Will Heath had started as a carpenter with a local firm, but then became its outside manager. In 1930 the owner of this small firm died and Will Heath took it over, changing its name to 'W. G. Heath, Builder and Decorator'. The firm was run from an untidy room in the Heath house, with Will Heath working hard and late to keep his small team of craftsmen fully occupied in what is normally seasonal work, in an even more seasonal wont. 'I have seen my parents struggling in the 1930s, having to do without holidays or luxuries to give my brother and myself a decent start in life,' Ted later recalled.[11]

Teddy Heath's emerging ideas were, as a result, coloured by the problems faced and prejudices developed by a small entrepreneur trying to make his way in a competitive world without any financial backing. Will Heath, who had started his political thinking as something of a Liberal, became increasingly Conservative. 'I was never Labour – I had too much to do with labour to vote Labour.'[12]

This attitude was helped by Broadstairs's isolation. Initially this had much greater social than political implications, partly because Broadstairs was geographically immune to the great socio-political struggles of the time. There was no radical tradition among Kentish farmworkers as there was, for example, among those in East Anglia, just across the Thames estuary. The miners' struggles of the twenties and the General Strike of 1926 had had their echoes only in the tiny Kent coalfield behind Dover.

Young Teddy Heath had already begun climbing his own 'ladder' at ten, when he secured admission to the best local grammar school, Chatham House School in Ramsgate down the coast. Built in 1909, it was imbued with the idea that it should provide an educational 'ladder' to the brightest and most hardworking boys of modest background. The best grammar schools at this time were scaled-down models of public schools, with imitation 'houses' and the prefect system. The school uniform was a badge of budding middle-class status, to be envied and pilloried by the 'scruffs' who had failed to make it. Students at Chatham House were expected to absorb too the middle-class virtues of neatness, punctuality, politeness, learning for the sake of learning and respect for the social pyramid they were aspiring to climb.

The pressure of Heath family hopes that Teddy would win a scholarship to Chatham House had run fairly high. Just before he was to take his examination, he fell ill with a feverish cold and was sent to bed. When the doctor called, his temperature seemed to go up further, so anxious was Teddy to be well for the examination. On other occasions the tensions were reflected in bouts of sleepwalking.[13]

Teddy passed his written examination and went for his interview with Chatham House's outstanding headmaster, H. C. Norman. Mr Norman was every inch the 'old-fashioned' grammar-school headmaster who thought his boys could conquer the world if they worked hard enough. He was favourably impressed by the neat, well-scrubbed and earnest little ten-year-old before him, who said he wanted to be an 'architect' – the professional equivalent of his father's job.

The Heath family were naturally thrilled. Winning the scholarship saved his parents twelve pounds a year in school fees – the fees that the fee-paying three-quarters of the school had to cough up. On top of that Kent County Council made the Heaths a grant to cover the cost of his school uniform because, when Teddy started at Chatham House, their income qualified them. When they moved into their own house a little later, they did not mention this grant to their new neighbours.

For nine years – from when he was ten in 1926 until he was nineteen in 1935 – Teddy Heath spent his formative years donning his green blazer, travelling on the tram across the fields to Ramsgate and immuring himself within the monastic walls of Chatham House. He imbibed its ideology in strong and habit-forming gulps.

Partly because he was over a year younger than the average in his form, Teddy Heath made a sound but by no means brilliant beginning. This was a time when the headmaster, Mr Norman, insisted on his masters giving a weekly mark to each of their pupils. Reference to these records shows that he never in these first five years achieved 'honours', only rarely a 'first' and nearly always 'seconds'. 'He was never a genius, never brilliant,' his master Cecil Curzon told the author. In forms containing about thirty students he was ranged between fifth and sixteenth.

One incident suggested that he might have been hiding part of his ability from his masters. At that time the principal examinations taken were those called 'LUGS' for London University General Schools. The Ordinary level was generally taken at fifteen, which was the minimum age. But Heath felt he was qualified to take it with the rest of his form when he was thirteen-plus. He pleaded with the headmaster, who reluctantly persuaded the London University examiners to allow this exception. 'It can only be by God's providence that he passes,' the head said to one of his masters. In fact, of the seven subjects young Heath took he secured five 'distinctions'.

His family were very proud of their bright and bookish son, the first on either side. 'He was such a good scholar,' recalled his aunt, Mrs Emily Wickens, 'which is a surprise when you realise his grandfather could neither read nor write.' His parents did everything they could to help his further development; Mrs Heath suppressed her hesitations and paid for his schoolboy trip to France when he was thirteen.

They were always ready to make excuses for his solitary immersion in books, although they were no readers themselves. 'He read and read . . .', his father later recalled. 'His bedroom was like a library. When he was reading – or for that matter playing music – to try to talk to him was like speaking to a brick wall.'[14] Sometimes this obsession with books could be embarrassing for the family. When family or friends called, Teddy would often arrive home, greet them with the politeness of a well-brought-up lad and go right up to his room to read. 'Teddy likes to be alone,' his mother would explain tenderly.

His parents would accommodate themselves to his sudden changes of mood. 'Then suddenly he would stop what he was doing and say, "Let's go for a walk, Mummy." And the rest of us would have to stop what we were doing and go out with him,' his father later recalled.[15] This pattern of lack of communication, alternating with a sudden desire for Teddy-directed family activity, was to last for years.

Because of the closeness and affection in the family, the normal 'generation gap' and that between an educated son and less well-educated parents was minimized. Will Heath was proud of his bright and solitary son without quite understanding him. 'I didn't have to encourage him,' he later reflected, 'I just had to work ruddy hard to pay the expenses.'[16]

Even Teddy's doting mother was a bit concerned about the extremes to which her ambitions for him had brought her son, and sometimes bothered by his high-falutin tastes in music. Once she brought him the music for the prewar favourite beginning, 'Little Old Lady, Passing By . . .' But Teddy snapped that he was not playing 'that tripe'.[17]

Teddy and his mother were more on the same wavelength about church. 'I was brought up in a Christian home, as they say in the obituaries,' he later half-joked.[18] For Teddy churchgoing and music blended. He sang in the choir every Sunday from the age of ten until his voice broke at fourteen. 'I became a chorister in the parish church,' he later recalled, 'and this really gave me a basis of church music.'[19] He also turned pages for the church organist, Arthur Tatham, who taught him to play the organ – an exceptionally important 'break' for young Teddy – and introduced him to Bach.[20]

He belonged to the young people's club attached to the 800-year-old church, and attended tennis parties in the vicarage garden on Saturday afternoons in the summer. 'He seemed to enjoy the game in itself and as a means of exercise,' recalled Tony Weigall, who played with him.

THE SCHOOLBOY SHAPE

When Teddy passed into the fifth form at sixteen, his future character was substantially apparent. And one of these was that he did not 'waste' any time on schoolboy sports. 'He took no active part in anything that required physical effort,' recalled his former master, Cecil Curzon, who coached cricket for twenty-five years at the school. The groundsman on the school's cricket field was Bill Pantony, Teddy's mother's brother.

'The nearest Teddy ever got to playing cricket,' Mr Curzon mused, 'was when the cricket eleven elected him as scorer. This was regarded as a great honour given to a non-player who had contributed to the school in other fields.' He also shared the Leslie and Douglas Prize awarded by the joint votes of the fifth and sixth forms.

Teddy had already demonstrated his form as an 'organization man', a debater and a musician. He got his training as an 'organization man' as a prefect and then 'captain' of his 'house' – Coleman's. As a prefect he showed the prim disciplinary toughness he was to display later. He kicked one boy in the backside for fighting. Another he gave 'six of the best' with a gym shoe. He was so strict in stopping boys from larking about on the tram going home that some would deliberately miss the tram on which he was riding. 'He was anything but popular,' recalled his friend Ronald Whittell. 'He never tried for popularity. He wasn't actively liked or actively disliked. He was respected and accepted, thought a little bit intolerant.'[21]

He also showed his musicianship, quite an important thing at Chatham House, which prided itself as the only grammar school with an orchestra pit! Heath carried off the valued Belasco Prize after playing a prelude and fugue of Bach and Mozart and Chopin selections.

Within the school Teddy was better noted as Secretary of the Debating Society, at a time when interest in politics and international affairs was rising sharply. The coming to power of Hitler in 1933 had local ripples in Broadstairs. Nazi agents were active there, because of nearby Manston Field; in 1935 a Dr Hermann Goertz was arrested there as a Nazi spy.[22] Sir Oswald Mosley and Unity Mitford rode around in their black shirts in open Mercedes cars. The Fascists even had a store in town selling their literature.

This challenge had an early impact on Teddy. 'As I got to seventeen, eighteen years old, the country as a whole was moving out of the period in which it was preoccupied with the sufferings of the unemployed – things were looking up – and moving into the period of the threat of the dictators. . . .'[23] Just after the Oxford Union passed the pacifist 'King and Country' resolution in 1933, Chatham House debated the same motion. Heath, leading for the side which favoured fighting 'for King and Country', carried the day.[24] Cecil Curzon recalls another debate, in 1934 or 1935, which he feels was the starting point of Heath's early 'Europeanism'. Heath pointed out that the bulk of the world's wars had stemmed from rivalries within Europe; this tendency could only be reversed by European unity.

It was inevitable that such a prematurely serious young man should find more profit in the company of older people. One of the people Teddy liked to cycle out to visit in Kingsgate was Alec (later Sir Alec) Martin, who became Chairman of Christie's, the art auctioneers. 'When I was a boy,' Heath later remembered, 'he tried to teach me about pictures.'[25]

Teddy also liked to visit Royalton Kisch, a London solicitor of German Jewish background, who grew roses in his Broadstairs home. Kisch, a perceptive man, thought Heath had great qualities. At Kisch's house Teddy Heath encountered a young solicitor who worked in the Kisch office, Arnold (later Lord) Goodman. 'I remember him as an alert young man,' Goodman later told George Hutchinson. 'I didn't get an impression of an intellectual but of a keen general intelligence . . . a keen, questing person who was looking for founts of experience, founts of sophistication, founts of knowledge . . . outside his own world and often from people older than himself. He was very genuine. He was not at all a young man on the make. . . .'[26] But the father of a friend said at the time 'Teddy's a social climber!'

Teddy was also taking his first timorous steps with girls. He tended to be thrown together only with nice middle-class girls, whom he met in church, at the vicarage tennis parties, or in the carol party which toured the streets for a fortnight before Christmas raising funds after practising in the Heath home.

Teddy took quite a fancy to Joan Stuart, a pretty young blonde. During the summer he would say 'I'm going swimming tomorrow. What are you doing?' If she said she was also thinking of swimming, she would see him scan the beach from above to see if she was there before joining her. He took her to the last dance at Chatham House School, where they moved around the dance-floor rather inexpertly.

Although Joan was sweet on Teddy, and Mrs Heath thought Joan a very nice girl, Joan found it rather uphill work. It was difficult making conversation. Joan would try starting one with 'Do you like the music of so-and-so?' Teddy would answer abruptly 'No!' and lapse into a prolonged silence. He never got his arm beyond her shoulder – not even around her waist. She carried a torch for him for years, and only realized she had ceased to be his 'girl next door' when later he assigned another local girl, Kay Raven, to the car in which he was sitting when he was down from Oxford.

TARGET: BALLIOL

At eighteen Teddy Heath decided on one target which he had to make: entry into Balliol College, Oxford. To enter Oxford was the highest prize sought by ambitious grammar school boys of that day, particularly those in whom political ambitions were budding. His headmaster and others advised him that he had a chance at Balliol which its new Master, A. D. Lindsay, had made much more accessible to grammar school boys of talent. When even his doting mother was surprised that he should try to aim so high, Teddy reassured her that it was a college for hard-working undergraduates. 'It's a *workers*' college,' is the way Mrs Heath explained it to family and friends.

Having entered for the Open Scholarship to Balliol, Teddy had to concentrate harder than ever on the three subjects which were required: economics, Latin and French. Unfortunately for Teddy, he 'would only bite on the subjects that really interested him', as his French teacher, Dr E. A. Woolf, commented later.[27] Economics *did* interest him, and he had absorbing arguments with Cecil Curzon, who took him in this subject. Thus, in discussing the role of monopolies, Curzon took the line that monopolies tended to exploit their position to keep prices high. Young Heath argued that, because they could spread their unit costs over so many more units, they could lower their costs.

When the results came back, there was great disappointment. Young Teddy had failed to make the grade for the Open Scholarship in economics. Inquiring, Cecil Curzon learned that he had been up to scratch in economics and passable in Latin, but his poor French pulled him below scholarship level.

His disappointed headmaster and masters strove to see what they could do. They secured a loan for him of ninety pounds a year from the Kent County Council. Then Mr Norman called in Teddy's parents. He told them that Teddy could go far if given the opportunity. 'He told me that Teddy might be Prime Minister,' Will Heath was fond of recalling later. 'It *was* the sort of thing the head would say,' Cecil Curzon later agreed, but insisted that it was not meant to be believed literally. The year 1935 was hardly a time when one thought it was possible that a carpenter's son could be a Conservative Prime Minister – even if he had won the school's mock election as a 'National' candidate that year.

It was a hard decision to commit another £120 yearly to Teddy's higher education for three years, on top of the County Council's loan. Other members of the family warned against ordinary working-class people trying to aim so far beyond their reach. 'For a while it was touch and go,' recalls Cecil Curzon, who was a friend of the family, as well as Teddy's master. But his hardworking and ambitious parents decided to listen to his headmaster. His worshipping mother decided that, in case of need, she would raid her hard-earned savings. 'So his mother and I decided that he should go,' Will Heath recalled. 'It would have broken his heart had we refused. I had to work damned hard though. . . .'[28]

3 THE OPEN DOORS OF BALLIOL

There are those among the Conservatives who are poor enough to regard the party chiefly as a means to success.

Balliol opened all the doors for me. Patrick Anderson, *Oxford Tory*, pp 20–1

Edward Heath[1]

'Mr Heath is more than an ineffectual young man with a charming smile.' Within a year of the publication of this in *Isis*, on 2 February 1938, he had carried the Oxford University Conservative Association first into the Eden camp and then into the anti-Hogg, pro-Lindsay camp. He had added to his Presidency of the Conservative Association the Presidency of the Oxford Union and of Balliol's Junior Common Room. And by 25 January 1939 he had achieved the summit of undergraduate regard, being named an '*Isis Idol*', or pin-up boy of that undergraduate journal. In the 'profile' which accompanied this designation, Teddy Heath was compared to a tank in his 'force of utterance and ability to surmount obstacles'.

Teddy Heath clearly had the inexorable drive of a tank. But he was helped in his 'breakthrough' by the impact of stirring outside events on Oxford's own evolution. When Teddy Heath made the 130-mile journey up the Thames to where it is called the Isis, Oxford's 4,000 students were affected by outside stirrings about unemployment and fascism, but insulated as well. Oxford men felt themselves among the 'chosen few' who felt sure of influential employment on graduating.

In seeking the centres of Oxford's political power, Heath did not have to break lances solely with the less-competitive sons of effete aristocrats. The domination of the social élite had already been broken. The mainstream was already dominated by the professional middle classes that the world's greatest Empire had developed to manage it. There were quite a few sons of peers, like the handsome and elegantly dressed younger son of Lord Lovat, Hugh Fraser, a Balliol contemporary. Famous politicians like Leo Amery and Harold Macmillan also provided their sons as contemporaries. But doctors, lawyers and colonial civil servants provided many more of their sons.

This was particularly true of Balliol, where a long-legged Scot, A. D. Lindsay, was rapidly developing his own scheme of a 'democratic aristocracy'.[2] 'It wasn't merely that I went up to Oxford,' Heath later enthused, 'but that I went to Balliol. Balliol is a college of high academic standards and strong democratic traditions, where Old Etonian sons of dukes or millionaires are expected – and expect – to meet on equal terms with, well, the son of a carpenter.'[3]

It was not as though his tutors or contemporaries *knew* that Teddy Heath was the son of a carpenter at the time. 'Of the seventy-five or so we admitted to Balliol every year,' recalls his tutor John (later Lord) Fulton, 'about three undergraduates on the average who were of working-class origin were conspicuously loyal to their social background. For them it was a constant agony and clash of loyalties to decide whether to remain "true to the working class" in speech, style and outlook, or to conform with Oxford's style. One never thought of Ted Heath as one of those.'

Initially, it was not easy to keep up even lower middle-class appearances. At first he had to manage on £220 a year, £130 from his parents and £90 as a loan from the Kent County Council. Although more than an average workman's wage at the time, it was not the sort of money on which to mix with the sons of the wealthy. Even at 1935 prices they spent more than that on clothes, drink, gambling and cigarettes. Even if he had no interest in 'keeping up with the Frasers', there were some expenses he thought important even if he refused to smoke and hardly ever drank. He had intrigued the Admissions Tutor, Charles (later Lord) Morris, by saying he wanted to be a 'professional politician'. It was automatic that anyone wanting to be a politician should try to make his mark in the Oxford Union, whose fees of four pounds helped to deter an argumentative contemporary, Denis Healey, from joining. On top of this, if you wanted to make one of the leading 'paper' (prepared) speeches, you had to appear in white tie and tails. And there was no Oxford version of Moss Bros from whom to borrow formal attire for the occasion. Despite the strain, the family did not stint expenditure on such rungs on the ladder.

ORGAN SCHOLAR

His financial straits improved in his very first term. 'I came up to Balliol to read Modern Greats – which was politics, philosophy and economics – because these were the subjects in which I was interested. And then, just after I got here – the first month after I got here – it was announced that the organ scholarship was going to become vacant, and so I decided to put in for that. We had an open competition and I was awarded the organ scholarship . . . it meant that I played in chapel every morning at eight o'clock and then on Sundays we had the usual chapel services, so that it meant I was always tied here to chapel for every day of the week while I was an undergraduate.'⁴ To perfect his organ technique he continued to take organ lessons.

In the special atmosphere of Oxford and Balliol, the Broadstairs 'loner' blossomed. 'He was friendly and an easy mixer,' recalled Ashley Bramall, a Union colleague, 'without the shoulder-heaving effort to be "one of the boys" he later adopted.' 'I would have said that he was a gentle, amiable, kindly, competent man,' recalled Philip Toynbee, an active Communist at Oxford, 'but not one with a very striking personality.... It's very significant, perhaps, that we used to call him "Teddy" in those days, and I don't know quite when he graduated to being "Ted", but he was more, much more, of a Teddy than a Ted, really.'⁵ It is curious, in view of his aloof shyness both before and since Oxford, how many then undervalued him as merely pleasant and competent.

Young Teddy showed his organizing talent in music. 'I started the Balliol Choir . . . this consisted of people from Balliol and Trinity, which is next door, and the sopranos and altos from Somerville and Lady Margaret Hall.'⁶

As *Isis* soon recalled, 'he conducted with distinction at the 1,000th Balliol Concert. This success was gained in spite of [his] inability to command that bad taste and bad temper which is apparently indispensable to so many choral conductors.'⁷

He also joined the Bach Choir, with long-term results. 'I discovered at Christmas-time (1935) that the Bach Choir, of which I was a member, sang in the Town Hall at Oxford a concert which was conducted by Sir Hugh Allen and which had the Oxford Orchestra as well. . . . I thought to myself: "Well, if we can do this in Oxford, is there any reason why we shouldn't do it in Broadstairs?" And, of course, when you're nineteen you have all the nerve in the world and you don't worry about these things. And so I went home and I wrote to the Chairman of the council.'⁸ Since the Broadstairs carol concert started in 1936, he gave it every year thereafter, except for the war.

POLITICAL COMPARTMENT

On his arrival in Oxford, he not only joined the Oxford Union but did something required to get into the closed meetings of even those organizations with which you were out of sympathy: 'I joined all three major parties in my first term at Oxford, to see what they were up to, but by then I had accepted that I was a Conservative.'⁹ People from traditional, orthodox upper middle-class families were moving sharply to the Left, some of them as far as Communism. In fact, four of his fellow undergraduates, who were later to serve behind him as Tory MPs, were at that time Communists at Oxford. Teddy Heath felt at least as hostile to the appeasement policies of the Baldwin and Chamberlain Governments. His loyalty to the Tories at that time appeared to fit into a pattern which struck Anthony Howard: 'The best incubator for the Conservative philosophy [at University] is often to be found in the . . . first generation University student. Nothing makes more effectively for ardent and self-publicizing loyalty to the Conservative Party than a basic feeling of social insecurity.'[10] The Oxford University Conservative Association had been dragged out of the doldrums first by the sparkling Ian Harvey, a Scots public-school boy, and then by Ronald Bell, a Cardiff grammar-school boy.

Because Baldwin and then Neville Chamberlain were Prime Minister, the Left was able to make most of the running at Oxford. The Labour Club, actively encouraged by dons like R. H. S. Crossman, Patrick Gordon Walker and G. D. H. Cole, secured the best speakers. In his first week in the Labour Club, Teddy Heath heard Clement Attlee, then the new Leader of the fairly feeble Labour Opposition. Later he heard Sir Stafford Cripps and Aneuran Bevan. Because the Labour Club was being taken over by transient Communists like Denis Healey, he also heard Communist leaders such as Harry Pollitt and Willie Gallacher, the Scots MP.

For ambitious Teddy Heath the OUCA was important partly as a potential power base, partly as a context in which to meet senior Conservative politicians. There, in November 1936, he was introduced for the first time to Winston Churchill. Churchill, then considered a cranky back-bencher, was in Oxford to push the claims of his testy friend, Professor Lindemann (later Lord Cherwell).

UNION ACTIVIST

Teddy soon convinced his contemporaries that he too wanted to be a professional politician by the intensity of his activity at the Oxford Union, chief nursery of politicians. In shape the Union is one of the last remaining great Victorian gentlemen's clubs. But for the ambitious it is the antechamber to another debating club – the House of Commons.

Heath made his maiden speech in the Oxford Union within four months of reaching Oxford, on the motion 'that this House considers that England is fast following in the footsteps of ancient Rome'. In March 1936 he challenged the motion 'that this House considers the present system of education is unsuited to a democratic state'. 'Mr Heath pointed out that equality of education meant equality of wealth

D

and equality of wealth meant Communism,' wrote Ian Harvey in *Isis*. 'Mr Heath has plenty of confidence. He must be careful not to appear too aggressive.'[11]

TUTORS' VIEWS

Teddy's preoccupations with music and politics did not completely overshadow his studies. His tutors, Charles Morris for philosophy, Maurice Allen for economics, John Fulton for politics, found that he was 'extremely' competent, producing his excellent essays on time and showing that he had put in quite a bit of effort. But in their discussions on their undergraduates in the Senior Common Room, one of them later recalled, there never was any dissent from the common impression that he would achieve no more than a 'Second' in Modern Greats at the end of his time in Oxford.

Teddy Heath felt at home in Balliol, partly because he had a piano in his room and the organ in the chapel, partly because the atmosphere at the time was political-argumentative, which he enjoyed. The Master of Balliol's greatest contribution to the college was to encourage diversity. He welcomed undergraduates from different social backgrounds, different countries, different viewpoints.

'Over and above the Balliol tradition of hard thinking and easy mixing,' Heath later recalled, 'there was Lindsay's belief in discussion as the main tool of the democratic system. Once a week he used to have a kind of open house evening and anybody from the Junior Common Room could go and you could talk about anything.

'He was a completely nondogmatic and nondoctrinaire thinker and doer. Anyway, what influenced me most about him was that he was a great believer in democratic expression of views as central to the whole system of political democracy, which, in turn, he thought was the only political system which enabled men to apply the freedom which is the prerequisite for doing the only thing that really matters – the chance for each man to live a full life – not a prescribed life, but *his own* full life.'[12] If anyone could have seduced Teddy Heath from his already declared commitment to Conservatism, it could have been Lindsay, the non-doctrinaire Christian socialist who believed in a 'democratic aristocracy'.

Teddy had his mild undergraduate amusements. He learned to punt. He learned to play pingpong, although he amused his colleagues by wearing a glove and holding the pingpong bat 'as if it were a soup spoon'.[13] He learned to dance moderately well, but appeared to be a bit immature in his relations with the few girls he knew from Somerville and Lady Margaret Hall. Teddy's ideas about girls were also a bit on the naïve side. On one occasion he encountered another Balliol man in the quad and asked about a mutual friend who was active in the Labour Club and whom he had not seen for a day or two. The other Balliol undergraduate told him that he thought their friend was spending the weekend with his girl friend at an inn not far from Oxford much favoured by romantically inclined undergraduates. 'You don't mean they're actually *sleeping* together?' demanded a shocked young Heath. When his more rugged friend indicated that this might well be so, Teddy replied shaking his head: 'I couldn't imagine that happening to members of the Conservative Association!'

Teddy spent the momentous summer of 1936 quietly at home, in Broadstairs. In July 1936 the Spanish generals, led by Franco and backed by Mussolini and Hitler, challenged the Spanish Republican Government. Nothing gripped Heath and his generation of undergraduates like the Spanish civil war. From the outset, volunteers from the universities joined those from the mines and factories to make up for the refusals of the democratic countries to help the Madrid Government. For virtually all those of that generation who feared the onrush of fascism, Spain was the place to stop it. It was a feeling which took an increasingly important grip on Teddy Heath. Such ideas did not bother any large percentage of Broadstairs inhabitants, more interested in the local weather than the war-clouds across the Channel. Teddy did even more lonely walking than usual. He blew off steam at a Men's Discussion meeting held by his church.

ESTABLISHED VOICE

Teddy Heath returned to an established niche in Oxford political life when he arrived in October 1936 for his second year. In November he passed under the watchful eye of Christopher Mayhew who was elected President of the Union by a substantial majority.[14] Mayhew had a good opinion of Heath despite their political opposition: 'Mr E. R. G. Heath (Balliol) can always be relied on for a sound speech.'[15]

Although praise from an opponent was sweet, Teddy was more anxious to impress young Conservatives. He was happy to oppose the motion 'that the public school would be an anomaly in a civilized society'. He teamed up with Hugh Fraser, a Tory who had been at Ampleforth, against Ashley Bramall, a Labour supporter who had been at Westminster, and Philip Toynbee, then a Communist, who had been at Rugby. Heath, the only grammar school boy of the lot, claimed that flogging was decreasing at public schools and learning increasing: 'What one loses at one end, one gains at the other'.[16]

In June 1937, Heath set a pattern for unexpectedly winning elections by carrying off the Presidency of the Oxford University Conservative Association. Until noon on 9 June, the Presidency was expected to go, uncontested, to John Stokes, a traditionalist protégé of Professor Lindemann and supporter of Franco, who later became a Tory MP. At midday, Patrick Anderson, a brilliant but unstable young Tory who had just become President of the Union,[17] unexpectedly put in Heath's name against Stokes. Anderson disliked Stokes, largely because he was pro-Franco; Stokes spoke up for Franco again on 11 June. Next day the vote showed: Heath, forty-seven, Stokes, forty. Stokes's friend, Harold Soref, said that Stokes had carried Queens, the Carleton Club and the women's colleges, but Heath had won largely on the Balliol vote. Heath also became President of the Federation of University Conservative Associations for 1937.

NUREMBERG AWAKENING

Although the fighting in Spain had begun to have an impact on his anti-Fascist feelings, it was his experiences at the Nuremberg Rally in 1937 which really made his plastered-down hair stand on end. He went initially as part of the family exchange system then popular. A German boy from Dusseldorf came to stay at the Heath home in Broadstairs. In August 1937 Teddy went to Germany, first Dusseldorf then in Bad Homburg. He went on to Bavaria to stay near the Austrian border with a retired teacher and his wife, doing some climbing and learning a little German. Teddy's host detested the Nazis and urged him to go to the Nuremberg Party Rally, held every year early in September. 'This was when I realized what they were really like,'[18] he later recalled. He heard Alfred Rosenberg rant during the three days there and saw 250,000 uniformed Germans march purposefully through the square, at a time when England's standing army was only 150,000. Shocked as he was, he did not forget his family; he took home a walking stick with an ornately-carved Swastika decorating it.[19]

Back at University in the autumn, Teddy made a happy start to the year. As an enthusiastic Union man, he made a practice of approaching newcomers to sign them up for the Union. One of the first he was able to persuade in October 1937 was Madron Seligman, who came from a business family who were of German Jewish origin three generations before. His father had been a founder member of the Ski Club of Great Britain and had had the distinction of introducing skiing to Switzerland! Madron himself was an attractive and intelligent young man who shared two interests with Teddy: politics and music. In politics he was a Liberal and shared Teddy's anti-Fascism. In Teddy's room they enjoyed also playing four-handed duets on the piano, mostly Mozart. Teddy played better than Madron, partly because he could sight-read music. Madron sometimes irritated Teddy by his penchant for 'swinging' the classics, a fashion that was developing at that time. Teddy sponsored his entry into the Union and helped Madron with his first 'paper' (prepared) speech. As often as they could afford it they went to concerts, either in Oxford or London, frequently with girls. On one occasion they heard Toscanini conduct Beethoven's Ninth at the old Queen's Hall.

CROSSING SWORDS WITH DALTON

He entered the Union debating chamber to 'enthusiastic applause from Conservatives' in November 1937. The motion was 'that this House approves Labour's "Immediate Programme"'. Teddy was inevitably nervous because he was opposing Dr Hugh Dalton MP, the Old Etonian turned socialist, who had a great booming voice to emphasize his air of effortless superiority. Dr Dalton, supported by undergraduate C. G. P. Smith – later Labour Peer Delacourt-Smith – called for more Government control of the economy, especially to encourage economic growth in depressed areas. In reply Teddy welcomed Dr Dalton as one 'whose intimate knowledge of the working classes was no doubt gained on the playing fields of Eton'. With the typical laboured humour of the undergraduate, he recalled that at a Labour Party conference Dr Dalton had said 'Comrades, let us be logical!' 'So original was this remark that such a striking impression did it make on the delegates that he was at once elected Chairman for the next conference!' Heath then went through the Labour programme point by point, alleging mistaken principles and attacking nebulous proposals like 'measures will be taken to increase employment'. He contrasted this with the 'constructive' work' of the Chamberlain Government. His speech aroused the enthusiasm of more than his supporters. 'This was one of the best speeches by an Oxford Conservative that I have ever heard,' enthused *Isis* reporter Alan Fyfe. When the vote was taken, Heath's side had won by 162 to 125.[20] The Tory undergraduate son of a carpenter had worsted the experienced and professional Labour son of the Canon of Windsor! More than thirty years later Heath could still exult: 'We won the vote, and it was the first time the Conservatives had won in the Union on a political motion for many years – probably the first time in the thirties.'[21]

THE EDEN TRAGEDY

Amidst all this glow of growing confidence, Teddy's balloon was suddenly pricked by the February 1938 resignation of Anthony Eden as Foreign Secretary, when he could no longer tolerate the humiliations being inflicted on him by Prime Minister Chamberlain. Heath, like so many internationalist idealists, had somewhat glamorized the matinée-idol figure of Eden. He first heard the news on the radio in Phil Kaiser's Balliol room: 'We were all waiting for news of Eden's resignation,' Kaiser later recollected. 'I remember that Ted said very little that night. It affected him. Eden was important to him. When it happened – and the resignation wasn't even reported as the first item on the news – a *gravitas*, a great thoughtfulness, settled on him, more than was the case with anyone else. He thanked me and then walked out.'[22]

Heath succeeded in persuading the University Conservative Association to come out for Eden and against Chamberlain. There was a famous occasion on which Chamberlain's picture came sailing out of the Carlton Club. Heath's enthusiasm for Eden somewhat waned when the former Foreign Secretary's cautious, cliché-ridden speech to young Tories in Oxford offered no banner behind which idealistic young men could gather. Eden made it clear that he was not going to attack Chamberlain and join the forces of the Tory anti-appeasers – Churchill, Macmillan, Sandys and Boothby.

This created a special turmoil for young Heath. Because he identified himself with the free enterprise system which had given his family a chance to improve itself did not mean that he could stomach the smug, don't-rock-the-boat insularity of Establishment Tories. He considered complacent Chamberlain Tories to be dangerously ignorant in their foreign posture and hopelessly stick-in-the-mud in refusing needed radical reforms at home.

Initially he tried humour as an escape. Previously known as a political speaker, he suddenly tried his hand as a comic in the Union, where he had been elected Librarian, deploring the decline of frivolity and attacking Alan Wood as a descendant of criminal settlers in Australia. Despite such deviations, he was put on the spot in June, when the Union debated whether the appeasement-minded Chamberlain Government should be replaced by a Popular Front government containing anti-fascists of all parties. It must have been tempting for Heath to speak for a motion deposing the Chamberlain Government which, only the

previous month, had shown how panicky it could get over reports of
German army manœuvres against Czechoslovakia.[23] But this was
hardly the debating role for the President of the Oxford University
Conservative Association and the former President of the Federation of
University Conservative Associations. So Heath opted to speak against
the motion. He had to listen to Liberal Alan Wood attack the Government's foreign policy over the Abyssinian war, Spain and now Czechoslovakia. Rather lamely, Heath could only point out that a Popular
Front government, while united on fighting fascism abroad, would be
divided over home affairs. Observers of the talented young debater
were struck by the fact that, for once, he was reading, without spon-
taneity, from full typescript notes.[24] He was probably glad to be beaten
in his loyal defence of Mr Chamberlain.

HOMAGE TO SPAIN

After that appeasement of the appeasers it was a great liberation for
Teddy Heath to travel for a fortnight that summer to Loyalist Spain as
a representative of the OUCA. By then the Republican Government had
less than a year to go and was fighting along the Ebro River. The student
delegation was taken to the front and then back to Barcelona, where they
interviewed the Socialist Premier, Dr Juan Negrin, and the Leftwing
Socialist Foreign Minister, Alvarez del Vayo. Twice the Oxford delegation was in serious danger. The hotel in which it was staying was
bombed. Heath and his friends survived because they remained on the
top storey; the bomb went down the lift shaft and killed those who had
sought safety in the hotel's bomb shelter. Then they were machine-
gunned on the Taragona road, after viewing refugee work. After his
experience, 'I was just more than ever in favour of a government that
was trying to resist the fascists.'[25] He made this clear in a radio speech
supporting the Republicans, which got him in the bad books of the
Franco side. He returned to Britain with a copy of the Republican
national anthem.[26] His welcome in Broadstairs was dominated by his
mother's grateful thanks that her first-born had survived the dangers of
Spain's civil war.

Teddy Heath arrived back in Oxford for his 'bonus year' as somewhat of a hero. It was a 'bonus year' because a three-year stay was
normal and this should have come to an end in the summer of 1938. But
Balliol was happy to let him stay on, both because he was its organist
and because he had high hopes of becoming President of the Union. He
returned to Oxford full of grim forebodings.[27] Coming from the front

invested him with a certain glamour at a time when people were being fitted with gasmasks.

In September 1938 Chamberlain's appeasement of the dictators came to a climax with his meeting with Hitler at Berchtesgaden and Munich. After agreeing to the dismemberment of that 'faraway country', Czechoslovakia, Chamberlain had been welcomed back to Britain with hysterical relief as the bearer of 'peace with honour'. Heath's revulsion merged with all who felt that the appeasers, having betrayed Spain, were now in the process of betraying Czechoslovakia.

By a stroke of fortune, Oxford secured a chance to demonstrate its feelings. The Government, having five by-elections pending, decided to fight Oxford City first. Quintin Hogg was selected as the candidate of the pro-Chamberlain forces. On 10 October Roy Harrod asked that the Labour (Patrick Gordon Walker) and Liberal (Ivor Davies) candidates step down in favour of an independent anti-appeasement candidate. The Master of Balliol, A. D. Lindsay, was persuaded to stand, in protest against the 'smug hypocrisy' with which Czechs were being handed over to the organizers of the 'horrible, beastly and abominable' concentration camps. Harold Macmillan wrote to *The Times*: 'The times are too grave and the issue is too vital for progressive Conservative opinion to allow itself to be influenced by party loyalties or to tolerate the present uncertainty regarding the principles governing our foreign policy.'[28]

Heath had been an early and eager recruit to the Lindsay campaign. In mid-October he himself had led an assault on Chamberlainism by leading off in the Union debate in support of the motion 'that this House disapproves of the policy of peace without honour'. He attacked the 'muddled' policy of the Government which was largely responsible for bringing Britain to the verge of disaster. Hitler could not be trusted; that was clear to everyone save Mr Chamberlain. Heath's position was supported by Christopher Mayhew, who had just returned from Czechoslovakia. But he was attacked by a Chamberlain Tory, J. R. J. Kerruish, who said that he had previously regarded Heath as 'a promising young Conservative'. Sir Arnold Wilson also supported Chamberlain. But the anti-appeasers won by 320 to 226.[29] Heath won the admiration of a new arrival at Balliol, Roy Jenkins, the son of Arthur Jenkins, Labour MP and ex-miner. 'Heath's speech,' recollected Jenkins, 'was highly polished and very effective.'[30]

For Heath the more important and more moving experience that month was his activities in the Lindsay campaign, where the sharpest slogan was: 'A vote for Hogg is a vote for Hitler'. Heath deployed his organizational talents, cycling around Oxford helping to tighten up the impromptu organization of the spontaneous and loosely-knit Lindsay forces.

The campaign against Hogg succeeded in halving the Conservative majority in Oxford City. But the anti-fascist campaign continued in the other four by-elections, reaping a victory at Bridgwater, where Vernon Bartlett was returned.

In Oxford University the comparable Popular Front victory was the election of Teddy Heath as President of the Union for the Hilary term. This occurred because Heath became more and more anti-Chamberlain as the autumn wore on. In mid-November he led off in support of the motion 'that this House has no confidence in the National (i.e. Chamberlain) Government as at present constituted'. He asserted that 'everywhere there was the greatest distrust of the Government. It was nothing more nor less than an organized hypocrisy, composed of Conservatives with nothing to conserve and Liberals with a hatred of liberty. As for Chamberlain's foreign policy, it could only be described in the maxim, "If at first you don't concede, fly, fly again".' In reply, his friend Ian Harvey said of Heath: 'The Librarian is like the red, red robin. His heart gets redder as Christmas gets nearer.' The anti-Government motion was carried by 203 to 163.[31]

His election as President in the Hilary term, in the winter of 1938–9, was as an anti-Chamberlain Tory, with wide anti-Chamberlain support from non-Tories. 'He won the Presidency on his anti-appeasement line,' Roy Jenkins remembered. 'I almost certainly voted for him; in fact I'm sure I did. . . . I would have done so on political and personal grounds. . . .'[32]

Heath's self-confidence was so enhanced by his victory that he invited Madron Seligman's father as well as his own to his Presidential dinner. Any fears he may have harboured about how his father would get on turned out to be fruitless. Will Heath was a man who could grow into his son's opportunities.

Heath's friends too were increasingly outside Tory circles. Roy Jenkins introduced him to his father, a friendly ex-miner who had become Labour MP for Pontypool in 1935. Arthur Jenkins liked the young and rebellious son of a Broadstairs carpenter and took him out to tea and lunch on occasions. Teddy Heath also saw Arthur Jenkins on occasional trips to Westminster to listen to Parliamentary debates. The former President of the Conservative Association entered the public galleries mainly on the tickets provided by a Labour MP.

He was a great success as President of the Union, setting topical debates and persuading the famous to debate in them. 'No President for many years has provided a more interesting series of debates and visitors,' applauded *Isis*, 'no President has done more to re-establish the prestige of the Union not only as a debating society . . . but also as a club.'[33]

This same administrative ability was displayed when he was elected President of the Junior Common Room at Balliol. He redecorated the JCR, made it cheap and convenient. It became the most popular and active place in Oxford.[34] It brought him close again to the Master of Balliol, who normally conferred with the JCR President over breakfast.[35]

Teddy paid for his success as a university politician and administrator by not being as great a success as a scholar, although he had spent four years at Oxford. He secured a 'Second' in Modern Greats. 'He was probably disappointed by his school results,' Fulton later thought, 'but then he had done a lot of other things. . . .'[36] His family was also disappointed. Since Oxford was such an exceptional attainment for a Broadstairs boy of modest background, they thought he must be intellectually outstanding as well.

OVERHANGING CLOUD

For Heath the greatest emotional experience of his last year at Oxford, apart from the fight to elect Lindsay against Hogg, was to take a delegation of Oxford Tory undergraduates down to welcome back from Spain the survivors of the International Brigade at Victoria Station. This reception meeting in the spring of 1939 was a deeply emotional experience for all those there. But among the Socialists, Communists and antifascist Liberals there, Teddy Heath's small contingent from Oxford must have been in a tiny minority of Tories.

Where Heath was at one with his whole generation was in the foreboding that war was coming. This gave an air of unreality to decisions about future careers. 'I had to decide whether I was going to become a musician or whether I was going to the Bar' as part of becoming a politician. 'I thought the best thing I could do was to go and talk to . . . Sir Hugh Allen, . . . then Professor of Music in Oxford. And what he said was: "If you are going into music then you don't really want to become a concert pianist, you are not capable of that. You could go on and become a cathedral organist. But really what you ought to do is conducting, which is the thing you've enjoyed most here at Oxford and which you've done quite a lot of. If you are going to be a conductor then the real thing is you must be prepared to go right to the top and make it the be-all and end-all of life. If you are just going to take part in it with general objectives, if you are not fully determined to go right to the top, then you will find being a professional musician is very hard work with not a great deal of satisfaction. And so," he said, "really my advice to you is that if you are terribly keen on the Bar and on politics you can really get just as much out of music for your own satisfaction and enjoyment and carry on in your own way, combine it with a career in [the] Bar and politics rather than making the whole of your life a professional musician's career."'[37] So Teddy secured a scholarship at Gray's Inn, which he never took up.

Before settling in for a new bout of studies, Teddy and his great friend, Madron Seligman, decided on a last vacation together. 'It was our last long vac,' Heath later recalled. 'We knew it was likely to be the last free holiday we'd have, either because there would be a war which one wouldn't survive or else one would have a job and that would be the end of long vacs.'

They decided to go to Danzig in the hot summer of 1939. They crossed via Dover and went to Berlin by train, in third-class carriages with hard wooden seats. Finding the youth hostels occupied by troops, they stayed at cheap *pensions*. They hitch-hiked as far as Danzig and stayed at the YMCA, and Warsaw, where they talked to Hugh Carleton Green in the Embassy; then they turned around and went West.

As they crossed the border into Germany again, they could see German tanks on railway flatcars ready to go. Tension was mounting and they got a bit windy. German drivers were too chauvinistic to give foreign students a lift. They reached Dresden and went to a museum where they looked at Raphael's 'Sistine Madonna' for ninety minutes and talked about the world falling to pieces around them. At Leipzig station they heard a boy shouting news of the Molotov–Ribbentrop Pact and decided they had better hurry out. A bit tense, they had their first quarrel. As they walked along, Madron started playing a pennywhistle he had acquired. Because he was slightly out of tune, it offended Teddy's musician's ears. They caught a train heading for the French border, only to find themselves in a compartment full of wild-eyed Nazi-indoctrinated girls. Seligman, whose German was excellent, argued with them all the way to the border. Heath, whose German was weak, found it difficult to follow. Once across the border they found the French mobilizing. They hitch-hiked back to blacked-out Paris in a Hudson. There they parted. Heath went back to Dover, where Teddy's father was waiting for him in the family's first car, a new Hillman Minx. It was 1 September, two days before war was declared.

A few days afterwards Teddy went back to Oxford – where he was still registered – and volunteered. The Oxford Recruiting Board recommended him for the Royal Artillery, but made it clear he would not be called up until January 1940. Training establishments could only cope with a certain number of raw recruits at a time.

AMERICAN TOUR

This deferment made possible Heath's taking on a university debating tour of the United States. The Committee of the Oxford Union decided that the last two Union Presidents, Teddy Heath and Hugh Fraser, should go. But Hugh Fraser was already in camp with his family's regiment, the Lovat Scouts. So Heath set off with another Union debater, Peter Street, about the third week in October 1939, winding up at Christmas.

Since these debating teams are considered to be showing the flag, even in less troubled times, the Foreign Office briefed them on how to handle themselves in still-neutral America. They were instructed *not* to debate the war, so as to avoid offending American neutrality. But once they arrived, they found all their private discussions were about the war. Pittsburgh University rejected all the debating motions suggested and chose instead: 'Should America enter the war on the side of the Allies ?' A very literal-minded young man, 'I thought we should pack up and go home. Our instructions were that if we had any problems we were to ring the British Embassy in Washington. So I spoke to Lord Lothian, who was then Ambassador. He said it wasn't necessary to be so drastic. What we should do, he said, was to accept the debate [on entry] and one of us should speak on either side. That would prevent any trouble, he said. . . . One night I would speak for the motion while Peter Street opposed, and the next night we'd do it the other way around.'[38]

In later years, Heath was thought to be less 'pro-American' than his older Conservative predecessors. This was true in the sense that he became more objective about the realities of Anglo-American power relationships. As an ambitious young man who had kept coming up against prewar British class barriers, there were many aspects of American life which appealed to him. 'What I warm[ed] to most is the social freedom, the classlessness, the unconcern with the meaningless distinctions which still mean too much here.'[39]

4 THE RUNGS TO MASTER GUNNER

What he has shown is that he has nerve and will: once pointed in the right direction the cannon will batter down the walls.

The Economist

The incident occurred in Antwerp in the officers' mess of the 107th Heavy Anti-Aircraft Regiment of the Royal Artillery, which had just participated in the liberation of Belgium's main port in September 1944. The twenty-eight-year-old Adjutant was frowning at a bottle of champagne which had appeared on the luncheon table. 'Where did *that* come from?' he demanded brusquely of his friend, the Quartermaster.

The Quartermaster explained that, because their supply column had fallen behind them, he had persuaded the Belgian Resistance to lead him to the abandoned Wehrmacht dumps. There, in addition to the tinned meat and vegetables urgently required, he had also discovered some crates of brandy and champagne marked 'Reserved for the Wehrmacht'. While loading his two three-ton lorries with necessities, he had also 'liberated' some of the Wehrmacht's abandoned liquid refreshments.

'You mean you *stole* it?!' demanded Captain Heath rhetorically. 'I'm not drinking any of *that*!' Throughout the somewhat tense meal Heath refused to sample the 'liberated' champagne. Some of his fellow officers shrugged their shoulders over his strait-laced primness, which they felt more suitable to a padre than an artillery officer. One or two understood that Heath's enormous drive to excel also attached to the organization with which he was associated. He expected the 107th to be the best artillery regiment, and its officers to behave like officers and gentlemen.

The fact that Edward Heath fought the war as an artillery officer was accidental. Unlike his brother John, he had not joined the Territorials. 'When the war broke out in 1939 I was [just down from] Oxford and everyone had to report back to their universities for selection,' he later recollected. 'I had no strong preference for any regiment and the authorities in their wisdom decided I should become a gunner.'[1]

But not immediately. He had almost a year to wait while the Territorials, who already had some training, were made battle-ready. His brother John was seeing action while Ted Heath was kicking his heels after returning from his debating tour of the USA. John's unit had been posted to France as part of the British Expeditionary Force. When the Netherlands, Belgium and France were overrun by the Nazis in May

1940, no news of John was received for long, worry-laden days. Then the unit was evacuated from France via Boulogne to Dover. Even there the Military Police would not let John telephone the few miles to his parents' home in Broadstairs. There was great rejoicing when he finally did.[2]

In those dark days when Britain was left to stand alone, Ted Heath had one consolation: the emergence of the admired Winston Churchill as Britain's wartime Prime Minister in May 1940 instead of the Neville Chamberlain he had so long detested. In welcoming Sir Winston back to Margate thirteen years later, Ted Heath recalled: 'The last time the Prime Minister was here in Margate was in 1940 at the height of the Battle of Britain when . . . despite the best arrangements that Margate could make, he spent a considerable amount of time in a deep tunnel.'[3]

It was in August 1940 that Ted Heath was posted to the Royal Artillery training establishment. Initially he was assigned as a gunner to the 70th Searchlight Regiment of the RA then stationed on the Sussex Downs near Storrington. He was soon recommended for officer's training, and moved on to the Officer Cadet Training Unit at Shrivenham, in Wiltshire. After two months he emerged as 179215, 2nd Lieutenant Edward Heath of the Royal Artillery. He was green but eager.

In March 1941 2nd Lieut. Edward Heath was posted with several other subalterns to the 107th Heavy Anti-Aircraft Regiment, then sited in Lancashire as part of the ring of AA around the Merseyside, a prime target for Nazi bombers. He was received by Lt.-Col. Richard Barrow, a Regular Army officer. Also looking on was a warm and colourful character, Lieut. (Q.M.) William ('Harry') Harrington. Another Regular, Harrington had left school at fourteen and joined the Army, serving much of his period in India where his even more colourful 'Brighton Cockney' wife brought up their five children.

After the new subalterns had been collected by their battery commanders, Col. Barrow and Lieut. Harrington discussed the new recruits. 'Col. Barrow was of the opinion that 2nd Lieut. Heath stood head and shoulders above the others,' Major Harrington (as he later became) told the author, 'an assessment with which I fully agreed. Col. Barrow said, "I must get George Chadd to keep an eye on him, he may well make the regiment a good Adjutant one day."'

Lieut. Harrington was happy to hear this because at the time he was doubling as Quartermaster and acting Adjutant. An adjutant's job is normally a difficult job to fill because it requires great administrative ability and tact and, preferably, experience as well. An adjutant is the chief administrative officer of a regiment. He is responsible for conveying the orders from the CO, normally a Lt.-Col., to the battery commanders, normally majors, while only holding a captain's rank. An adjutant is also responsible to the CO for the movement of the regiment's men and materials from one assignment to the next. The 107th had had a quick succession of adjutants – therefore the eager eye of its CO.

Initially 2nd Lieut. Heath joined 335 Battery, under the watchful eye of Major Chadd. There he learned something more about practical gunnery and about living on a site with a half dozen other officers and some 300 men. 'I've never seen him put a foot wrong,' insisted Major (later Lt.-Col.) Chadd subsequently. 'He was always meticulously correct in his conduct and behaviour. The men liked him. He was never impatient with dullards or arrogant to people not as bright as himself. He drank a glass of beer in the mess and he read a lot; he was always reading in bed, but he didn't go out much except with his band.'[4]

This copybook subaltern was one of those nominated to a vacancy at the RA training establishment at Manorbier in Pembrokeshire. There 2nd Lieut. Heath spent a hectic fortnight in September 1941 learning more about the 3·7 gun and the Sperry Predictor used to aim it. Heath's instructor there was Captain R. M. Fraser, subsequently Sir Michael Fraser, Deputy Chairman of the Conservative Party. Although they later became friends, Heath did not make an enormous impact on him in that fortnight. But Captain Fraser kept records on the twenty officers in the course, of whom he failed four. 'The records show that I picked out four from the rest as best. . . . Within the four, the two who really caught my eye were Captain Reeve, who was extremely knowledgeable and fairly experienced, and 2nd Lieut. Heath, who showed most drive and incisiveness.'[5]

Heath returned to his battery as a troop commander – each battery is divided into three troops – in time to help prepare for their next move. This was to the Birmingham area. There, at the beginning of 1942 the regiment lost its CO through his promotion. The new CO was Lt.-Col. Frederick ('Fearless Fred') Slater, a Territorial officer who was a Birmingham solicitor by profession.

This was Col. Slater's first command and he was determined to prove his ability. Unfortunately, his rather fussy style and tendency for long aimless conferences did not suit his Adjutant, Captain Jack Wellstead, who asked to be posted to a new unit.

In March 1942, a year after he had joined the Regiment as a green subaltern, Heath – to his surprise – was made its Adjutant, with the rank of Captain. Col. Slater took Heath into the regimental orderly room and, according to the orderly room clerk, Gunner Frank Hayes, said: 'Boys, I have a new Adjutant for you, Captain Heath. He is going to be a future Prime Minister of Britain.'[6]

Captain Heath's enthusiasm was displayed by the rapidity with which he began to gobble knowledge. For this he turned to the Quartermaster, Captain 'Harry' Harrington, who was not only shrewd but had spent more than half his forty-two years in the Regular Army. He knew not only the proper procedures but also all the shortcuts devised by 'old sweats' to achieve desired objectives and avoid unpleasant repercussions. 'Heath didn't know much at first,' admitted Harrington, 'but if he didn't understand something he would ask how to do it, rather than make a mess of it. When he had been told once, he never needed to ask again.' 'He had a fetish for documentation and a genius for organization.' One field in which he showed both qualities was in the drawing up of movement orders.

Another of his responsibilities was to write up the regiment's secret 'War Diary' every week and post it to the War Office by registered mail. For the most part these 'diaries' make terse and dreary reading, consisting largely of entries about officers posted into or out of the regiment, or the movement of the regiment or one of its batteries. Even when there was an interesting item, Captain Heath's sparse prose left his readers suspended in mid-air with unanswered questions. Thus, early in 1943 a gunner is recorded without explanation as having 'died of a rifle-wound self-inflicted during a troop lecture'.[7]

'Heath never relaxed completely with his brother officers,' one of them recalled. 'His unsureness surrounded him like a cloud. It would manifest itself either in the shoulder-heaving laugh for which he later became famous, or in enormous stretches of silence.' 'In offering his friendship he was very selective.' 'He was a loner.' This aloofness was not immediately apparent on the surface. He would join in discussions in the officers' mess, where normally all but the Quartermaster had a university background, but he gave away very little about himself, even about his activities at Oxford. He was very close to the Quartermaster, 'Harry' Harrington, who was fifteen years older than himself.

If he avoided too close intimacy with brother officers, he kept women well beyond arm's length. He avoided contact with ATS girls attached to the regiment. When his mother urged him to see Joan Stuart, he only offered to meet Joan halfway, at Brighton (she was at Gatwick, he was at Chichester). Although sweet on Heath, Joan refused and married another.

This primness or starchiness did not help him when, as Adjutant, he occasionally had to prosecute in courts-martial. Initially, he probably enjoyed the idea since he had accepted a scholarship to Gray's Inn, with the idea of being a barrister as well as an MP after the war. While they were stationed in Blandford in 1943 he had to prosecute an unfortunate gunner. This man had received word that his wife was having a love affair with another man in his absence. In a fury, he jumped on a regimental motorcycle to race to his home, twelve miles away, to catch his wife and her friend in the act. On his return he faced charges of absence without leave and the theft of the petrol needed to take him home and back. In the court-martial, Captain Heath demanded six months' punishment for the offence. The gunner got off with three months' because the officer defending asked that the officers sitting in judgment put themselves in the place of the wronged husband.

If Captain Heath did seem aloof or strained, most of his fellow officers attributed this to his difficulties with the CO. Col. Slater was not the easiest of COs to get along with, partly because he had tried to import rather unmilitary ideas from his Birmingham solicitor's office. He liked a long, repetitive morning conference which irritated Captain Heath. Many another officer working at cross purposes with his superior, would have asked to be posted out of the regiment. But not Captain Heath. 'I think that at this time Teddy accepted his posting as Adjutant as a challenge, and went all out to make a success of it,' judged 'Harry' Harrington.

This 'creative tension' in regimental headquarters did not interfere with the efficiency of the 107th, which was being brought up to mobile battle standard, in competition with other heavy ack-ack regiments, for the star role of accompanying the landings on the Continent and the reconquest of Nazi-held territories. To achieve this role they had to slim down by dropping the less physically fit from their rosters. By January 1943 they were down to 1,099 men and 42 officers.[8] Among those they shed were their ATS girls, who had been employed at regimental and battery headquarters as cooks, clerks, drivers and telegraphers. 'It was the Adjutant's duty to bid farewell to the ATS Officer,' recalled Major Harrington, 'but on this occasion again he deputed this task to me.' 'Oh Christ,' said Heath, 'I don't want to have anything to do with *her*!'

Finally, in April 1943, the CO wrote to his efficient Adjutant and his other officers to tell them the good news: the reports on their battle and mobile training had led to 'our being given a fully mobile role, instead of a semi-mobile role, over the heads of other regiments. . . .' A period of intensive training ensued, including a month's battle training. This consisted of rock-climbing, swinging on ropes over rivers and clearing obstacles. Most adjutants, being administrative officers, would have remained in their offices. 'Not so, Teddy Heath,' recalled Major Harrington. 'He was out all day with the men, returning to his office desk in the evening when everyone else was relaxing. He was a glutton for work.'

WAITING FOR INVASION DAY

In the months before D-day, the regiment finally received its full complement of guns, vehicles and predicting and signalling equipment. While others were mastering their new 'toys', Captain Heath wrote a new and unique regimental drill book for a mobile heavy anti-aircraft regiment. It was based on an official handbook, only a few copies of which were available. But, with the help of the CO and his second-in-command, Major John Saunders, Captain Heath did an improved version, full of 'dos' and 'don'ts'. This copybook handbook, distributed to every officer, wound up with the following words on the back cover: 'I ask myself, at the end of the day, "How has my show gone?"' Because the regiment following Heath's orders got lost on one occasion, Col. Slater improved this to 'Where has my show gone?'

The regiment embarked on 3 July and lay off Southend that night before crossing in convoy next day. On 5 July they arrived off 'Gold Beach', Normandy, and unloaded on 6 July at Arromanches. They were deployed first in the Thaon area, to act in a ground artillery role in support of the 6th Airborne attacking Caen. They moved down to Oistreham, at the sea end of the canal leading from Caen. They began incurring their first casualties, some from enemy mines and shellfire, but the largest number from three premature bursts from their own guns.[9]

The more intense the fighting, the more complex the administration of an anti-aircraft regiment. In addition to the vital task in battle of receiving and passing on orders from higher authority, an adjutant has to see that all the dreary paperwork is correctly collated: the dead and wounded posted out, the reinforcements posted in. Heath was ruthless with his own energies and those of his subordinates. 'He had no time for anyone not up to his job.'

The efficiency of the 107th told when, after over five weeks, they broke out through the Falaise Gap and moved on to Amiens. Field-Marshal Montgomery decided to limit advancing anti-aircraft regiments to the most combatworthy. On 3 September, they were ordered to take part in the capture of Antwerp, Belgium's main port, and then to protect it against Luftwaffe retaliation. A brigade reconnaissance column, under Major Saunders, led off. This was 'preceded into Antwerp', according to Heath's 'War Diary', 'only by the recce [reconnaissance] armoured cars of the 11th Armoured Division.'[10] Lt.-Col. 'Fearless Fred' Slater led the first regimental column, and the second was led by the Adjutant, Captain Edward Heath.

'The second column,' he recorded in his sparse military prose, 'was marshalled by the Adjutant N[orth] of Arras and moved along the route

Arras–Lens–Tournai–Renaix–Ninove–Assche–Merchtem. It left Arras
at 1030 hrs and arrived at Merchtem at 2230 when the reg[imen]t was
sent into harbour [i.e., to sleep] for the night along the road at Lowder-
zeel, as the situation in Antwerp, where the whole of the dock area was
still in enemy hands, did not warrant the deployment of HAA that night.

'The column encountered no interference on the journey, although it
was halted for an hour and a half North of Lens while a minor battle
was fought on the left flank.

'The column received a tremendous welcome all along the route,
being the first t[roo]ps to pass along the road after the tanks of [the]
11[th] Arm[oure]d Div[ision]. The route rec[onnaissan]ce parties were
in several cases the first British t[roo]ps to enter villages – which they
captured! There were many instances of D[ispatch] R[ider]s being
pressed to take prisoners giving themselves up. And so the reg[imen]t
moved into harbour [bivouac] that night decorated with flags and flowers
and laden with fruit, before moving into Antwerp the next day, the first
British t[roo]ps to enter the city after the tanks and some 48 h[our]s
ahead of the infantry.'[11] For an adjutant, particularly for Captain Heath,
that was a recording of deep emotion because, for the young idealist
who had smarted under the appeasement policies of Chamberlain, this
liberation of Antwerp represented the repayment of a debt. This helps
explain why Heath was so indignant when, next day, the Quartermaster
'liberated' some champagne from Wehrmacht stores for the officers'
mess.

Heath was not infected by the 'enjoy life while you may' feeling
which attacked so many young soldiers, especially when confronted by
large numbers of young women grateful to their 'liberators'. The regiment held a 'liberation dance' at a local hall. There Ted Heath's band,
made up mainly of men from the first battery he had joined, provided
the music. 'To my recollection, Captain Heath did not stay at the dance
overlong,' mused Major Harrington. 'After the CO left, he retired to his
makeshift office in a local garage to do more planning.'

After three weeks the regiment was relieved and went forward. From
27 September they were deployed in defence of Nijmegen, guarding
both ends of the road bridge over the Waal River. The Guards
Armoured Division had joined forces with the 101st American Airborne at Arnhem just North of the Waal. A desperate battle was fought
to keep the route open to Arnhem against a German effort to cut off the
Anglo-American forces. The bridge link was under constant attack
from the air, from the ground and down the Waal. But they were in
good heart when Field-Marshal Montgomery came to inspect them on
1 October.[12] 'Captain Heath was always actively engaged in some

project or other,' recalled his friend the Quartermaster. 'He never seemed to tire or give up.' It was hardly a time for giving up because the German army, thought to be crumbling, had suddenly shown a burst of energy which had caught everyone by surprise. The gunners of the 107th were used in all sorts of capacities – field artillery, anti-aircraft, even infantry – to cope with the unexpected two Panzer divisions in the area which frustrated Montgomery's 'Operation Market Garden'.

In that cold and waterlogged Christmas, Captain Heath inscribed the book of Kipling's poems for his friend the Quartermaster, who had told him that he had bought a plot in Brighton for his retirement: 'May you long live to enjoy your "fair ground by the sea", and in the years to come may these tales recall to you not only your service in the land of Kim but also that in the nearby Continent, and remind you of the regiment in which we serve and one who was for three years "the Adj".'—'Teddy'

On Christmas Day 1944, the regiment learned that it would be pulled out of the line to withdraw to Nieuweport, near Blankenberg, in Belgium, to undergo training in a new type of Canadian radar. For most it was a tremendous relief. They welcomed the chance of relaxation. But Captain Heath saw to it that training was not neglected.

So much prolonged virtue was, at last, rewarded. Captain Heath became Major Heath when he was posted as battery commander of 334 HAA Battery, one of the three in the regiment. There were some doubts about how good a commander Major Heath would make. 'Until that point,' recalled the Assistant Adjutant, D. C. Bennett, 'Heath had been almost wholly an administrative officer. He had shown comparatively little interest in gunnery tactics.'

This hesitation also showed itself among the ranks of 334 Battery, which Major Heath was taking over. 'We were all wondering what sort of person he would turn out to be,' pondered James Hyde, a Canterbury man who was then the battery's orderly room Sergeant, 'and were none too happy. Up to then he had been an administrator. He hadn't done any fighting worth speaking of. I was suspicious of him. I felt my life was going to be upset. But . . . within a fortnight or three weeks he exercised such a persuading influence that one found – much as one had loved one's previous CO, who'd undergone all the privations – that Heath was first-class. So far as administration was concerned, he was perfect. The other reason he was first-class – and this was to my surprise – was that he rapidly understood the men and their reactions. He made no changes that were apparent on the surface, but underneath the surface, he'd make them. Within a month or two it was Heath's battery. The men liked him because they thought he was a fair man. . . . He didn't know tiredness. I've done operations orders with him all night.

He was a tough skipper. If he said the battery was going to do it this way, that was it. . . .'[13]

Major Heath had the opportunity of a good shoulder-heaving laugh when he went down to brigade headquarters at Weert in those days. There he found, as Brigade Major, none other than his witty friend from Oxford, Major Ian Harvey. Harvey had gone through Staff College at Camberley and had dodged studying Japanese by pointing out that, as a prospective Conservative candidate for the Don Valley, he would be serving in the House of Commons rather than in the administration of Japan. Major Harvey was surprised at how highly Major Heath was thought of, even by the 107th's CO, with whom he had long clashed. 'I think Teddy will one day be Prime Minister,' Colonel Slater predicted, to Major Harvey's complete disbelief.[14] Colonel Slater had recommended him for promotion to Major and, later, for the military MBE, which did not come through until the spring of 1946.

The first occasion on which his orderly room sergeant discovered that Major Heath was at all interested in politics was in the early spring of 1945, when an Army Council Instruction came around. This said that anyone interested in fighting the expected general election would have to fill out a form to secure the necessary three weeks' leave. Without explanation, Major Heath asked Sergeant Hyde to secure the form for him.

Major Heath may have hoped that the Conservative Association in the Isle of Thanet might be interested in a local boy who had become Chairman of the Oxford University Conservative Association, Chairman of the Federation of University Conservative Associations, President of the Oxford Union and was now a major commanding a battery. Although there was some talk about it back in Broadstairs, the call never came. It went instead to an Old Etonian in the Life Guards – 'Ned' Carson, son of Lord Carson, of Ulster fame. 'Ned' Carson's mother, Lady Carson, carried a lot of weight in the Isle of Thanet Constituency Association.

In March 1945, Major Heath had home leave in Britain, his first since he had gone overseas. His parents were still living in Sutton, where they had been evacuated at the beginning of the war. He did a number of errands for the men in his command, including telephoning the parents of his orderly room sergeant, in Canterbury.

LEAVE WITH ATTLEE

On his way back to his unit, Major Heath had an amusing encounter – with Major Attlee. Late one night he arrived at Liverpool Street

Station, on his way back to his regiment. There he encountered amiable
Arthur Jenkins, the MP father of Roy Jenkins who had befriended Heath
during his University days. Arthur Jenkins, who was PPS to Clement
Attlee, then the wartime Deputy Prime Minister, chatted with the
young Major, while waiting for Attlee. 'When the Deputy Prime
Minister arrived,' Heath later recounted, 'I was introduced to him. We
chatted together for some time, and [Mr Jenkins], having told Mr Attlee
of my somewhat rebellious Conservative tendencies at Oxford, suggested that I might be pushed a little further and be a promising member of the new Labour Party. . . . Mr Attlee adopted . . . his most
quizzical expression, sucked at his pipe, and we pursued the matter no
further.'[15]

When he returned to his regiment, there was still fighting to be done.
On 13 May the regiment held its victory parade in the market place in
Calcar, with awards being presented by the CO.[16] The MBE for which
Heath had been recommended had not yet come through. Heath was,
however, mentioned in dispatches.

Ten days later the regiment moved back to near Antwerp to prepare
to hand in their guns. It was there, on 31 May, that they received orders
to move to Hanover where, under the command of the 8th Armoured
Brigade, they would take over occupation duties. They arrived in
Hanover on 5 June,[17] with 334 Battery being housed in nearby Bemerode.

THE SHOCK OF TORY DEFEAT

The atmosphere in the officers' mess was overwhelmingly Tory in the
days before the election of 5 July 1945. The announcement, after three
weeks, that the heroic wartime leader, Winston Churchill, had been
ousted by his colourless deputy on a tidal wave of Labour support –
particularly from the other ranks in the Services – came as a shock. And
to none more so than to Major Heath, for whom Churchill had been a
hero figure since the first battles against appeasement.

Major Heath had an early opportunity to examine Nazi atrocities. He
visited Belsen, the notorious death camp, then guarded by a sister
regiment. His regiment presided over the hanging of six Nazis for
brutality to POWs, including the infamous Irma Greese, with her
penchant for lampshades of human skin. Perhaps the biggest impact on
Major Heath was his attendance at the Nuremberg war crimes trials.
Less than a decade before he had been in that city watching Dr Alfred
Rosenberg when he and the Nazis were at their peak of power. Now
after almost pulling the whole world down about their ears, they were
seedy, sagging figures.[18]

Until 15 August 1945, of course, Major Heath's stay in Hanover was thought to be an interlude between wars. Initially the regiment was being weeded out to exclude older men while retaining the young and fit for the war against Japan, then expected to take another two years.

BECOMING HONOURABLE

On 22 September 1945 the 'War Diary' of the 107th read: 'T[emporary]/ Major E. R. G. Heath, RA (17915) posted as 2 i c [second in command] to 86 (HAC) HAA Reg[imen]t RA under auth[orit]y HQ BAOR MS/21/8205 dated 12 Sep[tember].'[19]

At least one of his brother officers in the 107th suspected that this posting had been arranged as a way of giving Heath an additional gloss for his future career as a Conservative politician. Having served in the Honourable Artillery Company, the oldest regiment in the British Army, was something which might appeal to Conservative selection committees. Its headquarters in the City had become, in peacetime, so much of a club that, at the war's beginning, many of the gent-gunners in the regiment had pledged not to ask for commissions so that they could remain together. The War Office finally persuaded them that winning the war was more important than retaining a club atmosphere in the 86th.

'I have no reason for thinking that his original posting to the regiment in 1945 was other than an administrative one,' insists Lt.-Col. G. H. Champness, who recalled the way in which the 86th was losing officers at the time, including himself. 'He was posted as second in command of my regiment on the day that I was demobilized in September 1945. The new CO was demobilized on compassionate grounds some three weeks later, leaving Mr Heath to command the regiment as a major until a new CO was posted about three months later.' In fact, Major Heath made so successful an acting CO in the interim that most of the officers and men were hoping he would be promoted to Lt.-Col. and CO.

It was at once striking how much more Major Heath could relax in command than he had previously been able to do as Adjutant or Battery Commander. He was also amazing in the way in which he transferred his loyalties to the HAC. He read up its history and was so taken by its mystique that he applied to become a member of the HAC which required sending three pounds and an application form to its Court of Assistants, which accepted him on 17 December 1945.

When the new CO, Lt.-Col. J. G. Tyrrell, arrived in December 1945, he found that Major Heath had everything under control. There was no friction in taking over, partly because Lt.-Col. Tyrrell was a relaxed

Regular who believed that, after a hard-fought war, the officers and men should enjoy the pleasures of peace. There was harmony also because 'Heath knew how to get on with senior officers'.

Major Heath adapted himself successfully, for example, to the CO's lavish lunch-time hospitality in the midst of war-devastated Germany. Being the sort of regiment they were, they had inherited a considerable cellar. It was decided in the officers' mess that they would try to drink their way through their liquid stocks and share out the cost. The CO would invite guests for an early lunch, pour drinks into them for an hour or more, then have a wine-embellished luncheon, followed by three or four stiff liqueurs. Major Heath was no heavy drinker but managed to avoid being odd-man-out by spinning out his drinks. Heath would only complain when he was presented with his part of the tab: 'That's a bit thick,' he said, 'I've had very little of this.'

They had a comfortable, pleasant life on the outskirts of Osnabruck, on the Haase River, halfway between the Dutch border and Hanover. Major Heath relaxed by playing two-piano duets with another officer. He also organized riding lessons for those, like himself, who could not ride. He did not do very well on horseback because, as one of his colleagues commented, 'He was just one roll of fat too many.' The paunch which showed in photographs of the victory parade in Calcar had taken on additional dimensions.

Major Heath did not advertise his politics in the mess, although it was fairly obvious to the politically sophisticated. 'What do you think his politics are?' one officer asked Lieut. Arnold Jennings, who had been at Oxford at the same time as Heath. 'Tory Reform, I'd think,' replied Jennings. When Jennings later told Heath that interest was being shown in his politics, Heath replied: 'Yes, I know. And I know what your answer was. You don't think my intelligence system is as bad as all that, do you?' He left up in the air, however, just how strong was the reforming element in his Toryism.

When the demobilization of the regiment took place, in April 1946, both Major Heath and Captain Jennings had a month of military service left to do. 'We don't want to get posted to another regiment just for a month, do we, Arnold?' said Heath persuasively. So, with the typical organizational ingenuity of a 'Mr Fixit' he had them posted to the college being run at Gottingen by the Rhine Army. And just so that they would not have to work during the month they were there, Heath had them assigned as 'observers' rather than students. 'That,' recalls Jennings, later a Sheffield headmaster, 'was a supreme example or Heathmanship!'

While on his way home to the UK at the end of his stay at Gottingen,

Heath had an encounter with another major, Ashley Bramall, whom he had known on the Standing Committee of the Oxford Union. They met in the officers' bar at Tournai. The conversation turned to what they would be doing after the war. Bramall was fairly sure he would try again for something in Labour politics. He had unsuccessfully fought the hopeless seat of Fareham in the 1945 general election. Heath seemed less certain. He was still toying with the idea of being an orchestral conductor. As a result he was not sure whether he would be able to carry out his long-held ambition to go into politics.

By a striking coincidence, within five months Ashley Bramall was the Labour MP for Bexley, and within a year and five months Heath was adopted as his Tory opponent for the next general election!

5   THE PURSUITS OF PEACE

> Whatever the situation before the war, we have moved
> with the times. . . . We do not pander to the wealthy.
>
> Edward Heath

'I have no prejudice against matrimony,' the earnest bachelor candidate
replied at his formal adoption meeting. 'I just think that it is *not* a
matter that should be rushed.'[1]   It was a cunning reply to an anticipated question. After a year in the constituency-chasing game, he knew
that Conservative constituencies did not like bachelor candidates over
the age of thirty. This was the sort of shrewd caution that enabled
Edward Heath to be adopted as the prospective Conservative candidate
for the marginal seat of Bexley in November 1947. And twenty-five
years later it was still considered a useful magazine feature to pick for
the bachelor Prime Minister of Britain the 'perfect wife'. One magazine
doing this had to be shredded because of tastelessness.[2] Although his
target was 10 Downing Street, even being accepted as the candidate for
a Labour-held marginal seat seemed a very big achievement at the time.

The Heaths had been lucky. Both the sons, Teddy and John, had
returned from the war unscathed, although Teddy had aged. 'The first
time I saw Edward Heath,' his one-time sister-in-law wrote, 'I thought
he was his own uncle. He was thirty and looked all of forty-five . . . he
had put on so much weight . . . that his own brother hadn't recognized
him when he went to Broadstairs station to meet him on his return from
the army.'[3]

The Heaths were back in their little semi-detached at 4 King Edward
Avenue, Broadstairs, after the parents' wartime evacuation to Sutton,
Surrey. The father, Will Heath, had been able to re-start his building
firm as Broadstairs's inhabitants began to reverse the wartime evacuation of the coast. Although it was good to be home, Ted's demobilization
in May 1946 had released him from the security of a major's pay. Should
he continue to aim for a political career? If so, how could he earn a
living? At thirty it was rather late to begin studying for the Bar.

Ted had an early talk with a distinguished neighbour, FitzRoy
Weigall. Could the son of a builder, even a former President of the
Oxford Union and a major in an HAC regiment, make his way in the
Tory Party? Weigall thought that a modest background might no
longer be an insurmountable obstacle. The postwar party was being

reshaped nationally by Lord Woolton, and this would penetrate darkest Kent eventually.

Politics played a part in deciding which friends to seek out among his surviving Oxford contemporaries. He dined at the Coningsby Club, revived in 1946 by Ian Harvey, who insisted there should be no 'red-brick goons' and no women at their meetings at the Junior Carlton Club. Few of their generation of Oxbridge Tories, except Hugh Fraser, had yet become MPs.

It was, after all, a period in which politics looked much more hopeful for his *Labour* contemporaries at Oxford. Ashley Bramall had been elected for Bexley in the 1946 by-election. Christopher Mayhew was already a junior Minister in the Foreign Office. Harold Wilson, another Oxford contemporary, was a Cabinet Minister at thirty-one.

Heath meanwhile earned his living in the civil service. Candidates went in batches to a country mansion early in 1947 where they were tested and interviewed. Heath tied for top score in his age group with Balliol friend Ashley Raeburn[4] and was assigned, as a temporary and fairly junior civil servant, to the Ministry of Civil Aviation's Directorate of Long-Term Planning, headed by Peter Masefield.

He represented Masefield on the London Airport Planning Committee, trying to get Heathrow going. 'Ted Heath used to go and fight on the committee and come back and cry on my shoulder about all the spokes put in the wheel by bumbledom. . . .' In a note written at the time, Masefield predicted: 'I fear we shall not have him here for long because, outside the office, he lives and dreams politics and, with the civil service machine the way it is, as soon as he is adopted for a Parliamentary seat he will have to resign. . . .'[5] Heath made it clear to his friends that he did not think the civil service was for him.

He was consequently delighted when in February 1947 he was offered the command of a Territorial regiment. The Territorials, on the point of being disbanded, were restored with the growth of tension with the USSR. The Honourable Artillery Company was among the first to be asked to re-establish a heavy anti-aircraft regiment. Field Marshal Viscount Alanbrooke initially asked Lt.-Col. Champness to form the regiment. Col. Champness had commanded the 86th regiment for the three and a half years until Heath joined in September 1945. He recommended that the younger Heath should replace him in command. 'My reason for suggesting that Heath should be invited to reform the regiment after the war was simply that on the few occasions that I had met him during the war, he had always impressed me by his efficiency and enthusiasm. . . .'

Heath's new regiment was reformed on 1 May 1947 and eventually given the title of 2nd Regiment HAC (HAA). Heath was promoted to Lieutenant-Colonel to become its commanding officer. He then began trying to recruit other officers, approaching Michael Fraser, who had also served in the artillery throughout the war. Fraser was fairly recently married and showed no inclination for 'playing soldiers' in peacetime.

TIME OFF FOR WEDDINGS

There were some of his friends he would not think of approaching for peacetime soldiering. One of these was Madron Seligman. Madron was launching on the sea of matrimony and, as his closest friend *and* organist, Ted Heath was invited to play at his wedding. Heath also volunteered to play for the couple who were married just before the Seligmans. Madron had written a bit of music for his wedding, a 'Melody in F'. Because the bride was ten minutes late, Heath was compelled to play his friend's musical confection ten times over – to his disgust. When the service was over, Seligman was rhapsodizing over the minister's words. 'It was a verbatim repetition of what he said to the couple before you!' taunted Heath.

Although he was seeing something of Kay Raven in Broadstairs, the absence of any serious lady-love of his own enabled Heath to concentrate all the more singlemindedly on his own passion – to become a Conservative MP. Like so many other ex-officer hopefuls, Heath went through the standard political drill and was added to the list of aspirants. Although his prewar work in the Oxford University Conservative Association and the Federation of University Conservative Associations gave him seniority, he was not thought enough of a Butler-type intellectual to be put on the party staff, together with Michael Fraser, Reginald Maudling, Enoch Powell and Iain Macleod, most of whom had won 'Firsts' at university. Heath was included in the Conservative seminars which met one Saturday afternoon a month at Church House to be lectured on the emerging party programme and have a chance to practise speeches on one another.

The only places Ted Heath was short-listed were in his native county of Kent. He had his first selection in March for Ashford, as one of three. But there William Deedes, MC, a *Daily Telegraph* journalist, had the inside track. He came from a long line of Kentish squires who had provided MPs for the area. Deedes insists it was because he dressed as a country gent and Heath as a City gent. The next unsuccessful canter, the following month, was against Vyvyan Adams for East Fulham.

In August 1947, Heath was short-listed among four for the cushy seat of Sevenoaks, which had attracted over 200 applicants, including Randolph Churchill and Brendan Bracken. The short-list was largely for padding because the seat was intended for ex-MP James Duncan. Heath did not know this and got very upset when his car broke down en route. He arrived, all flustered, five minutes after he should have begun making the first speech. This did not improve his orthodox presentation. The speeches of Thelma Cazalet and James Duncan, also on the short-list, were rather sober too. John Rodgers had the advantage of being warned by an influential local friend that the seat was meant to go to Duncan. Infuriated by this, Rodgers made an uninhibited speech about why the Tories had lost the 1945 election and why they were in danger of losing the next. Fearing long years of boredom with the candidate prechosen for them, the Sevenoaks Tories opted for Rodgers.

BEXLEY BECKONS

Heath finally struck it lucky at Bexley, a rather drab lower middle-class suburb in the north-west corner of Kent, on London's fringe. It looked rather dicey to settle for Bexley; Mrs Jennie Adamson had won it for Labour by 12,000 votes in the 1945 floodtide. When she resigned in November 1946, the seat was narrowly retained for Labour by Ashley Bramall, with a majority of 2,000. The drop in the majority gave advance indication of a change in the social and political makeup of the constituency. During the thirties there had been an enormous growth of small semi-detached houses, which went for about £400 each, mainly to skilled workers in the nearby Woolwich Arsenal. The war over, many of these workers were retiring and selling their houses to white-collar workers in the City.

Something which operated in Heath's favour was the rule that the new candidate should be unlike his unsuccessful predecessor, Lt.-Col. John Cutts Lockwood, a rich eccentric. He emphasized his own modest background. He even explained his two addresses: one was his parents' and the other, in Old Swanley, Kent, was where he was rooming with the father of his university friend, Timothy Bligh.[6]

Heath's selection was helped by the fact that his witty friend Ian Harvey, also on the short-list, was chosen one week before by Harrow East. This helped Edward Dines, the local Tory chairman, who felt that his marginal seat could more easily be won by a well-educated local boy from an ordinary family. Someone suggested Heath to him and he sent for his official party biography. Heath, who was in camp with his Territorial regiment, received a telegram asking him to appear for an interview.[7]

'Sit down please, Mr Heath,' invited Councillor Dines when Heath appeared at the Victorian villa rented by the Bexley Conservatives on 18 October 1947. Heath sat down at a trestle table facing six women and two men. 'That half-smile of his is what I will always remember,' recalled Mrs Gladys Whittaker. 'Of course, he was good on policy. But it is the smile that sticks in my mind. It was not the broad grin which we are used to from him now, but a shy kind of half-smile.'[8]

Heath had two competitors. There was Mrs Patricia Marlowe, daughter of Sir Patrick Hastings, KC, and wife of Tory MP Anthony Marlowe; and Eric Harrison, of the Parliamentary staff of *The Times*. Heath, who was interviewed second, was an easy winner. At a subsequent meeting of the Bexley Tories' Executive Committee Heath won three-to-one overall.

NO KISS FOR THE BRIDE

Heath could go along quite happily to the wedding of his brother John to Marian Easton, a week after his selection as Bexley's Tory candidate. Both John and Ted had new suits – no mean achievement in a period when clothing was still rationed. John had wanted his friend, Tony Yates, to be best man but Mrs Heath insisted on Ted. So the organ had to be played by somebody else. Ted presented John and Marian with a pewter cruet, which Marian later described as unattractive and impractical. 'After the buffet lunch,' she recalled, 'Teddy as the best man made a most amusing speech saying that as there were no bridesmaids he felt he had in no way committed himself . . . he was the only one not to kiss the bride.'[9]

Heath was in good spirits again at his formal adoption meeting a fortnight later, on 7 November 1947. There was the feeling that the Tories were on the march in Bexley. In the borough elections the week before, they had won three seats from Labour.[10] Heath promised: 'I will carry the fight right into the enemy camp.' He attacked the 'lack of leadership' and 'specious promises' of the Attlee Government. Its 'dogma of nationalization', its 'controls which multiplied like rabbits', its 'centralization of power which was putting the ordinary citizen into a straitjacket'.

However, he stoutly defended civil servants, of which he was still one, as men 'of great integrity . . . the great majority – and I have never met an exception – have ignored their political opinions in their work. If I am adopted as your prospective candidate, then I shall hand in my resignation as a civil servant.' He admitted that 'there is still a suspicion of our party in the minds of the people' and promised that it did 'not propose to tread down any particular class'. This was an area in which they wanted to make Tories of ambitious people of working-class origins.[11]

Before the final acclamation he had been asked his views on matrimony. When he cleverly said that he had no objection to it – but that it should not be rushed – this encouraged his mother, who was present. She reported it back to Kay Raven, his Broadstairs 'girl next door'. A prep school teacher, she was the daughter of a local doctor. She had been interested in Ted since adolescence. They had played tennis together and she had been the secretary of his carol concerts. She was encouraged by Mrs Heath to drop in at their home and Ted would visit her. After 1939, when he indicated he was more interested in her than in Joan Stuart, she was locally considered his girl friend,[12] although it was never more than platonic on his side. 'You can't imagine Teddy kissing a girl,' his mother said. Miss Raven, tired of waiting, married someone else early in the fifties.

Some of Heath's friends thought his political ambition was so strong that he would make a 'political marriage', which was not exceptional in Tory circles. His Oxford and wartime friend, Ian Harvey, married Christopher Mayhew's sister, Clare, about that time. As Harvey later explained: 'This satisfied my supporters in the constituency who thought it was a mistake to have a candidate who was a bachelor and over thirty. . . . When I got married I had never had sex with a woman nor had I ever desired to have it.'[13]

SECRET CHURCH JOURNALIST

Ted Heath was more preoccupied with finding a job to go with his candidacy, now that he had to resign from Civil Aviation. He applied to the Oxford University Appointments who recommended him for the vacant post as news editor on the *Church Times*. The job paid £650 a year, £200 more than his civil service post.

At the time the *Church Times* was a serio-comic outfit, neither a good weekly nor a happy bunch of journalists. Its editor, Trevor Beevor, a leader of the Anglo-Catholic movement, was a difficult man, and certainly did not hit it off with Heath. John Trevisick, a former provincial journalist, did not welcome as his senior a man without any journalist experience. Nicholas Bagnall, later of the *Sunday Telegraph* but then just down from university, was the third member of the newsroom.

Heath did not try to win anyone over. He acted the part of the simple bluff soldier. He was not so much unfriendly as austere and hard-working initially. He was never polite, no more than a commanding officer would have been polite in handing out assignments. His staff had their worst suspicions confirmed about his ignorance of journalism and church affairs. He 'corrected' a report on the annual meeting of the UMCA – or Universities Mission to Central Africa – by altering its initials to YMCA!

'Despite this,' recalls Nicholas Bagnall, 'after a couple of months he had us eating out of his hands!' 'He did it by force of personality, mainly by making it obvious how hard he worked himself.' 'What are you doing with the rest of your time?' Heath would ask young Bagnall, implying that working for the paper was only a half-time job. On one occasion Bagnall brought a story about the deterioration in church graveyards. 'You know this stinks!' was Heath's reaction, accompanied by the shoulder-heaving laugh for which he later became famous.

Heath was a plain, no-nonsense writer who cut a swathe through the ecclesiastical jargon which he clearly disliked. He occasionally did some straight reporting – including competent coverage of the 1948 Anglo-Catholic Congress. But he avoided editorials or book reviews. Mostly he edited and prepared for the printer other people's copy. On one occasion Trevisick, who succeeded Heath as news editor, remembers Heath 'laughing like a jelly' at a colleague being bitten by a dog while on assignment.

Heath attracted one wholehearted admirer, a secretary who burst out: 'That man is going to be a Prime Minister one day!' 'My god,' said the journalist to whom she confided this, 'you *must* be in love with him!' And indeed she was. She followed him around the office with sheeplike eyes of devotion. 'What shall I do about the woman?' asked a worried Heath.

What bothered Heath was that this job was not leading anywhere. He could write political speeches in the office, but his companions on the paper could not help him up the political ladder. 'We didn't see him outside the office,' recalls Bagnall, 'except occasionally at the pub across the road.' Heath found it as unmentionable to tell people that he was the news editor of a religious weekly as if he had been a bouncer in a bordello. In his first two years as prospective candidate – while he was on the *Church Times* – his occupation was never mentioned in his local paper. He kept it so well shrouded that when he entered the February 1950 election, *The Times* made the mistake of referring to him as still a civil servant.[14] Heath later omitted this era of his life from his *Who's Who* entry.

Heath decided to chuck his comparatively well-paid and undemanding job. 'He didn't like it,' his father recounted. 'After a year he said: "This isn't going to lead to anything" and just packed it up.'[15]

MAMMON AFTER GOD

Heath knew that the road to power in the Conservative Party was more easily paved with knowledge of money than religion. He went from the newsroom of the *Church Times* to the counting rooms of Brown, Shipley and Company. At thirty-three the prospective candidate for Bexley began work as a trainee banker on 31 October 1949, at four pounds a week and free lunches at the staff canteen. Since he wanted to finish the course in a year – there had to be an election in 1950 – they began moving him around the bank's various departments very rapidly.[16] 'A very nice man who seeks knowledge and who should learn quickly,' read a departmental report after two months. 'Likely to profit by his course.' In fact, Heath never secured any depth of economic understanding, according to his Tory economist friends.

His drop in pay from £650 to £200 embarrassed him a bit at home and in his constituency. His family and friends knew that he was taking a rash gamble on winning Bexley, subordinating all to his political ambitions. Before, he had been earning twice as much as his brother and had been able to be generous in family treats. Now it was no longer possible. There was virtually nothing left after his rent and fares.

It was more embarrassing in the constituency. Conservative candidates were then still expected to contribute at least £100 a year to their constituency associations. Luckily, his first chairman, Edward Dines, did not like the traditional habit. 'I remember Heath coming to me one Saturday morning about the time when his [£100] subscription was due and asking if we'd mind waiting a bit. I told him to forget all about it and that it would be soon enough to think about a contribution when I asked him for one. Of course, I never did.' The Association's President, banker Martin Holt, came to the rescue with a cheque for £250. Heath persuaded five other people to give £50 each, whereupon Holt produced a further £250. This gave the Bexley Conservative Association a kitty of £750 with which to face the impending general election.[17]

THE PHENOMENAL CANDIDATE

Local men gave of their money because Heath was giving more than generously of his time and talent. If the Tories were to become again the governing party, they *had* to win back lower middle-class seats in the southern suburbs of London. In the 1945 floodtide they lost

F

fourteen seats in their safest area in Kent, Surrey and Sussex, which had previously returned forty-seven Tories in forty-eight seats. In 1945 the Tories had not only been beaten but they had also been demoralized.

Heath himself was first launched at an open – as distinct from a Conservative – meeting on 21 November 1947. He attacked the Attlee Government for having wholly misconceived the transition from war to peace, underestimating the difficulties. As a result they had started big projects which they could not finish. Labour, he insisted, was reaping the results of their prewar propaganda: 'It is not necessary to work. You are working for the boss, do as little as you can.' Controls were a danger to freedom.[18]

He also did exchange stints in neighbouring marginal constituencies. To the south, in Chislehurst, the hot-gospelling redhead Patricia Hornsby-Smith was in action. To the west William Stewart, owner of Veeraswamy's, an Indian restaurant in Regent Street, was trying to win Woolwich West.

Heath built up the prestige of the Bexley Tories by having an impressive list of speakers: Beverley Baxter, Brendan Bracken, Lady Violet Astor and Sir David Maxwell-Fyfe. He could exploit the Coningsby Club and was helped by the fact that Bexley was high on the list of winnable seats, which gave him Central Office backing for his requests.

Heath toured the constituency with a new mobile library van as part of the recruiting drive. The target was to bring party membership in the constituency to 10,000 – or every second person who had voted Tory.[19] By November 1948, from 800 two years before, they hit 6,000.[20] Heath also sought to reach local people through their varying professional and other interests. He early encouraged the establishment of the Bexley Business and Professional Men's Luncheon Club, as a scarcely disguised Tory 'front organization' to be addressed by Conservative speakers. He even organized a regular angling contest between Bexley anglers – of whom he was President – and the Broadstairs fishing club, of which he was a member.[21]

He was both a great consumer and great critic of party propaganda, attacking it at his single effort as constituency delegate to the Llandudno conference of October 1948. AT LLANDUDNO – BEXLEY DELEGATE OPPOSES MOTION – LORD WOOLTON UPHOLDS MR HEATH was the headline in the *Bexleyheath Observer* of 15 October 1948.

'For the first time, the voice of the Bexley [Conservative] Association was heard at the annual conference of the Conservative party at Llandudno. . . . Mr Edward Heath, prospective Conservative candidate for Bexley, appealed for a new approach to the question of party propaganda. He suggested that much more could be achieved if the many excellent pamphlets and leaflets were less academic and couched in simpler terms. It would also be of great assistance if the cost of these publications could be reduced, as many associations were unable to afford sufficient quantities to effectively disseminate party propaganda.

'Lord Woolton, in his summing up, made special reference to the suggestions made by Mr Heath and promised that simpler wording would be aimed at, while the Woolton Fund would be used to subsidize party propaganda so that the cost to constituencies would be cheaper.' Lord Woolton was clearly taken by the shrewd young candidate.

In his speeches Heath impressed Bexley as a very earnest young man with rather starchily orthodox views on social questions, rather prewar views on economics and a very serious student of international affairs. He denied the charge of his Labour opponent, Ashley Bramall, then Bexley's MP, that the Tories were a 'class party'. 'Whatever the situation before the war, we have moved with the times. We have come up to date. . . . We do not pander to the wealthy.'[22] He disclosed nothing about his own modest background.

Heath attacked as 'a low shady political intrigue between two sections of the Labour Party' the effort to curb the power of the House of Lords to delay legislation – in this case, the nationalization of steel. He agreed that the Lords were politically lopsided and that there must be less emphasis on hereditary influence.[23]

On 14 November 1948, Heath expressed the jubilation of the meeting and Bexley Conservatives at the birth of the Royal baby, Prince Charles: 'We are met tonight on a very auspicious and happy occasion. We are cheered and heartened by the news of the birth of a prince to Princess Elizabeth. As a meeting and a party we pledge our loyalty again to His Majesty the King, to the Princess, and to the baby Prince, one day to be a King. We wish him health and prosperity.'[24]

ECONOMIC RIGHTIST

His economic views had an even more prewar quality. He kept stressing the need for 'more production, less controls, fewer people interfering in industry'.[25] He was a great opponent of nationalization, including the already nationalized airlines, BOAC and BEA. 'The answer is to free the airlines and bring them back to a commercial basis to get more competitive spirit into the field.'[26] At the end of 1948 he attacked the idea of nationalizing iron and steel just as vehemently.[27]

'A large part of Government expenditure must be cut out,' he told an audience of 250 in the Playhouse in his home town of Broadstairs in January 1949. 'Reduce taxation and let the working man have a reward once again. . . .' 'Let us do away with this generation of spivs.' 'Production and exports can be increased – by working with private enterprise instead of against it.' 'Civil aviation and coal are inefficient. Parts of these and other nationalized industries could be restored to private enterprise. . . .' But he added: 'It must be our solemn duty to maintain full employment.'[28]

When devaluation came in September 1949, Heath attacked as 'humbug' Sir Stafford Cripps's statement that the cost of living would not rise substantially. 'Improved efficiency and more work from everybody in industry is the only answer, and we must face it. The catch is that wages must not rise. . . .'[29]

THOUGHTFUL ABROAD

From the outset, Heath made his suburban constituency a lecture hall for his changing attitude towards foreign affairs. The candidate had no cheerful pre-Christmas fare. He warned that the breakdown of the four-Power talks might wreck the whole of the recovery of Western Europe. There was suspicion everywhere. He felt Germany ought to be united if it was to develop efficiently, otherwise there would be a crisis in Western Europe. In ten, fifteen or twenty years two Germanies might play off the Powers against each other.[30]

'Before the war we always looked upon Germany as our problem and the key to that problem was Russia,' he told the Ladies' Luncheon Club in January 1948. 'Today, the position is reversed. Now the problem seems to be Russia, which appears to be obstructing and causing trouble. I think that the key to the Russian problem is in Germany.' 'The Foreign Secretary [Ernest Bevin] has got to show how we are to keep some sort of control on Germany to prevent them becoming a fighting unit again.'[31]

The situation in Czechoslovakia was a threat to the whole of Europe, he told the Bexley Tories on 5 March 1948, just after the Communist takeover. 'Come what may, we shall not yield to Russian tyranny or Russia with the Atom bomb,' he later added.[32]

This last speech, to 250 people in the Playhouse at Broadstairs, gave him an extended weekend at home. Normally he would arrive home in Broadstairs late Saturday night, quite exhausted. He would work during the week at Brown, Shipley, going off almost every evening to one or another part of the constituency he was contesting. Almost every Saturday there was canvassing or fund-raising events. Occasionally

he could invite his family. Thus, when Lady Violet Astor opened the
Bexley Tories' Christmas Bazaar in 1949, Heath brought his quiet
but proud mother along.[33] Otherwise she would only see him when he
woke up late on a Sunday morning, to spend the rest of the morning
in bed reading the Sunday papers.[34]

Heath had his opponent to thank for being able to reach a much
wider audience than a prospective candidate fighting a sitting MP had
any right to expect. Although Heath pretended to local Tories that he
hardly had known his Labour opponent at Oxford,[35] he understood him
well enough to realize that he could not resist a challenge. Almost as
soon as Heath was adopted, he offered to debate on the Local Government Bill. When Bramall accepted local Labour people objected.
It was not usual for a sitting MP to help his less well-known opponent
become better acquainted with the voters. They met at the Scout's
Hall in Bexleyheath on 19 January 1948, with over 400 in the audience.
Heath was well-prepared. He produced large charts to prove Bramall
had been wrong in claiming that the saving for Bexley would be a
shilling in the pound; it would only be a quarter of that. Whoever won
on points, the debate earned Heath front-page coverage in the local
weekly.[36]

Heath's next big debate came just before the February 1950 election.
In October 1949 Heath attacked as a 'pernicious allegation' and a
'grotesque distortion of the truth' Bramall's statement that, on past
form, the Tories would like a pool of 1,300,000 unemployed.[37] Heath
challenged Bramall to debate it.[38] The debate took place with 800 on
hand and hundreds more unable to secure entry to the hall. Bramall
pointed out that unemployment during the past four years had been the
lowest since 1873. Heath said that mass long-term unemployment was
a worse social affliction than tyranny. He blamed what unemployment
there was on Dalton's 'cheap money' policy. He warned that Britain
was relying too much on American aid for needed raw materials and
not doing enough to make herself more efficient and self-reliant.[39]

APPROACHING ELECTION

As the election neared, Heath worried that Tory policy had not been
simplified sufficiently in its presentation. He showed this by seconding
a motion by Ian Harvey at the March 1949 meeting of the National
Council of the National Union of Conservative Associations at Central
Hall, Westminster. 'First,' insisted Heath, 'we want a crystallization
and reinstatement of our policy as it has developed over the past.
It is too diffuse. . . .'[40]

As a winnable seat, Bexley already had a full-time Tory agent. The agent Heath found there suddenly left on a day's notice, four months before the election. A stand-in held the fort for a month until the arrival of Reginald Pye, who was to be his agent for the next generation. Born in India, he had returned to Britain for his education before going East again as a rubber-planter in Sumatra. During the war he had joined the Canadian Army and had been posted to Harvard University to prepare to administer Japan. After MacArthur banned all allied troops, Reg Pye had returned to Britain, becoming a stamp-dealer, and Tory activist in nearby seats. He became Bexley's agent two months before the February 1950 election.[41]

Heath went over and over his simple but rather obvious 1,000-word election address. His agent had difficulty in getting it away from him in time when Prime Minister Attlee unexpectedly decided to go for a general election in February 1950 – normally a bad month for campaigning. Heath himself had been very uncertain about when the election would come.[42]

The campaign started with Heath's adoption as the Conservative candidate – as distinct from a *prospective* candidate – on 1 February 1950 at Scouts Hall, Bexleyheath. When the chairman, banker Martin Holt, introduced him as a man who was 'born in Kent, went to school in Kent, lived in Kent and understood Kentish people', a voice from the back shouted, '. . . and for all we care, he can *die* in Kent!' When the chairman asked for someone to play the piano accompaniment to the national anthem, to everyone's surprise, Heath volunteered and astounded them by his musical ability, which he had kept secret.[43]

Unexpectedly, the weather was good in that February of 1950, enabling Heath's friends and supporters to turn out in full force. The largest number came from the Honourable Artillery Company, which seemed to treat the constituency contested by the CO of their 2nd Regiment as though it were an enemy salient. There was also a small contingent from Brown, Shipley, and a larger group from safe Tory seats nearby, particularly Beckenham, plus Heath's friends from Broadstairs and university days. Because Heath's new agent, Reg Pye, had not yet imposed his methods, that first campaign in Bexley was somewhat loosely organized. Heath's ex-Liberal friend, Madron Seligman, initially went out with a loud-hailer, addressing unheeding shoppers. Then Heath sent him to heckle the Labour candidate.

The campaign for Bexley was lively but friendly, partly because Heath and Bramall had long known each other, partly because all four candidates were of the same age. When they met to put down their deposits, they agreed that whoever won would invite the other three to dinner at the House of Commons. Bramall was pretty sure that Heath would pay the bill, because he had been conscious of the social and political shift in the composition of the constituency.

Heath tried to make this foreboding come true. He had a team of Tory girl stenographers recording every word of Bramall's to pick up any slip he made.[44] His own emphasis was very heavily on economics and unemployment. In between meetings – which were still important in those pre-TV days – Heath used the new-style Tory canvassing technique. He strode down the middle of the street while his canvassers knocked on doors ahead of him, inviting electors to come out to talk to him.

The biggest meeting was the last, one of 1,000 at the Girls' Technical School in Bexleyheath on 18 February. Heath and his agent thought they were lucky to get for this eve-of-poll meeting an MP who was a fine orator and who, like Heath, had been active in the Oxford Union and served in the Royal Artillery: Derek Walker-Smith. In his speech he recalled how easy it had been to buy a house in Bexley for £375 with a deposit of £5 – which sometimes the estate agent would lend you. 'I never found that agent!' a woman shouted up from the audience. 'Well, madam,' Heath replied, 'I just cannot imagine why!'[45] Later Heath returned to the problem of housing, 'I sometimes think,' he said, 'that this problem would have been solved if Aneuran Bevan [a housing Minister] and Jennie Lee had had to live with their in-laws.' Came a voice from the audience: 'They do!'[46]

TIGHT COUNT

The count was very exciting. Heath, in a blue sweater, was perspiring visibly and scratching his nose nervously. Halfway through the count, the returning officer collapsed and was carried out, to be given first aid by the Mayor. He recovered in time to whisper to the candidates that Heath was the victor by 166 votes. Bramall requested a re-count. At 1.45 a.m. the second count showed that Heath had won by 133 votes: 25,854 to Bramall's 25,721, with the Communist, Charles Job, having secured 481 votes, or almost four times Heath's margin over Bramall. The Liberal candidate, Mrs Doris Hart, had 4,186 votes. Heath pledged: 'I shall always do my best to serve everyone and every organization, regardless of party.'[47]

About 5 a.m. that same morning, there was a strange and joyous reunion in the street in front of the Chislehurst Conservative Association in Hatherley Road, Sidcup. There Edward Heath was able to exchange enthusiastic mutual congratulations with redhaired Patricia

Hornsby-Smith, victor at Chislehurst and William Steward, who had won in Woolwich West. They had won three adjoining seats for the Tories *by a margin of under 500 votes for the three of them*, after multiple recounts. As they joyfully exchanged experiences, they could not know that victories like theirs had come close to ousting the Labour Government but had not quite. They did not learn until the following afternoon *that Labour had survived by six seats.*

6 BEING NOTICED IN THE CLASS OF '50

A party is lost if it has not a constant reinforcement of young and energetic men.

Benjamin Disraeli

'At the entrance to the House of Commons,' Edward Heath recalled about his first day, 'I was stopped by the police constable on duty. "A new Member, sir?" "Yes," I replied, "Your name and constituency, sir?" I told him. "Ah, yes," he said – in a way which led one to feel that he was already well acquainted with those details. "Welcome to Westminster." It was a pleasant start.'[1]

Edward Heath was entering the House as one of a hundred new Conservative MPs, as a result of the sharp swing back to the Tories which had shrunk the Labour majority to a perilous six after the February 1950 general election. This 'Class of '50' was unique. It represented the loosening of the stranglehold of wealth and position on the selection of Tory MPs. The emergence of a number like Edward Heath demonstrated that the dominance of Old Etonians, squires and business magnates was breaking up.

The plump, greying newcomer, in his 'uniform' of black jacket and striped trousers, was also made welcome on his first day, 1 March 1950, by Derek Walker-Smith.[2] As the only MP to speak for Heath at his eve-of-poll meeting, Walker-Smith had promised that, if Heath won, he would show him around his new working quarters. Heath appreciated this. 'Anyone in the House for the first time has much to learn,' he observed at the time in a curiously naïve way, 'but everyone, friend and foe alike, tries to make it easy for him.'[3]

He observed the Speaker's selection in the same tone of small-town awe. 'The House was full for this traditional ceremony . . . The Speaker of the last Parliament (Col. Douglas Clifton Brown) was proposed and seconded by a Member from each side of the House. He was unanimously elected, but when his sponsors went to lead him to the chair he at first resisted them, showing how unworthy of the honour he considered himself. It was a pleasant little reminder of the tradition of the House.'[4]

'The full splendour of State ceremonial was seen a few days later when the King opened the new Parliament. It was an unforgettable spectacle,' Heath felt, 'full of light and colour.'[5] He was taken by the 'grey and red of peers' robes, the jewels and tiaras of the peeresses, the red robes of the Bishops, and the brilliance of the judges' apparel'.[6] 'It was a thrill to see how Mr Churchill works in the House, to see how he dealt with his interrupters. He must be one of the great Parliamentarians of his time.'[7]

The tiny majorities of Heath and the Government both compelled him to arrange his life efficiently. He moved into a tiny bachelor flat in Artillery Mansions, in Victoria Street. Normally he worked at Brown, Shipley, the merchant bankers, only in the mornings. 'The narrow margin between the political parties in the House keeps him away a great deal,' mourned the manager there, 'but he attends here whenever possible.'[8] Heath earned £200 as a Brown, Shipley, trainee on top of his £1,000 as an MP.

Some aspects of the House were easy to pick up: 'the new Member who has been a member of the Oxford or Cambridge Union, coming to those benches is like coming home . . .'.[9]

Heath soon had an identity problem. The Conservatives, even in 1950, were a very class-conscious community, divided largely between the self-made elementary school boys and the prep school boys who had gone on to the great public schools: Eton, Harrow and Winchester. 'It's the bed you were born into or the one you crawled into that counts here,' grumbled Cyril Osborne, a wealthy self-made Tory MP who was the son of a miner.

As a 'City banker', the CO of an HAC and a Balliol man, Heath was anxious not to be identified with those outside 'the magic circle'. 'He did not like to be identified with the other ESBs – elementary school boys – on the Tory benches,' a colleague recalled with a slight edge of malice. Another noticed that Heath was very close-mouthed about his family background: 'His life began at Balliol!' Even his drinking habits were noted because the House tends to divide into non-drinkers who use the Tea Room, the beer drinkers who use various bars and the whisky drinkers who tend to concentrate in the Smoking Room. 'He was a Smoking Room type from the beginning,' remarked Lord Carson's son, Ned, MP for Heath's native Isle of Thanet.[10]

Heath's well-concealed class-consciousness made him less anxious to introduce around his family when he invited them down to the House. In those days it was always a foursome: his mother and father, his brother and John's then wife, Marian. The family was thrilled to see, during their lunch in the Strangers' Dining Room, many faces previously seen only in the newspapers and newsreels. Heath was somewhat embarrassed when his large, extrovert sister-in-law, Marian, enthused in a voice that might be overheard by other Tory MPs about the truculent Liverpool Labour MP Mrs Bessie Braddock.

THE CONSTITUENCY CONNECTION

Heath applied himself to learning about Parliament with all the systematic intensity he had applied to previous important tasks. He bought books on Parliament and its history. He was anxious to know how the legislative apparatus worked. He also had to be knowledgeable when, as part of strengthening his precarious hold over his constituency, he showed parties of Bexley people around.

Heath attracted a substantial constituency mail from the very beginning. 'The number of letters each Member of Parliament receives daily varies,' Heath observed. '. . . a new Member . . . usually employs a secretary part-time to help him with it.' He selected Miss Rosemary Bushe. 'The normal post-bag contains one or two effusive letters, a number of requests for help in remedying injustices which have to be taken up direct with the Minister of the Department concerned, and a few expressing the views of constituents on current political issues.' After the facilities he had enjoyed in the Army and even on the *Church Times* he was not impressed with those provided MPs. 'Members have to carry on this part of their work in conditions which are not good. Many sit in corridors dictating to their secretaries.'[11]

Heath felt it important to reach as many people in his constituency as often as possible. He had had only a tiny majority in the February 1950 election and since the Labour Government itself had only a tiny majority, a new general election could come at almost any time. He reached his Bexley supporters initially by a monthly meeting at which he reported back on what was happening in Parliament.[12] One of the schoolboyish ploys of the period was for Tory MPs to drift away from the Commons at night without arranging for 'pairs'. Then, at some agreed time, when a vote was expected, the Tory MPs would rush back to the House in the hope that their Labour opposite numbers had called it a night and could thus be out-voted. One of those who joined in this game was Sir Henry ('Chips') Channon, the wealthy, American-born Guinness-married, playboy-politician. He arranged large parties of Tory MPs at his nearby townhouse, to be interrupted in time to vote.[13] Its first success was on 22 March 1950, when the Labour Government was narrowly defeated.

In his speeches to his constituents, Heath made it clear that he was not privy to this strategy of guerilla warfare. 'You can take my word for it,' he told his constituents nine days later. 'The stories about the Tories rushing in straight from dinner in their dinner jackets and of Tories hiding in the yard outside and so on, are all makebelieve. The reason why there were so many Conservatives in the House is because we have such a keen lot of Members, who are determined to be there to play their part in the business of the nation.'[14] Unfortunately for Heath, residents of Belgrave Square like Channon did not confide all their japes to those living in Artillery Row. Heath was more accurate and thoughtful about the real balance of political forces: 'So long as the Government has a majority of five or six and is prepared to carry on, it is quite capable of governing and passing any legislation it wants.'[15]

Heath had neither the majority nor the upper-class arrogance to dismiss strong local feelings. Almost as soon as he reached the House he began to get a heavy mail on crimes of violence as part of a campaign by the Bexley Chamber of Commerce.[16] The next few months were a classic example of how to listen to your het-up constituents with apparent sympathy without committing yourself to their 'gut' reactions. By early April, a petition circulated by the Bexley Chamber of Commerce calling for the return of corporal punishment for crimes of violence gathered 7,000 signatures locally. Heath told the local newspaper he wanted to hear all viewpoints on the subject.[17] In mid-April, a chubby figure clutching the lapels of his grey suit, he presided over a meeting of local people. During the discussion he occasionally intervened to ask a question – did the local headmaster believe in using the cane? But even after his summing up at the end his audience was none the wiser as to his own viewpoint.[18] In May he took the 7,800 petition signatures to the Home Secretary, Chuter Ede.[19] About a week later the Tories won three more seats from Labour in the local borough elections, and were able to elect the first Conservative Mayor.[20]

REG THE 'RIGHT-HAND MAN'

Increasingly Heath was able to leave local organization to Reg Pye, his shrewd constituency agent. When Heath wanted to meet the local doctors, or to meet teachers to discuss their problems, he left it to Reg Pye.

In order to aid the efficient Mr Pye, Heath helped find a house from which to operate. The 1950 election had been fought from a room in a supporter's home – hardly adequate for a marginal constituency. The Bexley Tories found one house at £1,600 but turned it down because of dry rot; there was much Tory glee when the local Labour Party later bought it. Heath and Pye found another one for £4,000 in Crook Log. This had a lot of land behind it. The top floor was converted into a flat for Mr and Mrs Pye and, after part of the land was sold off to finance modernization, enough was left for garden parties. Heath was able to raise the £400 deposit by extracting gifts of £250 and £150 from friends.[21]

Like many good agents, Pye was an administrator rather than a politician. He liked to have an orderly, cohesive association without any internal feuds. Therefore he frowned on factional politics or agitational speeches. Under Pye's administration, the Bexley Tories ceased to submit dissenting or agitational motions to annual conference. If there was a political discussion to be held, it should be held within the Conservative Political Centre, leaving the association proper to operate as a cohesive whole to fight the local Labour Party.

As part of his obsession with unity Pye helped persuade Heath not to dine in the homes of leading Tories. His previous experience in nearby associations had taught him that the social jealousies resulting were disruptive. In Bexley a strict rule was instituted. The MP dined either in the Pye's flat in headquarters or in the local pub, the King's Head, when sharing a meal with local activists. This was a wholly exceptional rule, practised only in Bexley. It amazed other Kent MPs and agents who found that one of the easiest ways for an MP to repay supporters' efforts was to grace their table. There was a certain amount of irritation among local Tories that Heath allowed himself to be guided so substantially by Pye's opinions. It sometimes seemed as though Pye was practising on Bexley Tories the administrative arts that MacArthur had not allowed him to deploy in Japan. But Heath found it worthwhile to indulge his able agent-lieutenant.

Heath could get away with keeping his Tory activists at arm's length socially because he was so active elsewhere. He worked hard to provide constituents with seats in the Commons galleries. 'A Member of Parliament who has a politically-minded constituency, especially if it is near London,' he observed, 'receives a constant stream of requests from his constituents of all parties for tickets to get into a gallery to listen to a debate for a few hours.'[22]

As an 'organization man' of talent, he soon found satisfaction in turning the right levers to provide satisfaction for his constituents. 'But,' he early observed, 'there are some problems, especially those concerned with housing accommodation, which make a new Member feel quite helpless. He tries every possible solution but the problem remains.'[23] As the Conservative son of a builder Heath was sure the Labour Government and its Minister, Aneuran Bevan, gave too large a proportion of scarce resources to council houses. Heath expressed his dissatisfaction with the April 1950 Budget. 'It is quite inadequate to cope with the present home problem . . . it is essential to be able to build more than 200,000 houses in the year.'[24]

IN SEARCH OF AN IMAGE

For an ambitious politician it was not only important to do good, but to be seen visibly to be doing good. That required publicity in the London or national press. Heath's first press contacts in the House were not uniformly successful. Robert Carvel, then with the *Star*, saw the unknown Heath talking to 'Stackie' Stacpole, of the Press Association. 'Who is that?' asked Carvel. 'He's one of the new Tory MPs, who lives over in Artillery Mansions,' replied 'Stackie'. 'What's he like!' 'Oh,' said 'Stackie', half-joking, 'he's a fascist!' Needless to say he soon changed his mind.

One day Heath rushed into his agent's office, grinning and chortling, 'I've made it in the nationals!' He showed Reg Pye a nine-line item in the *Evening Standard* of 11 May 1950, which described his efforts to have Bexley designated for a head post-office. Two days later he had a 12-line bonanza in the *Evening News* telling of his fight for a Registrar's Office. It all helped.

ONE NATION/ONE NOTION

Quite accidentally, Heath got his foot on another ladder. In March 1950, during a crowded debate on housing, Heath found there was no room in the Members' Dining Room. With three other new Tory MPs – Angus Maude, Cuthbert Alport and John Rodgers – he went to the Harcourt Room. This enabled Heath to be brought into a discussion that Maude, Gilbert Longden and Alport had started over the failure of the Conservative Party to evolve and project a convincing policy on the social services.

The upshot was a discussion group of nine thoughtful, newly-elected Conservative MPs who met regularly. Maude, Longden and Alport had recruited Richard Fort, Robert Carr and John Rodgers, and now Rodgers had brought Heath. These seven then invited Iain Macleod to join them. The eight then lunched at the old PEP premises, at 16 Queen Anne's Gate, where Maude had worked. Macleod informed them that he had been asked to write a pamphlet on the social services for the Conservative Political Centre. He suggested that this might be a joint production. This was agreed. Macleod also suggested that Enoch Powell, who knew a lot about housing from his Conservative Research Department days, be asked to join; this was also agreed. Macleod was appointed the joint editor of the projected pamphlet, along with Angus Maude, the only known journalist in the group. Heath kept mum about his experience on the *Church Times*.

They decided to dine together every Wednesday night. They read the next week's 'Whip' – the cyclostyled list of the next week's business, with the Whip's Office's indication whether the debate was routine (single underlining), important (two-lines) or imperative (three-lines). They selected suitable topics on which to concentrate and picked their spokesman. They discussed capturing Tory Back-bench committees.

Heath's contributions tended to be practical. 'Heath was no intellectual,' John Rodgers later admitted. 'He listened while intellectuals like Macleod, Maude or Powell pontificated. Then he would surface with something like, "Well, what are we going to do about it?"' 'However,' added another member of the group, 'I can't recall that he ever told us what we *could* do.'

Initially, the group had neither a name nor a chairman. Normally, the person who was reading his chapter served as chairman. By the 1950 summer recess corrected drafts of the pamphlet were ready, with Heath having made his contribution to the last chapter, on financing the social services. Maude did the rewriting, editing and press preparation work during the holidays. It was not long before its publication that they decided on a title for the thick pamphlet – 'One Nation – A Tory Approach to Social Problems'. This gave the desired effect: that they shared with Disraeli the ideal of a united nation rather than 'two nations' one rich, one poor. Heath went along in October 1950 to the Leicester meeting of the Conservative Political Centre, to help launch the pamphlet.[25] It was after this that they took to calling their Wednesday evening pressure group the 'One Nation Group'. One of their sardonic colleagues redubbed it the 'One Notion Group', suggesting that its one notion was to call Macleod to the attention of the leadership.

A BACHELOR'S FOREIGN 'MAIDEN'

Although Heath turned up regularly, his mind and heart were abroad because, as he put it, 'foreign affairs was my first love in politics'. He had a timely opportunity to revisit Germany in June 1950, as part of a Parliamentary delegation, to find out the German reaction to the Schuman Plan. In May 1950 the French Foreign Minister had offered his plan to integrate the coal and steel industries of Western Europe under federal control. It was a French scheme to control the burgeoning West German steel industry, intending to exclude or subordinate Britain. Initially, the British Government was asked to accept federal control as a *condition* of exploring the idea. The Attlee Government was cool. The Conservatives stigmatized Labour's coolness as 'anti-European'. A half-dozen Rightwing Tories – including Henry Legge-Bourke, Gerald Nabarro and Enoch Powell – decided to abstain from supporting their Leader's Europeanism. Heath decided to make his first or maiden speech on this subject, after four months in the House.

When Heath rose on 30 June 1950, there was more hanging on it than he knew. It was the last serious speech he was to make in the House *for over nine years*. It also established him as a thoughtful 'European' among the Tories, then still largely imperial in orientation.

Heath had the advantage of just having returned from Bonn, where he had spoken to German Ministers: 'I believe that . . . the German Government would be prepared to make economic sacrifices in order to achieve those political results which they desire. . . . Under Marshall Aid, France has been able to expand her steel production very considerably. She would like to see German coke go to Lorraine and German steel production to remain pegged; while the Germans see in the plan an opportunity for expanding their steel production. There, possibly, is a possible seed of conflict . . . and I submit that that is a very strong reason why we should take part in these discussions – in order that we may balance out the difficulties between France and Germany which are bound to arise on the economic side. . . . Under the German plan, Germany may very well become once again a major factor in Europe. Anyone going to Germany today is bound to be impressed by the fact that the German dynamics have returned. . . . I suggest that there are only two ways of dealing with that situation: one is to attempt to prolong control. . . . The only other way is to lead Germany into the one way we want her to go. . . . I appeal tonight to the Government to . . . go into the Schuman Plan to develop Europe and to co-ordinate it. . . .'[26]

Heath's speech impressed his elders in the House, particularly Harold Macmillan,[27] and the Chief Whip, Patrick Buchan-Hepburn, long an intimate friend of Winston Churchill. They saw the need of serious young men like Heath because the North Koreans had attacked on 25 June, five days before Heath spoke up for a strengthened West European unity.

In the wake of the North Korean attack, Heath was one of the first on the Conservative side to reach the conclusion that it might be advisable to rearm the West Germans as part of a European force: 'It may be that Russia is just probing to find the weak spot, or to see how far she could get short of war, or it may be part of a much wider plan in which Russia is trying to involve the West in the Far East, so that she can start probing for weak spots in the West. If that is the Russian plan, then the future looks very serious indeed.' He thought it might be necessary to have a German force as part of a European army. That was fraught with danger, but he believed there was a way of controlling the rearmament of Germany and to keep it in European hands. He did not think that the Labour Government was capable of doing this. It was becoming insular, as was apparent from its placing unnecessary obstacles in the way of the Schuman Plan. It seemed incapable of cooperating with any but other socialists.[28] Two months later Dean Acheson put the same proposal to a reluctant Ernest Bevin in New York.[29]

HEADING SOUTH

Heath had a two-part vacation that year. The first part was with the family at Broadstairs. He relaxed and read, apart from one dramatic incident, at the cricket ground in Canterbury. When teatime came, Mrs Heath lit the paraffin stove. After one kettleful, she poured in extra fuel, without turning down the flame. The flame shot four feet in Marian's direction, igniting her clothes. Ted and John dived at her with the car rug. In pain from the flames, she was rushed by fast-driving Ted to Canterbury Hospital.[30]

In September he set off for a Continental jaunt with John Rodgers, the MP for Sevenoaks. They drove through France in Heath's new blue car. Heath would not let Rodgers drive, although it meant very long driving stints. Rodgers, a Director of J. Walter Thompson, was a relaxed vacationer. But Heath would say, 'Let's turn off here, John, for a few miles; there is an excellent museum near here.' In the South of France, Rodgers took Heath along to meet Lord Beaverbrook. 'The Beaver' was impressed with the young Tory MP and wrote to Rodgers later, 'I liked your young friend. I think he should go far.'

From the Côte d'Azur they followed the coast to Sitges, in Spain. Rodgers was happy to relax at the beach, admiring the nubile figures of girl swimmers. But this had little attraction for Heath. After a brief span he would excuse himself and put in a couple of hours reading the heavy tomes of history and biography he had brought. They had a furious row when Rodgers tried to fix a 'double date'.

During the crisis over Korea at the end of the year, Heath supported the trip of Prime Minister Attlee to Washington to urge caution on the Americans rather than spread the war to China. Heath emphasized it was in Britain's interest to preserve peace. In the Far East this meant localizing the conflict. The only long-term hope for peace was through the UN. Britain must maintain its friendship with the USA. There was no

G

hope for the Empire or the world without it. Efforts to split the two Powers must be neutralized. 'We and the Americans are friends who must stand together in good or bad times.'[31]

BELATED CHRISTMAS PRESENT

One of his presents was late that Christmas. Soon after he was back in the House in January 1951, he was asked whether he would accept an invitation to join the Whips' Office as Assistant Whip (unpaid) for Kent, Surrey and Sussex. Chief Whip Patrick Buchan-Hepburn, a tall, patrician-looking man, was anxious to strengthen the Whips' Office against the stormy period he foresaw.

The Whips' Office had always been a sort of Tory Praetorian Guard whose loyalty was strengthened by a common background of military service. Loyal service in the Whips' Office had customarily been rewarded with a Cabinet post and peerage for the Chief Whip and perhaps the Governorship of an Indian state for his best lieutenants. Previously the Whips' Office had been old-fashioned both in social content and in the parade-ground sort of discipline handed out. If an MP did not turn up to vote, the Deputy Chief Whip, Brigadier Harry ('Beer') Mackeson, tended to tear him off a strip as if he had been a deserter.

Buchan-Hepburn wanted to move towards a more modern discipline by Whips from a wider background. One of the first he interviewed was Heath, whose experience as CO of an HAC regiment made him more acceptable to those already in the Whips' Office, who had to vote unanimously to invite him.

Initially, Heath was not over-enthusiastic. He had only recently made his maiden speech. An Assistant Whip in Opposition had a lot of unpaid chores. It also meant that you could not normally speak in the House. But Buchan-Hepburn was persistent. Heath asked whether there would be any hard feelings if he left after eighteen months.

Heath succumbed to the Whips' Office blandishments during a convivial dinner with Brigadier Mackeson. Before confirming his acceptance, he telephoned Lord Swinton, the *éminence grise* of the Tory party whose acquaintance he had made. Lord Swinton told him: 'Take the chance to get into the machine, at however squalid a level.' Heath accepted the advice of the most influential behind-the-scenes manipulator in Tory politics.[32] He went to see the Leader of the Opposition for the formal offer. Winston Churchill told him: 'This will mean much hard work and it is unremunerated; but as long as I am your leader, it will never remain unthanked'.

Heath described his new function as Whip to his local newspaper:

'The Conservatives have a "Shadow Cabinet" who decide on the policy on all business coming up in the House. The policy must be passed on to the 300-odd Tory Members, who must be fully informed on what is going to happen with any business. The Whips see that the policy is known to the Members. Roughly, it corresponds to an adjutant in a military organization. The Whips also sit on the Front Bench to assist members of the "Shadow Cabinet" . . . while they also see that Members are there to vote and that they do not get into the wrong lobbies.'[33]

Heath made up in his constituency the speech-making opportunities he was losing in the House by becoming a Whip. He complained that while the Government was pledged to rearmament, they nominated a pacifist at the Bristol by-election – meaning Anthony Wedgwood Benn, who had been a pilot officer in the RAFVR, 1943–6![34]

Heath kept reassuring his constituents that he was still speaking in the House. He cited his participation in the debate of 26 April with Strachey over the army's Z reserves.[35] In fact the debate was an adjournment debate raised by a Labour MP in which Heath asked a single question: 'What is the percentage of those actually being called up?'[36]

He was more accurate in his complaint that he had been the victim of a 'count out' when he raised the question of additional houses for Bexley. He did this on the adjournment, normally a device for having a half hour's talk on some constituency problem. Heath had only been asking for an additional housing quota for seven minutes when Labour opponent, Geoffrey Bing, called for a count. Because Heath could not bring forty MPs into the House in time, he was 'counted out'.[37] As a Whip he was expected to take better precautions.

There was a little malicious fun in the Whips' Office that the hard-working 'new boy' had been taken down a peg or two. There could be no complaint about the amount or duration of work he did. Moreover, he took less time out for a matey meal or a jar with his colleagues. But he had the bad habit of finding it difficult to say 'thank you' in a relaxed and personal way.

He worked well with his new 'flock' of Tory MPs in Kent, Surrey and Sussex. He soon had each of them tagged, knowing their strengths and weaknesses, and where to reach them in an emergency. He varied his appeal to the ear receiving it. 'Ted Heath would use more of a "soft sell",' recalled Ned Carson. 'If I had shown signs of not voting with the party, he would walk up casually and say something on the lines of "Now be a good chap. It's not really a matter of your conscience this time, is it?"' – a reference to Carson's rebellion on the American Loan in December 1945. '"Do come into the lobby with us. There's no point

in abstaining." I remember, however, one occasion when he was stern
in a tactful way and I was so surprised at this I went into the lobby at
his bidding.'[38]

TIME OFF FOR TERRITORIALS

Occasionally Heath had to give himself a little leeway. This happened
in June 1951, when he was at camp at Weybourne, Norfolk, for fourteen
days with his regiment, the 2nd HAC. Things went pretty badly in
the rainswept camp until Lt.-Col. E. R. G. Heath, MBE, arrived to put
them right. Towards the end of his time he received a call from the
Whips' Office. They needed him to vote against the banishment of
Tshekedi Kama by the Commonwealth Secretary, Patrick Gordon
Walker. Heath made the 150-mile dash to Westminster, voted, and
turned around and went back to the Norfolk mud.[39]

The HAC were so pleased with Heath's achievements that Viscount
Alanbrooke promoted him to Master Gunner within the Tower for
1951–4. This honour, normally reserved for commanding officers of
the HAC, gave him responsibility for supervising ceremonial salutes
by the Tower Battery. It would mean that he would be expected to
arrive ten minutes before the salute resplendent in the blue undress
uniform – blue tunic with high blue collar, blue trousers with red
stripe and spurs. The danger was that the cheeseparing officials insisted
on using prewar ammunition for these ceremonial salutes. This oft-
damp ammunition was likely to misfire, offering physical risk to the
gunners and 'image' danger to the Master Gunner.

Heath learned that he would be taking on the role of Master Gunner
on the eve of his six-week trip to the United States and Canada,
beginning on 22 August. He had been able to persuade Brown, Shipley
to finance his tour, although they could hardly learn from him more
than from reading *The Economist* and the *Wall Street Journal*. Heath
was helped by his Oxford friendships with American Rhodes Scholars.
He met Tom Watson, President of IBM and the father-in-law of an
Oxford contemporary, Jack Irwin. He went to Brown Brothers,
Harriman, the American link of Brown, Shipley, before going on to
Canada.

The September announcement of the impending October 1951
election found him still there. 'I was in Ottawa when it was announced,'
he remembered later. 'I remember getting into a lift in the hotel, the
Château Laurier, and finding myself followed by Herbert Morrison
and Edward (later Lord) Shackleton, then his PPS. They had just had
a message from Attlee that he had called the election. I flew to New York

and travelled home on the *Queen Mary*. I remember Shinwell, who was also on board, leaning over the rail and telling me that they would lose the election by a small majority.'[40]

MOTHER'S SHOCK

A terrible shock awaited Ted Heath when he arrived home, laden with presents. His mother was in the terminal stages of cancer. She had been ill for some time but had kept it from her family. She had been admitted to Ramsgate Hospital finally, but they could do nothing for her and sent her home to rest. He had gone away knowing nothing.

On his return the truth was broken to Ted by his father. His sister-in-law, Marian, witnessed the terrible scene: 'Teddy leaned against the kitchen dresser, his face suffused with pain, and John and I stood together like lost children. . . .' Ted talked to the doctors to make sure that everything that could be done had been done.[41]

His mother was determined that her illness should not interrupt his campaign for re-election. She was, she pointed out, in good hands. Ted went down to see her every night, after canvassing until ten o'clock. Almost the last act she performed before sinking into a semi-coma was to co-sign a loan of £1,000 so that her son could invest the money in Brown, Shipley. The blow fell on 15 October, ten days before the election. Mrs Heath fell asleep and did not wake up. Although the end had been foreseen, it came as a terrible shock. Like so many emotions in his life, he had to button up this one too. As soon as the cremation was arranged and the memorial service held in St Peter's – he had to hurry back to the election campaign. There was no word of Heath's loss in the local newspaper. It was restricted to a few top Tories and Ashley Bramall.

This time it was a straight Heath–Bramall fight, with the Communists and Liberals not contesting Bexley.

Heath had not been as 'soft' with his Labour opponent as the latter had been with him. In March 1951 Bramall challenged him to a debate on Tory policy for bringing down prices; Heath ignored it.[42] Heath finally shared a platform with Bramall on 10 October 1951 at St Mary's Hall. He said he was a Tory because there must be both order and liberty, which the Tory party could balance. The Tories had not solved the problem of mass unemployment between the wars, but neither had anyone else. On 15 October, the night his mother died, he spoke at the Scouts Hall, Bexleyheath. He ridiculed Labour for its split over the pace of rearmament and for Morrison's role in Iran.[43]

NO RECOUNT DOWN HERE

There was no need for a recount in Bexley on the night of 25 October 1951. As a result of his work and the further swing to the Tories nationally, he was home and dry with a majority of 1,629 in a straight fight. Just after the announcement, a grinning Heath was carried around the area on the shoulders of his enthusiastic supporters. Next day it was discovered that the Conservatives had won a narrow majority of seats in Parliament although they still trailed by half a million votes in the country.

7 PRAETORIAN MONK

> Eat or be eaten, beat or be beaten; this is the vital question in
> analyzing any society.
>
> Samuel Butler

'I never accept Sunday engagements now,' said white-haired Lord
Woolton, father-figure of the postwar Conservative Party. 'I broke
my rule because I admire your young man so much.' The 'young man'
was thirty-six-year-old Edward Heath, then in his second term as
Bexley's MP, already a fully-fledged Whip and spending his 'spare'
time as Chairman of the Conservative Political Centre for the true-
blue Southeast of England.

So tightly compartmentalized and buttoned up was Heath that fellow
Whips knew virtually nothing about his weekend carryings-on. 'He
would turn up promptly at ten on a Monday and we would hear not
a thing about what he had done over the weekend,' recalled one of his
colleagues. The Chief Whip felt so sorry for having silenced the
former President of the Oxford Union by making him a Whip that he
offered him a speaking engagement in his own constituency of Beckenham!

The Conservatives' October 1951 electoral victory had made Patrick
Buchan-Hepburn, the Government Chief Whip, or, more technically,
the Parliamentary Secretary to the Treasury. As Winston Churchill's
right-hand man, it was his job to keep the Parliamentary majority
voting in step with the Prime Minister and his Cabinet. Buchan-
Hepburn picked his Whips' Office lieutenants with particular care
because he did not think the majority of eighteen was adequate. He
had been trained in the prewar Whips' Office when a majority of
seventy was considered the lowest comfortable margin for a Conservative Government. Buchan-Hepburn was also a worrier, 'an old woman'
one of his lieutenants described him. He warned Churchill initially
that he could not count on remaining in power for more than a few
months.

Heath was delighted when Buchan-Hepburn, on 30 October 1951,
upgraded him from Assistant Whip, then unpaid, to a full Whip or
Lord Commissioner of the Treasury, with £500 as a Whip on top of
his normal MP's salary, then £1,000.

Unfortunately, Heath had to drop his Wednesday night dinners with the back-benchers' 'One Nation Group'. Heath was replaced, briefly, by Reginald Maudling. At the dinner after Heath's resignation Gilbert Longden suggested they call it the 'Feast of the Passed-Over'.

Heath did not resign immediately from his £200-a-year job as trainee banker with Brown, Shipley, although this was obligatory. Anthony Clifton-Brown, its Chairman and an enthusiastic Tory financial supporter, wrote to him in November, pointing out that the terms of service would be brought to an end 'on December 31, 1951 next and your small salary will also cease then'. 'We sincerely hope that this termination will not stop our seeing you. . . .'[1]

Buchan-Hepburn expected his Whips to put in full time because of the new Government's many problems. The Churchill Government had been elected on a 'set the people free' platform. Once in office they realized how big was the inherited payments deficit. Because they moved so slowly, the public appeared to repent of the narrow Parliamentary majority they had given the Tories. 'I remember very well, in 1951, how quickly that Government became unpopular,' Heath later mused.[2] In his own constituency he justified the Government by explaining that, unhindered, the currency reserves would disappear completely in twelve to eighteen months.[3]

The Whips also had their hands full with the third of new Tories. Prewar Tories from traditional middle-class backgrounds had had loyalism bred into them; all you had to whisper was 'don't rock the boat' to bring them to heel. But quite a few of the new lot thought they had the right to think for themselves or be persuaded. For this reason the Whips run a two-way intelligence system. They convey to the back-benchers the wishes of the Government. They also convey to the Chief Whip – and through him to the Prime Minister – the feelings of back-benchers. They earn, thus, the tag of 'double agents'.[4]

Early in 1952 Heath and his colleagues had the unpleasant task of conveying the dissatisfaction of Tory back-benchers with Churchill's style. The Prime Minister communicated only with his wartime and prewar cronies. There was wry amusement when Churchill, sitting on the Front Bench next to his Chief Whip, loudly asked the name of his President of the Board of Trade, Peter Thorneycroft – the only post-war recruit for his Cabinet!

Heath had entered Parliament with a high regard for the prewar crusader against appeasement and wartime Prime Minister. But the seventy-six-year-old who had recaptured office was patently a much older, less capable man. Although discreet criticism of the Churchill style of government came through from below loud and clear, Buchan-Hepburn, who had an almost feline sensitivity to Churchill's moods, had to pick the right time to put the message across to the Prime Minister. 'Thereafter Churchill became more receptive to suggestions and it was possible to relax a bit.'

They still had to fight quite hard. A group of combative Labour MPS were getting back at the Tories for the late-night tactics they had employed when Labour had had *their* small majority, in the 1950–1 Parliament. Tory MPS – and even more their Whips – had to be alert right until the House rose. One night, after a late division, Ned Carson, MP for Thanet, ribbed Heath: 'Why don't you get married and go home and let me get to bed?' 'I don't want to get married!' retorted the testy Heath.[5]

Although his frustrations sometimes exploded, Heath normally was silent in his efficiency. His colleagues admired him for his long hours. And for his power of well-organized thought. Since most of them were military in background, they did not mind that he was a man of action rather than of words. They resented the fact that he seemed rather aloof socially. He joined in the tactical discussions. But, after a few hard hours rounding up votes, most of the others enjoyed a convivial drink together or perhaps a meal in the West End. Heath rarely joined them. On the rare occasions that he did, it was usually on the invitation of others. 'I've never seen him buy a round,' recalled a contemporary Whip.

Heath was too intellectual to fit in fully with the other 'organization men' in the Whips' Office, while he was too much of an 'organization man' to fit in with most of the middle-class intellectuals in the Parliamentary party. He offered his friendship only to a few people who had shared his life at Balliol, in the Army, or his interest in music.

However aloof he may have seemed to his fellow Whips, he readily made time for fellow Balliol men. Philip Kaiser, a Rhodes Scholar at Balliol, now the chief US delegate to the ILO, often dined with Heath when stopping off in London between Washington and Geneva. 'We usually had a relaxed gossip about what was happening to our friends at Balliol,' Kaiser recalls. Heath would bait Kaiser about the 'mess' the American Administration was making of the world. Kaiser would silence him by retorting that Washington had not yet touched the depths of the Chamberlain Government when *Britain* was the world's leading power.

Heath also kept warm his relationship with his wartime friends in the 107th Heavy Anti-Aircraft Regiment. Soon after he became an MP, Major 'Harry' Harrington returned from occupation service in

Germany. With Heath as sponsor and Harrington as organizer, they had a regular annual meeting of ex-officers, held initially in the House. Heath did not, however, mix his wartime friends with political colleagues.

These tight compartments broke down occasionally when someone of Heath's acquaintance belonged to more than one category. Thus, he continued to see Michael Fraser, now chief of the Conservative Research Department; Fraser was also a music lover. Heath spent a weekend in 1953 at the home of Sir Edward Boyle in Hurst Green, Sussex, where they attended the local church together on Sunday. Sir Edward, a rolypoly bachelor who had gone to Eton, had entered the House a few months after Heath at the Handsworth by-election. He was not only very intelligent and friendly in a relaxed way but also a considerable musical scholar. Music could often remove Heath's mask of aloofness. Colleagues and political opponents who met him at Covent Garden found him much more relaxed and friendly. Next morning Heath would be beavering away at No. 12 Downing Street, the Whips' headquarters, never thinking of discussing the musical compartment of his life with the Whips.

The Chief Whip saw in Heath what Churchill called 'physical-mental strength' – the ability to sustain long hours of prolonged mental effort. Buchan-Hepburn decided to promote him to Deputy Chief Whip instead of Brigadier Mackeson. Mackeson's no-nonsense, orderly-room style of whipping had been useful, but something more flexible and subtle was now needed. In order to make way for Heath, Buchan-Hepburn recommended Brigadier Mackeson as Secretary for Overseas Trade. (In that post he proved such a calamity, having to be removed after nine months, that he brought down on Buchan-Hepburn a stream of snide attacks as 'the aging peacock' in the *Observer*.)

So, in May 1952, an incredibly brief six months after becoming a full-fledged Whip, Heath was promoted to Deputy Chief Whip. Initially he served as Joint Deputy Chief Whip with Henry Butcher, who ran the comically 'separate' Whips' Office for the Tory-linked National Liberal Party. But, even before this arrangement was terminated in 1953, Heath's partnership with Henry Butcher was rather nominal. At this stage Heath was largely a Buchan-Hepburn protégé. Lord Swinton, then Chancellor of the Duchy of Lancaster, was another one who was shouting his praises into Churchill's ear. But Churchill had not yet taken a personal interest in Heath. In fact, on one occasion after Heath became Deputy Chief Whip, Churchill asked his name!

'After Heath took over as Deputy Chief,' recalled one of his subordinates, 'there was a sea change in the Office.' Efficiency increased' substantially and the approach changed. Heath started a card-file on which the characteristics of each Tory MP were noted, including his strengths and vulnerabilities. Instead of the same 'don't rock the boat' clichés being barked at every Tory recalcitrant, individual psychology became the fashion. For the first time Tory MPs could see a Deputy Chief Whip prowling the Committee Corridor of a morning to make sure that enough Tory MPs had turned up so that the legislation could be pushed through.

Heath was also impressing Young Conservative leaders at Swinton College. His hour-long analyses, normally delivered without notes, made a big impact on a number of young Tories, later MPs.

His constituency activists were naturally thrilled their MP was securing recognition, particularly when he reassured them that it would not interfere with his ability to do things for Bexley.[6]

Heath's promotion did, of course, give him more leverage. The Bexley Chamber of Commerce announced that Heath had acted for them in seven different matters.[7] He obtained a disability pension for constituent, Dr D. H. Hall, a scientific officer in the Ministry of Supply, whose plane had crashed, crippling him permanently.[8] He pursued local problems vigorously. He visited inadequately housed local schools.[9] He inquired about an unsafe street-crossing.[10] He sought better football grounds.[11] He pushed for better bus routes,[12] and more frequent services on Southern Rail.[13]

Despite these calls on scarce resources, Heath loyally defended his party's decision to introduce commercial TV. 'I am not a viewer, so I am not biased,' he said in May 1952, 'but I think it might be good if you had competition for the BBC.' He saw little danger that Britain would follow the American road.[14]

Heath was good with Bexley's professional groups, selected for him by his agent. But there was one type of meeting with supporters at which Heath did not shine and which was scrapped very soon. This was the 'coffee morning' with women activists in a ward. Since Heath had little small talk, the result could be disastrous – either a long and serious lecture or a frozen silence. As soon as he became Deputy Chief Whip, this was used as the excuse for a complete ban.

SUEZ ON THE HORIZON

After the winter of 1952-3 the waters of the Suez Canal began flowing through the Whips' Office. The 'Suez rebels' began to gather just after a group of nationalistic Egyptian officers seized power in Cairo. This seizure raised doubts about the enormous British military base in the Canal Zone. A meeting was held in Julian Amery's home in Eaton Square to avoid the attentions of the Whips' Office.

Any doubt that Anthony Eden might have had about the Whips' warnings about resistance forming was erased when he addressed a back-bench meeting of Tory MPs on 11 February 1953 on his plans to prepare for the independence of the Sudan. Empire-minded Tories warned that the Sudanese were being 'sold down the Nile' to appease the military nationalists in Cairo.[15] Typically, these gentlemanly rebels were more restrained in the House next day when Eden announced the agreement in public.[16] They made it clear to the Whips they were holding their fire because they planned to take much more seriously any evacuation of British forces from their Suez Canal base.

Heath had little reason for identifying himself with these warnings. Nobody in his family had added bits to the Empire. His own military service had been wholly in Western Europe. He was very Atlantic-orientated; in January 1952 he had gone to Paris with twenty-three other MPs to observe favourably NATO's new headquarters, then commanded by General Eisenhower.[17] In his 1953 message to his constituents he had praised NATO because it would 'help to ensure the maintenance of peace in the Western world'.[18] He was then invited to spend the summer recess touring the United States for two months at the invitation of the State Department.[19]

CHURCHILL'S SECRET STROKE

For a period, the Whip's preoccupation with Egyptian stirrings was interrupted. At a June 1953 dinner for the Italian Prime Minister Sir Winston Churchill suffered a slight thrombosis, originally misdiagnosed as over-indulgence in brandy. A small panic ensued among top Tory leaders. The 'Crown Prince', Sir Anthony Eden, was in Boston undergoing an operation. A sick man could hardly take over from another sick man. Top Tories decided to keep their chief's thrombosis a secret, disguising it as overtiredness requiring a month's rest. Luckily, the summer recess was looming. By October 1953 Eden might be sufficiently recovered to take over.

This decision put a heavy load on the Whips' Office. Tory MPs learned about Churchill's stroke on the Conservative bush telegraph. The Chief Whip, a long-time confidant of Churchill's, knew how slowly the Prime Minister was returning to normal. But he told Heath and other Whips enough to enable them to reassure inquiring Tory MPs and to enjoin them to continuing secrecy. Sir Winston's stroke did not become public knowledge.

AMERICAN EMBARRASSMENT

Churchill's illness provided a minor embarrassment for Heath during his American journey. He was asked repeatedly in his coast-to-coast tour: 'How is the health of the Prime Minister?' He had to invent various euphemisms about his need to rest. Heath himself had little rest except on the ship on which he sailed on 30 July 1953. After New York he went on to Washington, where he learned that an average US Senator received 500 letters a day, compared with thirty for an MP. He flew to Pittsburgh, which impressed him, and then to Niagara Falls, which depressed him as a sort of 'American Southend' replete with waterfall. In Detroit he was staggered to find that of the 28,000 workers on one shift 24,000 arrived in their own cars. He appeared to be impressed particularly by the enormous spread of toll-paying turnpikes. Back in Washington he met President Eisenhower again before his voyage home.[20]

Heath was back in time to participate in a ceremony with a speech which meant little to his restless audience, but a great deal to him. He moved the vote of thanks to Sir Winston Churchill, whose speech to the Tory conference at Margate marked his return to active politics. Since the stroke had been kept a secret, Heath could only say 'we are wholeheartedly delighted to find him here today in such splendid form. . . .' Heath's speech made the audience restless partly because he was playing the 'local boy' over much. 'We welcome him not only as the Leader of our party, not only as Prime Minister, but also as Lord Warden of the Cinque Ports. . . .'[21]

It was lucky for the Conservatives that Sir Winston was able to start functioning again. At that conference, Julian Amery received a fervent reception for attacking withdrawal from Suez. The 'Suez Group' did not trust Sir Anthony Eden, whom they considered too 'soft'. When Parliament reconvened, the scene was set for another demonstration. 'Only Sir Winston Churchill's personal intervention in the 1922 Committee,' the *Economist* later disclosed, 'averted an open demonstration in October.'[22] In the debate on the Queen's Address in November, Enoch Powell, then still in the group, warned against the 'fatal step' of evacuating the Suez base. Amery made an even bigger impact.[23] It was the job of Heath and other Whips to minimize the effect of these ardently imperial anti-Americans on the bulk of Tory loyalists.

In December 1953 the 'Suez Group' decided the Government might try to sneak through a settlement with Egypt during the Christmas recess. They put down an anti-evacuation Motion on the evening before the Prime Minister's annual luncheon with the 1922 Committee.

Sir Winston appealed to the 1922 Committee on 16 December not to threaten the Tory majority, then about sixteen. He urged them to conduct their arguments within the confines of the 1922 Committee.[24]

INVALUABLE DEPUTY

In those difficult times, Heath proved an invaluable Deputy Chief Whip. He ran an extremely effective party intelligence system, partly by collating the views of Tory Whips, partly by listening himself and developing his own sources of information. He actively befriended Lobby correspondents. In part this was to make himself known to them at a time when he could not make speeches in the Commons. Sometimes this publicity emphasized what he had been able to achieve for his constituents. Important was the disclosure that the Minister of Housing, Harold Macmillan, had informed Heath – after two years at his prodding – that he had given permission for the LCC to start a £12·5m. sewage purification system for Bexley.[25]

Heath also befriended political correspondents, as useful sources of political intelligence. Some MPs tell more to newsmen than to their own Whips, partly to have their views publicized, and certainly much more than they would tell the Whips of the other side. The best of the political correspondents have a very shrewd and objective picture of the state of play on both sides. During the 1951–5 period it was extremely important for Heath to diagnose whether the 'Bevanite' rebellion was a case of political sniffles or a fatal political illness.

The Lobby journalists whom Heath befriended during this period found him much more convivial and amusing than did the Whips in his own office. He seemed to be more capable of relaxing with journalists like Guy Eden, Victor Knight, Derek Marks, Ian Trethowan, and Robert Carvel than with most Tory Whips, possibly because journalists tend to be rather 'classless'.

Heath was welcomed partly because he had a fund of funny stories about fellow Conservatives, including Sir Winston. He told of getting Sir Winston back from a Savoy dinner, with the explanation that his vote was needed to get through a clause on the commercial TV Bill; when Heath worried they would only win by two or three votes, Sir Winston said 'One is enough!' One of Heath's other favourite stories was about Sir Henry Studholme, CVO, an Old Etonian former Scots Guards officer, already Vice Chamberlain when Heath joined the Whips' Office. Sir Henry invited Heath down to speak in Tavistock. There they were met at the station by Sir Henry's chauffeur, Travers. 'Good afternoon, Travers,' said Sir Henry. 'How are the dogs? And how is Lady Studholme?'

Once again, Heath kept his friendliness with political correspondents well separated from his professional colleagues in the Whips' Office. And both of them separated from his Balliol links. Or his musician friends. Or his family.

FAMILY COMPARTMENT

Only occasionally did his political and family worlds overlap. One of these was the Coronation of Queen Elizabeth II, in June 1953. As an MP he had a seat in Westminster Abbey. But he found time to secure seats for the rest of the family to see the procession from the stands in The Mall. When the Coronation was over, Heath bought for £4 his royal blue Abbey chair for his back bedroom in Broadstairs.

One of the things that upset the Heath family was the unexpected announcement that Ted's widowed father intended to remarry. His choice, Mrs Doris Lewis, was a divorced West countrywoman. Initially, the idea came as a shock to Ted Heath, as well as his brother John, and the latter's wife, Marian. This led to an uncomfortable wedding ceremony. Ted, John and Marian finally arrived ninety minutes late, five minutes before the office closed. When the brief ceremony was over, nobody kissed the bride. And at the quiet celebration lunch at a local hotel, nobody proposed the health of the bride and groom. Then the two sons and the daughter-in-law drove back to London.[26]

After that, there were fewer trips to the family home in Broadstairs, particularly in the summer, when Mrs Doris Heath took in French students as paying guests. Heath was punctilious in his treatment of his new stepmother. When abroad he brought her the same present he brought his sister-in-law. It remained difficult to bridge the gap because his stepmother did not understand him at first. His preoccupation with politics seemed unnatural to her, because it excluded more usual interests. She was also disturbed that he took it for granted that when he visited Broadstairs the household should revolve about him, as it had when his own mother was alive.[27]

Heath resumed family expeditions. At Walmer Castle he told a disbelieving guide, 'I'm a member of the Government and I shall see to it that it is noted that you take such good care of this place.'

Heath was able to be generous to his family as he earned £1,750 as Deputy Whip and had expectations, both of promotion and general pay increases. In February 1954 a Select Committee on MPs' pay urged an increase from £1,000 for the ordinary MP to £1,750. In fact, the recommended pay increase was not accorded, largely because of hostility which Heath himself experienced. In March 1954, he gave a staged press interview in his constituency. The first question: 'Does Mr Heath think that MPs should vote themselves increased salaries and a non-contributory pension?' He said: 'Why should not an MP suffer from inflation the same as others have to, and if they want a pension they should contribute towards it.' If increases in salary were made due to the cost of living, he added, these increases should include everybody and MPs should be the last in the queue.[28] The Cabinet initially decided to allow MPs another £500 for expenses. But the 1922 Committee, dominated by men of private means, expressed considerable opposition. In May 1954, the Government put the £500 increase to a free vote – that is, with Whips off – with the result the increase was supported, since a minority of Tories joined the majority of Labour MPs. When Sir Winston capitulated to Tory opponents, Labour MPs shouted bitterly, 'Twister!'

The Whips' Office thought it dangerous to rub the narrow Tory majority the wrong way because of other problems. Quite a few Tories were wondering when Sir Winston was going to allow his 'Crown Prince', Sir Anthony Eden, to ascend the throne and elevate his own courtiers. This interested Heath because Buchan-Hepburn expected to leave the Whips' Office soon after Churchill left 10 Downing Street, and had recommended Heath as his successor. Sir Winston was expected to step down in November 1954 after his eightieth birthday celebrations.

Sir Winston's imminent retirement helped re-energize the 'Suez Group' who considered Sir Anthony 'soft' on Egyptian nationalism. The issue came to a head in July 1954, when Anglo-Egyptian talks were reopened. On 13 July, Sir Winston Churchill made an emotional appeal for unity to a private meeting of the Conservative MPs' Services Committee, explaining that the H-bomb, which had been exploded four months before, had made such bases obsolete. Butler, then Chancellor, emphasized that it cost £50m. a year to maintain the beleaguered base. That night the Suez Group told the Government through the Whips' Office that they would vote against 'any treaty with Egypt which involves the removal of all fighting troops from the Suez Canal area'. Next day, Major Henry Legge-Bourke resigned the Whip in protest against the reopening of the Anglo-Egyptian talks. In the 28 July 1954 debate on the withdrawal from Suez twenty-eight Tory MPs voted against the Government. To keep the rebellion even within those limits, the Government had promised that the retreat from the Middle East would stop in Cyprus.

During his efforts to persuade imperial-minded Tory MPs not to vote against the Government, Heath summed up the arguments: 'First, to

have a force in the Middle East. Second, to look after the oil installa-
tions and Canal. And, thirdly, in the event of world war, to have men
fit for world-wide fighting.' But this was vitiated, he argued, because
while Britain had the right to keep only 16,000 troops, it had to station
80,000 to protect the fifth of the contingent against the hostile Egyptians!²⁹ He could still speak with the authority of Master Gunner
although, in June 1954, his guns misfired in celebrating the first
anniversary of the Queen's accession because of old and damp powder.

OFF TO AFRICA

Partly to become better acquainted with the Canal problem, Heath
signed on for an African trip that summer. The Commonwealth
Parliamentary Association's fourth postwar conference was the first
ever held in Africa, in Nairobi. Since fares were paid, Heath went by
way of Cairo. There he went out to the Canal Zone, to seek out his
constituents in the Forces there. He dined with Egypt's new Prime
Minister, Gamal Abdel Nasser, at the British Embassy.

Heath went on to Kenya. Before the conference he went on a tour of
Kenya, then just managing to cope with its Mau Mau troubles. He
dined with European settlers in the 'White Highlands' of Kenya: 'You
sat facing the door, with a revolver on the table.'³⁰ He also visited the
Buffs, where his driver, Neil Casey, was the nineteen-year-old son of
the *Daily Mirror* sports editor, who lived in Sidcup on the fringe of
Heath's constituency. Heath asked his driver what the army food was
like; when young Casey said it was virtually inedible, Heath promised
to try to do something about it. In fact, the food improved very shortly
thereafter.

Heath flew along the Zambesi river 'at bulrush height' and had a
close look at the splendour of Victoria Falls, 'not spoiled by com-
mercialism like Niagara, with honeymoon couples drooling over it',
he said.³¹ He visited the Rhodesias and South Africa too. In the copper
mines of Northern Rhodesia (later Zambia), he was struck by the wage
gap. An unskilled European could earn £100 a month as an overseer;
Africans would be paid one-thirtieth as much for the same job.³²
While in Rhodesia he visited Bexley-born Sir Godfrey Huggins (later
Lord Malvern), then Prime Minister of the Central African Federation. The party presented a mace to the new and virtually still-born
Federation Parliament.

Heath hardly made an impact on his colleagues. When he did speak,
his views were rather orthodox, not nearly as liberal as those later
voiced by Macleod and Macmillan. When he returned to Bexley he

H

summarized opaquely: 'African problems must be dealt with by understanding, patience and goodwill.'[33]

PRIMA DONNA HOLDS BACK

Conservatives also required patience towards their Leader. November
1954 came and went without the expected retirement of Sir Winston.
Heath was as anxious to be top man in No. 12, the Chief Whip's head-
quarters, as Sir Anthony was to move into No. 10 Downing Street.
As divisions deepened in the Labour Party, early in 1955, it became
increasingly opportune for the Tories to have an early general election.
Finally, in April 1955, Sir Winston was persuaded to hand over to
Sir Anthony so that the Tories could hold a general election while
Labour was deeply divided. The Conservatives went to the country
in May 1955.

At Heath's adoption meeting at the Girls' Technical School in
Bexleyheath, the Conservative Chairman was in full flight pointing
to his 'truly remarkable' voting record. Of the 730 Parliamentary
divisions since entering the House, he had voted in 720 and had been
paired in 6. Came a harsh growl from the back of the hall: 'What about
the other four?'[34]

The efficiency of Heath's Bexley organization came under suspicion
on 14 May when Heath went to the Bexley Council Office to hand in
his nomination papers. As required by law, he had his proposer and
seconder, but he was waiting for the papers, which his agent, Reg Pye,
was rushing over. The Labour candidate, R. J. Minney, handed in
his papers and they were accepted. But when Heath's papers arrived,
Pye handed them to the returning officer. The Labour agent objected
because under the election law only the candidate, his proposer or his
seconder could hand in the papers. The objection was upheld and
Heath's papers were handed back, necessitating the correct procedure
being followed two days later. Photographers were on hand to take
pictures of both groups. But only the Labour people were photographed
because Heath and his party swept out in a huff.[35] Heath felt better at
the end of the count because he retained his seat on 26 May 1955
by a majority of 4,449 – as against 1,639 in 1951.[36]

ANOTHER WAIT

A further swing to the Tories throughout the country had almost
quadrupled the Conservative majority in Parliament to sixty. This gave
Sir Anthony Eden more political security and flexibility. But he proved

to have as much difficulty in reshaping his Government as Sir Winston had in handing it over.[37]

Even before the results were announced, every political pundit seemed to know that Heath would be promoted. 'Mr Patrick Buchan-Hepburn,' wrote the *Daily Express* on 1 May 1955, 'can . . . count on a coronet. In his place, Mr Edward Heath, now his Deputy, will crack the Chief Whip.' But Sir Anthony was as slow as an Irish fiancé. It was only seven months later, in December 1955, that Sir Anthony Eden finally persuaded everyone to join in a grand reshuffle. He moved the formidable Harold Macmillan from the Foreign Office to the Treasury, replacing him by the more pliant Selwyn Lloyd. Patrick Buchan-Hepburn was made Minister of Works, and his protégé finally came into his own as Parliamentary Secretary to the Treasury, or Chief Whip. He was thirty-nine, virtually unknown in the country and little known among Tory back-benchers except as an exceptionally efficient mechanic operating the party machine.

Yet one who had observed him closely for six years was sure he had an exceptional talent which could take him far. When they returned to the Chief Whip's office from Buckingham Palace after Heath had 'kissed hands', received the seals of his new office and the insignia of a Privy Councillor, Buchan-Hepburn put his hand on Heath's knee and said: 'If you are sensible you can yet be Prime Minister!'

8   EDEN'S SCOURGE

> It is extraordinarily difficult to tell whether his incumbency of
> the Whip's office during and after the Suez fiasco was an example
> of an extraordinary period that was bound to make a man, or of an
> above-ordinary man who made his mark upon a period.
>
> *The Economist*[1]

It was a tense moment just before the crucial Suez censure vote of
8 November 1956. Britain had accepted the cease-fire imposed by the UN
backed by US economic pressure. A number of liberal-internationalist
Tory MPs were now expected to show their feelings for the first time
by abstaining.

Suddenly, before the startled eyes of onlookers, the Tory Chief
Whip, Edward Heath, walked over to two young Tory MPs and exhorted them earnestly for five to ten minutes. The two MPs, Peter Kirk
and David Price, were known to be planning to abstain. Edward Heath
did not try to argue morality. He warned them their abstention might
help destroy the Government and open the gate to Labour. If they
helped do that, he warned, their future in politics was bleak. Heath
succeeded.*

Thanks to the pressures and persuasiveness mobilized by Heath,
only six Tory MPs abstained instead of three times as many. This
climaxed his achievements in the year since he had moved into the
Chief Whip's corner seat on the Front Bench. Initially he had been
virtually unknown, simply a chubby, grey-haired figure who entered
flashing his toothy smile to spend long hours on the Front Bench,
occasionally interrupted by a shoulder-heaving paroxysm of laughter.

Heath took seriously his responsibility to produce for the Prime
Minister at least the nominal majority of sixty the Conservatives had
over the other parties. '. . . you will find that the party in the country
certainly follows it carefully and will start complaining if your majorities
fall,' he explained. He also felt that the eyes of the world were upon
his performance as Chief Whip: 'The Government's majorities are
followed very closely abroad . . . and it's most important that foreign
observers, foreign governments should see that the Government is
getting its full majority on important issues.'[2]

---

* They survived to become junior Ministers in his Government fourteen years
later.

EDEN'S ABLE SERVANT

Because a Prime Minister depends so much on the Chief Whip's ability, the latter often becomes the Prime Minister's confidant as well. But not in this case. Most of Eden's confidants – such as Anthony Nutting – were Old Etonians like himself. Sir Anthony appreciated Heath's abilities and once praised him to the whole 1922 Committee as 'the best Chief Whip the party has ever had'. But his role was that of an efficient lieutenant rather than that of an intimate personal aide.

'While I was shaving, bathing and dressing . . .' Sir Anthony recalled, 'Mr Edward Heath, with whom lay the responsibility for guiding and marshalling our forces in the House of Commons, would arrive with some suggestion or point for decision. Though Mr Heath's service in Parliament had been short at that time, I have never known a better equipped Chief Whip.'[3]

Sir Anthony rewarded his efficiency and ability as 'the eyes and ears of the Leader' by having him on hand for every full Cabinet meeting. Before, Tory Prime Ministers had only called Chief Whips into meetings of the Cabinet for 'Parliamentary business'. But Sir Anthony introduced the practice by which the Chief Whip became a constant attender at full Cabinet meetings, although not a member.[4]

Heath's opinion showed itself to be worth weighing. A secret argument was precipitated by Harold Macmillan, then Chancellor. Macmillan wanted to abolish the bread subsidy inherited from the Attlee Government, even threatening resignation. Heath opposed the subsidy's end because of its possible impact on wage negotiations. The crisis was avoided by halving the subsidy.[5]

Heath took over as a new storm was whipped up. Just after New Year's Day of 1956, open season began on Sir Anthony in the shape of an editorial article in the orthodox Conservative *Daily Telegraph*. Sir Anthony's indecisiveness was ridiculed by pointing out that when he spoke he emphasized his points by flourishing a fist over an open palm. But the smack of fist on palm was never heard. This *Daily Telegraph* article, 'Waiting for the Smack of firm Government', started a fusillade.

This showed that with Sir Winston's resignation the immunity to attack had been lost by Tory Prime Ministers. Sir Anthony was being blamed – as Sir Winston had never been – for failure to solve the problem of inflation and sagging prestige in the Middle East. When Parliament reassembled in January 1956, the Tories were lagging with 44·5 per cent to Labour's 47·5 per cent in the Gallup Poll.[6] Tory activists in the country were demanding full-blooded imperialism abroad and a battle against inflation and for law and order at home.

Heath's first major problem as Chief Whip was the party's posture over hanging. Sydney Silverman, the Labour crusader against capital punishment, had won a high place in the November 1955 ballot for Private Members' Bills. An early government decision on this touchy issue was so vital that it was discussed in Cabinet on 9 February 1956, without awaiting Sir Anthony Eden, delayed on his return from Washington.

The Cabinet asked Heath how the Conservatives would vote on abolition, if allowed a 'free vote'. A free vote, in Heath's mind, was one in which you invited Conservatives to *be* in the House to vote, but did not instruct them officially *how* to vote. If you did not tell them to be there, Heath later explained, 'you won't get a democratic decision. You'll merely get a large number of Members making individual decisions whether or not they should be in the House. Those who are determined to get their measures through will organize themselves.'[7] At the end of the previous, 1951–5, Parliament, an amendment to suspend capital punishment for five years had been lost by only thirty-one votes, 245 to 214. Since then, a number of young Tory intellectuals opposed to hanging had been elected to the House in May 1955. Heath who had good contacts with these new entries through his work in the CPC and lectures to the YCs told the Cabinet that between thirty and forty Tory MPs were likely to vote against hanging, even if a three-line Whip was on. He therefore estimated that the abolitionists would win on a free vote.

Perhaps because there were two older, former Chief Whips in the Cabinet – Patrick Buchan-Hepburn and James Stuart – the Cabinet decided that it could get away with the appearance of a free vote while indicating that the Government wanted to retain hanging for the 'worst cases'. R. A. Butler, who had become Leader of the House when Heath was made Chief Whip, announced in the House that the Government would allow a free vote on the main resolution, that 'the death penalty for murder no longer accords with the needs or the true interests of a civilized society, and calls upon Her Majesty's Government to introduce forthwith legislation for its abolition or for its suspension for an experimental period'. At the same time Mr Butler tabled the Government's amendment to retain the noose for the worst killings.

In the interim between this statement and the vote, Heath went to work on the Tory anti-hangers, to try to persuade them to support the Government's compromise. As Chief Whip he was the complete professional, persuading or harassing Tory MPs back into the pack.

One of his main targets was Peter Kirk, a bright new young liberal-minded Tory MP who was unofficial whip for the Tory anti-hangers. Heath first tried persuasion. When Kirk refused to budge, Heath used the Chief Whip's 'ultimate deterrent', communicating with the chairman and agent of the Gravesend Conservative Association, informing them that Kirk was 'rocking the boat'. But this failed too.

There was great tension on 12 March 1956. Despite the Government's nominal majority of sixty, there was great uncertainty about how many would cave in to the Whips' blandishments and pressures. Tension increased half an hour before the decision when Mr Butler said the Cabinet would abide by the vote. The first division, on the Government's amendment, was lost by thirty-one votes. The next, for abolishing or suspending hanging, was carried by forty-six. As Chief Whip, Heath had to vote to retain hanging for the 'worst' murders. But thirty-seven Tories voted to end hanging.

Heath was naturally somewhat irritated. 'I met him in the Carlton Club,' recalled Ned Carson. 'I made the remark: "Teddy, how could you?" and he turned round a little heatedly, and rejoined: "Oh, shut up, Ned!"'[8]

The accuracy of Heath's prediction only came out through a curious conflict among top Tories. Randolph Churchill tended to push Macmillan's virtue of decisiveness against Sir Anthony's flabbiness. As part of his campaign against Sir Anthony, Sir Winston's son ran the following story in the *Evening Standard* of 29 February 1956: 'The new Chief Whip, Mr Heath, advised Sir Anthony Eden a week in advance of the Commons vote that the Silverman resolution would probably be carried. Sir Anthony and his colleagues, however, preferred to gamble on the supposition that the Chief Whip was wrong. . . .'

Lord Beaverbrook, on returning to London, determined to re-establish his influence in No. 10 Downing Street by becoming the leading publisher-defender of the Prime Minister. He asked his new acquisition, Robert Edwards, ex-Editor of *Tribune*, to defend Sir Anthony. Since Edwards was a former Labour candidate he used the pen-name of 'Richard Strong'. Edwards/Strong tried to defend Sir Anthony against the charge that 'he bungled the hanging question'. 'Certainly that has been a fiasco,' he admitted in the *Evening Standard* of 20 March 1956. 'But it is improper and indefensible to blame the Prime Minister. He has in his Government two ex-Chief Whips. . . . It is their job to advise Eden on the temper and disposition of Members of the House of Commons. . . .' It was easy for Randolph Churchill to remind 'Richard Strong' that had he 'perused my articles in the *Standard* he would have known that Heath had warned Eden correctly'.

MIDDLE EASTERN FURY

Just before the Second Reading debate on hanging on 12 March, Colonial Secretary Alan Lennox-Boyd, announced that Archbishop Makarios had been seized and deported to the Seychelles. This announcement was timed to win back the faltering loyalty of Rightwing Tory MPs who feared that Sir Anthony's Government was not only 'soft' on murderers but also on Arab and Cypriot nationalists.

There had been a strong upsurge of such fears from 1 March 1956 when King Hussein of Jordan had suddenly dismissed Lt.-Gen. Sir John Glubb from his long-held posts of Chief of Jordan's General Staff and Commander of the British-financed Arab Legion. 'Glubb Pasha' had been a symbol of the semi-colonial tutelage in which Jordan had been held by Britain. When he was dismissed on the very day of the arrival in Cairo of Foreign Secretary Selwyn Lloyd, it was assumed that it was all a Nasser conspiracy. The actual fact – that the touchy young Jordan monarch did not like being patronized by the elderly Proconsul – was generally ignored.

Heath's report on the force of anti-Nasser feeling was hardly needed by Sir Anthony. The 'Suez Group' began raising their heads in the House on 5 March. Two days later Sir Anthony had his uninspiring speech treated with considerable hostility. It was only after they heard of the arrest and deportation of Archbishop Makarios on 12 March that they cheered Sir Anthony when he entered the Chamber. They roared their approval when he asserted that Britain must hold on to Cyprus to defend Arab oil.

Although the 'Suez Group' toughies were appeased, businessmen were not impressed by Eden. Heath tried to reassure them in Bexley that the Government would be giving first priority to industrial expansion.

There were mutterings in Tory ranks in April 1956 on the arrival in Britain of 'B. & K.' – the Soviet leaders Marshal Bulganin and Party Secretary Nikita Krushchev. Heath himself could not resist the fascination of the Russian visitors. At a reception for them he approached Russian-speaking Tory MP, Henry Kerby, and asked to be introduced. Commented Kerby, a rebellious gut-rightwinger, 'Why, that's the first time Ted's spoken to me for years!'

Both Sir Anthony and his Chief Whip were developing new styles of their own. For some time there had been a running battle by rightwing Tories against a Bill to increase the Government's power to lend money to the nationalized National Coal Board. A couple of dozen 'fuel furies', skippered by Gerald Nabarro, had voiced their disapproval. On its Second Reading in May 1956, over a score of Tory

MPs voted against it. In the next few days more appeared ready to support rebel amendments. Heath then got to work. He secured minor concessions, including an increase in Parliamentary control. He offered the rebels the right to be able to debate Coal Board investments in each of the next three years, and again after five years. He also spent a lot of time explaining to them why certain parts of the legislation were needed. *The Economist* praised the Chief Whip's ability to talk to his 'young party in contemporary terms, and not in the language of the Edwardian era'.[9]

Trinidad Oil was thought to be even more of an achievement. On Thursday night, 28 June, just after Texas Company's offer for the British firm was announced, the 1922 Committee was against it almost to a man. But by the following Wednesday, 4 July, not a Tory voted against it and only one abstained. This was considered a textbook case of brilliant Whipping.[10] Heath as Chief Whip and R. A. Butler, as Leader of the House, were credited with having improved the atmosphere in the Tory Party.

They still had plenty of problems. Continuing inflation was robbing the Tories of their support among middle-class people with fixed incomes. At the Tonbridge by-election in June 1956 the May 1955 majority of 10,000 was slashed to 1,600. This setback was a shock to Heath not only because it was in Kent and his 1955 majority had been less than half that of Tonbridge but because his own agent, Reg Pye, had organized the by-election. While a cold douche for the party, it gave Heath good material for pulling his agent's leg.

Under such pressure Sir Anthony was moving towards a radical change in foreign, defence and domestic policies. He was planning to cut up to £500m. from the £1,500m. defence budget by halving the four divisions he had permanently assigned to NATO in West Germany. The Soviet regime, Eden thought, was changing. In Cabinet he explained he hoped to cut conventional forces and end the call-up before the next general election.[11]

Heath was so anxious to avoid 'rocking the boat' and irritating his high-strung Prime Minister that he told off deviants with whom he secretly sympathized. In July 1956 Geoffrey Rippon, supported by John Rodgers and Fred Corfield, launched a call for a Common Market in Western Europe. This motion was backed by eighty-four Tory MPs and three Liberals. It was this project – to which the Government sent a powerless observer – which resulted in the Rome Treaty. But Heath, knowing Sir Anthony's hostility to Europe, called in Rippon and his colleagues and told them off for 'rocking the boat' without indicating his own sympathies.

ASWAN CLASH

All prospects altered on 20 July 1956 when it was discovered that on the previous day the US Secretary of State, John Foster Dulles, had suddenly cancelled the promised American aid for the projected Aswan Dam in protest against Egyptian purchases of Soviet arms. Sir Anthony promptly threw down his little gauntlet beside that of Mr Dulles, withdrawing British promises of aid. There was no anticipation of Egyptian retaliation.

Heath was on hand at the 26 July meeting of the 1922 Committee when Sir Anthony spoke to back-benchers of his hope of recapturing middle-class support by fighting inflation. Sir Anthony went on to his state dinner for King Feisal of Iraq. During dinner the message arrived that Nasser had nationalized the Anglo-French Suez Canal Company and seized physical control of the Canal. This unexpected news broke up the party. The Prime Minister went into immediate consultation.[12] There was wide, bipartisan support for Sir Anthony's denunciation of Nasser's 'arbitrary action' next day. Labour's new Leader, Hugh Gaitskell, described the Egyptian action as 'high-handed and totally unjustifiable'.[13]

It was a summer full of diplomats and conclaves – such as the London meeting of twenty-two maritime powers in August to rubber-stamp the futile Anglo-French-American proposal for an international authority to operate the Canal.

Increasingly, the Americans and Canadians became worried that Britain and France were less interested in guaranteeing international access to the Canal than in overthrowing President Nasser. In fact, the military and diplomatic planning had already begun. Only a small section of the Cabinet, part of the Defence establishment and a tiny part of the Foreign Office, were in on the Anglo-French plot. To avoid an American veto, President Eisenhower was kept in the dark and the CIA representative kept misinformed.[14]

Heath had to remain available through much of the summer to brief his high-strung Prime Minister on the feelings of those Tory MPs with whom he was in touch. But there is no indication that he was let into the carefully-guarded plan for military landings, which was kept from the bulk of the Cabinet until 18 October. Too objective to share Sir Anthony's curious belief that militarily-impotent Nasser represented a threat comparable to Hitler, Heath kept his later-claimed scepticism very much to himself. This was also because of his colleagues. The Whips' Office was a 'Praetorian Guard' not only in its loyalty but also in its heavily military background. Heath's Deputy Chief Whip, Martin (later Lord) Redmayne, was a Brigadier.

The two new men Heath had recruited in April 1956 had both won MCS: Michael Hughes-Young, a former Lieutenant-Colonel of the Black Watch, and Paul Bryan, a former Lieutenant-Colonel in the 6th Royal West Kent Regiment. Heath never let them think he was 'soft' on Nasser.

There was a sudden spurt of work when the Government decided to reconvene Parliament on 12 September to let them know the *diplomatic* story. Heath started work on 6 September to bring back some 360 MPs from all over the world in six days' time.[15] He did not try to bring back every one. Martin Maddan was in Ottawa on a business trip. Maddan explained the trip would be wrecked if he had to return. Since Maddan was an anti-hanger whom Heath hoped to work on, he let him stay in Canada. (In fact, Heath later 'collected' for this favour, persuading Maddan to back the Cabinet's compromise on hanging.)

'As I took my seat,' Sir Anthony wrote of that 12–13 September meeting of the House, 'the Chief Whip, Mr Heath, murmured to me, "There will be no division if you announce that you are going immediately to the United Nations." '[16] But Sir Anthony was not about to do that. He was determined to try the Canal Users' Association. And, if the Egyptians did not accept that, he insisted on retaining the freedom to solve the problem 'by other means'.[17] The Tories managed to chalk up a majority of seventy at the end of the second day of debate. This majority, ten better than the real Tory majority over its opponents, heartened Sir Anthony. He was proud of Heath.

Heath's 'reserve' was such that, when he made his regular October tour of his constituency, he refused to commit himself to full support for the Prime Minister. When he was asked about Suez he said that 'considerable moral issues were involved . . . but he volunteered no opinion'.[18]

Whatever doubts moderate Conservatives might have had, it was difficult for them to voice in the face of the rapidly growing and loudly expressed Labour conviction that Sir Anthony was contemplating war on Egypt. Gaitskell, initially willing to back Sir Anthony in diplomatic pressure, turned on him furiously when he saw that Eden thought of defying both the UN and the US.

Whatever Heath's reservations, once the die was cast, it was impossible to do anything but fall in the ranks and help maintain discipline. Even R. A. Butler, the No. 2 ranking Tory and Leader of the House, did not learn of the project for invading Egypt in collusion with France until 18 October, a fortnight before the Suez landings. Selwyn Lloyd told him about it outside the Cabinet Room, just before the scenario for the attack was outlined to the bulk of the Cabinet for the first time. Butler was furious: 'The poisoned chalice was presented to us without warning. We had either to drain it to its bitter dregs, or dash it from the hand which proffered it.'[19] Until that point it was possible for Butler or Heath or others *not* in the tiny inner circle to believe that Sir Anthony was *playing* tough to *bluff* Nasser.

It was even more difficult for a dissident Conservative to speak up after 31 October, when bombing of Egyptian airfields followed up an Anglo-French ultimatum to the Egyptians to overthrow Nasser. For the first time since the Boer War the major parties were at daggers drawn over an issue on which Britain's troops were committed. The Establishment was sharply divided, with key parts of the BBC, *The Times*, *The Economist* and even the Foreign Office in furious opposition to Sir Anthony. Throughout this emotion-seared period, Heath remained a wholly professional Chief Whip. His job was to keep the party united in support of the besieged Prime Minister. This he did with complete professional devotion, without indicating to friend or colleague what he himself thought.

'I am sure he was not *asked* his opinion on Suez,' observed a shrewd Tory contemporary. 'I am even more sure he never *volunteered* it. He was a completely professional Chief Whip and nothing more. He was wholly loyal to the Eden Government. He was as loyal to its initial determination to go in as he was loyal to its determination to get out. He never gave any hint of hesitation. As a former military man he should have known it was a military shambles. As someone who saw Eden every morning, he should have known the Prime Minister was on the verge of a serious breakdown. But if he knew he never let on.'

It was a great tribute to Heath's skill as a Chief Whip that on 1 November – the most tumultuous censure debate for twenty years – he kept the Tory ranks absolutely solid. The censure debate turned stormy as Gaitskell asked whether Britain was at war. Sydney Silverman suggested it was murder to kill Egyptians without a declaration of war. The Speaker had to suspend the session, the first time in twenty years. At the end, all the Tories present voted against Labour's censure motion, even William Yates, the pro-Arab Tory MP who had spoken darkly of an 'international conspiracy'.

Heath had a disturbing experience that day. He had secured a seat in the Strangers' Gallery for his best friend, Madron Seligman. After Sir Anthony's speech, Heath went up to the Gallery to see Seligman. 'What did you think of it?' asked Heath. 'The man's *mad*!' retorted Seligman. This disturbed Heath; but not enough to shake him into saying what *he* thought.

By keeping his own opinions buttoned up, Heath was better able to keep his lines open to all three of the basic groups into which the Tory

MPs in his flock divided. 'Teddy is the only person I can talk to,' is the way it was put by anti-Suez Nigel Nicolson, MP, a contemporary of Heath's at Balliol. Nicolson, son of Sir Harold Nicolson and Victoria Sackville-West, was reminded by Heath that his very rightwing constituency of Bournemouth East might not stand for his anti-Suez views. In fact, when he stopped listening to Heath's pleas for party loyalty and abstained from supporting the Eden Government, despite Heath's intercession his constituency dropped him.

On the pro-Suez wing, Heath tried as hard to persuade another Oxford contemporary, John Biggs-Davison. Biggs-Davison, who had been very leftwing at Oxford, was now very imperial. Heath trotted out all the arguments. 'You're new here,' he told Biggs-Davison, elected in 1955, 'don't you think you should wait until you're more experienced?' 'You'll never get anywhere in politics by lining up with old has-beens!' 'You know how highly the Conservative Party values loyalty.'

He adapted each argument to the person he was trying to bring back into line. When Richard Body expressed strong doubts about the Government's capitulation, Heath persuaded him by lifting the curtain on Cabinet thinking to show that they really were thinking like Body, but had further information.

The press was reporting that he was a very 'tough' Whip. In fact, he was rarely tough, and rarely angry. One story was current that he had said to one Tory MP, 'You were a Communist at university and now you're nothing but a bloody Fascist!' Another version of the same story had Heath turning up at a reception and someone asked him, 'Is it true you called the "Suez rebels" Fascists?' 'No,' Heath was alleged to reply, 'I called them "bloody Fascists"!' The first story could only remotely apply to John Biggs-Davison, who had been very leftwing at Oxford. But Biggs-Davison denies that any such interview ever took place. This is confirmed by the people who worked under Heath in the Whips' Office. 'He was very seldom a "tough Whip",' one of them later recalled, 'and that was not an effective role for him anyway.'

Heath *did* explode at Patrick Maitland, later the Earl of Lauderdale, who was one of the leading 'Suez rebels'. According to another MP, Heath snapped at Maitland and one or two others: 'I'm fed up with your bloody consciences. I'm going to get on to your constituencies!' After this 'flaming row', as Lauderdale recalls it, Heath got on to Maitland's agent. 'We're worried about your Member,' the agent was told. To this the agent retorted: 'Well, we're not!' 'You want him to be a Minister some day, don't you?' asked the Whip. To this the agent replied in unprintable language that he would be very disappointed if his Member joined the ranks of those willing to knuckle under to the Egyptians. It was to this conversation that Maitland was referring when he complained about 'extraordinary and unexampled pressures – some of them altogether underhand – which have been used to force Tories into line. . . .'[20]

Heath unbuttoned himself only to one or two, explaining how he saw the role of a Left-of-Centre Tory. The Left, he explained, could only hope to be effective if it walked in step with the Centre. The alternative, he warned, was to leave the party open to the natural dominance of the Right. Therefore, while welcoming the need of the anti-Suez liberal-internationalists to complain to him privately – for transmission to the Prime Minister – he deplored any action such as abstaining or voting against the Government. Heath's favourite anti-Suez MP at the time was Alec Spearman, who gathered anti-Suez MPs in his London flat to discuss the situation mournfully, but voted with the Eden Government.

THE FAÇADE CRUMBLES

Almost as soon as the fighting stopped, the façade of unity began to crumble. On 3 November, the resignation of Anthony Nutting, Minister of State for Foreign Affairs, and Eden's confidant, was belatedly released. That same day *The Economist* blasted the Prime Minister: 'Sir Anthony Eden has isolated Britain, except for the company of France. . . . This is a gambler's throw; upon it the Prime Minister has hazarded not only his political future and that of his Government, but, vastly more important, his country's position, interest, and reputation in the world.'

Like a coach-driver riding four-in-hand, it is always more difficult for a Chief Whip when going down hill. The Eden Government began picking up speed and hitting rough bumps from that 3 November session, the first Saturday Commons meeting in decades. Sir Anthony emptily threatened that the British and French would only stop their military action if the UN sent in a force to keep the peace and if the Palestine dispute were settled.[21] Sir Anthony also broadcast his views on radio and TV.[22]

Heath's fierce loyalty was shown by the tenacity with which he tried to keep Labour Leader Hugh Gaitskell from replying. The Labour Chief Whip, Herbert Bowden (later Lord Aylestone) had warned Heath that he would ask for the right to reply. Heath refused the request, telling Bowden that the decision rested with No. 10 Downing Street. The Prime Minister's Office also refused the Labour request, leaving the decision to the BBC. Under the 1947 Aide Memoire which controlled such broadcasts, if the Government Chief Whip refused a demand for a reply to a controversial broadcast, the BBC made the ultimate decision. The BBC decided to give Gaitskell equal time next day. 'Only one thing can now save the honour of our country,' Gaitskell said. 'Parliament must repudiate the Government's policy. The Prime Minister must resign. . . .'[23]

For Conservatives there was false hope on 5th November. That day they were almost delirious with joy over the false report of an Egyptian cease-fire request at Port Said. For a moment it looked as though Sir Anthony might have won a bloodless victory.

Next day, 6 November, the Chancellor, Harold Macmillan, looked in at the Treasury before going on to a Cabinet meeting. He discovered that the US Federal Reserve had released some of its sterling holdings. To meet the US unloading of sterling, the Treasury would need $300m. for that day alone. Macmillan 'phoned Washington to ask for a $1,000m. loan. He was turned down. Until Britain knuckled under to the UN decision, Washington made clear, there would continue to be US pressure on sterling and no provision of US petroleum to make up for Arab oil blocked in the Canal. That day the Cabinet capitulated.

Heath played a walk-on role in the drama which took place on 6 November. The Rent Bill was supposed to be discussed. But it was forgotten as soon as Sir Anthony rose to announce that Britain was halting its military action. Tory MPs who had cheered the day before were now largely grimly silent. On the Labour side there was joyous relief that the Prime Minister's imperial gamble had failed. It was in this tense atmosphere that R. A. Butler suggested that the debate be adjourned. It was Heath's chore, as Chief Whip, to mutter the ritual words, 'That this House do now Adjourn'.

Once the Government's policies had failed and British lives were no longer in serious peril, opponents came out in the open. On 7 November, Nigel Nicolson disclosed his views. That same day, Sir Anthony's chief information officer, William Clark, left 10 Downing Street. On 8 November Sir Edward Boyle resigned as Economic Secretary to the Treasury.

Although initial protests came from the resigning liberal-internationalists, Heath knew his main problem lay in the tougher, more numerous rightwingers. Heath showed he understood by consulting them on the recommendations he made to Sir Anthony for the minor reshuffle required. In the Smoking Room Heath asked a leading 'Suez Group' figure whether the Group would accept Derek Walker-Smith as the new Economic Secretary to replace Sir Edward Boyle.

The 'Suez Group' welcomed Walker-Smith, who was duly promoted. Ian Harvey, who had supported Suez, was promoted to become Parliamentary Secretary at the Ministry of Supply.

CRISIS NIGHT

Meanwhile tension mounted before 8 November when the crucial vote was taken on the Labour move to censure the Eden Government for its Suez aggression. It was feared originally that as many as twenty Tory opponents of Sir Anthony's effort to overthrow Nasser would abstain.

Heath continued to pare down waverers. Some he could not see in time. Two of them – David Price and Peter Kirk – he only got to just before the vote, when they were already sitting on the Front Bench below the gangway, planning to abstain ostentatiously when the vote was taken. They capitulated to his persuasion. Instead of the fifteen to twenty abstentions expected, there were only six: Anthony Nutting, Sir Edward Boyle, Sir Robert Boothby, Nigel Nicolson, J. J. Astor and Sir Frank Medlicott.

'To whom does Sir Anthony owe most for keeping the party from falling apart this week?' asked Robert Carvel in the *Star*. 'I nominate Mr Edward Heath ... for the gold medal. He has handled turbulent groups of MPs with a remarkably successful mixture of toughness and charm.'[24] 'In all these delicate comings and goings,' agreed James Margach in the *Sunday Times*, 'the generalship of Mr Heath ... was superb. He never for a second lost command of the situation. ...'

It was good to have such references, because, after less than a year as his Chief Whip, Heath's chief was visibly crumbling. 'Sir Anthony's name is now suspect,' wrote *The Economist* as early as 10 November. 'The danger is that so long as he remains Prime Minister, Britain's name will remain suspect, too.' The illness that had impaired Sir Anthony's judgment could now serve as a reason for shelving him. On 23 November Sir Anthony and his wife flew off for a few weeks' rest from 'severe overstrain' in Jamaica.

All sides in the Conservative Party were looking for whipping boys on whom to vent their frustrations. On 21 November Angus Maude threatened a 'massive revolt' if the dispatch of UN troops were accepted by Britain. Mr Butler, warned Maude, knew 'very well that no man who had steered this country into so abject a surrender could ever hope to lead the Tory Party'.[25]

The Tory leadership fielded their most skilful duo, R. A. Butler and Harold Macmillan, at the 22 November meeting of the 1922 Committee. Macmillan made 'the speech of his life', warning that disloyalty might speed the descent of the dark ages. He wanted to remain on the Canal to curb Nasser, yet made it subtly clear that Britain might be compelled to withdraw.[26]

Next day rumours began circulating that the Cabinet had already capitulated. On 3 December, Selwyn Lloyd told a crowded and tense Commons that the French and British troops would be withdrawn from the Port Said area without delay. Julian Amery stigmatized it a 'humiliating withdrawal'. Sir Ian Horobin asked sarcastically whether the Americans would now allow Sir Anthony to return from Jamaica.[27]

Heath's next major test came on 6 December, on a motion of confidence in the Government's handling of the Suez intervention. It was no small test because, a fortnight before, some seventy Tory MPs had threatened to withdraw support from the Government if it withdrew from Suez. Heath did not panic. Instead he used his many-sided technique of persuasion. 'One by one the weaker brethren were summoned to Mr Heath's room. Some who could not be charmed off their perch were given a shove. Some were reminded of their past services to the party; others were abruptly told that every abstention would mean a drop of $10m in the gold and dollar reserves. . . .'[28]

Heath finally offered a bargain to the 'Suez rebels'. If forty of them abstained, the Government might have to resign. This would probably mean a flight from the pound, and the return of Labour. Would it not be just as effective a demonstration if, say, sixteen abstained quietly?

The 'Suez rebels' agreed to sixteen, but insisted on flaunting their abstention in the Chamber. In the end, four of the originally designated abstainers fell out, but three others unexpectedly joined, making it an abstention of fifteen.[29]

'So much for the tough men of the Right,' scoffed *The Economist* on 8 December. 'They do not really prefer disaster to retreat. It is true that the particular disaster with which the Right was threatened this week was the to them unspeakable one of a Gaitskell Government. This was the main bogey used, and used with remarkable efficiency, by . . . Mr Heath. Mr Heath will surely have earned a niche in the Tory pantheon as the man who gave the party a second chance; at a time when the spotting of a Tory who may some day move to a much higher office has become the most popular Westminster occupation, here is a name to enter on the list.'

Heath was infinitely more touched and impressed by the small dinner given him by a group of Ministers and former Ministers as their way of thanking him for his sterling work in keeping the party together. It was organized by Toby Low (later Lord Aldington), with Sir Winston Churchill as one of the guests.

I

9 ON MACMILLAN'S CHAMPAGNE TRAIL

Ted's a fellow I'd go tiger-shooting with.

Harold Macmillan

Over a decade later, Harold Macmillan still seemed irritated that the press had discovered him and his Chief Whip, Edward Heath, celebrating his appointment over oysters, champagne and game pie. It was the evening of 11 January 1957. That afternoon, Macmillan had accepted from the Queen the summons to become Prime Minister. 'I remember warning her, half in joke, half in earnest, that I could not answer for the new Government lasting more than six weeks.'[1]

Macmillan realized that his most difficult task was to reknit the fragmented Tory Party. He had cemented it together at the top, Cabinet level. He brought together his rival, R. A. Butler, the alleged 'king-maker' Lord Salisbury, and the Suez-time Foreign Secretary, Selwyn Lloyd.

Macmillan needed Edward Heath's advice to balance out the other three-score appointments across the whole field of Government. Few Prime Ministers would make Government appointments below Cabinet level without the advice of their Chief Whip. And Harold Macmillan was delighted to inherit, as Chief Whip, the forty-year-old Edward Heath, who had so greatly enhanced his reputation during the volcanic Suez crisis.

Heath was very much a 'Macmillan man' already. Both were Balliol men. As an undergraduate Tory at Oxford, Heath had lost faith in Eden when the latter had refused to fight Chamberlain after being ousted. Heath had rallied to Macmillan when they fought against Quintin Hogg in the great anti-Chamberlain by-election of October 1938 in Oxford.

What irritated Macmillan about being discovered celebrating was the implication that the champagne supper was somehow meant to thank Heath for his part in blocking Butler. It was striking that Heath and both the people who polled the Cabinet – Lords Salisbury and Kilmuir – had anti-Chamberlain backgrounds, while R. A. (later Lord) Butler had been Chamberlain's FO spokesman.

The role of the Chief Whip was considered crucial because this was still in the era when Leaders 'emerged' after a curious process of 'consultation'. In fact, consultation was at a minimum in the January

1957 transfer because of the top Tories' decision to hand over the baton in a hurry, to avoid the disruption of a prolonged battle with the inevitable *post mortem* on the Suez fiasco. On 8 January, before travelling to Sandringham for a farewell audience with the Queen, Sir Anthony telephoned R. A. Butler to inform him that he was going off to tender his resignation. Next morning, 9 January, he called in Harold Macmillan from his Chancellor's residence at No. 11 to astonish him with the news.

The Cabinet was dazed by the unexpected disclosure that afternoon. Lord Salisbury, the senior Cabinet Minister, urged that consultations begin by polling the Cabinet first. He proposed that he and Lord Kilmuir poll Cabinet Members one by one in the Privy Council Offices. This was accessible without going out into Downing Street, where a crocodile of Cabinet Ministers might arouse pressmen and photographers. As each Cabinet Minister entered Lord Salisbury's room, the Lord President lisped: 'Well, which is it, Wab or Hawold?' Only a couple voted for Butler. The remainder preferred Macmillan.

'As well as seeing the remainder of the ex-Cabinet,' recalled Lord Kilmuir, 'we interviewed the Chief Whip and Oliver Poole, the Chairman of the Party.' Poole reported the party organization leaned towards Macmillan. Heath informed them that, in his hasty sounding of opinion among MPs, there was strong resistance to Butler but little opposition to Macmillan.

Even if he had not been alerted to the fact that his professional opinion would be sought, Heath could hardly have been in the dark about the turmoil in Tory ranks. In the wake of the Suez fiasco and the prolonged absence of the ailing Prime Minister, the Christmas recess had been converted into a cauldron of secret discussions about the succession. The Whips' polling operation was assisted by the fact that many back-bench MPs took steps to convey their views to the Whips by word or letter before going off for their Christmas vacations.[2] Heath required only an alert to put the Whips' Office machinery into operation. He and his Deputy Chief Whip, Martin Redmayne, deployed their area Whips to count heads in their own area from knowledge or contact. But the head-count was far from comprehensive. 'I was never "polled" at all,' Enoch Powell informed the author.[3]

Having killed Butler's chances, Heath was also given a dirty job. 'Ted Heath,' Rab Butler recalled, 'was sent to inform me of the result.'[4]

Knowing that Heath's report had helped ensure his victory, Macmillan had a number of reasons for wanting to see Heath. He had been selected over Butler largely because he was considered more of a 'hawk' over Suez. The anti-American rightwing of the Tory party was riding high. Yet it was Macmillan who, as Chancellor, had told the

Cabinet that they could not go on without American supplies of oil and support for sterling. He knew, too, that he had to rewin the friendship of his wartime chum, now President Eisenhower. On his first day in office he promised the *New York Times* to make Britain a 'partner of the United States' as his 'first objective'.[5]

Macmillan needed Heath's advice on how rapidly he could turn the rightwing majority of Tory MPs to face the realities of the predicament of the Suez fiasco. Whatever ambivalent promises he had given back-bench Tories on 22 December, Britain and France would have to withdraw from Suez. But how could this be done, at what pace, and still keep the Conservative Party in one piece?

The Cabinet positions he had filled already helped show a united front to the outside world. To secure the support of R. A. Butler he had given him the Home Office – necessitating the sacking of friend Gwilym Lloyd George – as well as keeping Butler as Leader of the House. Lord Salisbury had agreed to stay on as Lord President and Leader of the Lords, reassuring the imperial Right. As Foreign Secretary he had asked Selwyn Lloyd to stay on 'because I felt one head on a charger should be enough. . . .'[6]

For Heath it was a tremendous change to work with Macmillan. Sir Anthony Eden had been a somewhat lofty and unapproachable person, unsure of himself and hiding a rather snobbish attitude behind good manners and a parade of clichés. He had not aroused the belief in his subordinate that he was either brilliant, stable or commanding.

Working with Macmillan was a revelation, partly because the new Prime Minister was enjoying a delayed flowering. Although Heath had heard Macmillan think out loud in Cabinet, in Parliament Macmillan had seemed a rather stilted Edwardian fop with hooded eyes. As Prime Minister Mr Macmillan seemed to drop ten years and expand his powers.

Macmillan was also a good chief because he believed in exploiting all talents, no matter the background. He had married the daughter of the Duke of Devonshire; but he was also the grandson of a Scottish crofter who had set up the family publishing house. 'It is only by giving opportunity and strength to the able and the strong that we will be able to protect the weak, the poor, the aged,' was one of his recurring themes.[7]

The new closeness of Heath's relationship to Macmillan was evident at the ceremonial party meeting to install the new Prime Minister as Leader. About 1,000 Tories were gathered at Central Hall, Westminster. Heath was in the little room behind the platform, waiting until the preliminary speeches cleared the way for Macmillan's great entrance.

First Lord Salisbury moved a resolution accepting Sir Anthony's resignation. Then another, seconded by 'Rab' Butler, proposing Macmillan succeed to the Leadership. Macmillan was suffering from his usual bout of nerves before an important speech. He was thus grateful to be 'attended and comforted – and even stimulated – by the Chief Whip, Edward Heath'.[8]

A more important demonstration of Heath's enhanced role was his invitation to the first weekend meeting at Chequers of the inner core of the Macmillan Cabinet, on 23–4 February 1957. All but Heath were senior Cabinet Ministers. The key problem was how to expand the economy and speed the increase in living standards. Because the Government's civilian expenditures were going up, there was considerable need to cut back on military costs. Duncan Sandys had received his first offer of US 'Thor' missiles. Macmillan was disposed to 'go nuclear' because this could cover a sharp reduction in military manpower. If manpower were reduced, it might be possible to end conscription before the next general election.[9]

The extent to which Heath had become 'Mac's man' irritated some of his colleagues in the Cabinet. 'Rab' Butler thought that, as one who had worked closely with him during the previous year in taming the 'gut Right' of the party, he could count on Heath's support for his reforms as Home Secretary. But early in 1957 he was sharply disillusioned. He proposed a reform to the Cabinet and was turned down, the rejection being strongly supported by Heath. 'Rab' went back to the Home Office in a fury, storming that Heath was an ingrate.

His growing intimacy with Macmillan helped Heath in his organization-building grassroots politics. Newly elected as Vice President of the Young Conservatives, Heath was due at a meeting of about fifty YCS from Sussex at a Commons dining room. Meeting the Prime Minister in the Member's Lobby, he told him of the party. Mr Macmillan – whose home is in Sussex – volunteered to join the party. His arrival was a great surprise. 'The Prime Minister was in great form,' said one of the guests. 'He was brimful of confidence for the future and imparted the same feeling to us all.'[10]

Macmillan was optimistic because he was about to take off first for Paris and then for Bermuda to see President Eisenhower. Like Eden and Churchill before him, Macmillan was anxious to cut a figure on the international stage. He was worried about a damaging dispute in the shipyards, and a threatened national railway strike largely because he feared that it might delay his flight to Bermuda. But he resisted this. To have cancelled the Bermuda Conference would have over-dramatized the industrial difficulties at home.[11] Heath's role in the scenario was to keep Tory majorities well up. Macmillan was happy with him. 'The Parliamentary party . . . was reasonably steady and when the vote of censure came in the middle of March, it was easily repelled.'[12]

Macmillan thought his success with Eisenhower enormous. At Bermuda he was able to bridge the great gulf that had opened up at Suez. He had restored Britain to the role he had envisioned in wartime, of 'Greeks in a Roman Empire': Britain would play the role of the weaker, more clever Power, persuading the more powerful United States to do what was in their common interest. At Bermuda he accepted the offer of American 'Thor' intermediate missiles, with nuclear warheads.'[13]

Because his lieutenants handled their problems so well, Macmillan cut his stay by only a day. For Heath the main problem was assessing the result of Lord Salisbury's sudden resignation on 28 March, as a result of the Cabinet's decision to release Archbishop Makarios from detention on the Seychelles. This resignation caused an enormous furore. The press had built up Salisbury, the last of the influential Cecil family, as a 'king-maker' – the man who had succeeded in shunting Butler to one side to make way for his friend Macmillan. His sudden resignation produced wholesale predictions that his nominee, Macmillan, would collapse. But Heath and his lieutenants discovered that Salisbury had miscalculated. Few Tory back-benchers shared his concern about the release of the wily leader of the Greek Cypriots. They were infinitely more concerned with Britain's humiliating failure to take the Suez Canal and topple Nasser and the impending necessity to resume payment to Egypt when the Canal was cleared. 'What a blessing he went over Makarios,' wrote Macmillan in his diary.[14]

Heath's main preoccupation in the spring was with the party reaction to the impending settlement with Nasser over canal dues. On 3 April Selwyn Lloyd prepared Tories for the impending retreat.[15] Grumbles in public in the House were subdued compared with the threats to the Government shouted into Whips' ears. On 17 April fifteen 'Suez Group' Tory MPs warned they would fight any 'sell-out' that left the Canal in Nasser's 'unfettered control'.[16] Slowed down by fear of this reaction, the Cabinet did not decide until 10 May to allow British shipping to pay their Canal dues to Egypt. Lord Salisbury attacked the 'capitulation' of his old friend Macmillan on 13 May. On the night of 16 May 1957 fourteen Tory MPs abstained with eight rebel MPs sitting defiantly in their places, refusing to oppose the Labour censure motion attacking the Tory Suez policy. What was less well appreciated was the battle which had gone on behind the scenes to shrink that number from its potential of thirty.

Heath and his lieutenants had made every possible approach to rebellious Tory MPs to win them back to a more 'realistic' policy. Potential rebels were approached by their area Whips or those in the Tory Establishment thought most likely to influence them. On occasion, if thought susceptible to logical argument, Heath saw them himself. There were some notable converts. Gerald Nabarro, who had been a founder of the 'Suez Group', decided to vote with the Government. As the day of the vote approached, the collation of statistics on how many would abstain, how many would be 'paired' and absent was in the hands of the 'Pairing Whip', Harwood Harrison. 'What will our majority be?' Heath asked him. 'Forty-nine,' replied Col. Harrison, the MP for Eye. 'Are you sure it won't be fifty?' challenged Heath. 'No, forty-nine.' Col. Harrison was glad when the majority *was* forty-nine.

Heath also had domestic problems. The Rent Bill being pushed through the House in the first half of 1957 was being fought tooth and nail by Labour back-bench activists, led by Ben Parkin and Bob Mellish.[17] They used all the Parliamentary stratagems to slow its progress, including trying to keep the House up all night. This meant Heath, as Chief Whip, had regularly to produce over a hundred Tories to move the closure of debate after 8 p.m. 'Well,' Heath would ask Mellish in the Member's Lobby, 'what are you going to try tonight?' 'It will be a late night again,' Mellish would reply, and Heath would have to show his numerical superiority to bring the debate to a close.

There was little correlation between the Government's relative strength inside the House and its relative weakness outside. In the May elections Labour captured 11 councils, two of them for the first time.[18] At the Hornsey by-election the Tory majority dropped from 12,726 to 3,131.[19] *The Economist* (18 May 1957) thought that any Tory seat with a majority of less than 5,000 was vulnerable in a by-election.

Heath, who had won his seat by 4,499, never let up in cultivating *his* constituents, and particularly the activists in his Conservative Association. At the Association's annual dinner in April he was able to produce Macmillan's pet industrialist, Lord Mills, the twelfth member of the Cabinet to have visited the borough of Bexley. He gave a tea party to the Tory women activists of the Bexley Association, producing the Prime Minister as a special attraction.[20]

At this stage the Heath–Macmillan mutual admiration society was still going strong. Heath again participated in the 'stag party' convened at Chequers on the weekend of 11–12 May. Something was needed to recapture popularity lost through 'weakness' abroad and 'toughness' at home in measures like the Rent Act which irritated middle-class Tories.

FAILURE IN EUROPE

Heath's admiration for his entertaining and deceptively able chief was based partly on the efforts he made to reverse Eden's anti-European policy. Macmillan's approach was rather over-optimistic. He hoped that Anglo-French collusion over Suez would make France more willing to have Britain in the Common Market then emerging. He preferred to forget that Britain had capitulated to US pressure virtually without consulting the French.[21]

Macmillan first sought an industrial Free Trade Area embracing the whole of Western Europe, including the emerging EEC. With the signature of the Treaty of Rome on 25 March 1957, Macmillan began talking of an 'impasse' between Britain and France. But he still had hopes of bypassing the impasse.

Macmillan went on with his selling campaign. In August 1957 he named Reginald Maudling his first 'Mr Europe' with the technical title of Paymaster General. Heath was the subject of conflicting emotions. As a 'European' he shared Macmillan's aims. But, as an ambitious young politician, he could not help envying Maudling his promotion. Almost as soon as Macmillan took over in January 1957 Heath made it clear that he would like to move from the Whips' Office to a department of his own, preferably in foreign affairs. He confessed his ambition and the need to wait to a former regimental colleague who lunched with him at the House: 'The Government is like a regiment. You cannot change the CO and the Adjutant at the same time.' But when Maudling was named to a job he would have liked, he could not help feeling a twinge of envy.

The additional disadvantage from which he suffered was that he could not establish himself effectively with the party in the Commons and in the country at large so long as he was half-silenced. Not only could he not make speeches in the Chamber, but his speeches outside were virtually ignored. This was partly because the press assumed that, because he could not speak in the House, he could not speak outside. It was also because, as Macmillan's 'trouble-shooter', he was privy to considerable 'inside knowledge' which he was careful not to disclose. This effort often made his speeches not much more intimate than a *Daily Telegraph* editorial.

Early in the summer of 1957, it was possible to be optimistic about the Macmillan Government. After Mr Thorneycroft's 'Opportunity Budget', production and exports began increasing. The Tories began to narrow the gap behind Labour in the opinion polls to a point or two.[22] In this buoyant atmosphere the Macmillan Government finally decided to increase MPs' pay by £500 to £1,750. Junior Ministers were allowed to keep £750 of their Parliamentary salary.[23] Heath's salary went up from £2,500 to £3,750. It was during this euphoric period that Macmillan said on 20 July at Bedford: 'Let's be frank about it – most of our people have never had it so good.'[24]

Suddenly, the foundations of prosperity began to slide away. The pound began weakening, due partly to India's heavy drawing down of its London reserves, partly due to the sagging of the French franc and the rise of the West German mark. This produced a flight to the mark of both the franc and the pound sterling. In Britain production flattened out while inflation moved on. In July the trade gap doubled. In August the French franc was devalued by 20 per cent, in effect. That month alone defending sterling parity cost about $400m., although this cost was shrouded with the help of the European Payments Union and the German bankers.

In mid-July the Cabinet began discussing anti-inflationary measures: credit restrictions, further economies. It was split between the Chancellor, Peter Thorneycroft, and the Defence Secretary, Duncan Sandys. Thorneycroft wanted more defence cuts than Sandys would agree.[25] Political observers expected a blow-up. When Heath went to the South of France in mid-August, it was thought that the situation had gone off the boil.[26]

But Heath had to return to Britain in mid-September, because of the ice-cold douche of the by-election at Gloucester on 12 September. There Labour candidate Jack Diamond increased the Labour majority elevenfold, from 748 to 8,374. It was clear that many Tories were abstaining on straight fights or voting Liberal when one was standing.

Macmillan called Heath back to advise him on the reshuffle. The main change was to shift Lord Hailsham to Lord President of the Council so that he could become Chairman – and chief bell ringer – to the Conservative Party. Derek Walker-Smith became Minister of Health and Reginald Maudling entered the Cabinet. But no promotion yet for Heath.[27]

Three days later this reshuffle was followed by shock moves to protect the threatened pound. Bank rate was jerked up by two per cent. Bank overdrafts were frozen. Public spending was pegged. The credit squeeze was intensified.[28]

Although Britain's economic power was sagging, this did not stop Macmillan's deft efforts to maximize his leverage in world affairs. In public Macmillan flaunted his old friendship with Eisenhower. In private Heath could observe how furious he was whenever Washington did not allow itself to be manipulated by Britain's cunning Prime Minister – over the Oman troubles, for example. For Heath it was a revelation to see how Macmillan masked from the world his fury with the unauthorized Stassen proposal, which would have cut Britain off from the nuclear fissile materials on which it was dependent.[29]

BANK RATE 'SCANDAL'

Heath's dislike for Harold Wilson began to deepen in the early autumn of 1957. In the wake of the steep, two per cent rise in the Bank Rate on 19 September, rumours were published that there had been some anticipation through a 'leak'. Harold Wilson, then Gaitskell's 'Shadow Chancellor', tried to build this into a campaign to depict part of the leadership of the Tory Party as involved in a conspiracy to tip off their Tory friends. Heath felt that Wilson was unscrupulously milking the suspicions he was sowing at a time when the Tories were at their lowest point of popularity ever. Thanks partly to the deflationary measures of September and imminent rent increases due under the Rent Act, the Tories were 18·5 per cent behind Labour.[30] Wilson kept nagging: at the annual Labour conference at Brighton on 30 September 1957, Wilson asked: if the Tory Government had nothing to hide, why was it refusing an inquiry?[31] Heath was marginally involved, largely through Macmillan's consulting him about the tactics of replying to Wilson.[32]

There were great dangers of being obscured as Macmillan's 'Mr Fixit'. At their party conference which followed at Blackpool the main figure appeared to be that of the bell-ringing Chairman, Lord Hailsham, who was photographed emerging from the sea every morning, belly bulging over swimming trunks. Heath's services to Macmillan were more discreet but no less useful. Within minutes after the end of Macmillan's climactic speech at the end of the Blackpool conference – his first as Prime Minister – Heath was outside the main exit of the Winter Gardens. As delegates emerged he polled a cross-section. 'Well, how did that strike you, Barney?' he asked a long-time activist in the Young Conservatives in the south-east. As Barney Hayhoe watched him over the next twenty minutes, Heath completed a poll of representative activists. A half hour after his speech finished, the Prime Minister knew what impact he had made.

Heath had the advantage that Macmillan liked to think by talking aloud and found Heath a good listener. Heath was thus privy to Macmillan's long-term strategy. Macmillan was anxious to keep the Tories in office until the autumn of 1959. He doubted if Gaitskell could keep both the Right and Left wings of Labour pulling in the same direction, especially over the H-bomb.

Macmillan's long-term optimism was astonishing. The public disliked deflation. A Labour candidate, Dingle Foot, swept the by-election at Ipswich, with the Tory vote dropping by 10,000. According to the Gallup Poll, Macmillan was the least popular Prime Minister since Neville Chamberlain.[33] On one occasion he surprised his supporters by being crudely rude to Hugh Gaitskell. 'Good gracious,' said a Conservative MP, 'Harold's breaking up even quicker than Anthony did.'[34]

HEATH'S NUCLEAR ADVICE

Macmillan consulted with Heath on how to handle the increasingly ticklish problem of nuclear weapons in the December 1957 debate. The Soviet success with their Sputniks in October 1957 had provided both opportunities and problems. By demonstrating that the USA was within range of Soviet-based missiles, the Sputniks had suddenly given Macmillan more leverage since he could now offer Britain as a new launching pad for the shorter-range US missiles. It was so important to station these missiles in Western Europe that President Eisenhower flew to the NATO 'Heads of Government' meeting in Paris in mid-December. They did agree to station US intermediate missiles in Western Europe, together with nuclear warheads. But Britain was one of the few countries willing to house either.

Nuclear pacifists in the Labour Party were very unhappy about this, and put down Motions of protest. Macmillan had foreseen Labour opposition and had persuaded the Americans to include in the communique an offer to discuss limiting nuclear armaments, provided the Russians agreed to inspection and control. After discussing how to handle the problem of Labour qualms, with Foreign Secretary Selwyn Lloyd and with Edward Heath, it was decided that the debate should be held on a formal motion for the adjournment. This meant that Heath, as Chief Whip, moved 'That this House do now Adjourn', which normally meant no formal vote. But on this occasion there *was* a vote, reflecting the anti-Americanism of the Tory Right and the growing influence of nuclear pacifism in Labour ranks. 'We had a bad [39] majority,' recorded Macmillan, 'with some sick (unpaired) and some deliberate abstentions (Lord Hinchingbrooke and the rump of the Suez group). Altogether it was rather dampening after all our labours.'[35] Heath was furious over six broken Labour pairs and the failure of Tories to vote despite a three-line Whip.

They were all rather depressed when Parliament adjourned for Christmas. Macmillan's reputation and Tory popularity were at a low ebb. Macmillan asked his Chief Whip how he was going to celebrate New Year's Eve. Heath replied that he would be doing the usual – going around from one YC party in Bexley to another. 'Well,' said the Prime Minister with shoulders high and eyes round with amazement, 'if you have nothing better to do than that! . . .'

Even during the Christmas recess the Prime Minister did not let his Chief Whip off the hook. Macmillan wrote to explain why he wanted Heath to secure for him TV time to explain his foreign policy before he took off on his projected Commonwealth tour. 'I am anxious about the misunderstanding in our party on foreign policy,' explained Macmillan. 'There are three main troubles: first, the anti-Americanism of many of our supporters, which of course reached its culminating point at Suez but has not yet died down. . . . The second form of this isolationism is directed against Europe, and of course inspires Beaverbrook and his followers. The third problem, not I think so much in the party but in the country, is all about the H-bomb, the American bomber bases, the fatigue and worry of the long-drawn-out struggle against Russia, the clever Russian propaganda for peace. So we are reaching a position in which the English people of fifty million, who in material terms are quite unequal to the new giants, will move neither towards Europe nor towards America. It is a stultifying policy.'[36] As Chief Whip, Heath secured time for the Prime Minister to do a party political broadcast on the subject on 4 January 1958.

REVOLT OF THE TREASURY TRIO

Even the year's end was not sacred. On 27 December Thorneycroft, Powell and Birch met and decided they would rather resign jointly than allow their spending ceilings to be breached. Thorneycroft carried these unseasonable tidings to the Prime Minister. Macmillan informed his Chief Whip that a storm was brewing, as they embarked upon a series of compressed Cabinet meetings. These meetings, between 28 December and 3 January, were necessary because the Prime Minister was leaving on his Commonwealth tour on 7 January. Therefore all the key Budget decisions had to be reached before then instead of being spread over January and February, as was normal.

These tense meetings began with the Chancellor separated from his colleagues by £250m. Controversy raged as large chunks were carved off. Finally, Duncan Sandys refused to cut Defence further. The Chancellor pushed for a further £50m. to be cut from the social services.

By Friday night, 3 January, the Cabinet meeting intended to be the ast before Macmillan's departure, Thorneycroft had been defeated. Next night Macmillan planned to make the broadcast Heath had booked for him, see Sir Winston at Chartwell on Sunday and fly off to India. The Treasury trio changed all that. On Saturday, 4 January, they conferred and decided to resign collectively unless their terms were met. Macmillan immediately called a special emergency meeting of the Cabinet for Sunday night, 5 January. Thorneycroft insisted on solvency above all, but all the rest of the Cabinet felt a further £50m. cut in social benefits would cost much more in wage increases in the nationalized industries alone.

Heath was at the dinner at No. 10 which interrupted the emergency meeting, along with Butler, Macleod and the Macmillans. 'We discussed the position – still confused as the Chancellor had left the door open,' Macmillan recalled. 'I still thought he would retreat, if we could get him a few more economies to save his face. . . .'[37] When the Cabinet resumed at 10·30 there was complete deadlock and Thorneycroft left, promising to let Macmillan have his resignation in the morning.

Heath was a key man that frenetic Monday morning, 7 January. The three Treasury posts had to be filled, presumably by promotions, and the holes that these promotions left had also to be filled, after interviewing all the people concerned. But the Prime Minister managed it all in that day, with Heath as one of the Prime Minister's key team of four: 'This remarkable feat was due to the way in which everybody helped me. . . . The Chief Whip superb . . .!'[38] Their teamwork strengthened Macmillan's confidence, reflected in his throw-away line at the airport that the resignations had been 'little local difficulties'!

Macmillan's departing flippancy at London Airport hid his turmoil as he flew off to leave others in charge of what might well have been a sinking ship. But only a tiny minority of Tory MPs shared the views of the Treasury trio that it was a resigning matter.[39] By 19 January Macmillan was confiding to his diary that the worst was over: 'Butler, Chief Whip and all the others seem to have kept things going very well . . . the worst is over. . . .'[40]

As he approached home, on 10 February, Macmillan was struck by the difference between the consolidation of Tory back-benchers achieved by Heath, and the failure to consolidate Tory feeling in the country: 'We seem to get excellent majority in the *House* – sixty-two, sixty-four, sixty-nine. But it is not, alas, the same in the country. We shall lose Rochdale, I fear, by a lot. . . .'[41] But the mulekick of Rochdale was far worse than expected: the Tory candidate ran *third* in a seat previously Tory-held, over 7,000 behind the Liberal candidate, Ludovic Kennedy, who ran second.

Heath filled the Prime Minister in with all the gloomy details when he landed after his six-week, 29,000-mile tour. 'I drove back to London with Rab,' recorded Macmillan, 'he stayed an hour with me at No. 10; then the Chief Whip; then the Foreign Secretary. All the same problems – all important, and all insoluble.'[42] Heath's main pre-occupation at the time was the Cabinet's decision to allow Archbishop Makarios to return to Cyprus despite his refusal to commit himself to an anti-terrorist statement. Heath was able to enlarge on this at the Chequers weekend held by Macmillan on 15–16 February, immediately after his return. 'Mr Heath,' wrote the *Daily Telegraph* on Monday, 17 February, 'appears to have been present for most of the consultations. He and Mr Lennox-Boyd stayed at Chequers on Saturday night and went to church with the Prime Minister yesterday.' 'Ted Heath,' another Minister insisted, 'is probably the most influential man around the Prime Minister today. The PM consults him about practically everything – not just his work as Chief Whip.'[43]

Macmillan was so preoccupied with foreign affairs that Heath had to persuade him to talk to the 1922 Committee, on 20 February. He told the Tory back-benchers that he hoped to sweep the next election through a combination of economic and diplomatic success, just as Eden's success at Geneva in 1954 had been followed by electoral success in 1955. 'Macmillan was very persuasive,' one Tory MP recounted. 'He said that we could not sink much lower in popularity, but that if we did the right things, we'd get the benefit by election time.'

HEATH FALLS FLAT

Suddenly Heath fell flat on his Chief Whip's face. For the first time in the fourteen months since Macmillan had come to power, Heath lost a vote on the floor of the House. It was on a clause proposed by Anthony Greenwood to the Maintenance Orders Bill. This was carried *against* the Government by three votes, by 158 to 155. 'Mr Heath, looked rather white,' recorded the *Guardian* next day. When he held an 'inquest' next day he discovered several things. Fully forty-three Tory MPs were absent unpaired, on a 2-line Whip. A further six 'Suez rebels', who had not returned the Tory Whip, were also away. Another fourteen Tory MPs were absent sick; two were on the rifle range in the basement, out of earshot. But the real miscreant was a faulty division bell. Some twenty-six Tory MPs on the terrace level had remained there, thinking from the sound of the bell that it was a count rather than a division. Having established the facts, Heath went to a meeting of the

1922 Committee and warned that slackness might upset the Government's timetable and give the impression that support for the Government was waning.[44]

Heath was also having problems with 'leaks'. By making Tory backbench committees the place in which the most fundamental discussion was taking place, he had placed a high premium on the press securing 'leaks' from them. In February and March 1958 the Beaverbrook press succeeded in penetrating the Finance and Housing Committee and that on Foreign Affairs. Fairly accurate summaries of the private discussions on the Rent Act and on nuclear policies appeared in the *Daily Express*. Heath gave instructions that the MP responsible must be found. There was dark talk of possible expulsions from the party. But nothing happened in the end, except that one of the suspects did not receive the knighthood on which he had counted.[45] Macmillan, a great cynic about the corrupting effect of honours, allowed Heath gradually to increase the percentage of honours given for political services from seven per cent at the beginning of his reign to fully ten per cent.

THE UNEXPECTED BREAKTHROUGH

Just when things looked darkest a ray of light appeared but was not immediately noticed. In March 1958 Walter Elliot's able widow was still unable to retain the seat he had held at Kelvingrove by 1,360 votes.[46] At the end of March, Torrington was lost by the Tories; Mark Bonham-Carter increased the Liberal total from five to six.

By then the initial breakthrough had already been made in the shape of Macmillan's first successful TV interview on 23 February. Macmillan spoke on 'summitry', which he was sure would pay off in the end. For once the sparkling personality of the 'Old Entertainer' which had made such an impact in the Commons, began to beguile voters outside. And not before time, because the party was scraping bottom with the support of twenty-nine per cent according to the Gallup Poll.[47]

In mid-June the 'little general election' in five seats – Weston-super-Mare, St Helens, Ealing South, Argyle and Wigan – showed that the tide was turning. By July the Gallup Poll showed those satisfied with Mr Macmillan had increased from thirty-five per cent to fifty per cent. The *Observer* agreed that his TV performances had 'transformed an Edwardian relic into a modern "character".' But, it added (13 July 1958), the unemployment figures had begun to fall for the first time in 1958.

Macmillan was demonstrating, to the delight of his apprentice, Heath, the advantages of having your hands on the levers of power. At the end of June 1958 the Macmillan Government decided to lift the limit on bank overdrafts. This meant, in effect, that it would be easier for the middle-class to finance the purchase of a new car, a new washing machine, a deposit on a new house. This would mean further reflation, further mopping up of unemployment.

UPSETS IN FRANCE AND JORDAN

However clever a manipulator of the domestic economy, much of Macmillan's attention was concentrated on the changing balance of power overseas. By mid-May 1958 revolting generals had set up a 'Committee of Public Safety' in Algeria. When de Gaulle emerged on top, Macmillan was dismayed and delighted. He was dismayed that an 'almost insane' egomaniac should be in charge of the affairs of Western Europe's pivotal land Power. But delighted that he could recall their wartime friendship. He sent his 'warm congratulations' to de Gaulle, who invited him to Paris in June 1958. De Gaulle showed no interest in Macmillan's all-European Free Trade Area. More important, M. Pinay, whom de Gaulle had made Minister of Finance, was 'completely dominated by the French "patronat"' or big business, in Macmillan's eyes. And French industrialists did not want, on top of their competition with Germany, to have to contend with an industrial Britain more cheaply fed on Commonwealth foods.[48]

Failing to push ahead with the French, Macmillan instead contrived to land in the Middle East in harness with the Americans. Western power in the Arab world was being eroded. The curious religious-political balance in the Lebanon was teetering under heavy pressure from radical Arab nationalists backed by President Nasser.

Prime Minister Macmillan appeared determined to rub the noses of Eisenhower and Dulles into the fact that they had been wrong in not backing Eden and himself in 1956. In mid-May the British Cabinet agreed that, if asked, Britain and America would help preserve Lebanon's independence. 'Fortunately, the Americans have learned a lot since Suez,' Macmillan confided to his diary. On 17 May he discovered that the Anglo-American plans to support the Lebanon had 'leaked' in Washington. Macmillan expected an explosion, at least from the Left of Labour. Heath was ordered to have his full complement of Tories on hand for the 20 May debate. But to Macmillan's surprise, Labour was gullible about his claims to have discovered a Nasser 'plot'.[49]

When Iraq's pro-British regime was overthrown in mid-July the Prime Minister was only too anxious to believe the scrappiest intelligence reports that this was part of a giant Nasser plot. The Americans decided to go into the Lebanon, even if they had to do it alone. 'You are doing a Suez on me,' said Macmillan to Eisenhower over an open trans-Atlantic telephone line. When the King of Jordan requested help, Macmillan's Cabinet decided to fly in two battalions of paratroops from Cyprus, although they could have no line of supply. The decision was taken at 3 a.m. on the morning of 16 July. When Macmillan awoke at 8 a.m. he suddenly realized nothing had been done to get Israeli permission to overfly their country with armed troops! The Cabinet Secretary, Sir Norman Brook, 'almost in tears' at this oversight, strove desperately to repair this omission. Gaitskell was due at 1 p.m., as part of Macmillan's effort to secure a bipartisan policy. 'I was just beginning to tell him about the political situation in Amman when a small bit of paper was brought to me. "The Israeli Government has agreed."'[50]

Heath suggested a strategy for the afternoon to which Macmillan readily agreed. If the Government simply announced its proposed paratroop landing in Jordan, anti-intervention Labour MPs would demand an emergency debate under Standing Order No. 9, including a public vote with MPs standing in their places. Instead, recorded Macmillan, 'Ted Heath . . . wisely suggested that we should ourselves offer the adjournment (debate) at 7 p.m. . . . When Gaitskell and his friends [James Griffiths and Aneuran Bevan] came, I suggested this. A short statement, not too many supplementaries, a debate at 7. This was accepted.'[51] This display of high-risk muscle-flexing had popular support, with the country dividing two-to-one (fifty-four per cent to twenty-eight per cent) in favour of the landings.[52]

Heath noted Macmillan's occasional lapses of sensitivity. The Prime Minister was so intent on eradicating the Suez-time clash with the Americans, that he hardly noticed treading on de Gaulle's sensitive toes. When the British and Americans decided to go into Jordan and the Lebanon – formerly a French protectorate – de Gaulle offered his support, which was ignored. When he sent along the French warship, *De Grasse*, US commanders on the spot said the French were not wanted.

ELECTION PREPARATIONS

Election preparations were at the top of the agenda when the British Cabinet met for the first time after the summer recess on 11 September.

K

The purpose was to put the final touches on the strategy for the last year of Conservative rule. The basic strategy was to offer opportunity for the ambitious as the alternative to Labour's egalitarianism for the underdog.

Conservative enthusiasm was because in October 1958 the Conservatives overtook Labour in popularity in the opinion polls, after lagging long and disastrously. The previous October they had been 18 per cent behind. Now they were ahead – 38·5 per cent to 35 per cent with 10 per cent for the Liberals – according to the Gallup Poll.[53]

And this was at the beginning of what *News Chronicle* Political Correspondent Douglas Brown described as 'the slickest, smoothest, most expensive pre-election campaign in the history of British politics. It has everything from the brash Americanism of the "We Back Mac" stickers now appearing in the country to the subtle suggestion implicit in the appearance of the Prime Minister, elegant in morning dress, standing among the throng in Whitehall to wave his top hat at the passing Queen. . . . Neatly interlocking with the Central Office campaign comes the Government's programme for the new season. At the head of the list, two important tactical exercises. The first will certainly give the Tories an advantage in the election in fleets of cars to get electors to the polling stations. The other discontinues certain controls for the openly-stated reason that they would be of assistance to the socialists if they won. Even some of the Government are uneasy about it. The *Daily Telegraph* calls the more-cars Bill "a tactical mistake".' A subsequent survey indicated that sixty per cent of car-owners voted Tory, nineteen per cent Labour and eight per cent Liberal.[54]

At Heath's suggestion the new session got off to a flying start. Within a couple of days of the State Opening of Parliament at the end of October fully seventy per cent of the measures announced in the Queen's Speech had been introduced.[55]

LUCIFER FALLS

In that first month, too, the Chief Whip had a shock. In November 1958 Ian Harvey, Under-Secretary at the Foreign Office, was arrested by the police in St James' Park in an alleged homosexual relationship with a young guardsman. When he was identified, there was consternation among the police and, among MPs. Harvey resigned his office and his seat. He also resigned from the Carlton Club and the Junior Carlton Club.

This must have been a particularly hard blow to Heath. Harvey had been a colleague since his first days at Oxford, his predecessor as President of both the Oxford University Conservative Association and the Oxford Union. Both had served in the Royal Artillery. Harvey had even been considered for Bexley. They had entered Parliament together in February 1950. However sympathetic he may have been towards Harvey in his personal tragedy, nobody in politics could afford to be identified publicly with Harvey. 'Most of my friends were kind,' wrote Harvey later, 'although only a few went out of their way to seek me out.' 'The Conservative Party, quite understandably because of its outlook and makeup, did not want to know anything more about me . . .'[56]

Heath was involved in the small consequential reshuffle which took place – all among Harvey's and Heath's Oxford contemporaries! John Profumo took over as Under-Secretary at the FO, Harvey's former post, Julian Amery succeeded Profumo as Under-Secretary for Colonies, and Hugh Fraser took over as Financial Secretary for War.

OUT OF ACTION

So hard did Heath work that even his strong constitution began to sag. 'He works tremendously hard,' recorded his local newspaper, adding: 'and some people attending the annual dinner of Bexley Conservatives . . . thought he was not looking his usual self. Mr Heath is certainly more serious these days. . . . It has been suggested in one quarter that a touch of arrogance is noticeable in his reaction to the acquisition of power. . . . Perhaps the impression is gained because of the manner in which he ends his telephone conversations. He gets right down to business on the line and cuts out the niceties and frills, which waste so much time in conversation. And when the object of the call has been concluded, Mr Heath wastes no more words and quickly ends the conversation. Time is precious to a Government Chief Whip.'[57] Heath's abruptness was noticed elsewhere as well. At a party in which political correspondents and Ministers mixed at Westminster, a group of journalists clustered around an indiscreet Lord Hailsham. 'Rescue Quintin!' snapped Heath. Lord Hailsham was 'rescued'.

When Parliament resumed in January 1959, the Chief Whip was not himself on hand. For the first time since becoming an MP his incredible record of attendance was broken by a severe attack of jaundice. This was severe enough to put him out of action for over a month, part of it spent in the King Edward VII hospital.[58] Its importance lay mainly in its psychological impact. As an ambitious politician who knew how many rivals were jostling at the ladder, being out of the race was a form of torture. He determined not to make himself again vulnerable to such afflictions through overwork and lack of exercise.

The immediate impact of jaundice was to make the drinking of alcoholic beverages impossible initially. After a while he was told that he could drink champagne in moderation. He put in a stock of half-bottles of champagne. Later he was told that malt whiskey was purer than blended. For many years thereafter he stuck to a single drink of malt whisky.

So far as his constituency was concerned, his first public appearance was on 28 February 1959, when he defended the Prime Minister's trip to Moscow as having been worthwhile as a reconnaissance effort.[59] Heath was at the Cabinet meeting four days later at which Macmillan reported on his trip.[60]

Heath demonstrated that his illness had not impaired his ability as Chief Whip. On 16 March the Labour Opposition reopened the Suez controversy. Gaitskell made a riproaring speech which Macmillan thought one of his best, although he called for Macmillan's impeachment. But Macmillan was equally impressed by the majority Heath was able to chalk up with a Tory majority of about fifty: 'We got – very strangely – a majority of seventy although both sides had three-line Whips and it was a vote of censure.'[61]

It was taken for granted in the press that Heath was one of four men Macmillan would consult about his election plans – the others being the Home Secretary, R. A. Butler, Minister of Labour, Iain Macleod, and the Chancellor, Heathcoat Amory. Opinion at the time was divided. Heath spent Sunday, 19 April, at the Prime Minister's Birch Grove home. Next day he dined with the Prime Minister, after a brief Cabinet meeting and before the Prime Minister went to Windsor for an audience. Mr Macmillan told Her Majesty what he told 200 Tory MPs at the 1922 Committee luncheon two days later, on 22 April: 'There will be no early election. . . .'[62]

The reason the Prime Minister gave for delaying the polling was highly idealistic: 'I think it would have been a betrayal of British interests to hold a highly contested election at the opening of what may be the most critical month in the history of Europe for many decades.' But he was also a bit more honest: 'Besides, if I may be quite frank, I think my party will do much better later on.'[63]

A leading Tory journalist, T. F. Thompson, gave the real story away: 'Lord Hailsham, the party Chairman, gave the thirteen area agents fourteen days in which to assess the outcome in their own area of a spring election. At a meeting in London (in April) they came out overwhelmingly for an election in October or November. They reported that the cost of living and unemployment were still too dangerous for the party to risk a spring election. Most of the Cabinet agreed.'[64]

CABINET FORMING

Having been deprived of an election, political journalists went ahead with forming a new Cabinet for Macmillan when he did hold and win an election. There was general agreement that Heath would finally be liberated from the Whips' Office. 'If the Conservatives are returned at the next election there can be little doubt that Mr Heath will ask to be given a departmental post and that Mr Macmillan will give him one and that it will be a senior one. Then . . . it will be possible to decide whether, with all the other qualities which I have mentioned, Mr Heath has that mysterious thing which is called "size" . . .' wrote Henry Fairlie.

'Mr Heath does not command, as other great Chief Whips have done, by bullying or overt toughness. He commands . . . because he has an uncanny and instinctive understanding of politics . . .'

'"Does Mr Heath wish to be Prime Minister?" I asked someone who knows him well. "He intends to be," came the reply. It was all that I wanted to know. A politician without ambition is a useless animal. Mr Heath clearly has it, though, like his shirt cuffs, it does not show *too* far below the sleeve.'[65]

Although widely considered a Macmillan disciple, there were points at which Macmillan cynicism did not appeal to him. 'It occurred in the summer of 1959,' Butler later recalled, 'when a group of leading Ministers and party officials were gathered together in the Prime Minister's room at the House of Commons to consider a preliminary draft of our election manifesto. We had reached the passage which stated, in unexciting but I thought unexceptionable language, certain of my legislative aims for the next Parliament. "We shall revise some of our social laws, for example those relating to betting and gaming and to clubs and licensing, which are at present full of anomalies and lead to abuse and even corruption." The Prime Minister picked up the document, held it out two feet from his face, hooded his eyes and said very slowly, "I don't know about that. We already have the Toby Belch vote. We must not antagonize the Malvolio vote." There were dutiful chuckles round the table. Then the Chief Whip, Ted Heath, ever businesslike and forceful, intervened by pointing out that we had committed ourselves to such reforms. "Well," said Macmillan resignedly, "this is your province, Rab. I suppose you think it's right."

I indicated that I did, and without further discussion we passed on to less contentious matters.'[66]

HAMMER AND TONGS

Within minutes of the 8 September announcement of the election date on 8 October, there was a hammer and tongs argument between the two Chief Whips over whether Labour had inadvertently secured an advantage. This was because, before the announcement, the BBC had earmarked time for four Labour political programmes, including two on TV, while the Tories had only one sound broadcast. At a conference in which Butler and Heath represented the Tories, Butler's line was 'scrap the lot'. But the Labour representatives said that the Tories had no right to object to broadcasts made before the dissolution of Parliament, when the election got under way officially. After more than an hour, a compromise was reached. The Tory sound broadcast was scrapped and all the Labour programmes except one. The Tories did not object to an ITV programme on Gaitskell and Bevan's trip to the Soviet Union.[67]

With no Liberal candidate in Bexley, the campaign there was pretty much a foregone conclusion. It certainly was a subdued affair, with meetings on both sides rather sparsely attended, despite visits by both Gaitskell and Macmillan. The Prime Minister urged the people of Bexley that Heath 'stands for the new philosophy and thought in the party. You send him back for he is a good man.'[68] He was hardly needed, because Heath almost doubled his majority to 8,633.[69]

By the Wednesday after the election, Heath's immediate future was known. Macmillan promoted him to become Minister of Labour in the wake of Iain Macleod.[70] *The Economist* hoped that as Minister for Labour he would become 'chief breakwater against inflation' (17 October 1959).

Heath had no difficulty in celebrating. This was because he had stocked up, at places where he ate regularly, with half-bottles of champagne. It made a good celebration drink.

There is no face in the world which is better suited to convey the
relief and pleasure of us all at the avoidance of a rail strike.

Douglas Brown, News Chronicle

'Here I am,' Heath confided to his PPS, John Howard, 'only a few
months in office and faced with a strike which may put paid to my
political career!' This was said jocularly, but was no joke. It was the
first indication that his PPS had that Heath was determined to use his
£5,000 post as Minister of Labour as a rung on his way up to the top.

It had long been predicted that Heath would move from being Chief
Whip to a Ministry of his own. But most had forecast something more
elevated than the Ministry of Labour, vacated by Iain Macleod. When
appointed in October 1959 Heath entered the Cabinet at eighteenth
place in a Cabinet of twenty, with Maudling sixteenth in the pecking
order and Macleod tenth.

Heath was given Peter Thomas, a Welsh barrister who had been at
Oxford with him, as Parliamentary Secretary. Heath chose as his PPS,
John Howard, a quiet accountant who had been PPS to Enoch Powell.
Howard had just returned from a trip to Australia in December 1959
when he was told Heath wanted to see him. Howard was surprised
because he had hardly spoken to Heath since the resignation of the
Treasury trio in January 1958. 'Did you have a pleasant trip?' Heath
asked and then, 'I'd like you to be my PPS,' Heath announced out of the
blue. 'Do you agree?' Howard was astonished because a PPS, a cross
between a political intelligence officer and a political errand boy, is
usually a colleague personally sympathetic to the Minister. But Howard
agreed.

Friendly directness was part of an image which Heath was trying to
create. On 15 October 1959, four days before he took over officially,
Heath and Macleod turned up at the Ministry of Labour headquarters
in St James's Square, heart of London's clubland. Heath walked up to
two of the commissionaires, smiled and offered his hand, 'Good
morning,' he said, 'I'm your new Minister, Heath.' Macleod followed
suit and thanked the commissionaires for their past services. The commissionaires tried to remember whether Macleod had been as friendly on
his arrival.[1] In the next day or so Heath went in to have a preliminary chat
with top staff and to look at the office he was taking over from Macleod.

On one occasion, when walking to the Ministry from his nearby flat in Petty France, he arrived with a group of civil servants. After he had entered the lift, the attendant barred it to the officials. On the way up, Heath asked why the others had not been let in. The liftman said it was customary that the Minister should have the lift to himself. Heath gave instructions that the practice should be stopped.[2] Although both he and Macleod had belonged to the 'One Nation Group', Heath was determined to build bridges between the 'two nations' at a more rapid rate.

Political observers noted the increasing influence of 'One Nation' Tories. Macleod was Colonial Secretary, Maudling, President of the Board of Trade, and Heath was at Labour. Sir Toby Low had just become Deputy Chairman of the Conservative Party. Sir Keith Joseph and Geoffrey Rippon had just received their first Ministerial appointments. And three 'One Nation' men were chairmen of back-bench committees: Enoch Powell (Finance), Gilbert Longden (Foreign Affairs) and Robert Carr (Trade and Industry).[3]

Through his PPS, Heath kept in touch with Tory back-benchers' opinions on trade union affairs. Howard was also happily situated to brief the Labour spokesman on union affairs, Alfred (later Lord) Robens. Howard and Robens lived in adjoining villages near Oxted, Surrey, and normally took the same train home.

Although Heath did not get on very well personally with the bombastic Alfred Robens, he soon made it clear that his approach to labour relations was closer to that of the Labour Opposition than that of some of the Rightwing businessmen on the Tory back benches. It took some time for this realization to break through to trade unionists because, although Heath tried hard to be friendly, he was not one of nature's back-slappers. His first formal encounter with trade union and employers' leaders was at the quarterly meeting of the National Joint Advisory Council. Heath broke the ice gracefully by consoling Sir Tom O'Brien, there as a theatrical employees' leader, for having lost his seat as the Labour MP for Nottingham West in the recent general election. But once the meeting got under way he gave more of the impression of a well-briefed senior civil servant.

Initially trade union leaders thought he might turn out to be a new breed of tough back-street Tory, who might bring in restrictive legislation to curtail wildcat strikes, then marring industrial relations. Sir Tom (later Lord) Williamson, chairman of the TUC Committee investigating these strikes, came away from his initial meeting thinking that unless the TUC worked out a cure, the Minister himself would try to attack the disease.[4]

Heath was soon respected by trade union leaders as an efficient and well-briefed Minister. But he was hardly popular. Union leaders usually prefer either a matey beer-drinking type of their own background, or a relaxed aristocrat who lashes out with whisky. Heath got on fairly close terms with Vic Feather, then deputy to George Woodcock, the General Secretary of the TUC. But his relations with the rest were correct rather than warm.

Heath also had difficulty in warming up relations with the industrial correspondents. One sympathetic pressman recalls how often he then failed: every time he produced a new conversational gambit Heath produced a killing conversation-stopper.

NO DOUBT ABOUT COMPETENCE

Heath's senior civil servants soon learned that he was exhaustive and exhausting in his preparations. Before his debut in the House on 2 November he had them all in to prepare the answers he and Peter Thomas would give to the thirty questions they would have to answer. It was not enough for Heath that his civil servants should prepare the answers to the questions and possible supplementary, or follow-up, questions. He had to canvass the whole of the many fields covered and be sure he knew all the implications. The senior civil servants discovered to their surprise that he had read all the piles of briefs they had left for him.

There was a big cheer for Heath on his first appearance at the Dispatch Box at 2.36 on 2 November 1959. Many MPs were curious after so many years of parliamentary silence as a Whip. Marcus Lipton congratulated him 'on his promotion to more vocal duties'. Heath seemed to be fully self-confident as he stood there with both hands on the Dispatch Box, reading rapidly from the answers in the Ministerial loose-leaf notebooks and then awaiting the follow-up. Heath was able to point out that unemployment was decreasing and that some 50,000 students and apprentices, who had feared they would be among the last called up for national service in 1960, would not in fact be required. At the end of his forty-minute stint, there was another cheer.[5] 'He'll never make a second Macleod,' commented Labour MP Charles Pannell to a colleague. 'He's never suffered.'

Heath made his first speech in the House eight days later in the Second Reading, of the Local Employment Bill, introduced the previous day by Reginald Maudling. Heath's speech was competent but not inspired. 'Well, how did it go?' Heath would ask his PPS after a Parliamentary performance. A kind person, Howard hesitated to tell him that his speeches tended to be too long and too boring. 'It went fine,' he would tell Heath, 'although it could have been a mite shorter.' This was a rough translation of what he had been told by George Crist, the Central Office publicist in the Press Gallery. Crist would explode: 'Tell him, for God's sake to make them shorter and more human!'

On one occasion he tore up his prepared speech and was first-rate answering questions spontaneously. He demonstrated in the House what he had long previously shown in his constituency – that he could be long-winded and dull if he had a prepared speech but infinitely better if speaking spontaneously against a background of knowledge.

PUBLIC RELATIONS

With his own Ministry – and its press office – Heath began to get the benefit of a 'build up'. Newspapers were willing to accord him space now that he had emerged from the Whips' Office. He did very well out of Christmas news. He was featured at the carol concert at St James's Church, Piccadilly, where he read the Christmas lesson and listened to the carols sung by a choir of almost eighty from his own nearby Ministry.[6] Next day the cameramen and newsmen were in Broadstairs in force as he again rehearsed the annual carol concert. 'I hope you have all come in good voice, and have not forgotten what we learned last year. Remember, deep breathing, good phrasing, hold your notes high and let me have words properly pronounced,' he exhorted, still wearing his black jacket and striped trousers. He worried that the lashing rain and wind might keep people away. But nearly 700 came to the small Bohemia Theatre.[7]

In pursuit of a more 'human' image, Heath turned up at the boozy pre-Christmas lunch of the Fleet Street Column club on 22 December. He wore a blue and green paper hat and punched a red balloon across the table. He recited a bit of Treasury doggerel which, for Heath, was quite 'blue':

> In Brighton she was Brenda,
>   She was Patsy up in Perth,
> In Cambridge she was Candida,
>   The sweetest girl on earth.
> In Stafford she was Stella,
>   The pick of all the bunch.
> But down on his expenses,
>   She was petrol, oil and lunch.[8]

Heath was able to worry about his personal and political reputation because he found that being a Minister was less demanding than being a

Chief Whip, always at the beck and call of the Prime Minister or a back-bench crisis.

Within weeks of his arrival at the Ministry, Heath had absorbed its ideology. He turned his back on the idea of improving industrial relations through legislation. The constructive approach, he was sure, was that good firms had good industrial relations. Over a good part of industry, he learned, relations were very good. Statistics showed that strikes were not the main problem. While between five and eight million man-days were lost annually through strikes, official and unofficial, eighteen million man-days were lost through industrial accidents and industrial diseases, and fully 220 million man-days were lost through other illnesses.[9]

He was moderate when he appeared at a meeting of the Tory MPs back-bench Labour Committee on 9 December 1959. He commended the unions for accepting wage restraint as a corollary of the Chancellor's 'lower prices' campaign. He stressed that the main reason for stabilized prices in the previous eighteen months was the more moderate increases in wage rates. This had contributed to rising employment in manufacture and distribution.[10]

Heath found he was seeing much, much less of the Prime Minister. He saw him at Cabinet meetings, in the House and at other odd occasions. But it was no longer a question of being, as Chief Whip, a combination of chief intelligence officer, 'Mr Fixer' and the Prime Minister's favourite audience as he talked out his analysis.

Like many efficient men, Heath liked arriving at trains with very little time to spare. On his December 1959 trip to the Northeast, he rather overdid this, missing the 'Talisman Express'. He tried to make up time by speeding from York to the ICI works at Billingham. He hurried around part of the works, dropped into the Middlesbrough Town Hall for tea and chat with the Mayor and went off to Newcastle. In a speech there he said the Prime Minister had not forgotten the ordeal of unemployment he had observed when MP for Stockton-on-Tees until 1945. Heath broke into his schedule and asked to see a shipyard. 'There is a recession in shipping and a reduction in the amount of world shipping being used,' he told a Newcastle press conference. 'We shall do our utmost to induce other industries to come into this area as soon as possible.'[11]

IN CABINET COMMITTEE

The place where Heath began to shine best was in Cabinet Committees. On the Economic Committee Heath was the first to point out that the

Macmillan Government was drifting, without grasp or direction. From early in 1960 he began urging a tighter grip on the machinery of economic decision, particularly fastening on the Railway Board which was being reshaped in a major bill.

Heath was concerned about the railways because, at the end of his fourth month in office, a national railway strike almost destroyed his reputation. On 29 January 1960 the National Union of Railwaymen gave notice of a strike on 15 February. This presented him with his first real challenge as a Minister.

Heath tackled the railway crisis with quiet competence. His personal intervention did not begin until Tuesday, 9 February, six days before the strike was due. This was the day after the *Evening Standard* had challenged him: 'The time has come for Mr Edward Heath to intervene, personally and decisively, in an attempt to save Britain from the threat of a catastrophic railway strike. Mr Heath made his reputation as the silent, self-effacing man of politics – working behind the scenes. Now he must confirm it by taking the stage himself. . . .'[12]

Heath invited the representatives of the three unions and the British Transport Commission to the Ministry. Gradually he increased the pressure for a settlement. Finally, after brief and unrevealing reassurances in the Commons that everything possible was being done, he gathered all the parties together in his headquarters in St James's Square and kept them there hour after hour, seeking an interim formula until the Guillebaud Committee reported some weeks later. While he kept the union and management people in the Ministry, the Cabinet met under R. A. Butler – Macmillan was in Africa – in the Prime Minister's room in the Commons. Finally, late in the afternoon Heath sent across a message to Butler: 'Please make your decision in the next half hour. After that the pubs will be open and we will never be able to gather this crowd together again.' Almost immediately the Cabinet offered an interim increase of five per cent, and the strike threat was off, to Heath's immense relief.

'There is no face in the world which is better suited to convey the relief and pleasure of us all at the avoidance of a rail strike,' wrote Douglas Brown in the *News Chronicle*, 'than that of Mr Edward Heath . . . the man who now collects most of the credit. . . . He has faced his first severe test as a Cabinet Minister in charge of a department. He has come through it well. . . .'[13]

Heath's experience did not make him into a hard-liner. Early in the year he had written to a number of Tory 'hawks' rejecting their request for a Royal Commission on Trade Unions to recommend tougher legislation. 'I think we must first give the TUC the opportunity to deal with its undisciplined minority.' He pointed out that the Tory election manifesto had read: 'Prosperity depends on the combined efforts of the nation as a whole.'[14]

Two months later, in an article in the *Director*, he again called for moderation and harmony: 'It will clearly upset industrial harmony if individual sectors of the population try to increase their share of the national income, whether in the form of salaries, wages or profits, without consideration for the rest. . . . It is not easy even for the trouble-maker to make mischief without something to fasten upon.'[15]

Heath played to the hilt the conciliate-the-unions role within the Cabinet. This was demonstrated when a special Cabinet meeting was called on 4 March 1960 to consider the Guillebaud Report recommending rail pay increases ranging from eight to twenty per cent. Heath warned that unless there was a speedy acceptance, there would probably be trouble. The Chancellor, Heathcoat Amory, wanted the fifty million pound wage increase phased over several months. But Heath preferred a showdown with rightwing Tory back-benchers to one with the rail-waymen.[16] *The Economist* wrote of his 'policy of avoiding any annoyance to the trade unions'.[17]

Heath's behaviour continued to be very much in the pacifying, Monckton tradition of postwar Tories. This showed again on the Report Stage of the Payment of Wages Bill, to allow wage payment by cheque. He was very courteous, highly complimentary about the 'very valuable suggestions . . . made with a view to improving the working machinery of the Bill. Some of those suggestions we were able to embody in the Bill. I undertook to consider the others and I think that, as a result of the amendments which are now on the notice paper, we have been able to meet almost all of them.'[18]

Heath also followed the Macmillanite 'pay the increase' philosophy in matters which affected him more directly and personally in politics. Towards the end of his period as Minister of Labour there was a row, which only later came out into the open, over a second increase in the salary of his long-time agent, Reg Pye. The agent was given a £250 rise, on top of a £200 rise in 1959, bringing him up to £1,450. He also received expenses, a car allowance, and, for a modest rent, a flat above his office in the association's building. Because this salary was paid by the Bexley Conservative Association, some objected that too much of the association's fund-raising efforts were devoted to finding Mr Pye's salary. Some of the women active in the association asked to see Mr Heath at the House of Commons. They complained they were working to pay Mr Pye more than their husbands earned. He answered sympathetically that he could not tell whether their husbands were paid adequately. But he knew that Mr Pye was extremely professional and Bexley was lucky to have him. It would be unfair not to pay him the going rate. This calmed the storm temporarily. Subsequently two women resigned from the women's advisory committee, and four men from the finance committee.[19]

HAPPENINGS AND MISHAPS

Some of Heath's efforts to build an 'image' came off better than others. He managed to get quite a bit of publicity mileage out of celebrating the fiftieth anniversary of Britain's labour exchanges. These dreary offices hardly seemed a PR man's dream. But careful research produced some interesting facts: when they had been started in 1910, Winston Churchill was the man in charge as President of the Board of Trade and William (later Lord) Beveridge in charge of the department. Sir Winston was abroad, but Lord Beveridge was willing to attend. All the former Ministers of Labour still living were invited to the opening of the new Edgware Road labour exchange in London. They managed to secure Ernest Brown (1935–40), George Isaacs (1945–51), Alfred (later Lord) Robens (1951) and Lord Monckton (1951–55) – but not Iain Macleod (1955–9).

The really glamorous celebration was on 18 February 1960 in the Westminster Women's Employment Exchange, where Princess Margaret, Dame Sybil Thorndike, Evelyn Laye and Norman Hartnell were the guests of the Minister. And to milk every last drop of publicity out of the anniversary, he and Peter Thomas attended fiftieth anniversary celebrations in Leeds, Scotland and Wales.[20]

In contrast he secured a strange crop of misleading publicity when he spoke to the CPC on 17 March 1960. He tried to capture attention by a description of the House written by Augustine Birrell in 1896. Unfortunately for him, *The Times* report next day *attributed to Heath* Birrell's view of the House: 'Nobody does anything vehemently. An air of languor pervades the whole place. Listlessness abounds. Members stroll from one room to another, turn over the newspapers, and yawn in each other's faces. In the summer from five o'clock to seven the Terrace is crowded with fine ladies and country cousins, drinking tea and devouring strawberries. Occasionally some parliamentary person of importance will choose to stalk by, and even – such is the affability of true greatness – have a cup of tea with a party of friends.'

After publishing Birrell's words as Heath's *The Times* published an apology in the form of an additional news story. Heath's speech had been mainly a defence of the Whips' Office as a bulwark of party government and a defence of party government as a pillar of democracy. He explained that whipping was needed to keep MPs in support of the Government when, without it, they would cease to support it often for non-political reasons. 'It would not be the prick of principle, it would be the attractions of Ascot or the lure of Lords.'[21]

More important for Heath was an effort to create a new-style role in the Labour Ministry. He knew that Macmillan would give him plenty of independence – so long as he did not risk unnecessary confrontations with the trade unions.

His efforts to learn more about the causes of wildcat strikes began to produce results in unsettling his own thinking. 'How little we know about the causes of so many of the things we are continually dealing with,' Heath told the Industrial Welfare Society on 24 March. 'We have a statistical cover. But over a wide field we have done comparatively little investigation into the causes of these things. On strike proneness, how much do we know about what causes certain areas to suffer and not others ? . . . What are the fundamental causes and origins ?' He hoped the TUC inquiry into unofficial strikes would produce results.[22]

He emphasized that the need for full employment had to be combined with changing industrial processes and the resultant change in demands on staff. 'It must mean that we must have mobility of the working force. It must be mobile in adapting itself to change, perhaps with the firm, perhaps outside.' There must be systematic retraining of men.[23]

After the Easter recess he convened another one of his National Joint Advisory Council meetings for the purpose of discussing the staggering of summer holidays. A more controversial issue discussed by Heath and the trade union leaders was the failure of the British Government to ratify an International Labour Office convention condemning discrimination in jobs on the grounds of colour or creed. Heath explained that the Government did not feel there was a problem of discrimination in Britain, and therefore did not want to sign a convention that might mean more Governmental intervention in industrial relations.[24]

Heath moved the Second Reading of the Dock Workers (Pensions) Bill on 11 May 1960, as part of the effort to eliminate conflict in the docks by decasualizing dock labour. That Heath had done his homework thoroughly showed clearly in his speech, a comprehensive history of dock labour. 'It is a far cry from this pension scheme to the strike of 1889, which won the "Docker's Tanner",' he began. But he trod the whole long road.[25]

Heath felt that he was doing quite well. His report at the end of June 1960 reported it had found 1,500,000 new jobs and that unemployment, which had been at its highest since 1947 at the beginning of 1959, had been reduced to a local phenomenon at the year's end.[26] He showed considerable interest in tackling the remaining black spots, such as Scotland. He toured Scotland and was able to sound very knowledgeable when he replied to a debate on Scottish industry on 13 July 1960. Every time a question was asked he inundated the questioner with facts and statistics.

Heath began working out a whole new approach to industrial relations. He was thinking of better joint consultation, better training of managerial and supervisory staff, the recruitment and training of apprentices and the redeployment of those made redundant. He was particularly interested in improving industrial health, and in involving Conservatives more effectively in trade union relations.

In a series of little-noticed private meetings he began urging Conservatives to get into the trade union movement. He urged them not to judge unions by the current scandal of Communist ballot-rigging in the electricians' union. Fully a third of trade unionists – 7·5 million men and 2 million women – already voted Conservative and if they were active in their unions the political orientation of the trade union movement might be very different. Conservatives should emulate the Communists, who had influence because they were good organizers. He even urged Young Conservatives to read the Communist *Daily Worker* to be well-informed on union matters.[27]

As part of his effort to increase Tory influence in the unions – particularly the white collar ones – he persuaded the Cabinet to take a bold initiative on the Gower Report urging better minimum office standards. To do this he had to overcome strong Treasury opposition.[28] His last public contribution was towards improved industrial health, in the 25 July 1960 debate on the Nuffield Grant for industrial health research. 'I am happy to say that the Trustees of the Foundation have decided to allocate ... £250,000 ... for industrial health services....' He felt this was better than a Government-sponsored scheme.[29] And cheaper.

Two days later, on 27 July 1960, he performed his last official act by convening in his private room at the Ministry a last meeting of the Joint Consultative Advisory Council. He had hoped to change this rather dull and powerless body into an industrial parliament.[30] As Heath knew, that was his public swan-song as Minister of Labour.

THE SUDDEN CALL

A month before, while he was on a tour of northern Wales, he had been called back to No. 10 Downing Street to learn from Mr Macmillan the new role in which he was hoping to cast him. For some time Derick Heathcoat Amory had made it clear that his third, 1960, Budget was his last. Thus, while the Finance Bill was going through the House, the Prime Minister had to work out his top-level reshuffle. The post of Chancellor had long before been promised to Selwyn Lloyd as a reward for his long service as Foreign Secretary. But who would replace Selwyn Lloyd at the Foreign Office?

This was an extremely difficult problem because the Prime Minister was carrying out, under conditions of substantial secrecy, his own effort to maximize Britain's remaining leverage. At the beginning of 1960 he had done a five-week, 20,000-mile tour of Africa, climaxed by his famous 'wind of change' speech in South Africa. In mid-March he conferred with de Gaulle at Rambouillet a few days before Mr Krushchev's arrival in Paris and the opening of the Ten-Power disarmament talks in Geneva. Much more significant was his conference a fortnight later, with President Eisenhower at Camp David. Britain's intermediate missile, 'Blue Streak', had failed the previous autumn. Macmillan wanted to cover this failure by a nuclear test ban, or to secure an inexpensive replacement, to keep Britain in the nuclear deterrent business. Eisenhower offered his friend a weapon still on the drawing board: 'Skybolt', an air-to-surface missile with a thousand-mile range which could be launched by Britain's obsolescent V-bombers. In exchange, Macmillan gave Eisenhower facilities at the Holy Loch for us 'Polaris' submarines.[31]

Macmillan's efforts to enlarge Britain's influence came crashing in Paris in May 1960. He had worked long and cunningly to get Krushchev and Eisenhower to the 'Summit'. But, unknown to Macmillan, the President had authorized the flight of yet another U-2 high-level reconnaissance plane over Soviet territory. On the eve of the Paris 'Summit' meeting, the Russians had succeeded in downing a plane. When an adequate apology was not forthcoming, the 'Summit' for which Macmillan had prepared so long broke up in disarray.

It was in this context of complex negotiations of many sorts, on many levels, that the Prime Minister had to decide on his instruments. He had the possibility of promoting one of his younger Ministers. Macmillan had, of course, the alternative of offering the post of Foreign Secretary to R. A. Butler, then Home Secretary and Leader of the House. Butler certainly would have liked the post.[32] But Macmillan could hardly hope to be *his own* Foreign Secretary with someone so intelligent and knowledgeable as Butler in command of the FO.

Under these circumstances there was little that Heath could do to advance his cause as a very junior Cabinet Minister except to make loyal

L

sounds. One of these was his speech to the Young Conservative rally at Llandrindod Wells on 19 May 1960. 'We all know,' Heath proclaimed, 'that no man could have striven harder for a Summit conference than our Prime Minister. It is a great blow to all of us that, having got to Paris, it was not held because of the attitude of Mr Krushchev.'[33]

Heath knew that Macmillan might put him in charge of European entry as No. 2 in the Foreign Office, but he had not yet had the word formally. This only came a month later. As soon as it began to be leaked on 21 July that Lord Home would probably be the next Foreign Secretary, it was suggested that his No. 2 and voice in the Commons would probably be Heath. It was guessed that this post would carry the title of Paymaster General rather than, as it turned out, Lord Privy Seal. 'Both Mr Heath and Lord Home are close personal friends of Mr Macmillan,' jabbed The Economist; 'critics say that Mr Heath gets on well with the Prime Minister by advising him and Lord Home by agreeing with him'.[34]

The fact that Heath was going to leave the Ministry of Labour after only nine months there went hardly noticed because of the storm which descended on the Prime Minister when the Guardian got advance wind of the appointment of Lord Home as Foreign Secretary. Home had avoided the limelight for the fifty-seven years of his life. Although PPS to Neville Chamberlain as a young prewar Tory MP for South Lanark, he had spent the previous nine years in the Lords as the 13th Earl of Home, between 1955 and 1960 as Commonwealth Secretary. An unassuming and natural Old Etonian border Scot, he had managed to avoid public gaffes. But when the Prime Minister put him forward as the next Foreign Secretary, the skies broke. 'Oh Lord!' shrilled the Daily Mirror, 'the ludicrous selection of the oh-so-dismal Lord Home' was 'the most reckless political appointment since the Roman Emperor Caligula made his favourite horse a consul.'[35] For the bulk of the Labour Opposition the main affront was that the new Foreign Secretary would be unavailable as a target in the House of Commons. Hugh Gaitskell censured the Government, pointing out that when Sir Anthony Eden had thought of making Lord Salisbury Foreign Secretary in 1955, he had avoided it, saying: 'I felt it impossible to ask a member of the House of Lords to be Foreign Secretary.'[36]

When Heath was named as Lord Privy Seal on 27 July, The Times was rather critical: 'To remove one of the ablest of the younger members of the Government from the charge of an important department after so short a time to be a spokesman in the Commons – on a subject on which he will have two masters where Mr Selwyn Lloyd had only one – is an extravagant use of the highest talent.'[37] Edward Heath did not mind as much as the newspapers being demoted to No. 2 in the FO, a department he valued more highly than Labour. Macmillan made it clear in his briefing that Heath would 'be specially concerned with European affairs in all their aspects'.

It was the *Sunday Times*'s political correspondent that weekend who made the shrewdest estimate: 'we have the fascinating case of Mr Edward Heath, who has always been regarded as Mr Macmillan's favourite political son. . . . Mr Heath has less first-hand experience as a senior Minister than many of his colleagues and has still to establish himself as a parliamentarian in major debates. This is precisely why Mr. Macmillan has decided to give him a wider field of experience as quickly as possible; if Mr Heath can establish himself in his present role during the next eighteen months we should see him steadily emerging as the next Foreign Secretary . . .'[38]

11 THE DOUBLY-HOBBLED 'MR EUROPE'

> He knows that the next months will . . . decide whether he can
> possibly keep his present place near the top of the Tory Party . . . .
> As an administrator he has fumbled. As a speaker he was mumbled.
> Like so many previous ex-Chief Whips, Mr Heath has been a
> dismal failure as a Minister. . . . If he fails . . . his claim to be a
> future Leader of the Tory Party will have vanished forever.
>   'Cross Bencher', *Sunday Express*, 20 August 1961

After he failed in his effort as 'Mr Europe', Edward Heath used to joke
that if he had trading stamps for the 100,000 miles he flew in pursuit
of entry to the Market, he could have had his own small plane. In
fact, his arduous efforts to achieve entry *did* enable him to 'take off'.
He left the ground level where he was an obscure Minister for the
heights where the eyes of supporters and antagonists were all fixed
upon him. And he did this despite his twin 'hobbles'. Not only was he
second to Lord Home in the Foreign Office, with the title of Lord
Privy Seal, but foreign affairs strategy lay firmly in the hands of the
Prime Minister.

In offering Heath the job, Macmillan made it clear that, while anxious
to avoid a political division of Europe, he could not be sure that anything positive could be done to unite it. The Cabinet was divided on
how far to go in trying for unity between the British-led 'Seven' in
EFTA and the 'Six' in the EEC. The Cabinet Committee under R. A.
Butler had decided that Britain should not sacrifice its economic
links with the Commonwealth or commit itself to the expensive
agricultural policy of the EEC.

Macmillan's idea was to mark time until the new American President
took office. Meanwhile his hooded eyes were sharp. When the news
emerged of a 'tiff' between Dr Adenauer and President de Gaulle at
their 29–30 July meeting at Rambouillet, Macmillan saw the opportunity. De Gaulle had frightened Dr Adenauer by being anti-American
as well as anti-British. 'The situation was changed,' Heath pointed out,
'by the initiative of the German Chancellor in inviting the Prime
Minister to Bonn.'[1] But Macmillan took Lord Home with him.

Heath's exclusion alerted his press defenders. 'This is a brush-off . . .'
stormed Robert Carvel.[2] '. . . it emphasizes how much the Prime Minister
has foreign policy in his hands, so that it seems hardly to matter which

puppet, in Lords or Commons, is tugged along by him.' In fact by the time it was clear Dr Adenauer would welcome a visit from Macmillan, Heath had started on a vacation in Venice. Home and Heath had decided to divide up the August vacation: Heath would have his fortnight in Venice in the first half, and Home would go off on 13 August.[3]

When Heath returned he settled down in the room vacated by John Profumo. He had taken over Profumo's responsibilities within the FO, and Profumo's former title as Minister of State was temporarily dropped. This room had been completely refurnished for Profumo and was not thought to require redecorating for the Lord Privy Seal, a Cabinet Minister and the Foreign Office's senior spokesman in the Commons.[4]

Heath soon realized what he had promised when he had undertaken to read the bulk of the FO telegrams. 'Having more than eighty countries with which to deal . . .' he explained, 'one has to deal with a remarkable diversity of problems.'[5] Heath learned to go quickly through the up to 50,000 words on pink paper which flooded in every day. He earned the FO professionals' compliment of being considered 'good at his reading'.[6] This weight of reading convinced him that he should emulate John Kennedy. 'Normal high-speed reading is 300 words a minute – I could always read faster than that,' he explained. But after investing three guineas in a rapid-reading course: 'I can now read 650 words a minute'[7] was his boast.

The FO chiefs welcomed playboy John Profumo's replacement by the more dedicated Heath. They were encouraged by the extent to which the Prime Minister had increased the influence of pro-Europeans. Sir Frank Lee had emerged as Joint Permanent Secretary of the Treasury. The new Commonwealth Secretary, Duncan Sandys, was a pro-European, as was Peter Thorneycroft, now Minister of Aviation, and Christopher Soames, Minister of Agriculture. The professionals began pressing harder for a more active and constructive approach to the EEC. Heath seemed a very apt and hardworking pupil.

Heath's very gingerly European probing initially was demonstrated on 20 September when he addressed the Finance Ministers of the Commonwealth at Lancaster House. 'You have asked a lot of questions,' one Finance Minister summed it up, 'but given us no answers.' Heath pointed out that no negotiations were in progress or immediately contemplated. The pieces stood on the board much as they had stood since EFTA had come into being. If the change of heart intimated by Dr Adenauer in August came to anything, some of the blocking pieces might be removed. Heath's cautious ambivalence received short shrift from the pro-EEC *Economist* when he gave a similar performance at the Consultative Assembly of the Council of Europe on 27 September: 'what is completely clear is that for us to sign the Treaty of Rome – and I underline these words – *would be impossible*'.[8] *The Economist* commented: 'He put up and knocked down the same Aunt Sally as Mr Lloyd, reiterating that Britain cannot accept the . . . Rome Treaty as it stands today. He voiced the same objections: Commonwealth exports to Britain would suffer; and British agriculture is protected by different methods from those used by the Six.'[9]

Although Heath rushed to Scarborough to be in time for his stint at the Conservatives' annual conference there, his conference was rather quiet compared with Labour's unilateral explosion ten days before. Heath's task was to reply to the debate urging further steps to unite Europe. The *Yorkshire Post* correspondent detected 'an air of slight nervousness and tension. After all, this brilliant backroom boy has never made a public appearance on this daunting scale before . . .' Heath suggested that the Six – even the French – were friendlier. But he roused cheers by saying that if it came to a choice between Europe and the Commonwealth, 'of course there is absolutely no doubt about the answer'. 'We have a very modest target,' he summarized. 'It is to try to find a position from which we can move into a negotiation.'[10] His FO assistants were delighted that Heath could reply to the debate off the cuff without putting a foot wrong.

His first major speech, on the Queen's Address on 4 November 1960, turned out to be a dreary disappointment, an uninspiring tour of obvious horizons. 'On one thing I found everyone in Europe agrees, and that is that negotiations must not begin until there is a genuine prospect of success. What Europe cannot risk is another attempt which then proves unsuccessful . . .'[11] Journalists were not impressed: 'Mr Heath . . . put in a firm and timely word for the United Nations in the Congo, which was not at all to the liking of some of back-bench [Tory] opinion behind him; but in nearly every other respect his speech was feeble . . .', commented Norman Shrapnel next day in the *Guardian*.

Heath could not explain: 'Britain cannot decide its foreign policy until the USA decides on its new President.' The US presidential election several days later sank Macmillan's main fear of a pro-French policy by a Nixon–Dillon administration. Kennedy was pro-British from his student days in London and also had a brother who had married into the Devonshire family of the Prime Minister's wife. British foreign policy had nevertheless to mark time until after the Kennedy administration took office in January 1961. The Prime Minister came increasingly to rely on Heath as they planned for the future when John

Kennedy had got past his inauguration. '. . . It is Mr Heath who is invited to Birch Grove for a long, intimate walk through the Sussex countryside with the master.'[12]

Meanwhile, there were plenty of chores in which Heath was able to show himself a well-polished, hard-grinding cog in the FO machine. His answers to questions were virtually all the dated responses of the FO at the time. Britain could not support Algerian independence because there were a million Frenchmen in Algeria and its economy had been tied to France's for a hundred years.[13] It was not advisable to discuss Communist China's entry to the UN because forty-five states recognized Taiwan.[14] Although fellow politicians and political correspondents judged him by his competent but boring appearances in the Commons, Heath had other judges who valued him higher. In the FO senior civil servants could see that he was becoming as well briefed as themselves.

Heath was off guard, however, when the problem of the three Bahreini prisoners came up on 19 December, two days before the Christmas recess. This was a hangover from the Suez crisis. In November 1956 local Bahreini merchants had led a demonstration against the Anglo-French invasion of Egypt, while Selwyn Lloyd was passing through the oil-rich island on the Persian Gulf. This infuriated the autocratic ruler and his British mentors, who realized the demonstration leaders wanted democratic reforms and freedom from British control. Five men considered leaders were arrested. Arrangements were made to find them guilty of sedition and rebellion before a packed jury. British law was speedily altered to make it possible to exile them on the distant island of St Helena, Napoleon's last home. When the Suez passions cooled down, the Foreign Office connivance in this became embarrassing. But Bahrein's ruler resisted requests for clemency.

Heath came into this problem publicly on 19 December. Labour MP John Stonehouse asked him whether he intended to release the prisoners. When Heath insisted they had to be sent back, Stonehouse attacked this as 'outrageous'. Tory MP William Yates asked for political asylum for them. Heath tried to end the discussion by saying firmly: 'I shall have nothing further to say to the House before we rise for the Recess.'[15]

Next day, John Stonehouse tried to adjourn the House on the return of the prisoners to Bahrein where – Tory MP William Yates intervened – they might 'have their heads chopped off'. The required forty or more MPs clinched an adjournment debate.

For three hours a battery of Labour MPs including lawyers 'had a go' at Heath. He attempted manfully to prove that the Government had tried for clemency but, without the agreement of the ruler, had to abide by the 1956 agreement. At the end he promised not to send the prisoners back before the end of the recess and not without notifying the House.[16]

AFTER-CHRISTMAS INTERLUDES

Heath left London by air for Singapore on 27 December to attend the annual conference of British representatives in south-east Asia, to be held between 4 and 7 January 1971. On the way back he stopped off at Aden and Bahrein. He discussed the problem of the prisoners with the ruler and the British Resident, visiting Jidda Island with George Brown. They spoke to the two Bahreini prisoners who had not been sent to St Helena. 'What I saw disproves the wild accusations about the way [the three Bahreinis] would be treated,' Heath explained. 'They do not work and they are free to move about during the daylight. They have never been shackled. They spend their time fishing and tending their garden. They are taken to the mainland each month to see their relations.'[17] In a statement in the House on 30 January 1961, he said that until the prisoners and their lawyers decided whether they would commence fresh *habeas corpus* proceedings they could remain on St Helena.[18] This appeared to satisfy most critics apart from Bernard Levin.

Heath's lack of flair was a source of dissatisfaction, but mainly among Tories. Lord Lambton complained he had 'certainly been disappointing in the House of Commons. He seems to lack authority and grasp of his subject....'[19] 'Mr Heath is ... unfortunate,' said Peregrine Worsthorne. 'Pitched into foreign affairs, about which he knows little, with his tongue tied because of Lord Home's seniority, he has made a sadly poor impression on the House.'[20] The unkindest cut of all came from Henry Fairlie. 'I once ran him as a future Leader of the Conservative Party,' Fairlie confessed. 'He has since told me that the piece embarrassed him considerably; not nearly as much as, in retrospect, it embarrasses me.'[21]

To add injury to insult, while his reputation was sinking, that of his much under-rated chief, Lord Home, was rising. He scored over Heath with his straightforward character and a capacity for simple, lucid presentation of issues. This had made him personally popular, whether or not people agreed with his right wing views. Thus, when Krushchev raised the Berlin question, trying to incorporate it in East Germany, Home wittily summarized the Soviet approach: 'What is mine is mine and what is yours is negotiable'.[22] 'The one star that has continued to

climb to a meridian of respect and influence has been that of a peer –
Lord Home,' wrote *The Times*.[23]

Heath did not readily forgive the journalists who were now giving
him such a hard time. They were judging like theatre critics, on the
basis of his boringly careful performances in the House. But Heath's
important role lay *behind* the scenes, where he was Macmillan's instru-
ment in discovering how far Britain had to bend to get European economic and political unity, and to help move the Cabinet towards that
bargaining position.

An effort to win over de Gaulle was part of the Cabinet strategy
worked out at Chequers on the weekend of 21–2 January 1961. That
month was decisive. Kennedy was taking over in Washington, and a
common external tariff was being imposed by the Six. Heath again did
not go along with Macmillan and Lord Home to see de Gaulle at Rambouillet the next weekend. But he did not miss much. Although Macmillan suggested a common outside tariff on all goods from outside
Europe and the Commonwealth, de Gaulle was not concerned with
these 'Quartermaster' details. He was more interested in whether
Macmillan was willing to declare Britain's independence of the USA.

Since Macmillan still saw Britain as linked to the United States
as the West's second nuclear Power, he had little patience with de
Gaulle's 'pretensions'. He still hoped that Bonn was alienated from
Paris and willing to help Britain into the EEC. This hope vanished
when Dr Adenauer visited London on 22–3 February 1961. The aged
Chancellor said Britain must accept the Rome Treaty if it wanted the
benefits of a united Western Europe.[24]

After these two cold douches, it was more warming for Heath to
attend the Admiralty House dinner for Averell Harriman, now the
new President's Ambassador-at-large. Harriman indicated the Kennedy
regime's interest in seeing Britain included in the EEC.

Heath was interested because he had just flown back from Paris,
where he had outlined to the WEU Britain's new approach, a product
of deep study by Sir Frank Lee and other senior civil servants. If
the Six could help Britain with its Commonwealth, EFTA and domestic
agricultural problems, Britain could then consider a harmonized
tariff system on raw material and manufactured imports from countries
other than the Six, the Seven and the Commonwealth.

The *Daily Express* headlined its story: 'Britain to Open Up Empire
to the Six'. *The Economist* welcomed the initiative: 'The proposals show
that British European policy has taken two steps forward. Either
would have been regarded as pure heresy a year ago. Since the prefer-
ences in the Commonwealth are declining steadily in value, it is no more

than common sense to use what is left to bargain a way into Europe. The Government no longer excludes membership of the Common Market. . . .'[25] Unfortunately these half-way measures did not convince the sceptical French.

This reflected the moderate advance in the still ambivalent Cabinet position. Reginald Maudling spoke for the 'cool on Europe' faction, Heath was the 'warm on Europe' group spokesman. There were 'hotter', more senior pro-Europeans such as Duncan Sandys and Peter Thorneycroft. Both Heath and Maudling were often sent to conferences so that Britain could be *heard* speaking with two voices.

To win this argument, the pro-Europeans sought Washington's aid. George Ball, the pro-Market US Under-Secretary of State, felt that he was being received with new warmth on 30 March 1961. 'I called on the Lord Privy Seal, Mr Edward Heath, at his request,' Ball later recalled. 'Present at the meeting were several British civil servants, including Sir Frank Lee . . . Joint Permanent Secretary of the Treasury.

'Mr Heath launched immediately into the purpose of the meeting . . . the British Government wished to ascertain how the United States would react if Britain were to apply for accession to the Rome Treaty . . . I reviewed at some length the reasons why the United States had consistently encouraged efforts toward unity in Europe putting great emphasis on the need for Franco-German rapprochement and the necessity of tying Germany firmly to the West. There were, I noted, latent dangers in the continuance of a divided Europe and specifically a divided Germany. . . .

' "If," I concluded, "Britain is now prepared to recognize that the Rome Treaty is not a static document but a process that could eventually lead to an evolving European community – something in the nature of a European federation . . . I am confident that my government will regard this as a major contribution to Western solidarity and the stability of the free world. So long as Britain remains outside the European Community, she is a force for division rather than cohesion, since she is like a giant lodestone drawing with unequal degrees of force on each member state. But if Great Britain now decides to participate in the formidable efforts to unite Europe, she can, and I am sure she will, apply her unique political genius . . . toward the creation of a unity that can transform the Western world." I left the meeting with a sense that something historic might have happened. . . .'[26]

Ball's encouragement could be cabled to the Prime Minister, already off to the West Indies, from which he was planning to go to Washington where he was eager to win the support of the new President. So anxious was Macmillan to retain American support that he almost 'sold the pass' on the FO's policy on Laos. Kennedy had inherited the Republicans' CIA policy for Laos. This had resulted in the flooding of $300m. into that mountainous country of two million relaxed hill people between Vietnam and Thailand to convert them into a 'bulwark against communism'. Kennedy rejected this policy but was worried about how to extricate himself. The Foreign Office proposed a neutralized Laos, sending Kennedy's old friend, David Ormsby-Gore, then Minister of State. He told Kennedy that Washington was backing a crooked rightwing gang instead of the West's best hope, Prince Souvanna Phouma. In March the President offered the Russians either a neutralized Laos or stronger American intervention.

Kennedy asked Macmillan to interrupt his West Indies tour at Key West. Macmillan reluctantly agreed that Britain would support limited intervention in Laos if necessary. The Russians decided to avoid the confrontation, Krushchev explaining: 'Why take risks over Laos? It will fall into our laps like a ripe apple.'[27]

Macmillan was willing to sign an open cheque for Laos in return for Kennedy's support in Europe. 'On the first day of that visit, when we had gathered around the table in the Cabinet Room,' George Ball recalled, 'the Prime Minister lost little time in repeating Mr Heath's question. How would we react to British entry? President Kennedy turned to me, and, at his request, I answered in the same terms I had used in London. . . . The Prime Minister then made it clear that Britain would try "very soon to go into Europe". We dined the following night at the British Embassy. Twice during the evening Macmillan drew me aside to repeat that he was determined to sign the Rome Treaty. "We are going to need some help from you in getting in but we are going in. Yesterday was one of the greatest days of my life."'[28] The Prime Minister asked the President to support the British application when he next saw de Gaulle.

Unfortunately for Heath, Britain had to pay off in Cuban silences as well as Laotian promises. Kennedy had also inherited a CIA project to sponsor an invasion of Castro's Cuba by anti-Castro exiles. On 18 April 1961 Heath had to stave off criticism from critics of the 'Bay of Pigs' invasion. 'We have no clear information,' he insisted, loyally quoting 'the American Secretary of State' who had 'said quite clearly yesterday at his press conference that they did not originate in the United States and that American forces were not intervening. . . .' He fended off Barbara Castle's quotes from the *Daily Mail* that the invasion was US-financed and US-trained.[29] Eight days later Heath still refused to accept in the House that the CIA had organized the Bay of Pigs invasion.[30]

MORE EUROPEAN 'MUSCLE'

Within about a fortnight of Macmillan's return from Washington, the Kennedy promises had persuaded the Cabinet to take a shallow plunge. In the Cabinet discussions Heath 'was said to have won the Cabinet over to a policy of quick action', said the first authoritative report. 'Mr Maudling, President of the Board of Trade, was stated to have advised a slower time-table. Mr Selwyn Lloyd, Chancellor of the Exchequer, supported Mr Heath and Mr Maudling was reported to have been overruled.'

At Strasbourg Heath informed representatives of the 'Six' that Britain would join the EEC, subject to agreement on terms regarding the Commonwealth, EFTA and British agriculture. When this 'leaked', Reginald Maudling was quick to emphasize in a weekend speech that the Cabinet had only decided on the *desirability* of joining, if Britain's special difficulties in the three areas were met.[31]

Although Lord Home proclaimed his conversion to entry quite openly, Heath tended to be even more cautious in disclosing the new Cabinet position than the ambivalent Prime Minister. When Heath spoke to the Tory MPs' Foreign Affairs Group on 10 May he assured them that the UK would not join the EEC unless British farmers' rights were fully guaranteed. At the Tory MPs' Agricultural Committee which met that same day, there were warnings that eighty rural seats might be lost by the Tories if the farmers' rights were not protected.[32]

ORDEAL OF THE TRAVELLING SALESMAN

As the British bid to enter the Market began to move into higher gear, Heath channelled his mental and physical energies into the task of Britain's leading 'travelling salesman' of EEC entry while answering for the FO in the Commons. Over his next eighteen months as 'Mr Europe' Heath flew 100,000 miles and spent one night in five overseas. So arduous was this stint that his expanded FO staff took it in turns to accompany him. Every encounter had to be converted into reports.

Heath worked his staff hard, demanding high levels of competence from his lieutenants. But he never shouted at them, as he did at the incompetence of some *outside* his private office. Although they were often able to relax and joke together, there was no real intimacy, as one might expect from a group of men who were working together as a nomadic team. 'At the end of three years,' said one of the team, 'I knew him little better than I did at the end of three hours.'

Ordinarily Heath was willing to listen to advice from comparatively junior people, if cogently put and effectively defended against his tough probing. His private secretaries were less successful in putting drafts of speeches or Parliamentary replies into crisper, more straight-forward language than was his custom. He would almost always convert this back into his 'Inland Revenue' style.

Although he worked his staff very hard, he worked himself even harder, returning to his eight-guinea flat in Petty France very late almost every evening. One of the few indulgences he allowed himself in the late spring was taking off an afternoon and evening to go to the opera at Glyndebourne, often squiring June Osborne, the music-loving widow of pianist Franz Osborne. It was a musical friendship and little more, although Mrs Osborne later boasted that the Lord Privy Seal *had* put his arm around her shoulder. . . . But Heath suddenly startled many who did not realize how romantic he was, musically, in a review he wrote of a Royal Concert at St James's Palace at the end of May 1961. He thought that Yehudi Menuhin had 'made the theme of the Andante sing for pure joy' although the first movement of the Kreutzer Sonata had 'lacked something of the confident robust-ness and wild surge which it requires'.[33]

Heath was developing a musical 'double life' partly because the greater the pressures on him as a Minister, the more he needed com-plete escape as a music-lover. He had to watch every word as a politician-diplomat in a world full of booby-traps. As a music-lover he could be uninhibited. His personal pleasure in this musical escape-hatch was enhanced when, in 1961, he met the Cornish pianist Moura Lympany at the home of Frederick Erroll, then President of the Board of Trade. After the party, Erroll asked Heath whether he would take Miss Lympany home. This was the beginning of a long friendship. A fine pianist with an international reputation and a very sympathetic person whose second marriage was just ended, Miss Lympany became Heath's favourite concert companion. She was very impressed by his extensive musical knowledge, even if it did not equal that of Sir Edward Boyle. Having lived in New York, she was not dismayed by his caustic sense of humour. She brought him into contact with a new range of musical and theatrical friends, including actress Joan Fontaine.

GETTING UP COURAGE

The Cabinet suddenly decided, in mid-May, to make public its inten-tion of clearing the ground for entry into the EEC. The decision came suddenly, when the Laotian situation was resolved. At the end of April, 'we all felt that there was grave danger that internal strife would spread and that there would be further intervention, with grave international implications', explained Heath, neglecting to tell of Macmillan's pledge at Key West. On 16 May the Laotian conference met. It was decided to announce the Government's decision to try EEC entry in the 17–18 May foreign affairs debate, although there was no mention of it in the motion governing the debate.

'Throughout our history . . . we have recognized the need to establish a relationship with the other countries on the mainland. Usually, it has been because we feared their military hostility. Our relationship has been part of the balance of power. Today, that is certainly not the case. It is the great blocs of the Communist world and the Western Powers which confront each other. . . .'

'We see today in Europe a powerfully developing group of nations,' Heath said at the core of his forty-minute analysis. 'The gross national product of the Six is two and a half times that of the United Kingdom. Their rate of industrial growth is much higher. The internal trade of the Six rose by 30 per cent in 1960 compared with 16 per cent for the internal trade of the Seven. . . . In the past, over 50 per cent of American investment came to the United Kingdom. In 1960 it was down to 41 per cent and in 1961 over 50 per cent of the United States investment in Europe is expected to go to the Six. . . .

'The new Administration in Washington . . . is prepared to accept additional discrimination against its goods provided that the arrangements reached can be shown to strengthen the political unity of Europe. . . .'[34]

Although Harold Macmillan patted Heath's back in congratulations, unconditional pro-Marketeers were disappointed about the conditions surrounding entry. Roy Jenkins: 'I thought that the speech of the Lord Privy Seal, though obscure in some parts, certainly marked a substantial step forward' after Macmillan's equivocation.

As requested by Macmillan, President Kennedy raised the question of Britain's entry when alone with de Gaulle for his final meeting on 2 June. De Gaulle expressed doubt that Britain really wanted full, unconditional membership. The door was open but Britain would have to choose between membership in the EEC or participation in the Commonwealth preference system. She could not have both.[35]

Heath also had to keep his mind and eye on all the problems for which he spoke in the Commons. On 19 June he answered questions on Angola, Kuwait, Berlin, the Anglo-Egyptian financial agreement and the release of the Bahreini prisoners. These prisoners had now been released after a British court had ruled their trial, conviction and detention illegal. Heath told the Commons that the British Government would pay their fares to any destination up to the distance from St Helena to Bahrein.[36] They subsequently went to Beirut. Even those Labour MPs who had criticized Heath initially, felt that he had acquitted himself very honourably.

For several weeks Heath tried to rebut the sharp attacks on the Government for being too 'soft on Portugal'. The attacks were aimed not so much at Heath as at his chief, Lord Home, who hardly hid his admiration for the Portuguese role in Africa.[37] Heath flatly denied that Britain supported 'repression and extermination' or concurred with 'atrocities' by selling frigates to Portugal. He angered the Portuguese by saying the Angolan revolt bore 'relevance to the aspirations of the Angolans themselves' rather than pretend it was all caused by outside 'terrorists'.

Heath spent a good deal of July 1961 in the Mediterranean, trying to clear the way for negotiations with the Six. He was in Cyprus, discussing with Archbishop Makarios the impact on Cyprus of UK entry. From there he went on to Vienna for six hours of talks,[38] using some spare time to steal away to play a famous cathedral organ, at St Stephen's.[39]

THE GREEN LIGHT

Finally, Heath was given his green light. The Cabinet decided on 27 July to apply for entry to the EEC, provided conditions to safeguard Commonwealth trade, EFTA partners and domestic agriculture could be negotiated. This was largely because the economy was so sluggish and inflationary that Selwyn Lloyd had imposed his 'Little Budget' on 25 July, including 'pay pause' and seven per cent bank rate.[40] Macmillan and Heath were more interested in the politics of a unified Europe, but it was economics which enabled them to 'sell' it to hesitant Tory Cabinet Ministers like Butler, who was persuaded that British agriculture might do well.

The first official announcement came on 31 July, when the Prime Minister rose to announce that conditions would be sought for EEC membership. 'But if European unity would disrupt the longstanding and historic ties between the United Kingdom and the Commonwealth then the loss would be greater than the gain.'

On 1 August Heath carried the news to the WEU in Paris. He felt the Six were 'very enthusiastic'; even Couve de Murville hoped the negotiations could be held 'with the maximum good will'.[41]

After the House rose, Heath took a holiday in Brittany, enabling him to be away on 18 August, when the announcement that he would lead

the delegation at the Ministerial level, was made. 'The Prime Minister
has probably made the right choice,' thought *The Economist*. 'The
other possibilities were Mr Maudling and Mr Thorneycroft. Mr
Maudling had the overwhelming disadvantage of having been over the
same course unsuccessfully. . . . Mr Thorneycroft is one of the most
enthusiastic Europeans in the Cabinet, but does not have the close
relationship with the Prime Minister which is enjoyed by Mr Heath.
Most members of his own party . . . regard him rightly as a convinced
but not a fanatical European. . . .'[42]

On the second weekend in September, Heath left London for a weekend in the South of France, with his friends the Seligmans. This gave
him an opportunity for a casual stop-over in Paris, for a three-hour
lunch with the French Foreign Minister, Couve de Murville. One of
the things discussed was the British Government's decision to appoint,
as the head of the official side of Britain's negotiating delegation, Sir
Pierson Dixon, the UK Ambassador in Paris. The deputy head of the
official delegation was Austrian-born Sir Eric Roll, who had the talent
of virtually being able to lip-read in German and French; this enabled
him to tell Heath or Sir Pierson what their opponents were saying to one
another. They were to be so much in movement by air between London
and Brussels that they were usually referred to collectively as 'the flying
knights'.

Heath had to learn to manoeuvre skilfully because he was under
constant fire from different directions. In Brussels, he was accused
either of 'holding back' by Eurofanatics or 'selling out' by Europhobes.
To make any headway the delegation had to pretend in Brussels to
be making the maximum possible concessions while pretending at
home to have given hardly anything away. Initially, Heath hoped that
this two-faced appearance could be avoided by keeping conference
documents secret. But this exploded in his face at the first official
meeting on 10 October 1961. He sought to reassure the Six: 'The
United Kingdom is ready fully to subscribe to the aims and objectives
of the Community,' he insisted. But when the Canadian Ambassador
asked for a text, he was refused.[43] Pressure kept mounting, particularly
after it became known that the Five had passed a copy to Washington.
On 25 November it was decided to issue the full text to Britain's
Commonwealth and EFTA partners. But on 27 November the text
started coming out of Brussels via Reuters. It proved unremarkable,
except for its enthusiasm.[44]

'I have no inferiority complex about our ability to influence the Community when we play our full part in it,' Heath told the Tories' annual
conference at Brighton. 'Our voice will be heard and our voice will be

welcomed by the European countries . . . We should not frighten ourselves by false apprehensions.' He sat down amid prolonged cheering.
His emphasis on the need to unite Western Europe to resist the advance
of Communism was well received at the conference because two months
before the Berlin Wall had been raised. The Soviet Union had also
resumed nuclear tests in the atmosphere. The vote for entry was carried
overwhelmingly, with only thirty or forty opposed out of 4,000 delegates.[45]

The intensification of the 'cold war' made more impact on Heath
than on Lord Home, who never expected anything of the Russians.
Heath secured international fame at Russian hands for warning about
war over Berlin in the House. Krushchev threw in his weight a fortnight
later: 'Mr Edward Heath threatens us with war. But he apparently
forgets that Britain is a small island' that 'may be among the first to
experience the destructive power of nuclear bombs.'[46] Heath retorted
by baiting the Soviet leader on 2 November for having taken too long
to learn the evils of Stalinism. 'Why did the Russians negotiate for
more than two years on a [nuclear] test agreement, and reject it at
twenty-four hours' notice . . . ? Why not carry out the tests underground,
instead of in the atmosphere, where they are poisoning the air ?' Heath
demanded angrily. He was pulled up by Denis Healey for not recognizing how much more conciliatory Krushchev was than Molotov and
for under-estimating the importance of the division between China
and Russia.[47]

In Brussels Heath's brisk but amiable style won him supporters
among the Five, if not the Six. During the negotiations there Heath and
his leading 'flying knights' – Sir Pierson Dixon and Sir Eric Roll –
normally had a working lunch in the back room of one of the smallest
restaurants in Brussels, which advertised 'cheap food cooked in best
butter'. As they discussed their case over lunch, the professional senior
civil servants grew to admire Heath for the rapidity with which he
learned and remembered highly technical subjects. They found he had
considerable intellectual power even if not an intellectual.

If Heath developed many of the skills of a senior diplomat in Brussels
he was still very much a politician, trying to keep on his side the public
opinion of a divided Britain. He held a daily press briefing for the British
pressmen and one for the international press as well. In the evening
he would drop into the bar of the Metropole Hotel, the normal press
hangout. He became very much publicity conscious. When he arrived
somewhere he would often ask: 'Where are the photographers ?'

As a politician he had to be at Admiralty House whenever the Cabinet
met on Europe. Heath had to worry about possible backsliders like

M

R.A. Butler and about getting Cabinet backing for necessary concessions.

As he got into the swing of negotiations, Heath also began to feel more 'at home' in Brussels. He developed a taste for good food and wine, even if he never became as great a connoisseur as Christopher Soames. In the evening he would normally eat at 'Comme Chez Soi', the best and most expensive restaurant in Brussels.

It should have been clear to him from the outset that the basic rivalry within the Six was over whether France or Germany would become the dominant power in Western Europe. Britain was regarded by both of them as a dangerous competitor *unless* she agreed to enter the Community stripped of her assets: mainly access to the markets and cheap food of the Commonwealth and the diplomatic support of like-thinking EFTA partners. The strategy of the French and Germans, therefore, was that Britain should be allowed to enter *only on her own*, without EFTA partners initially and without access to cheap Commonwealth food, or direct backing by the Americans.

CONGO HEADACHES

Heath often left Belgium's capital to worry about the headaches the Belgians had left behind in their abandonment of the Congo. In December 1961 there was tumult when Heath informed the Commons that the Cabinet had agreed to supply 1,000 lb bombs to the UN forces in the Congo, with certain restrictions about their use against Katangan air-strips. He worried about the UN's intention to force on the Congolese a form of government. Also bombs had been used on non-military objectives. 'Aspects of this policy would have to be clarified before Her Majesty's Government feel they can authorize the release of the bombs.'[48] Heath managed to survive attacks from the Tory imperial Right and the Labour anti-colonial Left.

As the season of good will approached, relations between Canada and the 'mother country' dropped to freezing. The Canadian High Commissioner boycotted a Heath briefing. Heath determined to spend part of the Christmas recess talking the Canadians around. He had the advantage that the Canadians had been shouting loud about a trade which amounted only to about two per cent of their exports. He flew from Ottawa to Washington to discuss trade problems with George Ball and Douglas Dillon, now Secretary of the Treasury.[49] He was satisfied enough with his North American trip to do the Boy Scouts a good deed while in New York. The Scouts there had long organized an annual fund-raising breakfast at 5 a.m. That year they had great difficulty in finding any guest of honour willing to rise that early. Heath volunteered. 'So today he got up at 5 o'clock,' cabled the astounded correspondent of the *Daily Herald*, 'to attend the breakfast in the Waldorf-Astoria ballroom. And 1,500 past and present Boy Scouts cheered . . . the ovation was the heartiest given to a guest speaker since Dawn Patrol Breakfasts began.'[50] He was also thought a good scout when the *Queen Elizabeth* ran into the 'worst storm in a hundred years', according to his fellow passenger, actress Olivia de Havilland. 'He was extraordinarily steady in the storm,' she could still recall a decade later.[51]

In the Brussels negotiations he was exciting wonder as a most unusual Englishman: a Minister better informed than his civil servants, willing to work any hour of the day or night. A leading diplomat of the Six telephoned for an appointment with Heath. 'Certainly,' he was told by Heath's private secretary, 'could you come at 5.30 tomorrow?' 'That depends,' the diplomat replied, having heard of Heath's breakfast with the New York Scouts. 'Does he mean 5.30 a.m. or 5.30 p.m.?'[52]

Time was of the essence because the Cabinet had asked Heath to work out the terms for entry by the summer recess of 1962. But he did not cut corners. In the Foreign Office he not only read through the mountains of telegrams but also insisted on seeing all of the mounting tide of correspondence on Market entry, including those which began, 'Dear Sir, you bloody well ought to be ashamed of yourself. . . .'

BETWEEN TWO NARROW WALLS

In January 1962 de Gaulle's men at Brussels enormously complicated Britain's entry chances with an agreement for a rapid reduction of internal agricultural tariffs. This ensured that French surpluses would find outlets among the food-importing nations like Germany. At the same time the French secured agreement to a high 'threshold price' for food imported from outside the Community. This was a blow to Britain because it meant that cheap New Zealand butter would be brought up to the cost of expensive French butter.

Heath seemed willing to keep the Commons in the dark, while pretending to enlighten them. He aroused a storm of protest on 7 March 1962 when he galloped into a statement of progress at well over 200 words a minute. Reporters threw down their pencils in disgust. 'Is there any precedent for a statement at such length and at such speed?' demanded pro-EEC Labour MP Charles Pannell.[53]

Heath's contrived optimism was misleading. By mid-spring of 1962, the Brussels delegation knew that they could only hold out for New Zealand dairy products, West Indian sugar and transitional terms for

British agriculture. Some were even more pessimistic. In May 1962 Sir Pierson Dixon wrote to the Prime Minister: de Gaulle would wait until after the October 1962 French elections; once re-elected, he would blackball Britain's effort with impunity. Macmillan noted on the margin of Sir Pierson's dispatch: 'Interesting but unbelievable.'

The Prime Minister had been back to Washington in April 1962 to try to get further American support for his effort. Macmillan had found the young President very sympathetic to the ideal of a politically united Europe, but more realistic about its economic impact on the USA.[54] Heath was not at all impressed at the outcome of the Macmillan–Kennedy talks. 'If you leave those two alone for a minute,' he told a friend, 'they get things all messed up.'

Heath was caught between Sir Pierson's suspicions and the bland self-confidence of Macmillan who tended to pooh-pooh them. At a Cabinet meeting in mid-May, it was decided de Gaulle was manageable, provided he was appeased. At French Cabinet meetings at the same time, the new Premier, Georges Pompidou, warned against too harsh a posture towards Britain, particularly before the election.

The 2 June 1962 de Gaulle–Macmillan meeting at Château de Champs was a confrontation of two confidence tricksters out to cheat one another. Macmillan spoke vaguely of future nuclear collaboration. De Gaulle spoke hopefully of the entry negotiations, knowing his hands would be free once he won the nearing elections.[55] The Prime Minister gave Heath and the delegation a misleadingly optimistic picture of his encounter with de Gaulle.

The frustrations of his position explained why Heath was often short-tempered when reporting to Parliament. He could provide technical answers off the cuff. But when challenged more fundamentally he could lose his temper. On 2 July, his routine report-back turned into a bare-knuckled argument. The spark was the statement the previous Saturday by Minister of Labour John Hare that Commonwealth countries were 'behaving in some respects like children'. Peppery Emanuel Shinwell provoked Heath with: 'Is he not an honest man who has just expressed the view of the Government as a whole that the Commonwealth is now expendable?' Heath burst out: 'You are very good at phrases like "The expendable Commonwealth" and "selling it down the river". They have no relation to reality . . . !'

MACMILLAN SLIPS

Heath was worried too by evidence that Macmillan was beginning to slip, due to the still-secret onset of his prostate troubles. Macmillan was showing this in below-par speeches and behaviour in the House. The real shock came when Macmillan carried out his 'July massacre', discarding a third of his Cabinet, including such stalwarts as Selwyn Lloyd. Heath accepted the need to push for more reflation because he had had evidence of restiveness in his constituency, shown in the May local elections. Local Tories had suffered serious setbacks in Bexley.[56] Heath's criticism of Macmillan's subsequent Cabinet purge was that it looked more like a massacre than a needed infusion of new blood. Alienating a large portion of party loyalists when unity was already under strain as a result of the EEC entry effort did not make sense.

Heath, of course, had his own troubles. At the end of July it became a contest between Heath and his team to rush things through, and Couve de Murville and his French team to stall things until after the French election. A marathon series of meetings began on 27 July. That night Couve de Murville made the new system's discrimination against Commonwealth food exports clear. The French farmer would flourish when prices were low enough to deter over-production in Germany and when levies were high enough to discourage Commonwealth imports. On this anti-Commonwealth note, delegations dispersed, agreeing to meet again the following Wednesday, 1 August, for a final session. Sir Pierson Dixon rushed back to Britain to report to Macmillan and the Common Market Committee of the Cabinet, presided over by R. A. Butler.

That Monday, 30 July, the Cabinet meeting in Admiralty House had a stark alternative. They could sign the Treaty of Rome without special guarantees for Commonwealth suppliers and thus virtually guarantee entry. De Gaulle was still facing a general election and barring British entry would be held against him. The alternative was to hold out for Commonwealth concessions, hoping that de Gaulle would be defeated in the election or that, under pressure, his resolve would weaken. The Cabinet decided it would hold out for Commonwealth concessions. On 31 July Heath addressed a private meeting of the Tory MPs' Foreign Affairs Committee, just before flying back to Brussels. He blandly emphasized that although negotiations had reached a difficult stage, this had been anticipated all along and there was no crisis.

Back in Brussels on 1 August, Heath said 'we must underline the importance of ensuring that the essential interests of Commonwealth countries are safeguarded'. The next two days saw skirmishing in which the French prevented any substantial advance. Saturday, 4 August 1962, was to be the final day of the discussions, with most delegates anxious to be away on vacation. Couve de Murville had the task of making sure the last gap was not bridged until after the French elections. He constantly underlined the 'financial regulation' or levy on external agricultural imports, making it clear that France intended to keep out Commonwealth butter and wheat and thus block Heath's ability to carry out Cabinet instructions. In the early hours of Sunday, 5 August, Heath rounded on the French Foreign Minister: 'Mr Couve de Murville has now said that nothing could be settled without the financial regulation!' When they met for the fifth time at 6.30 a.m. Couve de Murville was still adamant. Exhausted by fifteen hours of debate and discussion during the night, they agreed to meet again in October and walked out into the morning light of Brussels at 7 a.m.[57]

Any realist would have accepted that Britain could not enter carrying New Zealand butter and Australian wheat in her baggage. But Heath was a never-say-die man, as shown by his discussion over drinks the next evening with Balliol chum Phil Kaiser, then American Ambassador to the African republics of Senegal and Mauritania, formerly French colonies. When Kaiser arrived in London there was a note from Heath asking him over for a drink at the FO. They had little time for the normal gossip about other Balliol men. Heath concentrated on finding out just how the preference for former French colonies with associate status in the Community operated in fact. He was searching for a fall-back position – equality for the Commonwealth and France's former colonies. He also gave Kaiser a message for George Ball: 'Tell George to stop pushing,' asked Heath. 'We know how he feels!'

SEPTEMBER EFFORT

Heath sat alongside as Macmillan tried to persuade the Commonwealth Prime Minister's Conference that EEC entry would help them in the long run. 'We have to consider the state of the world as it is today and will be tomorrow, and not in outdated terms of a vanished past.' Although the normally chummy Conference was unprecedentedly bitter, the slanted British press briefings made it sound as though the Australians, New Zealanders and Canadians were anxious to see Britain in the Community!

The Prime Minister continued his high-pressure campaign with a pamphlet, published a few days before the Tories' annual conference at Llandudno. Heath himself took off for Llandudno from his tour of Europe to assure the Six that Britain had not undertaken new obligations to the Commonwealth. Although he rushed from the Continent he arrived two hours late to address Tory agents. His appeal: 'You have great influence in the constituencies. Make sure that on this Market issue your local party does not rock the boat.'[58]

His big moment came with his reply to the debate on Market entry on 11 October. His principal target was Hugh Gaitskell, who, nine days before, had come out with a resounding rejection of entry. Gaitskell should have asked whether the opportunities created by entry would enable us to become stronger and therefore would we become weaker by staying out? The answer, Heath said, was 'Yes'. Heath sat down to loud applause. Only about fifty hands were raised in the crowded hall in support of no entry.[59] 'Ted really seems to believe in every word he says,' conceded one anti-Market Tory MP. 'That's what frightens me.'[60] It was generally conceded that he had enormously enhanced his prestige within the party.

The extent to which the political world had been polarized over EEC entry was shown by Gaitskell's reply to Heath in the EEC debate of 7–8 November 1962. Heath made a very curious speech. Knowing that his policy was coming under strong attack he chose to give a display of his mastery of obscure customs terminology. It was not the sort of speech which would enable even a bright MP to know how far he had succeeded or failed in protecting the interests of British agriculture, EFTA and the Commonwealth.[61] He showed irritation that he should be judged on 'provisional arrangements as they are at the moment'. He spoke vaguely of special trade arrangements for India, Pakistan and Ceylon. He admitted that he had failed to get 'comparable outlets' for food exports from the old Commonwealth, but claimed there were hopeful agreements still in the making.

Gaitskell punctured Heath's claims brutally. He started from a much more pro-American and pro-Commonwealth position than Heath. In his speech Gaitskell said he thought, until the previous Spring, that Heath was being tough enough, 'but in recent months, particularly in August and September, we have heard less and less of the conditions and more and more of the general arguments in favour of entry'.

'On examination, I must say, after studying the White Paper of August and examining the previous statements made by [Mr Heath] that we are driven to these conclusions: first, that the agreements so far made do not fulfil the conditions and pledges laid down . . . he asked that the status of associated overseas territories should be granted to all the less developed members of the Commonwealth . . . [Mr Heath] did not get it. That was turned down, as we know perfectly well because of the competition which was feared from Indian manufacturers. . . . Under this agreement there is no possibility of Commonwealth products being allowed to undercut European products, because they are more cheaply produced. . . .' Gaitskell's summation, he admitted, was 'crude': 'What is the alternative to cutting one's throat? It is *not* to cut it. What is the alternative to throwing oneself over a cliff? It is to stay on top. . . .'62

If Heath's opponents did not love him, his chief still did. Opening a Bexley bazaar for him on 1 December, Lady Dorothy Macmillan described him as a devoted colleague and friend of her husband. 'I do not suppose anyone realizes the overwhelming regard and affection my husband has for Mr Heath.'63

BACON AND EGGS

Heath spent most of December in Brussels discussing pigmeat and eggs. The Five were initially sympathetic about the British need to continue deficiency payments to their farmers for a while. But Couve de Murville refused to discuss these problems in detail; he accused Heath of trying to secure special treatment for Britain. When the negotiations resumed on 20 December the Six had lined up behind the French to decline concessions.64 It was hardly the omen for a happy Christmas.

The Brussels air had been cooled by the currents from Rambouillet where Macmillan and de Gaulle had had a chilly meeting. For some reason, Macmillan expected sympathy from de Gaulle for informing him that he was going to Kennedy to ask him for 'Polaris' missiles to replace the scrapped 'Skybolt' promised to Macmillan by Eisenhower. Instead he hardened the French President's belief that Britain was only an American 'Trojan horse'. De Gaulle asked Macmillan to break, once and for all, the 'special links' between London and Washington. Otherwise Britain's entry into the EEC would result in division in the Community and the isolation of France.

Macmillan ensured de Gaulle's hostility by his brilliant performance in Nassau as America's wounded but still loyal ally. Britain would stay in the nuclear race with or without US help. But if the US refused to supply 'Polaris', a dangerous Anglo-American rift was inevitable. 'Europeanists' among Kennedy's advisers warned that providing Britain with 'Polaris' would block EEC entry and maintain the division of Western Europe. Macmillan pretended that de Gaulle and Europe would understand, since America and Britain had built the A-bomb together.65 After Christmas in Broadstairs, Heath was able to get the whole story from Macmillan at Chequers, on the weekend of 5–6 January, where they discussed the Brussels negotiations.

Heath flew to Paris to lunch at the British Embassy with Couve de Murville on 11 January. He put to Couve de Murville a question which he repeated twice, and both times got the same negative reply. 'If Britain and the Six reach an economic agreement, is there any danger of a political veto?' Twice the French Foreign Minister said emphatically, 'No!'

That night, Heath dined with George Ball. 'In ebullient spirits,' Ball later recorded, 'Heath detailed his conversations with various members of the French Government. "I should not", he said, "pay attention to rumours emanating from newspaper sources . . ." While some serious obstacles remained, he seemed reasonably confident that the British application was in no serious trouble.'[66]

Heath still seemed optimistic when the Brussels negotiations reopened on 14 January. They even agreed to arrange for an official English translation of the Treaty of Rome. 'We all seem to be generally in complete agreement,' said Heath, bringing the meeting to a close.[67]

Unfortunately for Heath, the curtain was being brought down at that same time by de Gaulle at his dramatically-staged press conference in Paris. Britain, he insisted, had little in common with the Six and would not give up her 'special political and military relations' with the Americans. If Britain and her EFTA allies were admitted, the EEC would be transformed: 'The cohesion of all these numerous and very differing states would not last long and what would emerge in the end would be a colossal Atlantic Community, dependent on America and directed by America. . . .'[68] In Brussels the Five sought for fifteen days to persuade the French to relent. Then on 29 January the British delegates – Heath, Soames, Sir Pierson Dixon and Sir Eric Roll – heard the expected verdict: 'The French delegation has refused.' 'This is a sad moment,' said the Belgian Foreign Minister, Paul-Henri Spaak. After the Dutch and Germans had echoed this, Couve de Murville wound up his explanation with: 'We want to make a *European* Europe!'

'The end of the negotiations is a blow to the cause of the wider European unity for which we have been striving,' Heath retorted. 'We are a part of Europe, by geography, history, culture, tradition and civilization. . . . There have been times in the history of Europe when it has been only too plain how European we are; and there have been many millions of people who have been grateful for it.' He ended: 'I say to my colleagues: they should have no fear. We in Britain are not going to turn our backs on the mainland of Europe or the countries of the Community. . . .'

Heath was applauded by the press – mostly non-British – at his last press conference. That night, Heath walked coolly into the bar of the Metropole. Among the journalists, many of them heavily committed Europeans who had often talked with Heath during the previous eighteen months, there was a mixture of heavy disappointment and fury with the French.

But the highest compliment came from a Frenchman – the prediction of de Gaulle, which Heath soon heard on the diplomatic grapevine: 'The Labour Party will come to power for a short and disastrous period, to be followed by the Conservatives, with Heath at their head. It is he who will enable Britain to enter Europe.'[69]

12 OVERTAKING FROM BEHIND

> When you go into politics, either you take the view that you have got to please the maximum number of people all the time, or you can believe, as I do, that you are in politics to get rid of a lot of these 'nonsenses'.
>
> Edward Heath, *The Times*, 24 September 1969

'I suppose I might be more acceptable if I had a wife,' Edward Heath joked to his PPS, 'but I'm not likely to find one in the next fortnight!' This was at Blackpool in October 1963, where Harold Macmillan had just thrown the Conservatives' annual conference into confusion by informing them his prostate was pushing him into retirement.

Heath sent his PPS, John Howard, to sample MPs' opinion. Howard found that those traditionalists who wanted Lord Hailsham could not stand the idea of R. A. Butler as the next Prime Minister. Butler supporters bridled at the prospect of Hailsham. Lord Home did not raise the same hackles. Among younger men, Maudling was well in the lead, with Heath back among the also-rans with Macleod and Powell.

This was not surprising, considering Heath's decline since de Gaulle had vetoed Britain's EEC entry. Initially Heath had been welcomed home as the vanquished bearer of the national flag. Those who had wanted to see the Union Jack planted among the flags of the Six had praised him for the doughty fight he had put up. Those who had never wanted him to succeed now felt safe in applauding him.

Heath became the temporary symbol of Britain's wounded pride. The funeral ceremonies were quite long, with a two-day debate to bury the attempt held on 11–12 February. Even when buried in public, the attempt kept being exhumed in private. Heath invited Professor Walter Hallstein, then President of the European Commission, together with the available members of the British team, to Chequers to examine just why they had failed. They agreed that the members of the French team were taken by surprise by de Gaulle's veto and that he may have blackballed Britain as much because they were on the point of entry, as because of Macmillan's tie-up with the Americans over the 'Polaris' missiles.

FIRST HEATH BOOM

Heath's pro-EEC enthusiasm won him the enthusiasm of a small group of pro-Marketeers among the 1959 intake. A boomlet for Heath started in February 1963 with which the *Sunday Express* frightened its readers: COULD HEATH REALLY BECOME OUR NEXT PREMIER?[1]

In fact, Heath was having a thin time. There was a sharp rise in unemployment in February 1963. Heath offered himself as the head of a 'task force' to replan the economies of the old, declining regions. Macmillan was in no mood for another wounding Cabinet reshuffle. When Heath was left vegetating as No. 2 under Home in the Foreign Office, many thought he was finished.

This had its compensations. He needed spare time initially to find a place to live. At the beginning of 1963 he had been ousted from his little furnished flat in Petty France. He finally found a new place in the Albany where, for the first time, he had his own furniture including: two Churchill paintings and some of the objets d'art he had picked up in his wanderings. Because Sir Eric Roll and Sir Pierson Dixon also found flats in the Albany, it almost became 'Brussels in London'. Heath would walk by Sir Eric's ground floor flat and wave and be invited in for a drink, and the talk would turn back to: why had it failed? Unlike others in the Foreign Office, Heath did not turn anti-French, even during the period when Princess Margaret's Paris visit was cancelled. Heath's own anxiety not to worsen Anglo-French relations was shown in March 1963 when he asked the BBC not to use an interview with Georges Bidault, leader of the anti-de Gaulle 'Secret Army'.[2]

CHARLEMAGNE PRIZE

It was a much-needed pep-pill for Heath to learn on 2 April that he had been awarded the £450 Charlemagne Prize for services to European unity. The only previous British recipient had been Sir Winston Churchill in 1956. The award was to have been given to de Gaulle, but when he blocked Britain's entry Aachen decided to give it to Heath.[3]

Heath's decision to spend his Charlemagne Prize money on a Steinway grand indicated the increasing interaction between his European and musical interests. When in Hamburg to talk to businessmen, he played the baroque organ in a local church. Later he arranged to play on an organ in Utrecht. In mid-May he returned to Balliol to hear a Brahms recital by Yehudi and Hepzibah Menuhin. 'Brahms . . . had a close personal link with Balliol,' Heath recalled. 'It's wonderful to feel part of such a real link.'

For a period everything was dominated by discordant sounds of shrill indignation and raucous laughter over the Profumo case. Heath was interested beyond the fact that he had to answer questions about why Christine Keeler was in Spain and whether she was being extradited. He had long known Profumo, whose office and job he had taken over in the FO. He asked one of his private secretaries what was being alleged. When told the seamy stories circulating in Fleet Street, Heath, who was very naïve sexually, refused to believe them. He preferred the story concocted by Profumo, Macleod, the Attorney General and Chief Whip Martin Redmayne, announced to the House on 22 March by Profumo, with Macmillan at his side.

Heath's wilful *naïveté* was understandable. As one who was so 'buttoned up' himself it was difficult for him to believe that a colleague would be so riskily self-indulgent as to employ the same call girl as a Soviet intelligence agent. Also by that time it was clear to most top Tories that they would need about eighteen months of clear sailing to hope to overtake Labour's lead. Part of their unpopularity had derived from a series of security scandals: the Krogers, Gordon Lonsdale and George Blake in 1961 and William Vassall in 1962. Heath himself had had the embarrassing chore of defending the Foreign Office for having planted Harold ('The Third Man') Philby on the *Observer*.[4] Profumo finally confessed early in June. Heath was furious partly at his own *naïveté*, partly at the way in which the case had been 'mishandled' by the Prime Minister, the Chief Whip and others, and partly by what this would mean to hopes of a Tory comeback. Unlike Enoch Powell he never even contemplated resignation.

Although Macmillan survived the 17 June censure vote – despite twenty-seven Tory abstainers – a tremendous 'Mac Must Go!' campaign followed. This was fanned by a poll conducted by Maudling supporters. This showed how 100 Tory MPs had divided in their preference for Macmillan's successor: for Maudling 45; Hailsham, $13\frac{1}{2}$; Butler, 12; Heath, $6\frac{1}{2}$; Powell, 6; Home, 1 and Macleod, 1, with nine undecided.[5]

Although Heath knew that Macmillan was no longer the Prime Minister he had first known, he neither attacked nor defended him. The Prime Minister punctured press stories of Macmillan–Heath alienation by sending Heath with Lord Home to Moscow to sign the Test Ban Treaty in August.[6] 'Mr Krushchev is a realist,' Heath found. 'Of course he has not abandoned his intention of furthering the aims and interests of the Soviet Union. But if he has forsworn running the risk of nuclear war to achieve them, there is common ground between us.'[7]

SECRET ISLAND VISIT

Heath himself spent the end of August furthering his own aim. He kept quiet his visit to John Morrison, the wealthy and influential chairman of the 1922 Committee. When the Beaverbrook papers learned of it: 'It was simply that I was holidaying in Scotland at the time and just popped over to Islay' – Morrison's private island – 'for a few days. It was my first visit there.'[8]

At the time Macmillan was reluctantly thinking of his successor as his prostate trouble increased. He was determined not to hand over to the obvious 'crown prince', R. A. Butler, but did not believe that the front-runner among the younger men, Maudling, had the 'charisma' to overtake Labour's lead. If he *did* go before the end of the year, he told Lord Hailsham on 30 September, he thought that 'bell-ringer' had the best chance of rousing the Tory troops.[9] There was no evidence that the possibility of Heath as a successor was seriously considered by Macmillan.

Heath stopped in at No. 10 to see the Prime Minister just before the 8 October Cabinet meeting and thought he looked ill. Macmillan, under sedation after a sleepless night, only told Heath and the others that he would give his winding-up speech at Blackpool the following Saturday: 'There has got to be a decision and I must announce it at Blackpool.' They took the conference train to Blackpool not knowing that they had attended Macmillan's last Cabinet.

Heath had a speech to Tory agents scheduled for the same evening. It was a come-down to have only this speech after having been the 'darling' of the Llandudno conference the previous year. One of Heath's paragraphs was misinterpreted as aimed at Macmillan having run out of steam. 'After twelve years in power it is no bad thing to ask the question, "What would we want to do if we were coming to power for the first time at the next election?" This calls for a clear eye and a fresh mind, uninhibited by the achievements, and unencumbered by the legacies of the past.'[10]

Even before Heath had spoken, Iain Macleod was called out to speak to 10 Downing Street. He then called Heath and other Cabinet colleagues outside and told them that the Prime Minister had been rushed to hospital for an operation and would not be coming to Blackpool. They were to keep mum until the public announcement at 9.30 p.m. Heath was silent as he contemplated the impact of Macmillan's illness on his own future. The wife of the agents' chairman, sitting next to him, reproached him: 'Mr Heath, are you feeling well? You're not very talkative, and you're eating nothing at all.' 'I'm afraid,' he replied, 'I'm always nervous before a speech.'

The public announcement caused an uproar. Was Macmillan going? Who would replace him? The TV boys were after Macleod to comment. But Macleod, bruised by the fact that he had not been told of Macmillan's illness until after his press conference, declined. So Heath stone-walled in a late-night programme.[11]

Next morning's conference opening turned into a form of 'decibel democracy', with delegates showing their feelings by their applause. Lord Hailsham stole the show by bouncing in late as the chairman was introducing the others on the platform. But Heath, with six seconds, was second to Hailsham's thirty seconds; Macleod received five seconds' applause.[12]

Among the younger leaders, Maudling appeared to be well ahead of Heath, partly because of Heath's bachelor status. The Gallup Poll in the *Daily Telegraph* showed Heath running fourth with the support of eleven per cent of Tory voters and six per cent of all voters after Hailsham (18/10), Butler (15/14), and Maudling (11/10). Macleod, Selwyn Lloyd and Lord Home (with 3/2) were after him.[13]

On Thursday Lord Home arrived with a letter from Macmillan saying he would be unable to continue and calling for 'the customary processes of consultation' to start. He had already agreed with the Chief Whip a procedure whereby a straw poll would be taken of Tory MPs, Tory Peers, and the party in the country as well as the Cabinet. The Macmillan letter produced the loud sound of Hailsham throwing his coronet in the ring before an audience of 2,500 at a CPC meeting. This form of emotional exposure hardened Heath against Hailsham's candidacy. Heath preferred an older candidate, who would not be on the scene too long, because he was not yet ready to stand himself. Since he did not like Hailsham and had never been one of Butler's favourites, he moved quietly towards Home. Because Heath could see Home as a stepping stone to No. 10, he showed none of the indignation towards him displayed by Enoch Powell or Iain Macleod who considered it a plot by the 'magic circle'. On Saturday Home was prevailed upon to think seriously about standing. By Monday Heath and Selwyn Lloyd were the leading Cabinet Ministers in Home's corner. And John Morrison hovered in support.

In those peculiar Tory 'customary consultations' they not only asked MPs and others for their *first* choice but also for their *second*. This was Macmillan's inspiration because both Hailsham and Butler had many opponents, while Home had very few. Heath spent fifty minutes with Macmillan at the King Edward VII Hospital for Officers deciding how best to present Home as the compromise choice most widely favoured.[14] Heath himself also attracted a certain amount of support as a compromise candidate. But, 'party officials . . . are deliberately encouraging the idea that ten MPs would support Lord Home for every one who would support Mr Heath.'[15]

Heath regarded the resistance of the pro-Butler faction to Macmillan's plans to bypass Butler with amused disdain. One of his close friends, Lord Aldington (formerly Toby Low), the Deputy Chairman of the Conservative Party, was a Butler supporter who was present at Powell's home on 17 October, trying to work out how to resist 'Macmillan's plot'. Heath telephoned Aldington, reproving him humorously: 'I thought you were a friend of mine. . . .'

By this time Heath was serving Home as an honorary 'Chief Whip', advising him on how to break the threatened boycott of some of Macmillan's former Ministers. Hailsham, Butler, Maudling, Sir Edward Boyle, Macleod and Powell had all indicated they would not serve under Home. If the first three held out, Home could hardly form a credible Government, and indicated his doubts to the Queen when invited to try. 'My sincere hope is that all our colleagues will be able to serve with him,' Heath said.[16] In fact, all except Powell and Macleod found it impossible to resist Lord Home.

LONGEST LABEL

When he won, Lord Home was a Prime Minister in a weak position on whom Heath had a substantial claim, as one of Home's strongest backers. Moreover, he was bright and young and certainly no aristocrat. Heath's 'image' as a thrustful modernizer was just what Home required to eliminate the taste of the '14th Earl' and the Powell–Macleod boycott.

Heath had had a hankering to be Foreign Secretary. But he knew Home had to tempt Butler with this one senior post he had never held. He knew too that he had to succeed in a major domestic department which would give him a firm base from which to climb. He asked for a jazzed-up version of the old Board of Trade, strengthened in its regional development. Home gave him what he wanted – by down-grading Frederick Erroll, its former President, to the Ministry of Power. Home also moved Heath up the Cabinet ladder from No. 12 to No. 8, only three places below Reginald Maudling at No. 5.

The title Heath chose was a bad joke. A cartoon showed Butler with a simple case marked 'FO'. But Heath's case was marked 'EHSOSFITARDA-POTBOT', for 'Edward Heath, Secretary of State for Industry, Trade and Regional Development and President of the Board of Trade'.[17] He explained to Home that he wanted not only to stimulate the old trade activities but to try a wholly new co-ordinated attack on the country's backward regions. This appealed to Lord Home as a Scot, also as a Prime Minister who had a year in which to restore Tory popularity. He appreciated the enthusiasm of a 'young statesman who makes things hum', as he told audiences in Kinross, the seat he was trying to win as Sir Alec Douglas-Home.[18]

When Heath moved into the old Board of Trade building on 22 October, things did begin to hum. He had as his principal lieutenant and Minister of State, Edward duCann, the pioneer of unit trusts who had just come over from a successful stint as Economic Secretary to the Treasury. Heath inherited as the other Minister of State Lord Drumalbyn (ex Niall Macpherson) and as Parliamentary Secretary, David Price. Initially, Heath tried to work as a four-man team. After a while he dropped the other two from his consultations and relied largely on duCann.

From the very beginning the rival departments of state recognized Heath's efforts to put muscle on the Board of Trade as an empire-building effort to take over all industrial expansion policy.[19] Heath lost no time in the battle for press attention, which he had missed in his nine months out of the spotlight. Three days later he was photographed licking the raw whiskey off his fingers opening a new bonded warehouse in Dumbarton.[20] On one occasion when his Minister of State secured widespread publicity for releasing some trade figures, he instituted an inquiry to discover why *he* had not been given the figures to release.

Heath knew that they had only a year before the next election. The one field in which he could get going immediately was regional development, where he had accumulated expertise when Minister of Labour. Many of the problems in the field had first been analysed by Lord Hailsham and others. Heath put forward the idea of 'developing the region as a whole to make it a place where people want to go on living, instead of migrating'.

Heath announced on 14 November the additional investments he had already been able to pry out of the Cabinet for 'growth zones' in the older industrial areas. In the North-east there was an immediate welcome. 'I feel sure Mr Heath is the man who is going to get things done,' said George Chetwynd, ex-Labour MP and Director of the North East Development Council.[21]

In his simultaneous pursuit of expanded foreign markets he was not afraid to step on the toes of allies. He determined to sell British heavy engineering in Eastern Europe. Because it required credits longer than the five years agreed within NATO, Washington protested. His friend, George Ball, spent ninety minutes trying to argue him out of giving the Communists 'a form of concealed economic aid' in long-term credits. Heath remained unconvinced.[22]

N

THE ANTI-RPM WAR

Heath was as anxious as any ambitious new Minister to place some masterpiece on the statute books. He asked duCann to draw up a list of needed laws that could bring them merit in the next year. On the list was the repeal of RPM (Resale Price Maintenance) recommended as long ago as 1951 by Harold Wilson. Many traditional shopkeepers considered RPM (the selling of goods at the prices fixed by manufacturers) an important protection against price-slashing supermarkets. Heath knew too that RPM was against the rules of the EEC regarding price competition, although he did not think Britain would have a new chance to enter until 1968. He was forced into a sudden decision when John Stonehouse and John Osborn won first and second places in the ballot for Private Members' Bills. Stonehouse announced he would sponsor a Bill to ban RPM. Osborn announced he would go for a Bill to compel cash redemption for trading stamps – which would also undercut fixed prices. If a Labour MP succeeded in abolishing RPM, the Government could hardly claim credit for it. If they opposed Stonehouse's Bill, they could hardly claim to be modernizers. Heath made up his mind to present his own anti-RPM Bill before Christmas. But the Cabinet proved sticky.

When Heath proposed to abolish RPM with some exceptions, he found opposition from R. A. Butler, Lord Hailsham and Selwyn Lloyd. He was backed by Maudling, Sir Edward Boyle, Erroll and Sir Keith Joseph. His opponents complained that his timing was all wrong. This was the sort of reform for the *beginning* of a Government's term, not when it wanted a united party for the impending elections. Heath pointed out he had to take a position on the two impending Private Members' Bills.

Heath's opponents in the Cabinet did not like the idea that he had already briefed the Sunday papers of 12 January that the reform was going through. Nor did they enjoy the way he 'leaned' on them on Tuesday, 14 January, as if he were still battling the French at Brussels. He finally won his Cabinet battle on Wednesday morning, 15 January, with the crucial support of Sir Alec who wanted this modernizing 'image' but also saw that Heath's dynamism derived from his personal competitiveness. Heath was, as a rural Tory put it, 'threshing his horns among the other bullocks, anxious to be first through the gate'.

Even with Cabinet backing, his compromise Bill was regarded as his personal crusade. 'The trouble is that Ted Heath is trying to steam-roller it through,' complained senior and moderate Tory MPs.[23]

Even before the Bill was published on 16 February, the opposition to Heath's efforts showed itself in two forms. One was the moderate, Establishment view that RPM had to go but that it should be done carefully. This was led by Sir John Vaughan-Morgan, Chairman of the Tories Trade and Industry Committee. The other was a root-and-branch opposition, which defied Heath to keep 'hands off the shopkeeper' as the bulwark of the local Tory associations. The Beaverbrook press, which had not forgiven Heath for leading the EEC entry negotiations, played up the attacks on Heath for their back-street Tory readers. Heath was surprised and shocked by the bitterness of the attack on him. He reacted like a strong man hit in the face for the first time, feeling anger and disbelief mixed with distaste for the *canaille* who were attacking him. As the Second Reading of his Bill on 10 March approached, he threatened to resign if the Cabinet weakened.

The Second Reading was one of Heath's worst hours. Apart from taunts from Douglas Jay, Labour did not oppose the Bill. Instead it watched as the Tories split into three. Heath's own speech was dull and technical. The only stirring speech was the anti-Heath attack of a traditionalist rebel, Sir Frank Markham. Where were the warnings, the consultations, the respect for the traditions of the party? demanded Sir Frank.[24]

The vote was catastrophic. Twenty-one Tory MPs voted against the Bill and another twenty-five or more deliberately abstained. Its scale far outstripped the Suez revolts. Many of the rebels, feeling Heath was 'arrogant' in not submitting, spoke hopefully of forcing him to resign. After the Chief Whip, Martin Redmayne – himself an opponent of the Bill as a former shopkeeper – failed to find a compromise, a 'Steering Committee' was set up to negotiate compromises acceptable to Heath. The Bill still remained in danger. On one amendment, dealing with the position of chemists, the rebels lost by only one vote. Had they carried the day, Heath later admitted, he might have been compelled to think of abandoning the Bill and resigning from the Cabinet.[25]

'My mistake,' admitted Heath, 'was to assume that the basic philosophy of the party, with its emphasis on competitive enterprise, was sufficient to ensure that the great majority of the party would go along with RPM. I wanted to get on with the legislation; time was running out, the election was looming, so I set a fast pace, and did not leave enough time for a thorough discussion within the party . . .'[26]

'In the smoke-filled rooms he was stern and stony. On the Treasury Bench he was cool, unruffled and courteous.'[27] Heath got the credit much later, when the Act worked successfully, for having achieved what nobody before had even dared try.[28]

Heath did not enhance his reputation with his dreary speech on 6

July defending the Government's plan to take limited anti-monopoly powers *after* the next election. 'If your conversion on monopoly is so complete,' asked Douglas Jay, Labour's spokesman, 'why did you deal with the small shopkeeper so promptly and leave the big monopolies until after the general election?'[29]

As the election campaign hotted up Heath turned very coy. He admitted that the July trade figures were bad. But he would not comment on the (under) estimate that there would be a £500m. deficit for the year. 'People should not ask what the Government is going to do...' Private firms got the orders. 'Our job is to create trading conditions to help them.'[30]

CAMPAIGNING TO SURVIVE

There had been predictions Heath would organize the election campaign. But when the election campaign staff was announced in September, he turned out to be one of four. He and Maudling represented the Parliamentary politicians, while Lords Blakenham and Poole represented the party organization. Sir Alec felt that naming Heath as Chief of Staff might arouse resentment. Heath was very conscious of the cold, meritocratic 'image' he projected. He jumped at the chance of using his own professional public relations man in his Bexley campaign. This was a bluff Canadian, Ted McAlister, who had been recommended to Heath by Lord Swinton. Heath was fascinated by the problem of how to get more adequate and favourable publicity than his rivals. On one occasion he kept McAlister on the telephone for ninety minutes while the Canadian analysed for him why the speeches of others were getting better 'play' in that Sunday's newspapers.

As Heath campaigned in the streets of Bexley, also in his entourage was a very blond young man with a famous name: Winston S. Churchill II, the grandson of Sir Winston. Heath had been asked by Lady Churchill to show her 24-year-old grandson the political ropes.

While Maudling handled the national press conferences, Heath was the 'anchor man' on TV for the Tories. The general verdict was that he tried too hard and never reached the right level of direct communication.[31]

Heath was embarrassed by a Butlerian pre-election indiscretion. In a newspaper interview with George Gale, Butler said of the election: 'Very close. We're running neck and neck. I'll be very surprised if there's much in it, say twenty seats either way. But things might start slipping in the last few days.' Slipping away? 'Yes, they won't slip towards us.' Asked about Sir Alec's praise for 'young, dynamic'

Edward Heath, Butler replied: 'That's interesting. I think Alec's a bit bored by him – not as a Minister, of course.'[32]

Heath told a meeting of canvassers in Bexley on 12 October: 'The most up-to-date public opinion poll out today shows that the Conservatives should have a majority of 30 to 50 seats.'[33] When the results began coming in three days later with Labour's tiny slight lead hardening, he took the blow very hard, harder than he took his defeat by a much wider margin as Leader fourteen months later. He sat in the lounge of his agent's flat above the association headquarters in Crook Log, and shook his head, saying 'They can't do it, they just can't do it!'

Not for Heath the tradition of the 'honeymoon' in which a new Government would be given immunity to attack for a month at least. Eight days after the election he was describing the Wilson Government as 'old, fat and immensely disappointing . . .'. 'When Mr Wilson drove to the Palace the one thing foremost in his mind was how to win the next election with a much larger majority,' said Heath the thought-reader.[34]

SIR ALEC REDISPOSES

When Sir Alec organized his forces for the battle against the precarious Wilson Government, he named Reginald Maudling his Deputy Leader.[35] This accorded with feeling among Conservative voters. Most Tories thought Sir Alec should stay on, but if he left thirty-five per cent supported Maudling as his successor, twenty-eight per cent Butler and ten per cent Heath.[36]

Heath himself was named economic spokesman and assigned Butler's old job, as Chairman of the party's Policy Advisory Committee, to recapture the policy momentum, especially in modernization.[37] Heath was supposed to provide the defeated and dispirited Tories with new slogans and new targets. He soon showed a tendency to provide new blueprints.

Heath did not hide his contempt for the new Labour Government's handling of the inherited economic crisis. When he unleashed his attack in the debate on their proposals on 10 November, the tag 'hatchetman' was applied to him by most Parliamentary writers. Thus, he said of Sir Solly Zuckerman, an expert on primates and long a scientific adviser to Tory Governments: 'I think it most appropriate that an expert on tadpoles should be adviser to the present administration.'[38]

On 1 January 1965 he rushed up to Coldstream to see Sir Alec about readying an emergency manifesto. 'I think it is possible there will be an election before Easter.' Pollsters working for the Conservatives indicated that Labour could substantially increase its majority then.[39] 'Mr Wilson is an opportunist and he may take the chance of a quick election if he thinks it will suit him. . . . We have got to be prepared.'[40]

To produce his emergency manifesto Heath deployed his 23 policy groups with speedy efficiency, uniting them in an Advisory Committee on Policy under himself and Sir Edward Boyle. Heath's refusal to confirm that Selwyn Lloyd headed one policy group on immigration and Anthony Barber another on consumers fed the suspicions of his opponents. He justified it, saying that chairmen would be pestered by TV and pressmen, and that civil servants like Sir Timothy Bligh (government structure) or Paul Chambers of ICI could hardly participate if their help was disclosed. This fed the suspicions of anti-Marketeers like Harmar Nicholls, who warned the 1922 Committee of 'Heath cabals'.[41] Lady Douglas-Home also worried about the emergence of a 'shiny, bright new party' in which 'no one will recognize the true Conservatives . . .'[42] The worry of traditionalists that Heath would commit them to EEC entry was strengthened by the publication 'One Nation' urging a Minister for European Affairs in the next Tory Cabinet. This 'One Nation' pamphlet was signed by Heath and others and written mainly by Nicholas Ridley and Enoch Powell.

While Lady Douglas-Home nurtured deep suspicions, Heath continued to impress Sir Alec mightily. Unlike the other Tory ex-Ministers, Heath had hardly shown the loss of his civil servants. He continued to act as a fighting professional, instead of an amateur dilettante. Unlike Maudling he was more willing to forgo a good meal or a good wine to attend a meeting on taxation policy.

Sir Alec either ignored or was ignorant of Heath's covert support of the 'Alec Must Go!' campaign started in January 1965 by PEST (Pressure for Economic and Social Toryism). Its 22-year-old Chairman said Sir Alec 'should go and must go'. In public Heath defended Sir Alec as a modernizer who had supported his anti-RPM measures 'right up to the hilt'.[43] But Heath made a quiet donation to PEST after its splash provoked the *Sunday Times* into a survey which showed that an election for the leadership would 'yield more than 100 votes each for Mr Maudling and Mr Heath and some 25 for Mr Macleod . . .'.[44]

Sir Alec made clear which horse he was backing in that two-horse race by redisposing his forces in February 1965, with Heath as spokesman on the economic front and Maudling covering international affairs. Since foreign affairs were his own field, this gave Maudling a chance to put in more time in the City, where he was Executive Director of Kleinwort, Benson the merchant bankers, among other things. In

October 1964 Heath had become a Director of Brown, Shipley, also merchant bankers; but he spent little time there.

There was no indication that Sir Alec had any intention of stepping down soon. Ladbrokes were giving odds of 8 to 1 against Heath being the Tory Leader at the next general election.[45] But Sir Alec's new dispositions gave Heath a chance to show his new attacking style during the Budget period when he was sure to have prolonged periods in the spotlight. Moreover he had a chance to do this when the business community was becoming more anti-Labour and pro-Tory as a result of new Labour taxation schemes. Heath was able easily to adapt himself to this rightward swing of the current of Tory opinion, which found Maudling immovable. Some of Heath's long-time colleagues were surprised to find how strongly he believed in the curative ability of liberated capitalism. He believed that dreary old declining industries would be replaced by shiny new competitive industries.

Heath did not limit his attacking style to the Budget and its Finance Bill. When Roy Jenkins, now Minister of Aviation, wiped out the BOAC operating deficit of £80m., Heath hit out, 'You made a petulant and arrogant speech which is becoming all too characteristic of you. . . .'[46]

It was not only in language and in economics that Heath swung to the right. On 2 March Heath and the rest of the Shadow Cabinet marched into the division lobby behind Sir Cyril Osborne, whose fiercely anti-immigrant motion had been toned down by Peter Thorneycroft.[47] Heath could not quite bring himself to vote against Sydney Silverman's Murder (Abolition of Death Penalty) Bill. Maudling voted to retain hanging, Macleod voted against hanging. Heath stayed away.[48]

Heath recognized the opportunity that James Callaghan's mammoth reforming Budget would provide. He selected a team – Peter Walker, Anthony Barber, William Clark, Peter Emery, and John Hall – all of whom had made their own way in business and were not products of famous public schools. It was the job of this 'task force' to make a 'professional' assault on the Callaghan Budget. They met at noon every day to co-ordinate their operation, based on information and advice from trade and industrial organizations. They virtually silenced the amateurish company directors on the back-benches. 'We never really permitted our sillies a look-in,' claimed one of Heath's team.

Heath could laugh uproariously when he was working. His lieutenants came to feel quite close to him. But he would not let them get too close. One lieutenant dared suggest he should change his shirt after a steamy TV exchange and was for some time in bad odour himself.

What Heath demonstrated to Tory back-benchers was an end to bipartisanship, both in word and style. In words he made a bare-knuckle attack on the Budget on 6 April. 'The Budget soaks the rich. It also soaks the poor . . . it is nasty, brutish and long.' 'There is nothing in it to produce efficiency and more exports . . .' Maudling cheered him and Hogg drew blood poking himself in the face.[49]

More revealing, he aroused the fears of Wilson and Callaghan that they might not get their mammoth Budget through. As advocates of bipartisan government, Maudling and Callaghan had been accustomed to let one another know just how many days of debate they would go through before letting the Government have its Finance Bill. But Heath, never conceded 'defeat' until the next to the last day on Report Stage.[50]

Heath was now battling against a new backdrop. Ten days after naming him chief economic spokesman in February, Sir Alec Douglas-Home unexpectedly embraced the democratic process for the next Leader which had been proposed months before by Humphrey Berkeley, then a maverick Tory. There was no great pressure for it. But Sir Alec had been hurt by the accusations that he had emerged in October 1963 from the 'traditional consultations' as the product of a shady 'fix'.

Maudling knew that there was a battle on, but handled it in his own relaxed way. At the end of March he made a speech in Barnet designed to appeal to Tory traditionalists: 'We are a party of the Right'. On 1 April he made a speech on foreign affairs, proving a match for Wilson in his usual chummy way.[51]

Heath's bare-knuckle blows made it look as if Maudling had been hugging the Labour punching bag. On 29 April Heath made a slashing attack on Labour's housing policies, climaxed by throwing torn-up bits of paper to the chant of 'paper promises', 'paper promises'. He was personally abusive to Callaghan, suggesting he had forgotten what he had learned 'under tutorials from Nuffield'. Callaghan retorted that Heath was also a visiting Fellow of Nuffield; 'he shares their hospitality with me and I hope that he will not sneer at them'. Two days later the Chancellor said resignedly: 'the sooner we get this leadership battle over, the better it will be for all of us'.[52]

One of Heath's best-publicized coups was a repeat of the guerilla raids used by the Tories early in 1951 and by George Wigg in 1953. On the night of 6–7 July, Heath and Whitelaw laid their trap. At the end of an 11.30 division, Tory Whips told their charges that they could go home if they could find a pair. Then a group of Heath's partisans went to their normal pairs and said, 'Well, there won't be any more divisions tonight, so I'm pushing off . . .' They then went to their cars and drove off into the night, taking care not to *write* an official 'pair', which would have prevented their voting again that night. One of the houses in which they waited was that of party chairman Edward du-Cann in Lord North Street. During the next hour or more the Opposition did not press its amendments to a vote. Then, after the old *franc tireur*, George Wigg, had checked up that Tories were not lurking in out-of-the-way corners, some fifteen Labour MPs were allowed to leave, including George Wigg. It was at 1 a.m. that Heath's partisans came back and carried, against the Government, an amendment which gave unit trusts the same rate of capital gains tax as individuals. While Heath and his friends patted themselves on their backs, the Government accepted its setback.

'After 211 hours of debate in twenty-one and a half days, the longest and most complex Finance Bill of modern times has passed through the Commons,' Heath recorded. In all, 1,222 amendments were placed on the Order Paper, 440 by the Chancellor of the Exchequer himself and 680 by the Conservative Opposition. 'There were 108 divisions, in three of which the Government was defeated and on one of which it tied. (This was the first Government defeat on a Finance Bill since 1924.) Observers agree that it was the most intensely argued Finance Bill in living memory. . . .'[53]

THE DROP-ALEC CAMPAIGN

The importance of Heath's combat record increased as the 'Drop Alec' campaign again got under way. A new dimension was given the campaign by the victory of the Liberal, David Steel, at Roxburgh, considered Sir Alec's own corner of Scotland. Sir Alec was also hurt by the clumsiness of his 'defenders'. Sir Gerald Nabarro asked his colleagues not to 'shoot the pianist, he is doing his best'; he warned that a leadership crisis would 'give hostages to Wilson, precipitate a snap election and lead to another Labour Victory by a larger majority'.

Heath's combat team became anxious to see him in command of the whole Tory attack on Labour. He knew of this and did not stop them. But there was no indication that he encouraged them, at least not directly. Veteran Tories did note that Heath was cultivating the 1964 intake, stopping for a quip and a pat on the back. Commented one MP: 'The difference between them is that Reggie smiles when he's happy and Ted smiles when he is being watched.'[54]

The Heath campaign went 'over the top' because of a splash in a hostile paper. On 27 June, the day after Sir Alec announced in Glasgow there would be no Tory Leader selection that year, the *Sunday Express* headline read: 'BID TO OUST SIR ALEC BY 100 MPs'. Keith Renshaw told of 'intensive lobbying' by Heath's supporters, who had found one hundred Tory MPs willing to support a bid to oust Sir Alec immediately and replace him by Heath. This was not taken seriously by other newspapers. Sir Alec accepted Heath's word that he had not encouraged anyone to campaign to jettison Sir Alec. 'I acquit him absolutely,' said Sir Alec. At a private lunch they both attended Sir Alec pointed to an empty chair beside that of Heath, 'For one of your hundred men, I suppose?'

A week later, on 5 July, Sir Alec's future was suddenly raised at a routine meeting of the executive of the 1922 Committee. Widespread feeling was voiced that Sir Alec's early replacement would improve the party's chances. This view came not only from Heath supporters but also from at least one Maudling backer (Neil Marten). The Chairman, Sir William Anstruther-Gray, agreed to see Sir Alec. He came back and said Sir Alec was staying on. Then a misleading press 'leak' suggested that a move to oust Sir Alec had only been narrowly averted. For Sir Alec the idea of standing in the way of a more effective and popular leader was increasingly a torture.[55]

One of the overlooked boosts which helped precipitate change was an anti-Alec piece in *The Economist* edition of 10 July. This suggested that the Tory squirearchy were reluctant to hand over the leadership to someone 'from lower down in the middle class than the people who run the Tory party quite like. . . . Neither of them went to the right school. Neither of them to this day carries the faintest whiff of gentry . . .'[56] *The Economist* admitted that Heath was the 'riskier choice'. 'Mr Heath's predicament is not just a personal one; it is much more the classic situation of the abrasive man of change in what are still British political parties predominantly staffed by men of no change. . . . But if the choice had to be made between the two men now, it would have to be for Mr Heath. To those who believe that Britain's place is inside Europe, and to those who believe that the greatest single need . . . is the encouragement of competition, Mr Heath has the better record. . . . What he has shown is that he has nerve and will: once pointed in the right direction the cannon will batter down the walls. . . .'

The Heath forces were thought to be hurt by Sir Alec's sudden decision to go, disclosed on Thursday, 22 July, at 6 p.m. Nobody, he, insisted, had 'suggested to me that I should go but there are those, who, perfectly properly, felt that a change of leadership might be for the best'. He was too proud a man to stay where he was not unanimously wanted.[57]

That evening, Reginald Maudling met his main backers at the Barton Street house of William Clark, MP. He decided to fight a completely gentlemanly fight, taking advantage of the indignation that would attach to the Heath forces for having forced Sir Alec out of office. He told his lieutenants on no account to pester MPs or offer deals, pacts or promises of patronage to come. As a sign of his self-confidence, he put his campaign in the hands of a diffident aristocrat, Lord Lambton. The Maudling campaign took on the lethargic appearance of its candidate.[58]

At his flat in the Albany, Heath put his campaign in the hands of a tough and efficient general staff led by Peter Walker, Peter Emery and Anthony Kershaw. They canvassed systematically, with City backing. 'He has the support of the younger, forward-looking bankers, brokers and investment experts,' reported David Malbert, City Editor of the *Evening News*.[59] 'Heath understood the Finance Bill much sooner than many in the City. He directed the Opposition in the Commons that secured so many useful concessions.' Maudling had been the reckless Chancellor, who had kept the economy going full-out until the October 1964 election, despite the mounting deficit.[60]

The bulk of the Conservative Press came out for Heath: *The Times* (which had supported him for Leader as early as 1963), the *Daily Mail* and *Evening News*, *Sunday Times* and *The Economist*. 'What Conservative MPs have to choose . . . is a national leader, not a future hostess for No. 10 Downing Street,' wrote *The Times*. 'It is sometimes said Mr Heath is too ruthless and too much of a juggernaut to run an Administration comfortably. The same criticism was made of him when he pushed through the abolition of resale price maintenance before the election. Today the benefits of his drive are being felt by the public as a whole.'[61]

Maudling was more popular among the voters outside, both the general public and Conservative voters. It was only among Liberals – because of his pro-EEC and anti-RPM stances – that Heath was in the van.[62]

When nomination day was over on 26 July, there were only three candidates, Heath, Maudling and Enoch Powell. Iain Macleod, assured he would get no more than 20 or so votes, declined to stand (but voted for Heath). At the last moment Peter Thorneycroft decided against standing. The next day the National Opinion Poll in the *Daily Mail* showed twenty-eight per cent of those polled for Heath, forty-four per cent for Maudling and three per cent for Powell. Their campaign managers gave both Heath (152 'solid') and Maudling (159) a majority of the potential vote of 305.

Next day, between 11.30 and 1.30, 298 Tory MPs went into the Grand Committee Room where, under the watchful eye of the 1922 Committee

Chairman, Sir William Anstruther-Gray, they cast their ballots. It was a secret ballot but Sir Alec allowed one of Heath's lieutenants to see that he was voting for Heath (although his wife did not approve).

Just before 2.15 p.m. the figures were announced to the members of the 1922 Committee: Heath (150), Maudling (133) and Powell (15). Heath had secured an overall majority by two, and 50.3 per cent of the poll. But he had not achieved the lead of 45 required under the new rules to dispense with a second ballot. Maudling decided not to ask for the second ballot. He telephoned Heath to congratulate him, and assured him of his support. 'We have elected a rough rider,' said one senior Tory, 'and it is time to fasten our seat-belts.'[63]

I'm not thinking in terms of beating Mr Wilson. Surely this is
what is wrong with British politics at the moment, and in the
comments on it. It is seen entirely in terms of personalities
trying to beat each other.
                                    Edward Heath, Tyne-Tees TV, July 1966

Edward Heath, only a few days old as the new Conservative Leader,
came out for his first sparring match with Prime Minister Harold
Wilson, on 2 August 1965. Not even his best friends thought it was
a brilliant speech for a censure debate. He surveyed the postwar
contribution of Conservative Governments to the economy. Then he
turned on the Prime Minister and, with his sharp index finger pointing,
hurled: 'It is my regret that you have never been prepared to recognize
these achievements. No matter what jibes you may hurl, nothing can
detract from the achievements of the British people in the past fifteen
years.'
    When Wilson wound up, he poked fun at Heath's one feeble joke –
that Labour had 'a tortoise in its tank'. 'I must say I liked that. I
liked it the first time I read it in a *Sunday Citizen* cartoon on 27 June.'
He then went on to claim that his prices and incomes policy was something that the Tories had been afraid to tackle when in office: 'Let
not the House think that all we need is the cheap sneers at the problems
we face in introducing it.' Talking straight at Heath, Wilson said:
'He and his colleagues knew the facts last October. They knew what
to do.' An infuriated Heath sprang to his feet and, pointing at Wilson,
said: 'That is absolutely typical of everything which has characterized
you. . . .' The last two minutes was drowned out as a flushed Heath
faced an equally angry Prime Minister across the Dispatch Box.
When the closure was moved, Wilson picked up a bundle of papers and
flung them in the direction of the Conservative Front Bench. This
confrontation began something more like a Sicilian vendetta than the
normal Parliamentary pillow fights. Heath and Wilson clearly detested
each other so much that it was the courtesies that rang false rather than
the vituperation.
    It was not easy to disentangle why these Oxford contemporaries,
products of modest homes and grammar schools, should so utterly
provoke each other. It was partly a contrast of identification. Wilson,

lower middle-class by origin, identified himself with the working class in his Northern nonconformist way. Heath, working class by origin, identified himself with the middle class. For Wilson, Heath was a 'climber', a 'rich man's lapdog'. For Heath, Wilson was a leveller-down, a tricky opportunist, who would sacrifice the national interest for cheap party advantage.

On 4 August Heath fielded his new Front Bench team. He kept Maudling as his Deputy Leader. Sir Alec became his foreign affairs spokesman and Edward duCann remained as party chairman. Iain Macleod took over as economic spokesman, with Anthony Barber replacing him on steel. Sir Edward Boyle remained in charge of education, Sir Keith Joseph was put in charge of the social service. Heath defended himself against charges that he had been predictable. 'Having had three years of differences within the party – Harold Macmillan's final year, then two under Alec Home – I wanted to continue the unity established at the time I was elected leader.'[1] There was one ingenious appointment: Enoch Powell as defence spokesman. When Heath and Powell discussed the appointment, Heath offered to set up the normal arrangement whereby the Opposition spokesman on defence is briefed on confidential information to know which sensitive areas to avoid. Powell declined the offer, not to have his hands tied. Powell came away from the meeting happy thinking both of them were 'Europeans' and Heath was not in thrall to the United States; they were, Powell thought, agreed in wanting to extricate Britain from its imperial commitments.

UNUSUAL VACATION

Although Heath took off with his father and stepmother to join his friends, the Seligmans, at Villefranche, it was not wholly a vacation. Every morning at eight he received a telephone call from his new assistant, John McGregor. At midday another call came through from the press department of Central Office, telling him what Wilson was doing. For political discussion he had Edward duCann and Iain Macleod nearby.[2]

On 14 August, Heath drove down to Nice Airport to greet David Howell, CPC Director, who had come down with the draft policy documents. On the same plane was Sir Eric Roll, one of Heath's chief aides in the Brussels negotiations, but now serving George Brown in the DEA. Sir Eric seemed slightly embarrassed to walk through the barrier almost into the arms of Heath. Muttering politely, Sir Eric went off to the sumptuous villa of Harold Lever, millionaire Labour MP.[3]

These things were observed because the new Leader was the centre of an enormous publicity operation trying to make him better known to the great British public. A TV company came down to film Heath on vacation. Heath was filmed in a dinghy off the French coast. One bit had to be cut, however: at that stage he still had difficulty bringing the dinghy about. Heath did not tell TV men *why* he had taken up sailing. 'It was upon my doctor's advice that I first took up sailing,' he explained later, 'a decision which reduced my demand on pharmaceuticals.'[4]

As soon as he returned to the fray, Heath showed he was moving to the right. He had changed his mind on strikes, he admitted. As Minister of Labour he had thought them less disrupting than industrial illness and accidents, but 'strikes disrupt production through a whole firm and through a whole industry, whereas sickness is allowed for in working arrangements and does not disrupt in the same way'. He had also hardened against Labour's credit squeeze and other efforts to save sterling. 'This is the biggest "stop" since the war,' he complained en route to a Tory policy conference at Lord Swinton's home. 'All the forecasts are it will be a long time before they can get the "go" again.'[5]

He attacked George Brown's five-year National Plan as a 'Brown paper' plastered over the holes blown in the economy by Callaghan's budgets. Wilson was living in a 'private dream world' in which his Cabinet had saved the pound. Instead it had really been saved 'by the brilliant planning of the Bank of England and by the international bankers . . . who were contemptuously described by the Deputy Prime Minister as "the Gnomes of Zurich".'[6] This claim startled *The Economist*, Heath's most influential supporter: 'most independent commentators would judge that the Bank did make some mistakes in its handling of exchange control last year, that two of the Governor's public speeches have been singularly ill-timed, that the long and rather neurotic war between the City and Labour was managed on the City side with less than consummate efficiency, that there have been some criticisms to be made even of the Bank's operations in exchange markets. For a Conservative leader to give blanket approval to the Bank's "brilliant" record is as unwise as it would be for a Labour leader to give blanket approval to the "brilliant" record of the trade unions.'[7]

The Economist was also worried about the speed with which Heath was privately moving away from an incomes policy: 'some foreign visitors have apparently had the impression, after private conversations with Mr Heath, that he thinks incomes policy is all tosh, that he is a Rightwing advocate of "keeping a curb on the money supply and then everything will be solved", that he is almost an old-fashioned [economic] Powellite in this respect'.[8] He was also increasingly hostile towards militant unions and their leaders. He paid lip-service to unions as 'one of the major estates of the realm' but was sharply critical when they behaved as though they were. He stigmatized Frank Cousins, the transport workers' leader on leave as a Cabinet Minister, as 'the silent enemy within the gates' of the Cabinet. 'A man can be loyal to his Cabinet colleagues. He can be loyal to his union comrades. But he cannot be loyal to both when they are opposite sides of an industrial and political conflict. To Mr Cousins I say: if you are a man of principle . . . resign from the Government or resign from the union.'[9] Heath had just resigned as a Director of Brown, Shipley, merchant bankers.

Where Heath was fearful of moving at all was over Rhodesia, then coming up to the UDI boil. He was pulled between the pro-Smith Monday Club lobby on the right, led by Lord Salisbury, and the anti-Smith, anti-racialist Tories on the left, including friends like Sir Edward Boyle. He was immobilized in the middle ground by Sir Alec's 'five principles'. If he moved at all he risked tearing the party apart, Suez-style, and making himself vulnerable to a snap election by Wilson.

Heath saw Ian Smith, the Rhodesian leader, after the Shadow Cabinet had decided in favour of further Anglo-Rhodesian discussions. Then, on 10 October, Heath and Sir Alec were called into a private discussion with Wilson and Arthur Bottomley, the Secretary of State for Commonwealth Relations. Heath and Sir Alec were anxious to keep the talks going, partly to avoid splitting the Tories. But Wilson was adamant that there should be no retreat on any of the five principles. Not only Heath was suspicious that Wilson was as interested in splitting the Tory Shadow Cabinet as he was in splitting Smith's Cabinet.[10]

Heath was wounded by a shift in public opinion. He had taken over a party revelling in a seven per cent lead in the Gallup Poll. Yet 100 days later – after unprecedented publicity about him – the position had been reversed. 'It is the normal trend of the holiday season, when the Opposition can't keep the Government under scrutiny in Parliament,' he explained. 'Mr Wilson has been constantly in the headlines over Rhodesia. During September the Government pegged bread prices and mortgage rates. It appeared to be tough with the unions, and got a 1,000m. dollar standby loan – all of which pleased people without their realizing the full implications.'[11] The public was also having difficulty in identifying with the new-type Tory Leader, with his curious speech and preference for piano-playing instead of grouse-shooting!

Because he was so 'buttoned up', he could not be sold as a warm man. Despite seaside pictures with his father and stepmother, he was hardly a 'family man'. So he could only be merchandised as a 'man of principle'.

OVERHANGING ELECTION

The timing of the election was in the hands of the Prime Minister. He had no doubt that Wilson would encourage and exploit Tory disunity. He felt at a disadvantage because he had so little time in which to impress himself on both the party and public consciousness.

Heath tried to kick off by launching his new policy statement 'Putting Britain Right Ahead', the collation of the work of the 23 policy groups he had been supervising. After the press conference his prepared opening statement was flat and boring. But his replies to questions showed a degree of preparation unprecedented in a Tory Leader. How would the Tories help mortgage payers? 'We have been looking at the Merrett-Sykes proposals and also the Australian system.' Even *The Economist* was impressed. 'This is a vast difference from the Douglas-Home style of leadership. This was a push-button computer bidding for office at Number Ten.'[12]

Still combating the overhanging threat of an election, Heath decided to exploit the Conservative conference in a new way. Previously, Tory leaders had only descended at the end of the conference to give the final speech. Instead he decided to sit through the whole conference – as Labour leaders did. This would enormously increase his TV 'exposure'.

When Conservative delegates arrived at the Brighton Sports Stadium for their conference on 13 October they saw a slogan, 'RIGHT AHEAD WITH HEATH', the first time they had put their Leader's name into a conference slogan. This compensated a bit for the fact that the Prime Minister had gone that same day to Balmoral, thus stealing the headlines with speculations about an election. The delegates soon made it clear that they would enjoy going into battle behind Heath. In winding up a debate, he explained his credo: 'Our task is to change the mood of the country – to make it exciting as a country in which to live and in which people can achieve their ambitions. . . . Let us encourage the pacemakers by all means, for they are the people with particular skills, greater imagination, foresight, inventiveness, administrative ability who can give a lead. Let us recognize the part they can play.'[13]

Heath was reluctant to be the pacemaker on the Rhodesian crisis, knowing the fragility of Tory unity. Lord Salisbury tried to move a resolution opposing sanctions against an independent Rhodesia. This

o

was ruled out of order. Instead, Heath hid behind Selwyn Lloyd and Sir Alec who helped the conference steer a safe middle course.

Enoch Powell almost piled the conference up on the anti-imperial rocks. Since he was then himself as 'European' as Heath, Powell thought he was entitled to put an anti-imperial defence policy. He insisted that Britain's own defence, and after that the defence of Western Europe, had an 'overriding claim' on Britain's resources. Powell, well-applauded by a largely uncomprehending audience, was shocked when he was privately disavowed by Heath, who had proclaimed only a few days before, 'The immediate threats to peace are now in the East. . . .'[14]

This temporary embarrassment was erased by the thunderous applause Heath evoked with his closing speech on Saturday, 16 October. Part of the applause came from fairly easy Wilson-baiting: 'I will give you the name of the man who in the past year has done far more than any other to sell sterling short. It is Mr Harold Wilson himself, by his politically motivated exaggeration of the £800m. deficit. . . .' At the end he gloried in a four-minute ovation which he climaxed by grabbing the chairman's bell and ringing it as Quintin Hogg had, years before.[15] It was one of the first of his big speeches where he really got going, departing from the prepared speech. 'I responded to the audience, rather than stick to the text I had prepared,' he said. 'It developed as I went along.'[16]

Heath was on trial from the resumption of Parliament on 16 October, the day on which the Smith regime in Rhodesia proclaimed its independence. He was careful to avoid supporting Wilson's counter-measures so wholeheartedly that he would provoke the Tory Right. He asked for a publication of the records of the conversations between the Prime Minister and Ian Smith in Salisbury. He urged that Smith's proposals be put to the people of Rhodesia to see whether they had their approval. After a Royal Commission had ascertained that, then Parliament could decide whether to give Rhodesia its independence under Smith.[17]

The vendetta quality of Heath–Wilson relations was so firmly established from the outset that Heath was incapable of handling gracefully Wilson's report on his sudden dash to Salisbury to attempt negotiations with Ian Smith. He found it impossible to *seem* generous and to congratulate Wilson for following the policies for Rhodesia laid down by R. A. Butler and Sir Alec. It was a small incident, but revealing.

Heath went far to re–establish himself as the Tories' best Wilson-baiter in his 9 November onslaught on the legislative programme in the Queen's Speech. This he dismissed as an 'electioneering pamphlet'. He sneered at Wilson's omission of steel renationalization. He ridiculed

George Brown, 'rushing up and down the country rather like a Prince Monolulu shouting "I have got an incomes policy"'. He sneered at the whole Labour Cabinet, 'There they sit where they have for a year, overweight and over-numerous,' grossly overpaid on the basis of payment by results. It was the sort of speech which enraptured his supporters.[18]

ABANDONED BY COLLEAGUES

While the spotlight of public attention was on these Heath–Wilson salvoes, Heath was much more troubled by the evidences of his isolation within the Tory Front Bench. His victory, the ensuing publicity and abrasive command style soured a number of his contemporaries. The result was a distinct dropping off of the activities of his colleagues as if they were saying, 'Well, Ted's the Leader, let him get on with it!' Maudling's diagnosis was that Heath would soon burn himself out and wear everyone else out.[19]

It hardly helped that Heath's most active lieutenant was Enoch Powell. Powell not only differed from Heath on Britain's defence role in Southeast Asia and the Middle East, but ranged far and wide into different fields. He compared Heath's programme for industrial peace through legally enforceable agreements with 'the corporate state of Fascist Italy'![20]

This internal Tory tension was not immediately 'leaked' to the press. But it had a depressing effect on Heath. He came to lean increasingly on his avuncular Chief Whip, William Whitelaw. Whitelaw was a completely complimentary contrast to Heath. An extrovert Scottish squire in manner, he had inherited wealth and the background of Winchester, Trinity College, Cambridge, and the Scots Guards. He was one of those Establishment Tories who recognized Heath's strengths and the need to put up with his weaknesses. A wartime friend of Whitelaw tells of arriving to pick him up for their annual night on the town, during which they ate well, drank their copious fill and reminisced of shared experiences in the Italian campaign. Whitelaw came out to meet him in the Central Lobby and asked apologetically, 'Would you mind terribly if I brought a friend? I know that we enjoy doing this on our own together. But just this once. . . . He's very depressed and he has no other friends he can turn to. . . .' Reluctantly, Whitelaw's friend agreed. The Chief Whip went away and came back with Heath.

Heath was depressed over Rhodesia. He felt no emotional involvement, neither the 'kith and kin' feeling of the traditional imperial right or the identification with African rights of the internationalist left.

He thought much of the furore an irrelevance since Britain would eventually have to live with the tiresome white settlers of Rhodesia. His main fear was that a split would make Tories more vulnerable to Labour victory at a snap election which might put off the time when a Heath regime could modernize Britain and bring it into the EEC. On 11 November he twice appealed for party unity at the 1922 Committee. The whole of the white Commonwealth were opposed to the Smith regime, and would be 'mortally offended' if the Tories split on this issue.[21]

Heath made clear his own priorities when he flew to Paris on 22 November 1965 to see President de Gaulle for an hour's talk on his 75th birthday. He told de Gaulle that a Tory Government would apply to join the EEC, accepting the Treaty of Rome and the Community's agricultural policies.

Heath returned to a new stage on Rhodesia as the Government moved towards sanctions and investigated the possibility of an oil embargo. When, with UN encouragement, the Government decided on oil sanctions, it had a much more immediate impact in splitting Heath's than Smith's supporters. To try to hold the Tories together, Heath and the Shadow Cabinet urged abstention. But – to Heath's mortification – the imperial right, led by Julian Amery, chalked up 50 MPs voting *against* oil sanctions. And the liberal-internationalist left lined up 31 in favour of oil sanctions. Only a former Chief Whip could realize what a defeat this represented.

The Prime Minister's sudden decision to impose tighter sanctions, base an RAF contingent in neighbouring Zambia and consider sending a battalion of British troops to Zambia intensified Heath's discomfiture. Convinced Wilson was only trying to *look* tough, Heath feared the Africans might exploit those measures to precipitate a military clash between British troops and those of Rhodesia. When Heath tried to question Wilson on his actions in the House on 2 December Wilson exploded: 'All the time you are trying to find some point to raise . . . and you have been ever since you came under attack from Lord Salisbury at Brighton. You had better decide, do you support the policy of the Government? If not, put down a motion of censure – provided you are willing to abide by the consequences.'[22] 'I must say plainly to Mr Wilson,' Heath said next night on TV, 'that he must not allow himself to be dragged into using force in Rhodesia because of some incident . . . engineered by those who only wish to create havoc.' Force against Rhodesia would not solve the problem.[23]

Tension over Rhodesia mounted further. Heath feared that Wilson was committing his prestige to toppling Smith much as Eden had committed his to toppling Nasser. He and his colleagues heard that the aircraft carrier *Eagle* was off Mozambique. They feared that the oil embargo, which they accepted, was being converted into an oil blockade, which they considered a step towards military force. Heath put down a motion rejecting 'the use of blockade or of force in any other form in an attempt to obtain a settlement of the present dispute'. On 21 December Heath voiced his fears of war over Rhodesia.

Wilson taunted Heath from a position of strength. The previous day's *Daily Express* opinion poll had given the Labour Government the support of fifty per cent of the public, with only thirty-six per cent for the Tories, and six per cent for the Liberals.[24] Wilson had succeeded in arrogating to himself the traditional Tory role of 'standing up for Britain's rights' on the rim of Empire!

WELL-COVERED VACATION

Heath had a curious 15-day vacation starting on 29 December 1965, spent largely in a charter aeroplane travelling from Britain to Pakistan to India to Malaysia to Singapore to Borneo to Vietnam and back. It was not surprising that he should have wanted to see those countries. What was curious was the chartering of a large enough plane to take half a dozen journalists along. Taking the journalists was described as a way of splitting the costs. But had Heath wanted only to brief himself, it would have been cheaper to go by scheduled airline, with an aide or two. This trip was seen as a way of stealing back some of the Rhodesian limelight from the Prime Minister while Parliament was in recess. Heath took two Tory MPs (Christopher Chataway and Anthony Barber), the head of his private office, John McGregor, a PR man and two pretty girl secretaries. The recapture of attention and popularity was very much needed. Wilson and Labour were well in the lead and the odds on a March election were hardening.

The process of deflation started in Istanbul where even the military governor was unwilling to meet Heath after an anti-British demonstration over Cyprus.[25] In Pakistan's capital Heath was luckier with General Ayub Khan – because of Wilson's anti-Indian statement during the Indo-Pakistan clash. Heath did not lack naïve bravery: 'The main purpose of my visits to Rawalpindi and Delhi has been to help ease the way to a better understanding at Tashkent.'[26]

Heath began to show signs of nervous strain – jiggling his foot in conversation – as it became clear that he was being taken less seriously and getting less press coverage than he had hoped. In Kuala Lumpur he was initially boycotted by the 'mediating' Prime Minister, a pro-British conservative. He was more relaxed in Borneo in the field with British officers and men scouring the jungles for Indonesian 'infiltrators'; but even there he was more an inspecting officer than a glad-handing politician seeking information. He was worried about the situation in Vietnam, but largely accepted American optimism about the forthcoming build-up.[27]

Those who talked with him after his return found the trip had strengthened his convictions rather than deepened his understanding. He was all the more determined that British forces should be retained in Southeast Asia and the Persian Gulf and the Americans in Vietnam – curious postures for a man considered 'European' rather than imperial. It resulted in a number of bitter arguments at off-the-record lunches at the *Sunday Times* and *The Economist*.

COLD DOUCHE RETURN

Heath returned to the chill of a double-headed attack on him by one of his own spokesmen. Angus Maude had already criticized Heath for going for change-for-the-sake-of-change in a *Sunday Telegraph* article on 14 November. Maude believed that Conservatives had governed for three-quarters of the period after World War I because they had been 'the party of gradualness' of 'resistance to radical change'. He thought the conversion of the Tories to Heathian 'radicalism' spelled disaster. Because nobody but rival editors had paid attention to these views, Maude agreed to write again along substantially the same lines for *Spectator* and *Encounter*. He started his 16 January *Spectator* piece with a blockbuster: 'It is obvious that the Conservative Party has completely lost effective political initiative. Its own supporters in the country are divided and deeply worried by this failure. . . . How far the decline is due to misfortune and how far to ineptitude is debatable. . . .'

Heath went over to the counter-offensive. 'The job of all members of our party, including Mr Maude and any who think like him, is to get out to stomp the country. They should stop attacking their own party and attack the Government.'[28] Heath's defensiveness was apparent on the Robin Day interview on 17 January. 'Have you sacked him?' asked Day. Heath insisted stiffly that this was 'a matter for me to discuss with Mr Maude and not for discussion on television'.[29] Since he parted company with Maude next day, it would have been simpler to smile and say, 'Not yet. . . .'

Heath also refused to be drawn on rumours that he was about to drop the party chairman, Edward duCann, who had served under him at the Board of Trade. Although duCann was an extremely efficient party chairman and had the loyalty of the organization, stories about their differences had started circulating weeks before. These had an essential core of truth. DuCann appointed by Sir Alec was not only more traditional and rightwing, but he thought that the party as a whole came first, with the Parliamentary party being a subordinate part of it. Heath in contrast, thought the Parliamentary party and its Leader should dominate the party in the country. DuCann represented a significant challenge to Heath while he was in Opposition. Previous Leaders had been able to dominate the party machine largely because they had been Prime Ministers first. His position was so weak that he did not dare sack duCann at that stage. Not when an election was expected at any time.

RHODESIAN SUSPICIONS

Heath remained touchy about Wilson's efforts to crucify him further on the Rhodesian issue. When the Prime Minister invited Heath and the Liberal Leader, Jo Grimond, to meet the Chief Justice of Rhodesia, Sir Hugh Beadle, Heath initially reacted with suspicion because Wilson had blocked an earlier contact with Sir Hugh Beadle. Heath, together with Selwyn Lloyd and Duncan Sandys, then saw Sir Hugh for three hours in Heath's Albany flat. Sir Hugh helped convince them that there was no better choice than to negotiate with Ian Smith. Next Tuesday in the House Heath warned against demanding 'unconditional surrender' of the white Rhodesians. [30]

Heath again lost his temper with Wilson in the House on 31 January. During the small hours Wilson had tightened Britain's measures against the Rhodesian regime: stopping all trade and warning that Britain would pay no Rhodesian bills. Heath attacked this as 'a complete failure of psychological understanding', concluding that 'so long as the Prime Minister is there, there can be no honourable settlement in Rhodesia'. Wilson retaliated by recalling the Tories' three-way split and jabbing that if Heath was doing nothing more than playing to his right wing he should put down a censure motion. 'If the Prime Minister was in earnest – in his desire to see a national policy,' Heath gritted out, 'he would refrain from this continued abuse.' [31]

Heath hoped for a 'middle way' with Rhodesians returning to a modified form of the 1961 constitution, with guarantees against either white or black domination. [32] He dispatched Selwyn Lloyd on a fact-finding mission to Rhodesia. Lloyd came back saying that links could be restored through talks with no prior conditions – presumably no 'five principles'. [33]

THE CALL FOR HOPELESS BATTLE

One of Heath's pluckiest performances was when he demanded on 8 February 1966 that the Prime Minister put his government to the electoral test as soon as possible. The Labour capture of Hull North the week before had shown a swing away from the Tories of four per cent. The opinion polls showed Labour a dozen points ahead. Heath was asking to be slaughtered.

When Wilson agreed to his request in March, Heath went to war initially with all the wooden gallantry of the C.O. of the 600 charging into the enemy guns. His leadership style was solitary, hardly consulting Maudling or Macleod. From the beginning he let fly with his radical reforming policies. On 5 March at Southampton he said: 'We want to clear away the debris of half a century,' and proposed the new Industrial Relations Act he was to carry through five years later.[34] He demanded immediate talks with the Smith regime in Rhodesia. While the attacks were slashing and the proposals radical, the gestures were wooden and the style hesitant. Pressmen were initially bored by Heath.

In public he exuded confidence. In private he was pessimistic. Sometimes his real expectations broke through. 'No doubt it will be only another month now before we read of Mr Wilson having tea at No. 10 Downing Street with a pregnant panda,' he said in a Freudian slip.[35]

Initially the fascination for those watching Heath was the knowledge of an impending massacre: 'For those who relish a lost cause, his tour started in a way which looked as though it would satisfy even a Billy Bunter appetite,' wrote Gordon Greig. 'Silent, almost somnolent audiences, drawn by curiosity, departing unconvinced. . . . There was one appalling moment when he was introduced as "a magnificent television personality". There were two seconds of laughter. . . .'[36]

Suddenly, on 15 March 1966, he surprised his news conference by criticizing those who went 'around complaining, bellyaching and condemning de Gaulle and the French'.[37] Wilson immediately exploited Heath's utterances by describing him as 'rolling over like a spaniel' at one kind gesture from the French. The text of Wilson's speech caught up with Heath at Rhoose Airport, Cardiff, late on the night of Friday, 18 March. As he flicked through Wilson's Bristol speech, he spat out angrily: 'This is too sordid for words . . . what a poisonous speech . . . I lie on my back like a spaniel? What a revolting bit! This is a lie . . . Wilson must be out of his mind. . . . Abuse like this is unforgivable when you're dealing with international relations.' He began referring to Wilson as 'a squalid little man'.[38] When Wilson alleged that Macmillan had misled de Gaulle at Rambouillet in 1962, Heath nailed him: 'President de Gaulle himself told me in November last year that Mr Macmillan had given him the relevant facts about Skybolt and Polaris at Rambouillet.'[39]

Heath suddenly began unbuttoning, began developing his own style. He dropped his quickfire monotone and his reliance on clichés. He then began to attack Wilson personally and for his 'unhealthy dependence on American power and money to which this Government has condemned us'.[40]

The Tories became frantic to overcome the large but shrinking Labour lead. One of the members of Heath's private office asked Enoch Powell to take up the existence of a contingency plan for sending a token British force to Vietnam. Powell made the provocative speech requested, but was infuriated on 27 March, when Heath dismissed Powell's statement as strictly his own personal view. Heath had never been informed of his office's request to Powell.[41]

Another effort to smear the Wilson Government did not come to light. A couple of days before the election, the Maudling office telephoned Heath's private office to inform his PR consultant, that the Government was understood to have seized an issue of *Paris-Match* allegedly containing a scandalous and lying story about Harold Wilson. Heath urged his PR man to get on to the magazine's headquarters in Paris. When he reached its news editor he discovered there never had been any such article.

Typically, Heath was able to relax completely at the end of his campaign. He knew that it was lost. But he felt sure he had done all that was reasonably possible. 'In his final news conference of the campaign at Central Office yesterday Mr. Heath convinced a fairly rugged and disabused audience that he has been notably matured and toughened by his campaigning,' wrote David Woods in *The Times* on election day, 31 March. 'He was scarcely recognizable from the unrelaxing technocrat who introduced the Conservative manifesto three weeks ago. He was urbane, witty, and in rapport with all comers as we have never seen him before.'

Heath also won praise for the grace with which he early conceded defeat, when the votes were counted Wilson had beaten him by 363 seats to 253, by 47·9 per cent of the poll to 41·9. It was almost an exact reversal of the 1959 elections. He even had the personal humiliation of having his majority in Bexley halved to 2,333. Heath was compared to Hugh Gaitskell as a 'born loser'.

SAVED FROM THE COUNT-OUT

Two things saved Heath from being replaced as Leader immediately after the 1966 general election. First, in the end he had performed much better than expected and far better than any of his potential rivals in the top ranks. Second, having had three Leaders in three years, the party was in no mood for another struggle over the succession. 'That would benefit only one person,' warned *The Economist*, 'Mr Wilson.'[42]

Heath was faced with two interacting problems when he returned prematurely from a Roman holiday in mid-April because the Rhodesian crisis again boiled up. How could he best hold together a broad coalition party like the Tories when issues like Rhodesia repeatedly threatened it with a three-way split? How could he field a cohesive team which would still look credible at the time of the next general election around 1970.

The latter problem was most pressing because he had to have his new team ready when Parliament reassembled. His friend on *The Economist*, Ian Trethowan, was already urging him to drop those who would be in their sixties by 1970. And he again had a disciplinary problem in the shape of Enoch Powell. Powell, still very anti-East-of-Suez, had clashed in January 1966 with Maudling over incomes policy. Just before Heath returned to London, Powell had again angered Maudling by putting out, through Central Office, a statement attacking the Rhodesian oil blockade without any consultation with his Shadow Cabinet colleagues. Heath called in Powell to point out to him that individual forays confused the Tory rank and file more than they damaged the Government. Heath wanted coherent team attacks.

Powell thought there was more to be gained by individual grenade launchings. But Powell was not thinking of resigning, nor was the just-defeated Heath strong enough to sack a man with his own following.

Heath took the advice of *The Economist* and, apart from Sir Alec, whom he retained as foreign affairs spokesman, dropped veterans Selwyn Lloyd, Duncan Sandys and John Boyd-Carpenter. He switched Quintin Hogg to Home Office affairs, vacated by the defeat of Peter Thorneycroft. But the most distinctive change was his promotion of able younger 'Heathmen' from modest backgrounds: Geoffrey Rippon, who had returned for Hexham, and Peter Walker who, at 34 was the 'baby' of the 'Leader's Committee', as Heath renamed the Shadow Cabinet.[43]

Heath also followed another bit of *Economist* advice and set up a purge of the Tory candidates' list to retire the country gentry and increase the percentage of go-getting 'pacemakers'. Heath put the task into the hands of the party chairman, Edward duCann. When duCann sent out letters emphasizing the need to 'cut out the dead wood' veteran Tory MPs became frightened that they themselves might be sacked. Heath had to soothe the 1922 Committee on 12 May. He insisted he was not trying to stuff the House with 'technocrats' in his own 'image'. Just the best and ablest representatives of all walks of life. Few doubted that there would be a higher percentage of 'Europeans' among these new candidates.

One of the ways to hold the Tories together, Heath decided, was keep firing with all guns at the Labour Government, giving less chance that the Tories would turn their ideological guns on one another. This attacking strategy explains why Heath immediately attacked the new Selective Employment Tax, although the Tories were considering a similar employment tax.[44]

In this post-election period Wilson was at his peak: 'He can't seem to put a foot wrong!' was a common remark. And Heath was scraping bottom, rather testy and prickly. His lack of self-confidence led him to challenge Wilson first too often and, having been clobbered, to withdraw into a cocoon of silence. His failure to perform led to depression among his supporters and further intensified his lack of self-confidence.

To refurbish his image, he flew off to the United States to play the 'alternate Leader' role during Whitsun. But when asked at the National Press Club, how he would have handled the national seamen's strike, he replied briskly, 'The situation would not have arisen.'[45] Partly because he supported the President's position in Vietnam, Mr Johnson kept him at the White House so long that Heath missed his planned luncheon appointment with Senator Fulbright, an opponent of the Vietnamese war.[46]

Heath returned to a renewed attack by the Beaverbrook press. 'SUPPOSE THE TORIES WANTED TO DITCH THEIR LEADER . . .' was the headline over a *Sunday Express* editorial article.[47] This suggested that because he had been elected democratically, he should have to renew his mandate annually (like the Labour Leader in Opposition).

Heath was saved from any intensive development of this campaign by the economic difficulties into which the Wilson Government suddenly stumbled, beginning in June 1966. Heath was able to recall his 'vote now, pay later' slogan and forecasts of bankruptcy in the election. 'Once again the pound is only being sustained because the central bankers are propping it up. Once again the Bank of England begging bowl has had to go round,' he said in Bexley.[48]

Labour's economic troubles inspired him into making a fiery attack on the Chancellor, James Callaghan. 'You are a new quack, who is draining off the blood of industry and then suddenly giving it a shot in the arm. First the leech, then the hypodermic.'⁴⁹

However mock-heroic he might become in internal battles, Heath always took foreign affairs seriously. He remained particularly concerned that the gulf that had developed between Britain and France should narrow. When Defence Secretary Denis Healey attacked de Gaulle as a bad ally, Heath tried to get Wilson to repudiate Healey, without avail. Wilson quoted his own attack on de Gaulle in 1963: 'The high hopes of so many have thus been thwarted for political reasons by the will of one man.' Both Heath and Sir Alec tried to recover the situation, to Tory despair and Labour delight. Maurice Edelman recalled the time when Heath had entertained M. Tixier-Vignancour, the lawyer for the would-be assassins of de Gaulle. 'It is not for me,' said Wilson suavely, 'to comment on [Mr Heath's] social life.' 'Slander and innuendo!' shouted Heath furiously. 'Typical of the character of the Prime Minister!'⁵⁰

Heath was intolerant of any attacks on France because he had come to believe an Anglo-French alliance crucial. He later demonstrated this at the Hague meeting of the European Parliamentary Congress. 'We would be wrong to seek to isolate France,' he insisted. 'Even if it were to succeed, which I doubt, such a policy would only repeat in different form the errors which we in Britain have suffered these last five years. A Europe without France in the long run makes as little sense as a Europe without Britain.' When liberal-internationalist Tory MP, Peter Kirk, disagreed with Heath's pro-Gaullism, Heath did not speak to him for six months.

Heath never applied Anglo-French teamwork to Vietnam, where de Gaulle opposed US policies. When Wilson dissociated the Labour Government from the US bombing near Hanoi and Haiphong, Heath rushed in to attack the Prime Minister. His pro-American attack prevented an anti-American attack on Wilson by Labour leftwingers. For Heath, standing together with the Americans on Vietnam was infinitely more important than splitting Labour.

While arguing in public with Wilson, Heath was also arguing in the Shadow Cabinet with Enoch Powell. Powell was alone in opposition to the American role in Vietnam. Some of their colleagues wanted to send a token force to fight alongside the US forces there. Heath, impressed by the immense commitment of American material felt that an American defeat in Vietnam could not be contemplated.

THE RUNNING FIGHT WITH POWELL

Heath's running fight with Powell continued behind the scenes for long months before it erupted in the open. Heath was much more the organization man, anxious to keep the Tories united to fight Labour; Powell was much more the intellectual, anxious to pursue any idea which fascinated him to its illogical end. Heath was a modernizer, Powell a traditionalist. Both were anti-Establishment, but Powell preferred to fight it from the outside, while Heath preferred to infiltrate it. The contrast in their speech was evidence of this: Powell's speech was straight Birmingham, Heath had put a 'posh' top-dressing on his native Kent coast.

This produced wide-ranging arguments. The Labour attempt to bring in its mild Prices and Incomes Bill to defer price and wage increases split the Tory Shadow Cabinet. Maudling and Boyle rather favoured it while Powell opposed it; Heath was rather ambivalent. He accused Labour of trying to impose a 'totalitarian society'.

They managed to avoid a clash at the October 1966 Tory conference, largely because Sir Alec persuaded Powell to delete a passage from his speech which might have been interpreted as abandoning the defence of New Zealand and Australia. Despite mutterings Heath had an easy run at that conference. He proclaimed his undying confidence in the party chairman Edward duCann and spent most of his time slating Wilson's integrity and Labour's threat to freedom. The Tories stood and cheered the 'new Ted Heath'. He had, in fact, changed. He had lost about 25 lb. The following winter his failure to win popularity in the country produced some secret discussions about 'dumping' him. But there was no agreed alternative Leader.

In the House, his style remained so much of single-handed combat with Wilson that peppery Manny Shinwell asked, 'Is this a private row or can I join in?'[51] Behind the scenes Heath continued having considerable trouble with Enoch Powell, who seemed to be trying to see how far he could go without being sacked. In 1967 Heath decided that a CPC pamphlet Powell was writing on defence was not in line with party policy. He deputed Sir Michael Fraser, deputy chairman of the party, to tell Powell that it could not be published.

Heath and Powell even argued about Black Rod. When this black-clad messenger from the Lords arrived in the Commons in November 1967 in the middle of an interesting debate on Wilson's new effort to join the EEC, there was considerable irritation with his interruption, which Heath shared. In his next Shadow Cabinet, Heath said that this ceremonial 'nonsense' must be stopped. Powell defended this ancient institution, dating back to the fourteenth century at least.

Although he had difficulty making his oft-predicted 'break-through' before, Heath was finally 'made' by devaluation. Wilson had resisted devaluation desperately; but by November 1967 he had been forced into it. Heath, making a furious attack on this 'defeat', insisted that there had been no need for it apart from the Government's incompetence.

Labour fell further into unpopularity early in 1968, when it was compelled to make post-devaluation social and defence cuts to turn the economy around. Labour reversed many of its old policies including prescription charges. As its popularity fell, that of the Tories rose, although Heath's did not rise as fast.

BATTLES OVER RACE

Just as the Tories' prospects looked increasingly rosy, the behind-the-scenes battles in the Shadow Cabinet over race came out in the open. Quintin Hogg, the spokesman on Home Office affairs, was against exploiting 'an emotionally-charged atmosphere' through 'disagreeable racial overtones'. In contrast, Powell, was responding increasingly to the fears of the back-street Tories in the Midlands. Heath sided with Hogg.

Powell baited Hogg and alerted his Midlands audience to the possibility that another 200,000 Kenya Indians might be flooding in, through a little noticed speech in Walsall on 9 February 1968. Heath almost sacked Powell over this. But two weeks later the Government decided to rush through a Bill to keep out the Kenya Asians. The Shadow Cabinet reluctantly agreed to support the Government. But 15 Tory MPs, led by Iain Macleod, voted against the Bill.

The next split came over a strengthened Race Relations Bill of March 1968. There was a strong tussle in the Shadow Cabinet, with Sir Keith Joseph and Robert Carr against opposition. But Heath, fearing renewed party splits, decided to resist the Bill by a 'reasoned amendment'. Humphry Berkeley resigned from the Tory Party, evoking a letter from Heath justifying his decision on the ground that the Bill would be unworkable and unpopular both.

Into this smouldering situation Enoch Powell threw his explosive 20 April speech in Birmingham, a classic example of misjudged brinkmanship. 'I deliberately include at least one startling assertion in every speech in order to attract enough attention to give me a power base within the Conservative Party,' Powell had explained. 'Provided I keep this going, Ted Heath can never sack me from the Shadow Cabinet.'[52]

Heath *did* sack him after the speech in which Powell transformed British politics by telling the doubtful story of a never-found white constituent being hounded out of her house by Asians pushing excrement through her letterbox. When he saw it in the Sunday papers at Broadstairs Heath was furious. He tried to reach Powell, who was not on the telephone in Wolverhampton. He then reached Powell's agent and asked him to get Powell to phone him. At the Albany, he received Powell's telephone call and told him brusquely that he would be issuing a statement next day sacking him for delivering a speech which Heath thought 'racialist' in tone.

Heath's decision cut the Tory party like a cleaver. The Establishment supported him to the man. 'In dismissing Mr Powell, Mr Heath takes the known risk of having Mr Powell as an enemy,' wrote *The Times* next day; 'that, fortunately is less grave than having Mr Powell as a colleague.' But on 23 April thousands of dockers stopped work, hundreds marching on Parliament under slogans like 'Don't Knock Enoch' and 'Back Britain, not Black Britain', led by Fascist organizers. Heath's mailbag became swollen with protests, often from mentally-sick racialists. On his tour of the Midlands the following weekend, the Fascist, Colin Jordan, was thrown out of a meeting in Dudley, where Heath admitted the 'natural fears' of all living in communities with a high proportion of coloured immigrants. Tension rose so high that, when Heath and Powell attended the 1 May meeting of the 1922 Committee, *both* had Special Branch men to guard them. Heath managed to joke about his action. He said that he had feared that divisions in the Labour Party might be contagious. 'Fortunately,' he added, 'we have been Enoch-ulated against it!'[53]

The immediate impact of Powell's challenge was severe. After Heath had decided that the Tories should *not* oppose the Race Relations Bill, the majority of the executive of the influential 1922 Committee tabled an amendment to throw the Bill out. Fully 45 voted against the Bill's third reading. Heath met the 1922 Committee. 'I will not tolerate any discrimination.' But also emphasized that his party policy had become one of the most rigorous control of new immigrants and their dependants.[54]

Despite such concessions, Powell seemed to be set on sinking into Heath's back every ideological stiletto he could fashion. In March 1969 he made a sudden reversal and came out against joining the Common Market. In June he ridiculed the idea that there could be a 'European deterrent', an idea that Heath had floated in his 1966 Godkin lectures. It was a curious situation in which Powell, the 'pure' intellectual, was providing the justifications for the chauvinistic reactions of the 'gut rightists' among back-street Tories. They were the people from whom Heath stemmed, but who opposed most of his policies.

One of the many clashes came on 17 January 1970, when Heath denounced as 'un-Christian' and an example of 'man's inhumanity to man' a speech by Powell at Scarborough. Powell appeared to be saying that he was opposed to special aid for cities with immigrant-swollen slums unless immigrants were also encouraged to go home. Heath put an even harsher interpretation on Powell's convoluted speech. An incensed Powell sent Heath a copy of his speech pointing out he had not said what Heath had claimed. Heath refused to budge, despite Willie Whitelaw's efforts to bridge the gap.

THE ROAD TO SELSDON PARK

Heath was furious with Powell for his constant guerilla raids. He too could be the slashing controversialist on occasion, but was more at home, however, making ready to take over the machinery of Government. This had seemed pretty inevitable, particularly since May 1968, when Labour had fallen twenty per cent behind in the opinion polls and, except for a brief recovery in the autumn of 1968, remained well behind.

The meeting of Heath and his Shadow Cabinet at the Selsdon Park Hotel near Croydon from 30 January to 1 February 1970 had elements of a publicity stunt, designed to show that the Tories were ready to take over. And to demonstrate that their well-prepared policies were mostly hard-line rightwing. Some of this was evident from the people present. As Shadow Minister for Education, Heath now had Mrs Margaret Thatcher, a grocer's rightwing daughter, instead of his long-time friend and colleague, liberal Sir Edward Boyle.

Sir Edward had been an embarrassment because of his liberal line on race relations, Rhodesia and education, including tolerance for comprehensive schools in new areas. Opposition to Sir Edward had made itself felt at the October 1967 party conference. The next month his supporters had been ousted from the back-bench Education Committee by rightwingers. Heath who was against private schooling, largely supported Sir Edward's progressive ideas. To get Boyle out of the firing line, Macleod and Carrington suggested that he be made spokesman on the social services, but Heath resisted this. But as the party moved steadily to the right, Boyle became more and more of an embarrassment to Heath. In October 1969 Sir Edward's appointment to Leeds University was announced. Heath named as his successor Mrs Margaret Thatcher, much more acceptable to the right.

One of the other concessions to the right announced at the Selsdon Park meeting was to strengthen the under-manned police force and to bring in law changes – including that on trespass – to make impossible the sort of anti-Apartheid demonstrations which had succeeded in banning the South African 'Springboks'.

It was in promising to dismantle economic 'Wilsonism' that this meeting was most emphatic. Direct taxation would be sharply cut, possibly replaced by heavier Value Added Tax. SET would be abolished and Regional Employment Premiums be phased out. Trade union agreements would be made legally binding. Immigration controls would be tightened. Heath insisted they had to have a draft manifesto ready and an outline of their first five years of legislation, although he did not expect Wilson to dare to have an election until 1971.[55]

THE SUDDEN DROP

As late as 10 April 1970 Heath felt secure, because of Tory advances in the county council elections. When Wilson baited him about allegations of an unofficial Tory emissary having been sent to Salisbury, Heath snapped: 'The purpose of these exchanges is to enable Her Majesty's Opposition to carry out its duty of keeping itself fully informed on the situation in Rhodesia. . . . If Mr Wilson considers that any offence has been committed by Her Majesty's Opposition, or that there has been any breach of the Official Secrets Act, let him prosecute me and my colleagues forthwith. If not, let him shut up. There are no lessons in patriotism to be learnt from Mr Wilson.'[56]

But on 29 April, the Harris Poll in the *Daily Express* suddenly showed Labour in the lead – *the first time since 1967*. Next day Marplan gave Labour a 0·8 per cent lead. A week later municipal elections gave an enormous swing from the previous year. 'Labour's recovery has taken the party almost back to 1966,' wrote *The Economist* sadly.[57] On 12 May the Gallup Poll showed Labour seven per cent in the lead.

'I have never seen a party plunged more suddenly and irrationally into such black despair as happened to the Conservatives the other night when the Gallup Poll figures showed Labour ahead,' reported James Margach in the *Sunday Times*. 'In the Conservative Party,' said Sir Alec in Perth, 'we always do our best with our backs against the wall. And all I can say is that it's a damned great wall we're up against now.'[58]

What had happened? Heath's virility-quotient should have been increased by his victory in the Australian ocean races. The public could not know how boring he could sometimes be about it in private, as in Heath's first meeting with Viscount Hall, a steam yachtsman then head of the Post Office. After sitting silently at the lunch, Heath suddenly said: 'And now I'm going to tell you how I won the great yacht race.' 'I'm sorry,' interposed Hall, 'I haven't congratulated you on your win. I'd like to hear about it because I'm a sailor myself.' 'Yes,' replied Heath coldly, 'in ships with engines. . . .'[59]

Heath was afraid of making himself a Wilson target as an into-Europe-at-any-cost man. Because M. Pompidou had given the green light, negotiations for Britain to enter the EEC seemed likely to begin. Heath was scheduled to travel to France and Germany, beginning with a speech to the British Chamber of Commerce in Paris on 5 May. He emphasized that Europe had to unite if it was to enhance its voice in world affairs. The Russians and Americans were talking about strategic arms limitation 'on European soil but without any European participation'. But, he warned, British opinion would 'remain sour and uncertain' if they felt the settlement reached was 'unequal and unfair'. 'Nor would it be in the interest of the Community that its enlargement should take place except with the full-hearted consent of the Parliaments and peoples of the new member countries.'

When he returned home, he seemed completely self-confident. 'Nervous? Not me,' he said when asked about the unsettled election date. 'Not us. Wilson is the one who has had to make up his mind. And he hates having to do that. He's the nervy one.'[60] 'All we have to do is press the button and everything we have laid on will happen.'[61]

Heath sounded confident when Wilson asked the Queen for a dissolution on 18 May. But for the first two weeks of the campaign, only one or two of his close friends, Anthony Barber and Lord Aldington, particularly shared his confidence. Even the planned publicity fell flat. When he took a pretty girl aboard his *Morning Cloud* to alter his image relating to women, she turned out to be a PR girl. And the yacht ran aground off Ramsgate, as the newspaper headlines gleefully recounted.[62]

Heath promised a new-style government, not Wilson's 'cheap and trivial' 'government by gimmick'. 'I cannot promise to stop roaring inflation overnight, but I will give it priority,' he said.[63] He promised no 'miracles'. He promised to cut the number of ministers and civil servants. 'We have had only two Labour Prime Ministers since the war. Each one in turn has devalued the pound, and created inflation as a result.'[64]

Heath was under heavy pressure from Central Office to concentrate more on the Tories' ability to curb price rises. He resisted, knowing this was largely dishonest. The Tory market researchers persisted, having found that working class wives were receptive on this issue. On 15 June, three days before the election, Heath agreed because, after a long run of favourable trade figures, that day a deficit of £31m. – which later proved to be exaggerated – was announced. This meant that the virility symbol that Wilson had erected as an economic manager had gone limp.

Next day, 16 June, at 11.15 – *after* his press conference – reporters were handed a statement signed by Heath claiming that tax cuts and curbs on nationalized prices 'would, at a stroke, reduce the rise in prices . . .'.[65] A Labour win might bring a new devaluation.

By then virtually all the political commentators and all his friends, except Anthony Barber, Iain Macleod and, belatedly, Willie Whitelaw, thought he was still a 'born loser'. Those not so friendly speculated on how to 'dump' him. Lord Carrington telephoned Lord Aldington to suggest he arrange a consolation party. Aldington said not to worry. Ted would be giving *them* a party, at No. 10.

> Our purpose is to bring our fellow citizens to recognize that they
> must be responsible for the consequences of their own actions
> and to learn that no one will stand between them and the results
> of their own free choice.
>
> Edward Heath, Blackpool, 10 October 1970

When he took over 10 Downing Street on 19 June 1970, Edward Heath's style was more like a victorious commander moving into a command post he had stormed than the Leader of an Opposition party taking over the reins of government.

Partly it was the swagger of the conquering hero whose victory was such a surprise. Since all about him had lost heart and many had begun to speculate on how to jettison him, he had 'made it on his own', as he had so long dreamt. His every command was every Tory's wish, to be obeyed with uncritical gratefulness. 'Ted Heath,' said one aide, 'lost most of the battles and won the war.'[1]

Such a successful commander could be forgiven his occasionally curious appointments. His senior officers were predictable and understandable. As Home Secretary, Reginald Maudling's placid bulk could cool the law-and-order brigade and straddle the bipartisanship needed on Northern Ireland. As Foreign Secretary Sir Alec Douglas-Home could give a false sense of Conservative continuity while promising to bridge the Anglo-Rhodesian gap and restore better relations with South Africa. Iain Macleod's long preparations to bring the Treasury under control and prepare the economy for EEC entry made him the obvious choice as Chancellor of the Exchequer. The persuasive Robert Carr was just the sort to gentle down the skittish trade unionists while settling in place the bridle and bit of the new industrial relations legislation. Heath had long appreciated the humanity of Sir Keith Joseph and the go-getting talents of Peter Walker. Predictably, his close friends William Whitelaw and Lord Carrington would make a fine Leader of the House and an excellent Defence Secretary respectively. Heath had to put up with Quintin Hogg, so he dressed him up as Lord Chancellor, renamed him Hailsham and sent him back into 'exile' in the Lords on the Woolsack.

More indicative was Heath's promotion of those who depended more on loyalty to him and his ideas than to proven ability. Geoffrey Rippon as Minister of Technology, Anthony Barber as 'Mr Europe',

Jim Prior as Agriculture Minister and Peter Thomas as Secretary of State for Wales *and* chairman of the party seemed chosen favourites rather than obvious choices. Their promotions seemed to reflect Heath's determination to provide opportunity for loyal 'meritocrats' anxious to rise.

Even more revealing was Heath's exclusion of the able men whose chief sin appeared to be that they had 'crossed' him. He could hardly work with Enoch Powell, his would-be political assassin. But Edward duCann? Hugh Fraser? Angus Maude? And why leave out Peter Emery, one of the leading campaigners for Heath in 1965? Heath also left out independent-minded youngish MP, John Biffen, thought to be too sympathetic to Powell. A fast-moving commander required those whose single-mindedness is focussed in the same direction and whose loyalty is beyond doubt. For Heath, politics was warfare carried on by other means. His strategic intentions differed as much from the traditional Tory Prime Ministers who had preceded him as the mobile warfare of a Rommel, Montgomery or Patten differed from the trench-bound generals of the First World War.

However much he had glossed over in the election, his targets were scarcely hidden from his Cabinet: an efficient Britain in the van of a West European super-Power able to confront the Americans and Russians as an equal. To achieve this he knew that he had to transform Britain as radically as the raw recruits had been transformed into an efficient and mobile regiment in wartime. If he was rather brusque and businesslike at Cabinet meetings it was because this was the style he preferred as C.O.

It is in this context that he spoke of 'One Nation' on becoming Prime Minister. He was not being ironical, in view of his intention to bridle the unions. He really meant 'One Combat Team', fighting its way to wealth and power in the vanguard of Western Europe. Leftwing Liverpool dockers had served loyally under his command in the RA. Why not that leftwing Liverpudlian, Jack Jones? New industrial relations laws were to be another sort of 'Queen's Regulations', imposing a needed discipline on a fractious army of workers. Once the new discipline was accepted the whole nation could advance in unity to new affluence.

In private Heath made it clear that for him inefficient industrialists and stupid shareholders were at least as poor combat material as lazy and greedy unionists. They should be treated with even less consideration, allowing below-par enterprises to drop out, to give place to the efficient and combative. And to help them get ahead, the government should stop propping up the incapable and stay out of the hair of the able.

This simple approach to an old and complex economy shows the directness which often characterizes successful commanders. Heath approached militant trade unionists and hidebound manufacturers much like an old-fashioned officer approaching a soldier having a breakdown under fire. The idea appeared to be that shouts of 'pull yourself together', a slap or a threat of a court martial might restore him to combat fitness.

To Heath's dismay, his command team was thrown back from its first target. This was 'stagflation' – stagnant production and roaring inflation – which he had promised to tackle immediately in the hope of slowing price rises 'at a stroke'.[2] The Treasury mandarins insisted that virtually everything that Iain Macleod wanted to try would only speed inflation. They claimed that there were enough expansionist factors already working their way through the economy. The defeat of 'Heath's Raiders' in their first behind-the-scenes scuffle was signalled by Iain Macleod's 7 July statement that 'it would be premature at this moment to take action to stimulate demand'.[3]

However disappointing, Heath accepted Macleod's judgment because it was his command style to appoint men he trusted and support them. Heath's reliance on Macleod as a shrewd, combative politician and able administrator received a brutal blow on 20 July, when Macleod died next door in 11 Downing Street from a heart attack.[4] Nobody envied him the task of replacing Macleod. When he named Anthony Barber the new Chancellor, made Rippon the new 'Mr Europe', and promoted John Davies to head the Ministry of Technology after a few weeks in parliament, not a few doubted Heath's judgment.

It was the absence of a policy that made Heath so vague when he saw the TUC general secretary, Victor Feather, and the CBI chief, John Partridge, early in September. At that point he talked of putting a check on consumer demand and was certain only of the need to control excess wage inflation.[5]

To provide him with longer-term strategic alternatives he brought in Lord Rothschild and his 'think tank' as a sort of intellectual commando squad to outflank the desk-bound immobilized civil servants.[6]

From the outset he showed determination to face down demands for large wage increases. 'We might be faced next week with a very grave situation which we shall have to handle with coolness and determination,' he said of the impending dock strike to his first 1922 Committee meeting in July 1970. 'We must never go on the defensive.'[7] He brought back some of the troops sent to Northern Ireland to cope with the dockers. In fact, the dockers got another seven per cent after the Pearson Report.

The Cabinet had decided that the best way to squeeze down the rate of wage inflation was to be tough in the public sector to give heart to private industrialists. Heath was willing to face a winter of grave inconvenience, even hardship, feeling he would win public support for his willingness to hold the line.[8] Heath was not moved by the three dustmen who called on his family home in Broadstairs to point out that, although they had gone to the same primary school, St Peter's, they were earning £16 while his pay was £240 a week, mostly untaxed.[9] He refused to intervene in the unofficial strike of 5,000 GKN-Sankey workers after five weeks, not thinking intervention 'helpful' – and too much like Wilson![10]

Union problems he had delegated to Robert Carr, as he had put Northern Ireland in the hands of Maudling, and education in those of Margaret Thatcher. This delegation sometimes did not work out – as when Mrs Thatcher put through a new instruction reversing policy on comprehensive schools without going through the usual consultation ritual. But Heath seldom butted in unless there was a real crisis. Even then he was more likely to hand over to his two most trusted henchmen, Lord Carrington and William Whitelaw.

He still liked to keep the ultimate reins firmly in his own hands and could be furious if anyone tried to usurp power. This was the reason behind the sacking of Viscount Hall, the Post Office chief. Hall went ahead and printed more expensive stamps – even transferring the metallic sorting strip – without getting the authority of the Minister of Posts, then Christopher Chataway, much less that of Heath and the Cabinet, for increasing postal rates. Chataway and Heath were furious, both for usurping their authority and because they suspected that Hall, a Labour supporter, had been playing politics by not demanding increased rates *before* the election. Hall was dismissed at the first opportunity, four months later.[11]

Heath did not want to have anything to do with anyone or anything selected by Wilson. A startled salesman, coming to 10 Downing Street to find out whether he wanted to continue the TV rental begun by his predecessor, heard Heath telling his housekeeper that he wanted nothing to do with anything chosen by 'that man'. He called in Jo Patrick, the designer who had redecorated his Albany flat, to redo Downing Street to remove the lower middle-class taste of the Wilsons – as well as the country-house flavour left by Lady Dorothy Macmillan.[12] He replaced the housekeeper Wilson had selected for Chequers. Heath had the Principal Private Secretary, David Isserlis, who had been selected by Harold Wilson, transferred from No. 10 Downing Street.

MISLEADING PICTURE

The style of 10 Downing Street changed, but not quite in the manner it was generally interpreted. Because of the music and the yacht, many got the idea that Heath was playing the upper-class dilettante. In fact, he was playing the 'to the victor belongs the spoils' game common to soldiers and other organization men.

Heath lived quite high on the hog at Downing Street and Chequers, much as his last C.O. had done in the Honourable Artillery Company in Germany. The cost of Chequers soared as guests increased to an average of sixty a week and the average meal – often procured from Fortnum and Mason – came to £3.50 a head.

Even his pleasures he took hard. The yachting, now played up more than ever, was above all an exercise in command and victory. He was out to win, not to enjoy a day's cruising in the sun.

His enjoyment of music could also have a 'command' quality. Soon after he had moved his Steinway into No. 10 he invited his personal staff up to his flat for drinks. As his guests arrived, Heath walked over to the grand piano and launched into a sonata. His guests shifted uneasily in silence as he played it straight through. 'Sorry,' he apologized at the end, 'but when I start something I like to finish It.'[13] (It was like one of his favourite stories about being 'ordered' down to Alton, Hampshire, to hear an analysis of the world strategic situation from Field Marshal Lord Montgomery.)

All that summer there was considerable wonder about what Heath was up to, partly because his reduction in government intervention and his sharp cut in government disclosure made a nonsense of the 'open government' he had proclaimed. His press officers began pumping material out in September 1970 when he took command of the crisis involving Arab skyjacker Leila Khaled in Britain and three skyjacked planes, one of them BOAC, in Jordan. Heath kept secret, however, his private messages to President Nasser. It became known that Heath was being quite tough, insisting that *all* the detained passengers be released, including Jews. Heath became furious when Mrs Golda Meir became tougher, detaining 475 Arabs in Israel. Heath was so pre-occupied with the crisis that he missed a concert at Chequers.[14]

Heath found music an escape in another way too. 'The devoted team of secretaries in No. 10 are constantly lying in wait to fill every moment of the Prime Minister's time with red boxes, Parliamentary questions, Foreign Office telegrams and all the other demands of the office,' Heath recalled. 'But I have noticed that the best way I can fend them off is to go and play something on the piano. They creep up to the door with their red boxes and creep away again with the boxes unopened, "Heath is at his exercises," they murmur to themselves. . . .'[15]

Apart from planning the restructuring of the Government, Heath spent most of that summer's 'hibernation' on his foreign plans. He had outlined his rather two-dimensional strategy in his comments on the Queen's Speech, in what sounded like a military appreciation. He would build a position of strength in Western Europe, hold on to the 'strong North Atlantic alliance' which provided Britain's nuclear umbrella, retain positions of strength in the Persian Gulf and Southeast Asia, where Britain had interests Labour was prepared to abandon. And he intended to rebuild 'vital defence interests' in South Africa 'which we cannot ignore'.[16]

In his effort to persuade the French to open the door to the Market, Heath made public his offer of nuclear collaboration with the French.[17] He agreed with the proposition 'that if one day Western Europe is to be endowed with a military capacity which is not ultimately dependent on the willingness of the United States to commit suicide on our behalf, such a capacity must be built on a basis of Anglo-French cooperation'. 'I put forward this proposal . . . as long ago as the spring of 1965 in a lecture at Oxford,' Heath told the House, 'and I have developed it since then . . . in the Godkin lecture.'[18] Heath was anxious to win over the French to avoid a third veto – about which he was anxious enough to ask his Ambassador in Paris, Christopher Soames, to investigate.[19]

Heath ran into mounting difficulty with his plans to restart selling frigates and helicopters to the South Africans. Heath welcomed Richard Nixon to Chequers together with the Queen during the US President's five-hour stay in Britain on 3 October 1970. But even that was long enough to discover that the Americans thought that arming the South Africans would play into Communist hands in Africa.[20]

After Nixon's visit, Heath began increasingly to feel his isolation on the issue of South African arms, over which Wilson was making heavy weather. Most officials in the Foreign and Commonwealth Office opposed the sale. Sir Alec remained favourable, partly because he was an old-fashioned anti-Communist, partly because he expected the South African government to help him with his Rhodesian 'deal'.

A week after Nixon, Julius Nyerere, President of Tanzania, was very much more vehement at Chequers. Heath and Sir Alec warned that the Russians were trying to build their strength in Africa as they had in the Arab world. 'A couple of frigates in the Indian Ocean will not make the slightest difference to a Soviet presence in the Indian Ocean,' replied Nyerere, 'but it will make a big difference to the South Africans.'

South Africa, he insisted, would treat this as a certificate of respectability, which they lacked.[21]

That meeting was friendly compared with the 16 October confrontation with Kenneth Kaunda, President of Zambia. Heath tried to explain that half of Britain's oil and a quarter of its trade came around the Cape. This trade was menaced by the growth of Soviet influence in Africa. Kaunda retorted that Communist influence was growing mainly because the West was unsympathetic. Portugal was using NATO arms against Mozambique and Angolan freedom fighters – which would hardly make the latter pro-Western. Heath became angry at this 'lecture', reacting as if his manhood was threatened by Kaunda's telling him where Britain's national interests lay. At the end, Kaunda was so angry that he left saying Britain should be 'chucked out' of the Commonwealth if it sold arms to South Africa.[22]

Heath was also under bombardment by the Church of England, not only the archbishop and his bishops, but experts like Admiral Sir Anthony Buzzard they brought to make mincemeat of his strategic arguments. Heath received them with thinly-concealed impatience, wrote polite letters explaining himself, but did not enjoy the attempted brain-rinsing. His attitude was reflected by his joke on receiving the Catholic primate, Cardinal Heenan: 'Good morning, Cardinal, I suppose I can't offer you Canterbury by any chance?'[23]

OVERSHADOWING ECONOMICS

Even more uncomfortable was the economic strait-jacket in which he found himself. He had taken over knowing that wage inflation was roaring at ten per cent. What he had *not* known previously was that, instead of money issue increasing at five per cent, as announced, Jenkins had allowed it to increase to sixteen to seventeen per cent. The classic, capitalist cure for this, to which Heath inclined, was cutting back the money supply and other deflationary techniques. But Sir Leslie O'Brien, Governor of the Bank of England, warned that this would bring bankruptcies and push unemployment beyond the 750,000 already registered. He urged a wages policy, anathema to Heath.

The Cabinet Heath convened at the end of September and early October was by no means unanimous. Maudling was one of nature's reflationists and also an advocate of a wages policy. But the new Chancellor, Anthony Barber, saw things identically with Heath. They decided that they would make marginal cuts in government expenditure and taxes, as a sort of 'clubs and carrots' operation. They would begin to get the Government out of industry's hair. But primarily they would use psychological shock to force people to realize that the cosy old days were over and a new 'stand on your own feet' era had dawned.

Heath's 10 October speech to the Tory conference was therefore the verbal equivalent of a gallant cavalry charge with shiny capitalist sword drawn and Victorian pennant flying. He proclaimed a patriotic 'revolution' restoring 'freedom' and promising 'to change the course of history'. 'Our fellow citizens,' he proclaimed, 'must realize they are responsible for their own actions.' If private employers did not resist excessive wage claims, he warned, 'the Government is certainly not going to rescue them'. He was enthusiastically applauded, as had been John Davies's earlier promise that industrial 'lame ducks' would be allowed to fall flat on their faces.[24] Heath later admitted this was conceived of as psychological warfare: 'Nothing is more difficult than to persuade people to cast off their chains.'[25]

It was because the contrast between the metaphors and the measures was so marked that Anthony Barber's 'mini-Budget' statement of 27 October raised such a storm. Government expenditures would be cut on school milk, council house subsidies, prescription costs and dental treatment. In six months income tax would be cut by 2·5 per cent. Lesser depreciation allowances would replace investment grants in the regions. Banks were asked for £100m. in special deposits.[26] It infuriated Labour as socially divisive, helping go-getting executives at the expense of industrial workers. But it did not impress Heath's own friends either. *The Times* wrote of 'growing doubts whether the Government was losing its economic grip' and warning that 'a strategy without an incomes policy would be ruinously expensive to the economy in terms of jobs, profits, output and indeed bankrupted enterprises . . .'.[27]

Heath's attempt to fight back against these critics turned the 9 November 'Panorama' programme into a type of political 'bear-baiting'. His main fury was directed at the Scamp pay award which, with 'blatantly nonsensical' arguments, had awarded fourteen per cent increases to the dustmen for 'dirty work'. He hardly disputed that the average worker would be worse off under Barber's new proposals, while executives would enjoy tax cuts. 'What surely matters,' he insisted, 'is that we have incentives so that we have greater national wealth and everyone can benefit from it.'[28] He extolled the same Victorian virtues at the Guildhall dinner a week later: 'It was the acceptance of personal responsibility, not dependence upon the central government, that made this small island with its comparatively small population so dominant in the world.'[29]

Heath's discomfort that he was relying largely on 'words, not action' at that stage made him prickly when baited, particularly by Roy Jenkins. When the former Chancellor jabbed him with his 16 June 'at a stroke' statement again, Heath snapped that he had inherited not only £1,500m. of overseas debt but also Jenkins's abandonment of monetary control.[30]

Heath felt his government was making progress with its programme to reduce the role of government interference in private industry. The Prices and Incomes Board had been told to keep its nose out. The Industrial Reconstruction Corporation was being wound up. And 'the casualty list is by no means complete . . .' he told the Institute of Directors.[31]

Heath also began trying to get transferred back to private hands selected state-owned concerns or parts of the nationalized giants. The first 'success' was the announcement that Thomas Cook and Son would be sold. The NCB was asked about selling its brickworks, British Rail about its hotels, and the nationalized gas industry told its exploration of the North Sea gas and oil fields was over.[32]

Heath's approach suffered a sudden blow in November when Rolls-Royce came begging for help with the RB 211 engine whose cost and technical problems the firm had grossly underestimated. Very reluctantly the Government promised £60m. in support. As if to prove that Rolls-Royce was a one-off operation, Heath in Cabinet refused, at the end of November, to bail out the Mersey Docks and Harbours Board, after his Ministers, John Peyton and Peter Walker, had agreed to do so. The unhappy investors and the inefficient management suffered most.

Heath's main pressure, however, was on how to squeeze down mounting wage claims. By early December the Cabinet had its Industrial Relations Bill ready and the challenge of the electricity workers, demanding twenty per cent instead of the ten per cent offered. The Cabinet decided to stand firm, no matter what public hardship was caused. It was thought that public opinion would be with it. Heath pledged on 5 December that the Government would not yield; hints were leaked of a willingness to use troops.[33] The electricity workers staged a one-day strike. Heath countered by persuading top civil servants, judges and generals to forgo for six months wage increases of £2–3,000 due them on 1 January. It was initially considered a great victory for Heath when Robert Carr persuaded the electricity workers to go to the Wilberforce wage tribunal. With difficulty, Heath was prevented from crowing.

Heath showed, by the way he unveiled his Industrial Relations Bill like a new siege-gun, that he preferred the style of confrontation. 'Let

me promise you this: your government will not bow before the storm.
We will persevere and we will come through it.' 'It is the storm before
the calm.'[34] Heath and his Cabinet decided to take the Committee Stage
of this contentious Bill on the floor of the House. This was partly to
help widen Labour divisions, already shown on Mrs Castle's earlier
effort in the same field. Also to embarrass Wilson by identifying him in
the public mind with the militant unions. When Whitelaw unveiled this
strategy on 3 December, Heath grinned like a Cheshire cat.[35]

Before Christmas, Heath had convinced most people that he was no
carbon-copy postwar Tory Prime Minister. He had deliberately
fractured the cosy consensus. He had preferred to arouse the enthusiasm
of his rightwing friends, rather than dampen the fears of his leftwing
opponents. 'We are beginning to realize that we have swapped an India-
rubber ball for a spanner,' said a senior civil servant. 'The new man at
No. 10 is the toughest operator since Neville Chamberlain. He knows
what he has gone there to do; and nothing will stop him. Nothing.'[36]
The public seemed to like decisiveness. The Tories crept back into the
poll lead by 1·5 per cent.[37]

Heath saw his attempted shock treatment at home largely as preparation for a larger British role abroad, particularly in the EEC. He had
talked briefly with M. Pompidou at de Gaulle's memorial mass on
14 November.[38] He worried about growing evidence that the entry
negotiations would compel Britain to swallow too harsh terms. At
the same time Heath was concerned that links between the White
House and 10 Downing Street 'had deteriorated badly' in Wilson's
last years. Heath's EEC interests had never dimmed his understanding
that Western Europe would, for a decade at least, need the US troops
and nuclear 'umbrella' to protect it. He had already done his 'bit'
by reversing the 1968 Wilson decision to pull out of Southeast Asia,
at least to the extent of leaving a token British force in Malaysia.

After several personal letters to Nixon, Heath was invited to Washington, 16–17 December. The main disagreement was over Britain's
£10m. computer sale to the USSR, vetoed by the US in NATO. On the
main issue, however, Nixon assured Heath that for the US the economic
disadvantages of Britain's entry into the EEC were far outweighed
by political advantages. At the final press conference, Heath grimaced
when Nixon spoke of the Anglo-American 'special relationship' instead
of the 'natural relationship' which sounded better to his (and M.
Pompidou's) ears. Heath showed his gratitude to Nixon by saying, on
American TV, that US bombing of North Vietnam would be 'justifiable'
to cover Nixon's 'honourable withdrawal' from the South.[39]

The Washington meeting looked all the smoother as seen from

Singapore the next month. Heath went to the Commonwealth Prime Ministers' Conference determined to explain that he was no racialist but that he needed South African help to prevent the threatened Soviet domination of Britain's trade 'arteries' in the Indian Ocean's sea lanes to prevent Britain being 'choked'.

Almost as soon as he reached Singapore his anger started smouldering quietly as he viewed the emotional efforts of the twelve African states, led by Dr Obote, Kaunda and Nyerere, to isolate and attack him as insensitive to racial domination. He remained courteous, punctilious and silent initially, earning the title of 'Edward the Silent' from Dr Obote (a former student of Harold Wilson). Heath was able to deploy his Edwardian view of the Soviet naval threat to a private session of the thirty-one Prime Ministers, where he was heard politely even if he won hardly any converts. He seemed unable to answer the rhetorical question of Canada's Mr Trudeau: 'What will have been gained if, to ensure the security of the sea lanes, we encourage the British to take steps which make the assurance of Soviet penetration even greater?' The 'final straw' for Heath was when the African Prime Ministers insisted on going back into plenary session to deliver their prepared speeches so that their exaggerated attacks on Britain and Heath could be released for the papers back home. Heath did the same, informing British correspondents of his contempt for the ignorance, emotionalism, verbosity, crowd-pleasing lack of sophistication of the African chiefs of state. Heath left the conference unchanged by anything he had heard, uncommitted to any modification of his policy, and having made the point that Britain too was independent and able to pursue its own national interests. But he convinced onlookers – partly by the contrast between his behaviour and that of Sir Alec – that the old Establishment knew better how to handle Africans. They could take African rudeness with forbearance in public and puncture it with humour in private. 'Mr Heath,' wrote The Times' Commonwealth Editor, 'seems not to be secure enough for that. . . .'[40]

REVERSING WITH ROLLS-ROYCE

On his return, Heath found a pile of problems. These sorted out into those whose solution he counted a success, for which he took credit. Others, which seemed to turn out failures, he tended to play down.

At the end of January 1971 the postmen were on strike. Labour's screams over the 'guillotine' on the Industrial Relations Bill dramatized the sharp resistance to this measure in Westminster and among trade unionists in the country. At Brussels, Geoffrey Rippon was finding the going unexpectedly tough, with the French demanding a much higher contribution than Britain could afford.

Heath's tough, unbending posture began to produce results in some areas. By the beginning of March the postal workers capitulated. This 'victory' overshadowed the Wilberforce award to the electricity workers, which had been presented as an increase of 10·9 per cent but turned out to be eighteen to nineteen per cent, according to *The Economist*.[41] By the summer the Industrial Relations Act reached the statute book. In the long run, Heath hoped, that would change the balance of forces in industry and curb the ability of unions to demand inflationary wages, if bosses, too, could learn to be tough.

But Heath's own 'image' was suddenly fractured by the Rolls-Royce crisis. His 'no subsidies' bark had been muted the previous November when £60m. in aid had been promised the famous firm. But by the end of January Rolls-Royce had no money for wages, owed tens of millions to creditors, and faced penalties of hundreds of millions for late or non-delivery of the RB 211 engines it had been expensively developing for the Lockheed TriStar. Heath's initial instinct was to let them go bankrupt, as a lesson to feckless managements that relied on government help. But it was pointed out this would bring to a halt 81 airforces, 200 airlines and Britain's own nuclear submarines that relied on Rolls-Royce engines and servicing. Apart from escalating unemployment in the Midlands, a Rolls-Royce collapse would bring tumbling the teetering American giant, Lockheed. Heath tried to telephone Nixon, who was away, and spoke to Dr Kissinger instead. Heath finally decided to accept the device of an arranged bankruptcy, which would dodge Rolls-Royce's obligations to Lockheed. The key aeroplane, gas turbine and marine engine segments would be nationalized in Rolls-Royce 1971 Ltd. This state-owned firm would renegotiate with Lockheed on a profitable basis the RB 211 engines it needed for TriStar. Nixon telephoned in the middle of the 3 February Cabinet meeting deciding this. Heath told him what had been decided and why, and promised the British Government would keep Rolls-Royce going on the RB 211 and would help finance it if the bulk of the money came from the American side. In the end, this 'amazing poker coup' came off, saving the industrial heart of Rolls-Royce.[42] But not Heath's over-simple 'image'.

After Heath declined to announce or defend this reversal in the Commons, the Political Editor of *The Times*, David Wood, almost wept at the cynical jokes hurtling around Westminster about the Government that insisted on denationalizing the Carlisle breweries but nationalized Rolls-Royce. 'Mr Heath will almost certainly be the main victim. For in the seven months since the general election, Mr Heath has put a particular stamp upon the Government . . . here is a Government led by a Prime Minister almost constitutionally incapable of compromising, of cooking up expediencies to make life easy for everybody, of bowing to any storm that blew. . . . Scarcely a day has passed without some reminder that here is a Conservative Government that scorns the old easy compromises of the 1950s and 1960s and the cynical alternation between the private face and the public face. . . . The man of principle will seem to many to be a pragmatist and a fixer of a familiar kind. . . . Mr Heath has been robbed of something of great value to him.'[43]

TACKING TOWARDS THE
TARGET

When people agree with your policies they admire your firmness.
But when they disagree they damn your obstinacy.

Edward Heath[1]

The Conservatives gathered at Brighton to enthuse in October 1971
could hardly see that their ocean-tanned Prime Minister had changed
his course as drastically as if he had changed his sex. Only one subtle
word gave away how far he had tacked to port since he had addressed
them a year before, as he proclaimed: 'A Government must have the
vision to look ahead, the intuition to point a path, the courage to lead
the way.' The word was 'intuition'.

Heath was saying, in effect, that when a policy appeared to threaten
to pile the Government up on the rocks, he would use his 'intuition' to
change course, regardless of what was previously announced. His
destination was unchanged: a modernized Britain leading a West
European Super-power. But when the starboard tack had threatened
disaster, a confident skipper was entitled to shift course without
notice or contrition.

The tough skipper could hardly boast to that audience that, after
City pressure had produced a modestly reflationary 'incentive Budget'
largely to benefit businessmen, he had to put on much more reflationary
sail in July 1971. He could boast that the total reflation of £1,900m.
was the greatest amount ever pumped into the British economy. But
it was uncomfortable to recall that previously he had been *against*
reflation until wage inflation was beaten. And that he had only been
converted when industrial stagnation, rising unemployment and growing unpopularity had threatened to sink the Tories.

Heath had been willing to change course because he had been
persuaded that, while accelerating, the British economy had a better
chance of winning the race within the EEC. He realized, of course, that
it might be necessary to devalue again, as the French had in 1959.
But by Conference time he knew, at least, that he was almost certain
to be in the EEC race. In March and April 1971 Heath had had more than
a qualm or two. The French had demanded too high an entry fee.
Heath had even gone to Bonn in April to ask Willy Brandt's support.
A whole series of alternative plans were contemplated, including an
emergency 'Summit'. But all this had proved unnecessary after the

Q

20–21 May Heath–Pompidou meeting at Chequers. After that every-thing was fairly plain sailing, although Britain's contribution would have to be heavy enough to slow it down, perhaps dangerously.

A capable skipper is supposed to be able to foresee difficulties. Therefore Heath was forgivable for telling his audience: 'I must tell you today that the change which I and others foresaw is now coming upon us. The United States, faced with deep-seated problems at home and abroad, is working . . . towards direct arrangements with the Soviet Union and with Communist China.' In fact, Heath had been furious in July, when he was caught by surprise when Dr Kissinger travelled to Peking to pave the way for Nixon's later visit. An hour's notice was hardly adequate for an ally that based its whole defence on the reliability of the United States. And the rapid shift of Nixon towards recognizing Peking and dumping Taiwan made Britain look like a 'running dog': Britain had been unable to raise its mission in Peking because it had insisted on retaining a consulate in Taiwan out of deference to American feelings. . . .

'Even more important, the United States is acting drastically to protect its own balance of payments and its own trading position against the erosions which they have suffered.' Heath had become more philo-sophical since the first rude shock of the Nixon–Connally 'new econo-mic policy' on 15 August. Since Heath had thought he and Nixon were on good terms and were keeping each other informed, the unexpected imposition of a ten per cent surcharge on imports into the US and the slamming shut of the American 'gold window' had been a trauma both to Britain's foreign trade and Heath's ego. Heath was vindictive towards John Connally, the Texan wounded when Kennedy was assas-sinated and now Secretary of the US Treasury. Connally was trying to bully Britain and others to revalue their currencies upwards. 'I knew they killed the wrong man in Dallas!' fumed Heath.

'Everyone agrees, of course, that the level of unemployment is too high – far too high,' Heath told his Brighton Tory audience. But he had only gone into high gear to tackle it the previous July, when the second quarter reports had shown another 200,000 added to the unem-ployed total, moving towards a catastrophic million the following winter. A government which cajoled the country into the EEC *without* tackling unemployment head-on was doomed. Heath had dropped his anti-inflation priority over the side and pumped a dramatic £1,300m. into the economy, with special provision for areas of heavy unemployment.[2]

Heath's marked preference for *pretending* he had not altered course was shown that same conference when a convivial colleague confirmed that Sir John Eden and Nicholas Ridley ought to be sacked for resisting the new tack. Sir John Eden had just sneered about the current 'obsession' with unemployment. This story, including the names of other 'duds' due to go over the side, dominated the news from an otherwise dull conference. Heath, 'hopping mad', demanded that Whitelaw investigate the source of the leak. He then put off the sackings for seven months.[3]

VOLTE FACE

Heath caused consternation when, on 18 October, he put out a statement giving Tory MPs a free vote at the end of the 21–28 October debate on EEC entry. People had taken seriously his statements in the Commons and to the press that EEC leaders were expecting his government to 'use its majority in the Commons to carry this through'.[4] He had also wanted to whip his supporters to make sure he had a majority made up of Tories, with any Labour or Liberal votes being extra. One of the reasons for putting off the entry debate from July to October had been the hope of talking round or 'twisting the arms' of enough dissident Tories. As late as 11 October he still said he would have a whipped vote: 'on a major issue such as this, the Government is absolutely entitled to ask for its support'.[5] By mid-October, however, thirty or so Tory MPs remained anti-entry. In the country as a whole half of the people were opposed to entry and only a third were in favour.[6]

Two days after he had secured a pro-entry vote of 8-to-1 from his tame Conference, Heath faced a moment of truth in his room at Brighton's Metropole Hotel. William Whitelaw and Chief Whip Francis Pym informed him that 30 to 35 Tory MPs would rebel against a three-line whip. On the other side, only 20 to 25 Labour Marketeers could be expected to cross over while the Tories maintained their three-line Whip. This meant that this key vote might only be carried by a majority of about 15, even with Liberal and Labour support.

Heath decided to put about and allow the Tories a free vote, to encourage between 60 and 90 Labour MPs to abandon their anti-Market ship. To avoid embarrassing the Labour Marketeers, this was announced not from the Tory Conference but from 10 Downing Street on 18 October. It aroused the consternation expected in Labour ranks. There, the reversal was recognized as a defeat for Heath, who had so long stuck to his original course. But Heath managed to carry off the propaganda honours, since the pro-Market press largely treated it as a generous concession.

The six-day debate on EEC entry – the longest since the war – had a number of dramatic curtain raisers. Jasper More, Vice-Chamberlain

of the Household, resigned in protest, as had another anti-entry
MP, Edward Taylor, in July. Anthony Barber announced the Cabinet
would resign if defeated in the vote. As Heath rose, the last of 176
speakers, the House and its galleries were brimful. 'After ten years of
negotiations, after many years of discussion in this House . . . the moment
for decision for Parliament has come . . . many millions of people right
across the world will rejoice that we have taken our rightful place in a
truly united Europe.'[7] He had to shout his last words, drowned in an
uproar as the voting began. Just before the vote was announced,
Francis Pym rushed in to tell him the good news of an unexpectedly
large majority of 112 – 356 for entry to 244 against. Roy Jenkins had
led 69 Labour MPs into the pro-entry lobby; there had been a further
20 Labour abstentions.[8] The free-vote strategy had worked. Heath
was transported with joy, even without the waving papers and Tory
cheers. He spent the next two hours in 'Annie's Bar', where MPs and
journalists meet, talking relaxedly of his hi-fi set at 10 Downing Street.

Over dinner at No. 10, on the evening of 3 November, Heath and six
of his Ministers – Barber, Whitelaw, Carr, Walker, Prior and Sir
Keith Joseph – discussed what further they could do to change the
economic climate. Despite hundreds of millions poured into the
economy, unemployment was still inching its way upward towards
the million mark to be achieved two months later. It was proving
difficult to persuade industrialists to step up their capital investments,
although Barber had told the Institute of Directors that day the economy
was expanding at the rate of 4 to 4·5 per cent.

Convinced that businessmen could respond to exhortation and
flattery, Heath invited eight leading industrialists to Chequers on 4
December. He urged them to step up their expansion so that when
Britain joined the EEC they would be going flat-out. He then marched
them into the music room and exposed them to Bruckner.[9]

DOWN FROM THE MUSICAL SUMMIT

Heath could be forgiven because he was still descending from his
musical summit. This had occurred on 25 November when he had
conducted the London Symphony Orchestra in Elgar's 'Cockaigne
Overture'. Although invited as a gifted amateur who had been chairman of the LSO Trust for seven years, he had been a pleasant surprise
to the LSO at his first rehearsal, where the professionals applauded
him at the end, knowing they had played under worse professionals.
On the night the whole musical Establishment – and most of Special
Branch – was in the audience, both appreciating that it is not every night

that a Prime Minister turns conductor. At the end there was virtually unanimous praise, not least for his self-confidence.[10]

Like a Bavarian monarch, Heath lightened his official duties with music. When the choir of St Margaret's, Westminster, performed madrigals for the visiting Australian Prime Minister, it turned out this had been the sixth or seventh time they had performed at No. 10.

CLOSER TO FRANCE, COOLER TO USA

Heath went so far out of his way to make pleasant the visit of the French Foreign Minister, M. Maurice Schumann, in November that it fed Bonn's growing suspicions of an Anglo-French 'axis' to replace Adenauer's Bonn-Paris 'axis'. Heath met French desires about costing on the 'Concorde'. As a final 'sweetener' it was proposed that Her Majesty would again visit France on a state visit in 1972.[11]

As the Indo-Pakistan conflict began at the end of November, Anglo-American relations deteriorated sharply. Heath sided with the Indians, having improved relations with Mrs Gandhi during her London visit after the coolness of the Wilson era. In contrast, under Dr Kissinger's influence, Washington was very *anti*-Indian, partly because India was seen as an extension of Soviet power, partly because of intelligence reports that India would attack West Pakistan as well as free 'Bangladesh', and partly to 'sweeten' the Chinese. The Foreign Office urged the State Department to forgo its pro-Pakistan 'tilt'. At Heath's instructions, Whitehall briefings became increasingly hostile to US intervention on Pakistan's side. Finally, Nixon made a 90-minute telephone call to Heath on 25 November, setting up a conference in Bermuda on 20–21 December.[12]

Heath paid Nixon back for his consultation failures in July and August by 'telegraphing his punches' in unprecedented fashion. Heath was bitter about failures of consultation and the American 'bungling' of the Indo-Pakistan conflict, which would strengthen the Soviet position in the Indian Ocean. Although he knew Nixon was going to Peking, he let him know through his briefings, of the *Daily Telegraph* and *Sunday Telegraph* in particular, that he should 'sup with a long spoon' with Chou En-lai. Heath hoped that the one-sided decisions of 15 August would lead to the existing dollar-dominated monetary system being replaced by one independent of the dollar. Once Britain was in the EEC, Western Europe would gradually assume a larger part of the Atlantic defence burden. But the West could only be defended if North America and Western Europe acted in unity.[13] Heath treated much more correctly M. Pompidou, who was to see the President first, in the Azores. The Heath–Pompidou consultations, kept secret, enabled them to walk so closely in step that, according to one high French official, 'it would not really have made much difference which of them had spoken first'.[14]

In fact, the Heath–Nixon meeting was not as chilly as Heath's advance briefings led people to expect. The world monetary crisis caused by the US actions of 15 August had been partly resolved in the Washington meeting of the Group of Ten, enabling the US to withdraw the 10 per cent surcharge on the eve of the Nixon–Heath meeting. Nixon freely admitted that such surprises were unpleasant for allies, and promised to do better. Heath did not accept his insistence that only the movement of a US naval task force into the vicinity had deterred the Indians from invading West Pakistan. Nixon was presumably as sceptical about Heath's promise to make Western Europe a more cohesive ally.

Heath returned to enjoy the advantages of having been pro-Bangladesh. When Shaikh Mujibur Rahman was freed in January 1972, he turned up first in London, where he thanked Heath for his attempts to save his life. Heath promised him eventual recognition, when it could be achieved collectively, and put an RAF 'Comet' at his disposal for his flight home.[15] At least the leader of Bangladesh would not think that only the Russians were friendly.

MINTOFF STANDOFF

Shaikh Mujibur was a pleasant contrast to the difficulties Heath had been having with another leftwing nationalist, Dom Mintoff of Malta. Almost within hours of winning a one-seat majority in June 1971, Mintoff had been in touch, demanding a much higher rent for the facilities Britain had long enjoyed in Malta and now shared with its NATO allies. Heath had thought their mid-September meeting at Chequers had gone well. An agreement had been made to pay £4·75m. immediately for six months from 30 September 1971, with some chance of supplementary payments to be decided by the end of the year. By November Mintoff was demanding that Britain surrender facilities and land but employ more Maltese. Finally, on Christmas Eve, Mintoff sent an ultimatum: all troops out by 31 December.

Heath's 29 December message to Mintoff had been curt: 'we [are] prepared to continue to talk in a genuine attempt to seek a basis for a new agreement. . . . But . . . we will not, of course, seek to keep our forces on the island against the wishes of the Malta Government. In the light of your latest message, we shall undertake preparations for withdrawal straight away. . . .'[16] Heath was as good as his word, ordering the accumulated stores of scores of years shipped off the island which had suffered so from its alliance with Britain in the Second World War.

Heath then became very angry when attempts by the US and NATO to avoid a break that might open Malta to Soviet penetration, appeared to be queering his pitch. On 10 January, Dr Joseph Luns paid a secret visit to Chequers to reassure Heath.[17] The day before, Archbishop Gonzi of Malta had turned up there as an intermediary to explain that Mintoff was only blackmailing Britain because Malta was flat broke. Finally the differences were patched up. But not before all of Britain's NATO allies had developed a new respect for Heath's no-nonsense qualities.

It seemed to be a period for troublesome nationalists. In January 1972 the Pearce Commission began operating in Rhodesia, to discover whether the deal arranged between Sir Alec Douglas-Home and Ian Smith was widely acceptable to the people of Rhodesia, particularly the ninety-two per cent of black Africans who had not been parties to the talks. Heath had come into office with new Anglo-Rhodesian talks as a key part of his plans. He was sure that something could be arranged, once Wilson with his 'double-dealing' efforts to trifurcate the Tories was out of the way. But almost as soon as the Pearce Commission began operating, it became clear that politically-interested Africans either did not like the deal negotiated or that they would not trust the Smith regime to carry out those parts of it favourable to black Africans. The nettled Smith regime soon made it difficult for the Heath Government by detaining Garfield Todd, the liberal former Prime Minister of Rhodesia. Heath said that the Government could make requests but could not impose their acceptance on Smith. Heath seemed less disturbed than many expected at this impending setback to a policy he had long emphasized. It was little appreciated that for Heath the main importance of the negotiations with Smith was to remove this issue as a constant threat to Tory unity. If Smith could not 'deliver the goods' the pro-Smith Tories on the right would no longer have a leg to stand on and Tory eyes could turn away from Southern Africa.

FOCUS ON BRUSSELS

Heath had hoped to end 1971 with a double 'bang', by flying from Nixon in Bermuda to Brussels to sign the Treaty of Accession to the EEC before Christmas. But, despite his personal letters to the Norwegian Prime Minister, the final issue of fisheries rights was not settled until 12

December. It was not until 17 December that it was decided to stage the signing on 22 January 1972.

From the outset Heath determined to make a big occasion of it, travelling personally to sign it along with Sir Alec and Geoffrey Rippon and veteran Marketeers of all parties, with a big party to follow. Unfortunately for Heath, he had to have a further debate, on the Treaty of Accession, on 10 January 1972. There he only had a majority of 20 – 296 to 276 – on the Government's procedure of only providing the full texts *after* accession.

But Heath dismissed this narrow squeak on which both sides were whipped as 'a bogus thing, a phoney thing'. He preferred the vote of 28 October. 'On that we had a majority of 112. It was a free vote on our side. . . . It is what Parliament really thinks about coming into the Community.'[18] (In February the majority fell to eight.)

In fact, his signature at Brussels on 22 January was curiously anti-climactic. The only personal drama came when a neurotic German woman threw ink over him as he entered Egmont Palace – in protest against plans to redevelop the Covent Garden area! When Heath arrived an hour late in an ill-fitting replacement suit, it turned out to be a boring occasion as he read a speech which could have been composed by a Foreign Office computer. But he signed the accession documents for the Rome Treaty, joining the Coal and Steel Community and Euratom, all in eight languages.[19] Heath became human again that evening when he was interviewed for the following Monday's BBC-TV 'Panorama' programme in the bar of the Metropole Hotel. He made it clear that the larger EEC he envisaged would be giving the USA a run for its money. 'I never felt they really understood what would happen when it was enlarged.'[20] Poor George Ball!

BACK TO 'REALITIES'

Heath had a rude welcome when he returned to the Commons on 24 January. Wilson's sarcasm was bitter: 'Back to reality – the reality of the Government's attainment of one million unemployed.' Wilson described Heath as the 'first dole-queue millionaire to cross the Channel since Neville Chamberlain'. Heath replied that his government's spending was beginning to show results but that it would take time to put the situation in reverse. He did take credit for having almost halved wage settlements; a year before they had run at fourteen to fifteen per cent; now they were down to seven to eight per cent.[21]

Heath had his rudest awakening yet to come. It was his capitulation to the National Union of Miners, giving them increases of £5–6 a week after a five-week strike which brought the whole country close to a dead stop. When the miners went out on their first national strike since 1926 on 9 January 1972, they were virtually ignored. Poor coal sales the previous year had left plenty of coal above-ground. The power stations using coal said they had eight weeks' supply. Nobody in authority in the Government thought the miners could last that long. The Prime Minister, although born a few miles from the Kent coalfield, had no idea of the normal solidarity of the miners' caste, nor their special indignation about having been overtaken as the 'aristocracy of labour' in the wage race. The Government were even more culpable in accepting the power stations' slack estimate of their reserves. Even their coal reserves were often not immediately to hand and could be hit by a sympathetic response to miners' pickets. And other supplies needed to run a power station – lighting oil and hydrogen particularly – were more vulnerable still. The picketing began sporadically as a grassroots activity; initially, men from the Kent coalfields looked no further than Brighton or Maidstone; some time later they took over picketing coal movements in London. By the end of January men from other unions – particularly lorry drivers – began to respond; three stations were halted, one with three weeks' supply of coal still in its bunkers. By 31 January the Generating Board realized that danger was threatening, but it was unable to persuade the Cabinet's Emergency Committee, headed by Reginald Maudling. This was partly because power cuts were averted temporarily by the onset of warm weather. On 3 February John Davies asked the Cabinet to declare a state of emergency and impose rationing. But the bulk of the Cabinet was opposed to it, preferring to play down the danger to improve chances of negotiating with the miners (as well as the power workers, also on the verge of a strike). But when negotiations were attempted, Coal Board chairman Derek Ezra offered a fifth of the increase that NUM president Joe Gormley demanded. The state of emergency came into effect on 10 February, with the first power cuts being forced on the Generating Board and unprepared industry and the public. There was immediate chaos in every factory and home as drastic cuts meant that virtually everyone was without electricity for half the time. With coal running out, and more and more stations closing down, the country was grinding to a halt.

The Cabinet, in effect, capitulated by setting up a Court of Inquiry under Lord Wilberforce. He could move quickly. And he had shown in his recommendations for the electricity workers a year before that he had a realistic approach to the value of workers in a strategic industry. He produced a report which offered the miners as a 'special case' increases of £5–6 compared with the £4–7 they had originally demanded. Realizing they had won, the miners' leaders tried to squeeze out a few further advantages while they had the Government crying 'uncle!' They asked Robert Carr for an additional £1 a week on top. Carr took it to the Cabinet, which turned it down and made lots of standby 'preparations'; to invoke a compulsory secret ballot of the 280,000 miners, to import foreign coal, to use troops to prevent picketing; everything in fact short of using bayonets to mine coal.

It was only at this last moment that Heath came into the picture. He had so loathed seeing Wilson on the TV and in the press having strike leaders in for a beer and sandwiches at No. 10 that even in this grave emergency he had remained in the background except for a portentous warning to Liverpool Tories that probably increased public sympathy for the miners. Heath finally came into it because Gormley and Lawrence Daly insisted on seeing him after Carr turned down their request for a further £1 a week. 'We had to go to the top of the tree before deciding to go round it,' explained Gormley. Heath was not welcoming when they arrived at No. 10. 'It was not "Smiling Ted" by any means,' said Gormley later. 'We didn't see much of his teeth at all that night. I wouldn't say he was humiliated by the settlement, but he was very subdued.' However weak his position, Heath refused to retreat from the Cabinet decision to reject a further £1. 'We pushed Heath, we pushed him like hell, but he wouldn't budge. We were facing a united Cabinet decision. In the end I realized there was not a cat in hell's chance of getting the extra £1 we were demanding.'[22] Heath was entitled to his small face-savers, for he had contributed more to the realization of working-class power in a few weeks than the syndicalists had done in as many decades.[23]

RECOIL FROM LONDONDERRY

The difficulty with being a Prime Minister is that the job must often seem like that of a man having to juggle hand grenades without knowing whether any of them has had its pin pulled. This must have been Heath's feeling on 30 January 1972 when, as the miners' strike was moving towards its conclusion, British soldiers in Londonderry killed 13 civilians in controversial circumstances. This 'Bloody Sunday' suddenly transformed British troops in Northern Ireland into the traditional villains of Irish history. It also brought tumbling the slow-moving initiative that Heath and his Ministers had long been trying to get off the ground.

Heath had succeeded, in the previous September, in bringing the

Prime Ministers of the Republic and Northern Ireland together for the first time in fifty years, at Chequers.

A new crescendo of IRA attacks had started in February 1971. Heath had resisted the demands of the Ulster Unionist Prime Minister, Major James Chichester-Clark, for heavy reinforcements to be stationed in the heart of the Catholic slums. When he was refused Chichester-Clark resigned. 'I didn't realize it was as critical as that,' Heath said over the telephone. 'Why on earth didn't you tell me?' 'Short of leaping on the Cabinet table at No. 10, I thought I could hardly have made it clearer.'[24] When Brian Faulkner succeeded Chichester-Clark, Heath had come to the end of the road so far as serviceable moderate-right Ulster Unionists were concerned. Faulkner could be nudged, but could not be pushed too hard, because he had to drag with him a sectarian party mired in the Orange politics of Irish history. Despite this, Heath and Maudling thought they were making moderate progress and planning more when 'Bloody Sunday' – 30 January 1972 – erased the impact of all the hard-won concessions on the Catholics. 'Bloody Sunday' made impossible any further military pacification, it left only a political initiative as a possibility.

Heath demanded of the Cabinet Committee dealing with Ulster a policy 'breakthrough' which would win back the Catholics. A package began being put together on what would meet the demands of the moderate-Republican forces led by Gerry Fitt and the SDLP. This started out with the dismantling of internment which the Heath Cabinet had 'bought' from Faulkner the previous August as the only answer to the mounting tide of IRA bomb attacks. It included the suspension of Unionist-dominated Stormont, and the transfer of all security responsibility from the sectarian incompetents in Ulster to London. If Brian Faulkner would not 'buy' this package, it would mean the dispatch of a Minister to Northern Ireland to run the province for a year at least. The Cabinet Committee – chaired by Heath, but including Maudling, Carrington, Sir Alec and Willie Whitelaw – decided Whitelaw was the best able to cajole the Catholics back into the fold, when Faulkner rejected the proposals.[25]

The announcement that William Whitelaw was taking over direct rule of Northern Ireland and that the Stormont was being suspended after fifty-one years exploded like a political blockbuster on the Irish scene when announced by Heath on 24 March. For the first time there appeared to be a small glimmer at the end of the Irish tunnel as Whitelaw started winding down internment. By the end of May 1972, a bare two months later, an open peace movement began baiting the IRA in Londonderry and the official IRA called for a truce, knowing that this was what its sympathizers were demanding. By the end of June 1972 the Provisionals had also agreed a ceasefire. In Westminster Heath was applauded by Labour for doing what the Wilson government had contemplated but had not quite dared to do.

EATING HUMBLE REGIONAL PIE

Heath's Labour opponents could be forgiven for forcing his man John Davies to eat humble pie on the 23 May 1972 second reading of the Industry Bill. It was one of the most dramatic reversals to which Heath had agreed, the throwing overboard of most of Heath's objections to state intervention to help industry, particularly in the regions. Anthony Wedgwood Benn, the former Labour Technology Minister, so often under attack by Heath for his interfering largesse, enjoyed himself pointing out that Heath's projected spending of £650m. was over four times larger than the £150m. allotted the much-abused IRC. Benn was unkind enough to point out that the Government were taking powers under the Industry Bill that they had dismantled with the IRC. Benn's former junior Minister, Edmund Dell, summarized it: 'Our pragmatic Prime Minister, having marched his troops up the hill to *laissez-faire* and disengagement, is marching them down to selective intervention on a massive scale.'[26]

There was something about Heath's unswerving determination to reach his targets which provoked Labour opponents into humour at his expense. On 24 May 1972 it was announced that the new Bexley–Sidcup Conservative Executive had agreed unanimously to invite Heath to become their candidate at the next election. Although Heath had ridiculed Wilson for not daring to bring in the boundary reforms, when he had himself brought them in, they had deprived him of his richest Tory areas, making what remained of his seat a 'Labour marginal'. He coveted Bexley–Sidcup, although he had offers from cushier Tory seats, because he had invested a quarter of a century in this lower middle-class area. Unfortunately, Dame Patricia Hornsby-Smith, seventy per cent of whose old Chislehurst seat was absorbed into Bexley–Sidcup, had a greater claim. Suddenly, Dame Pat stepped down amidst promises she would be found another seat, and Bexley–Sidcup went to Heath. With malicious wit, Labour MP Andrew Faulds wrote to *The Times* and *Guardian* of 25 May the brief letter: 'Once upon a time in Bexley a gentleman would have offered his seat to a lady who was standing.'

Heath was sure he would have the last laugh at the end of the decade beginning in January 1973, during which he would help put Britain at the head of a West European Super-power able to stare down either the Americans *or* the Russians.

NOTES

INTRODUCTION HEATH AND THE HEATHMEN

1. *New Statesman*, 16 October 1971   2. BBC-TVI 'Panorama', 24 January 1972

CHAPTER 1 THE BUTTONED-UP PRIME MINISTER

1. Patrick Gordon Walker, *The Cabinet*, revised edition, Collins/Fontana, London, 1972, p. 107

CHAPTER 2 MOTHER'S PRIDE

1. Conservative Party Conference, Margate, 10 October 1953, *Report*, pp. 116–17   2. Marian Evans, *Ted Heath*, Kimber, London, 1970, pp. 42–4 3. *Daily Express*, 11 March 1963   4. Evans, op. cit., p. 45   5. Kenneth Harris interview, *Observer*, 23 January 1966   6. Evans, op. cit., p. 48 7. ibid.   8. George Hutchinson, *Edward Heath*, Longman, London, 1970, p. 7   9. Bryan Magee (musical) interview, BBC-TV2 'Omnibus', July 1970, transcript p. 3   10. Evans, op. cit., p. 55   11. *Sunday Telegraph*, 6 February 1966   12. Anthony Sampson, *The New Anatomy of Britain*, Hodder & Stoughton, London, 1971, p. 84   13. Evans, op. cit., p. 60   14. *Sunday Express*, 15 August 1965   15. Ibid.   16. *Evening Standard*, 27 July 1965   17. Evans, op. cit., p. 65   18. *Observer*, 16 January 1966   19. Magee (musical) interview, p. 3   20. Evans, op. cit., p. 49   21. Hutchinson, op. cit., p. 14   22. Evans, op. cit., p. 52 23. ibid.   24. Hutchinson, op. cit., p. 14   25. *Evening Standard*, 27 July 1965   26. Hutchinson, op. cit., pp. 12–13   27. *Sunday Express*, 15 August 1965   28. ibid.

CHAPTER 3 THE OPEN DOORS OF BALLIOL

1. *Observer*, 23 January 1966   2. Drusilla Scott, *A. D. Lindsay, Master of Balliol*, Blackwells, 1971, *passim*   3. *Observer*, 23 January 1966 4. Magee (musical) interview, pp. 4–5   5. Bryan Magee (political) interview, ATV 'This Week', 20 March 1969, transcript p. 4   6. Magee (musical) interview, p. 5   7. *Isis*, 25 January 1939   8. Magee (musical) interview, pp. 7–8   9. *Observer*, 23 January 1966   10. *Guardian*, 24 February 1959 11. *Isis*, 1 March 1936   12. *Isis*, 25 January 1939   13. *Isis*, 25 November 1936   14. *Isis*, 20 January 1937   15. *Isis*, 24 February 1937 16. *Isis*, 5 May 1937   17. Hutchinson, op. cit., p. 23   18. Evans, op. cit., pp. 3, 66   19. *Isis*, 10 November 1937   20. Hutchinson, op. cit., p. 34   21. ibid., pp. 23–5   22. William L. Shirer, *The Rise and Fall of the Third Reich*, Secker & Warburg, London, 1960, pp. 442–7   23. *Isis*, 8 June 1938   24. Hutchinson, op. cit., p. 26   25. *Isis*, 25 January 1939 26. ibid.   27. *The Times*, 23 October 1938   28. *Isis*, 19 October 1938 29. Hutchinson, op. cit., p. 30   30. *Isis*, 23 November 1938 31. Hutchinson, op. cit., p. 34   32. *Isis*, 8 March 1939   33. *Observer*, 18 October 1959   34. Drusilla Scott, op. cit., p. 122   35. Hutchinson,

op. cit., p. 36   36. Magee, musical interview, pp. 5–6   37. Hutchinson, op. cit., pp. 39–40   38. *Observer*, 23 January 1966

CHAPTER 4 THE RUNGS TO MASTER GUNNER

1. *Evening News*, 26 May 1966   2. Evans, op. cit., p. 71   3. Conservative Party Conference, Margate, 10 October 1953, *Report*, p. 116 4. Hutchinson, op. cit., p. 41   5. ibid., p. 42   6. *Daily Express*, 4 June 1969   7. Public Records Office, *War Diaries*, 1943, 107 HAA, WO 166/7475, HF 323/3   8. ibid.   9. *War Diaries*, 1944, 107 HAA, WO 171/1152 10. ibid.   11. ibid.   12. ibid.   13. Hutchinson, op. cit., pp. 42–4 14. ibid., pp. 44–5   15. *Hansard*, 23 October 1967, 751/1361   16. *War Diaries*, 1945, 107 HAA, WO 171/4914   17. ibid.   18. *Bexleyheath Observer*, 30 January 1948   19. *War Diaries*, 1945

CHAPTER 5 THE PURSUITS OF PEACE

1. *Bex. Observer*, 14 November 1947   2. *Nova*, whose March 1972 issue was destroyed because a computer-selected wife was still married to a Pakistani   3. Evans, op. cit., p. 9   4. Colin Cross and Simone French, *Sunday Express*, 22 August 1965; Hutchinson, op. cit., p. 46   5. ibid., pp. 50–1   6. *Bex. Observer*, 14 November 1947   7. Hutchinson, op. cit., pp. 54–5   8. *Sunday Express*, 22 August 1965   9. Evans, op. cit., pp. 26–7   10. *Bex. Observer*, 7 November 1947   11. *Bex. Observer*, *Kentish Independent*, 14 November 1947   12. Evans, op. cit., p. 29 13. Ian Harvey, *To Fall Like Lucifer*, Sidgwick & Jackson, London 1971, pp. 66, 119   14. *The Times*, 10 February 1950   15. *Sunday Express*, 22 August 1965   16. Hutchinson, op. cit., pp. 23–5   17. ibid., p. 66 18. *Bex. Observer*, 28 November 1947   19. *Bex. Observer*, 3, 24 September 1948   20. *Bex. Observer*, 10 December 1948   21. *Bex. Observer*, 26 August 1949   22. *Bex. Observer*, 10 September 1948   23. *Bex. Observer*, 24 September 1948   24. *Bex. Observer*, 19 November 1948   25. *Bex. Observer*, 26 December 1947   26. *Bex. Observer*, 16 January 1948 27. *Erith Observer*, 3 December 1948   28. *East Kent Times*, 26 January 1949 29. *Bex. Observer*, 30 September 1949   30. *Bex. Observer*, 26 December 1947 31. *Bex. Observer*, *Erith Observer*, 30 January 1948   32. *Bex. Observer*, 30 September 1949   33. *Bex. Observer*, 9 December 1949   34. Evans, op. cit., p. 31   35. *Bex. Observer*, 14 November 1947   36. *Bex. Observer*, 23 January 1948   37. *Bex. Observer*, 4 November 1949   38. *Bex. Observer*, 27 January 1950   39. ibid.   40. *Erith Observer*, 25 March 1949 41. *Bex. Observer*, 4 November 1949   42. *Horley Advertiser*, 7 October 1949   43. *Bex. Observer*, 3 February 1950   44. *Bex. Observer*, 24 February 1950   45. ibid.   46. ibid.   47. *Bex. Observer*, 3 March 1950

CHAPTER 6 BEING NOTICED IN THE CLASS OF '50

1. Edward Heath, 'First Impressions of a New Member', *Britain Today*, July 1950   2. *Bex. Observer*, 3 March 1950   3. *Bex. Observer*, 24 February 1950   4. Edward Heath, op. cit.   5. ibid.   6. *Bex. Observer*, 24 March 1950   7. ibid.   8. Hutchinson, op. cit., pp. 69–70 9. Edward Heath, op. cit.   10. Evans, op. cit., p. 91   11. Edward Heath, op. cit.   12. *Bex. Observer*, 31 March 1950   13. R. R. James, editor, *Chips: The Diaries of Sir Henry Channon*, Weidenfeld & Nicolson, London, 1967, p. 443   14. *Bex. Observer*, 7 April 1950   15. ibid.   16. *Bex. Observer*, 31 March 1950   17. *Bex. Observer*, 7 April 1950   18. *Bex. Observer*, 21 April 1950   19. *Bex. Observer*, 12 May 1950

20. Hutchinson, op. cit., p. 70   21. ibid.; Evans, op. cit., p. 36
22. *Bex. Observer*, 21 April 1950   23. Edward Heath, op. cit.   24. *Bex.
Observer*, 5 May 1950   25. *Bex. Observer*, 6 October 1950   26. *Hansard*,
30 June 1950, 476/1959–64   27. Harold Macmillan, *Tides of Fortune*,
Macmillan, London, 1969, p. 197   28. *Bex. Observer*, 28 July 1950
29. Andrew Roth, *Can Parliament Decide ?*, Macdonald, London, 1971,
p. 35   30. Evans, op. cit., p. 76   31. *Bex. Observer*, 15 December 1950
32. *Daily Telegraph*, 16 December 1971; *Evening Standard*, 14 January 1972
33. *Bex. Observer*, 16 February 1951   34. ibid.   35. *Hansard*, 26 April
1951, 487/705   36. ibid.   37. *Hansard*, 10 May 1951, 487/2308–10
38. Evans, op. cit., p. 90   39. *Bex. Observer*, 29 June, 6 July 1951
40. Hutchinson, op. cit., pp. 77–8   41. Evans, op. cit., pp. 74–8
42. *Bex. Observer*, 27 April 1951   43. *Bex. Observer*, 19 October 1961

CHAPTER 7   PRAETORIAN MONK

1. Hutchinson, op. cit., pp. 79–80   2. BBC-TVI 'Panorama', 11 October
1967   3. *Bex. Observer*, 21 December 1951   4. Ian Gilmour, *The
Body Politic*, Hutchinson, London, 1969, p. 266   5. Evans, op. cit., p. 90
6. *Bex. Observer*, 6 June 1952   7. *Bex. Observer*, 18 July 1952
8. *Bex. Observer*, 14 December 1951   9. *Bex. Observer*, 25 January 1952
10. *Bex. Observer*, 1 February 1952   11. *Bex. Observer*, 22 February
1952   12. *Bex. Observer*, 13 May 1952   13. *Bex. Observer*, 19 September
1952   14. *Bex. Observer*, 30 May 1952   15. *Observer*, 15 February; *The
Economist*, 21 February 1953   16. *News Chronicle*, 18 February; *New
Statesman*, 28 February 1953   17. *Bex. Observer*, 25 January 1952
18. *Bex. Observer*, 2 January 1952   19. *Bex. Observer*, 31 July 1953
20. *Bex. Observer*, 31 July, 23 October 1953   21. Conservative Party
Conference, Margate, 10 October 1953, *Report*, pp. 116–17   22. *The
Economist*, 9 December 1953   23. *Hansard*, 5 November 1953, 520/342–9,
370–9   24. *Guardian*, 17 December 1953   25. *Star*, 9 November; *Bex.
Observer*, 13 November 1953   26. Evans, op. cit., pp. 83–5   27. ibid.
pp. 87–8   28. *Bex. Observer*, 26 March 1954   29. ibid.   30. *Bex.
Observer*, 15 October 1954   31. ibid.   32. ibid.   33. ibid.   34. *Bex.
Observer*, 13 May; *Daily Telegraph*, 16 May 1955   35. *Reynolds News*,
15 May 1955   36. *Bex. Observer*, 3 June 1955   37. Lord Kilmuir,
Political Adventure, Weidenfeld & Nicolson, London, 1962, p. 44

CHAPTER 8   EDEN'S SCOURGE

1. *The Economist*, 17 October 1959   2. ATV interview, 22 June 1958
3. Lord Avon, *Full Circle*, Casssell, London, 1960, p. 549   4. Patrick
Gordon Walker, *The Cabinet*, Cape, London, 1970, p. 105   5. Harold
Macmillan, *Riding the Storm*, Macmillan, London, 1971, pp. 12–15
6. *News Chronicle*, 26 January 1956   7. ATV interview, ibid.   8. Evans,
op. cit., pp. 90–1   9. *The Economist*, 7 July 1956   10. ibid.
11. *Yorkshire Post*, 21 July; *Hansard*, 23 July 1956, 557/37–47   12. Lord
Avon, op. cit., p. 424   13. *Hansard*, 27 July 1956, 557/777–8
14. Geoffrey McDermott, *The Eden Legacy*, Frewin, London, 1969, pp. 133–60
15. *News Chronicle*, 7 September 1956   16. Lord Avon, op. cit., pp. 481–2
17. *Hansard*, 12 September 1956, 558/2–15   18. *Bex. Observer*,
5 October 1956   19. *Reynolds News*. 21 June 1959 (from a letter to a friend,
who showed it to Randolph Churchill)   20. *Daily Express*, 7 December 1956
21. *Observer*, 4 November 1956   22. ibid.   23. *News Chronicle*, *Guardian*,
Daily Express, 5 November 1956   24. *Star*, 23 November 1956
25. *New York Times*, 22 November 1956   26. *Daily Telegraph*, 23 November;

Sunday Times, 25 November 1956 (Curiously enough, Macmillan did not find space for this famous speech in his enormously long account of that time: *Riding The Storm*)   27. *The Times*, 4 December 1956
28. *Observer*, 9 December 1956   29. *The Times, Guardian*, 7 December; *Observer*, 9 December 1956

CHAPTER 9   ON MACMILLAN'S CHAMPAGNE TRAIL

1. Harold Macmillan, op. cit., 1971, pp. 184–5   2. Ian Gilmour, op. cit., p. 76   3. Andrew Roth, *Enoch Powell: Tory Tribune*, Macdonald, London, 1970, p. 159   4. Lord Butler, *The Art of the Possible*, Hamish Hamilton, London, 1971, pp. 195–6   5. *New York Times*, 12 January 1957   6. Harold Macmillan, op. cit., 1971, p. 186   7. *Daily Express*, 2 February 1957   8. Harold Macmillan, op. cit., 1971, p. 201
9. ibid., p. 210   10. *Daily Telegraph*, 6 March 1957   11. Harold Macmillan, op. cit., 1971, p. 249   12. ibid., p. 345   13. ibid., pp. 249–62; *Hansard*, 1 April 1957, 568/37–68; *Daily Mail*, 23 March; *Sunday Times*, 1 December 1957   14. Harold Macmillan, op. cit., 1971, p. 235
15. *News Chronicle*, 4 April 1957   16. *Daily Express*, 18 April 1957
17. *Evening News*, 10 May 1957   18. *Daily Express*, 10, 11 May; *Daily Telegraph*, 11 May 1957   19. *Daily Telegraph*, 31 May 1957   20. *Bex. Observer*, 19 April; 3, 17, 31 May 1957   21. Harold Macmillan, op. cit., 1971, p. 431   22. *Daily Express*, 9 July 1957   23. *Guardian*, 5 July 1957   24. *Sunday Times*, 21 July 1957   25. *Observer*, 28 July 1957
26. *Star*, 17 August 1957   27. *Daily Mail*, 17 September 1957
28. *Daily Express*, 20 September 1957   29. Dwight D. Eisenhower, *White House Years*: vol. 2, *Waging Peace*, 1956–61, Doubleday, New York, 1966, Heinemann, London, 1966, p. 473; Harold Macmillan, op. cit., 1971, p. 307   30. *News Chronicle*, 1 October 1957   31. ibid.   32. Harold Macmillan, op. cit., 1971, p. 418   33. *News Chronicle*, 28 October 1957
34. *New Statesman*, 23 November 1957   35. Eisenhower, op. cit., p. 232; Harold Macmillan, op. cit., 1971, pp. 335–41   36. ibid., pp. 460–1
37. ibid., pp. 368–9   38. ibid., 1971, p. 373   39. *Daily Telegraph*, 8 January; *News Chronicle*, 13 January; *The Times*, 20 January 1958
40. Harold Macmillan, op. cit., 1971, pp. 373–4   41. ibid., p. 409
42. ibid., p. 411   43. *Evening Standard*, 17 February 1958   44. *News Chronicle, Daily Telegraph, Western Mail*, 14 March 1958   45. *Reynolds News, Sunday Express*, 16 March; *Sunday Times*, 23 March 1958
46. *Daily Telegraph*, 14 March 1958   47. *News Chronicle*, 26 February 1958
48. Harold Macmillan, op. cit., 1971, pp. 443–50   49. ibid., p. 506
50. ibid., p. 520   51. ibid., pp. 520–1   52. *News Chronicle*, 22 July; *The Times*, 24 August 1958   53. *The Times*, 6 October 1958   54. *News Chronicle*, 7 November 1958   55. *Sunday Times*, 2 November 1958
56. Ian Harvey, op. cit., pp. 101–11   57. *Bex. Observer*, 28 February 1958
58. *Bex. Observer*, 13 February 1959   59. ibid.   60. Harold Macmillan, op. cit., 1971, pp. 634–5   61. ibid., p. 64   62. *Daily Express*, 20, 23 April; *Birmingham Post*, 20 April; *Daily Telegraph*, 21 April 1959
63. *Daily Mail*, 13 May 1959   64. *Daily Mail*, 11 May 1959   65. *Daily Mail*, 20 April 1959   66. Lord Butler, op. cit., pp. 197–8   67. *Daily Express*, 9 September 1959   68. *Bex. Observer*, 2 October 1959
69. *Bex. Observer*, 2, 16 October; *Daily Telegraph*, 8 October 1969
70. *DailyTelegraph*, 15 October 1959

CHAPTER 10   BRIEFLY IN LABOUR

1. *Sheffield Telegraph*, 16 October 1959   2. *John Bull*, 30 January 1960

3. *Sunday Times*, 22 November 1959   4. *Daily Express*, 17 November 1959   5. *Hansard*, 2 November 1959   6. *Evening News*, 18 November 1959   7. *Sunday Express*, 20 December 1959   8. *Daily Mail, Daily Telegraph*, 23 December 1959   9. *Daily Telegraph, Guardian*, 30 November 1959   10. *The Times, Daily Telegraph*, 10 December 1959   11. *Newcastle Journal*, 28 November, 4, 5 December; *Liverpool Daily Post, Financial Times*, 5 December 1959   12. *Evening Standard*, 8 February 1960   13. *News Chronicle*, 13 February 1960   14. *The Times*, 4 January 1960   15. *The Director*, March 1960, cited *Daily Telegraph*, 2 March 1960   16. *Reynolds News*, 6 March; *Daily Mail*, 8 March 1960   17. *The Economist*, April 1960   18. *Hansard*, 30 March 1960, 620/1343–5, 1388–9   19. *Sunday Express*, 13 November 1960   20. *Daily Telegraph*, 26 January; *Daily Herald*, 1 February 1960   21. *The Times*, 17, 18 March 1960   22. *Yorkshire Post*, 25 March 1960   23. *Daily Telegraph*, 25 March 1960   24. *Daily Express*, 28 April 1960   25. *Hansard*, 11 May 1960, 623/495–9   26. *Daily Mail*, 28 June 1960   27. *The Times*, 2 June; *Daily Worker*, 23 July 1960   28. *Daily Mail*, 28 July 1960   29. *Hansard*, 25 July 1960, 627/1078–80   30. *Guardian, Financial Times*, 28 July 1960   31. Andrew Roth, op. cit., 1971, pp. 53–4   32. Lord Butler, op. cit., p. 231   33. *Western Mail*, 23 May 1960   34. *The Economist*, 23 July 1960   35. *Daily Mirror*, 25 July 1960   36. *Hansard*, 28 July 1960, 627/1973–83   37. *The Times*, 28 July 1960   38. *Sunday Times*, 31 July 1960

CHAPTER II   THE DOUBLY-HOBBLED 'MR EUROPE'

1. *Hansard*, 4 November 1960, 629/517–27   2. *Star*, 11 November 1960   3. *The Times, Daily Telegraph*, 13 August 1960   4. *Daily Telegraph*, 28 July 1960   5. *Hansard*, 18 May 1961, 640/1673   6. *Daily Telegraph*, 20 September 1960   7. *Daily Express*, 14 November 1962   8. *Daily Express*, 28 September 1960   9. *The Economist*, 1 October 1960   10. *The Times, Daily Telegraph*, 14 October 1960   11. *Hansard*, 4 November 1960, 629/517–27, 589–90; *Financial Times*, 1 November 1960   12. *Sunday Express*, 20 November 1960   13. *Hansard*, 4 November 1960, 629/617–20   14. *Hansard*, 16 November 1960, 630/375–8   15. *Hansard*, 19, 20 December 1960, 632/877–8, 1084–7, 1149–1208   16. *Hansard*, 20 December 1960, 632/1084–7, 1149–1208   17. *Daily Herald*, 17 January 1961   18. *Hansard*, 30 January 1961, 633/596–603   19. *Evening Standard*, 7 February 1961   20. *Sunday Telegraph*, 12 February 1961   21. *Time and Tide*, 24 August 1961   22. House of Lords *Report*, 20 July 1961, 233/773–818   23. *The Times*, 26 June 1961   24. *Daily Telegraph*, 24 February 1961   25. *Daily Telegraph, Daily Express, The Times*, 28 February; *Yorkshire Post*, 4 March 1961   26. George Ball, *The Discipline of Power*, Bodley Head, London, 1968, pp. 78–9   27. Arthur M. Schlesinger, Jr, *A Thousand Days*, André Deutsch, London, 1965, pp. 273–82   28. George Ball, op. cit., pp. 80–1   29. *Hansard*, 18 April 1961, 638/971–5   30. *Hansard*, 26 April 1961, 639/406–15   31. *Daily Telegraph*, 1 May 1961   32. *Daily Mail, Guardian, Daily Telegraph*, 11 May 1961   33. *Sunday Times*, 4 June 1961   34. *Hansard*, 17 May 1961, 640/1387–99   35. Arthur M. Schlesinger, op. cit., pp. 299–300   36. *Hansard*, 19 June 1961, 642/21–9, 926–40   37. Kenneth Young, *Sir Alec Douglas Home*, Dent, London, 1970, p. 130   38. *Yorkshire Post*, 1 July; *Daily Telegraph*, 10 July; *Financial Times*, 14 July, 1961   39. *Evening Standard*, 24 October 1961   40. Andrew Roth, op. cit., 1970, p. 260   41. *Yorkshire Post, Financial Times, Daily Herald*, 2 August 1961   42. *Financial Times*, 9 September; *Sunday Times*, 12 September 1961   43. *Daily Express*, 11 October; *Guardian*, 12, 14 October 1961   44. *Hansard*,

R

27 November 1961, 650/30–43; *The Times, Daily Telegraph, Daily Express*, 28 November 1961   45. *Daily Worker, Daily Express*, 13 October 1961 46. *Daily Mirror*, 18 October; *Daily Herald*, 25 October; *Daily Express*, 31 October 1961   47. *Hansard*, 2 November 1961, 648/330–48, 375–81 48. *Hansard*, 5 December 1961, 650/1142–8; *Daily Express*, 6 December 1961   49. *Hansard*, 24 January 1962, 652/193–203   50. *Daily Herald*, 11 January 1962   51. *Guardian*, 23 August 1971   52. *Sunday Pictorial*, 8 August 1962   53. *Hansard*, 7 March 1962, 655/405–16; *Daily Express*, 8 March 1962   54. Arthur M. Schlesinger, op. cit., p. 651   55. Piers Dixon, *Double Diploma*, Hutchinson, London, 1968, pp. 282–3; Alexander Werth, *De Gaulle*, Penguin, 1965, p. 324   56. *The Economist*, 19 May 1962   57. Piers Dixon, op. cit., pp. 282–92   58. *Daily Express*, 10 October 1962   59. *Guardian*, 12 October 1962   60. *Daily Telegraph*, 12 October 1962   61. *Hansard*, 8 November 1962, 666/1288 62. *Hansard*, 7 November 1962, 666/975–1028   63. *Daily Express*, 2 December 1962   64. Piers Dixon, op. cit., pp. 293–8   65. George Ball, op. cit., p. 84; Arthur M. Schlesinger, op. cit., pp. 666–8   66. George Ball, op. cit., p. 81   67. Piers Dixon, op. cit., p. 302   68. *The Times, Guardian* 15 January 1963   69. *Sunday Times*, 29 August 1965

CHAPTER 12   OVERTAKING FROM BEHIND

1. *Sunday Express*, 17 February 1963   2. *Daily Mail*, 6 March 1963 3. *Daily Mail*, 24 May 1963   4. *Hansard*, 20 March 1963, 674/363–4, 8 July 1963, 680/33–5, 864–70   5. *Daily Telegraph*, 21 June 1963 6. *Daily Express*, 1 August 1963   7. *The Times*, 24 September 1963 8. *Daily Express*, 6 September 1963   9. Randolph Churchill, *The Fight for the Tory Leadership*, Heinemann, 1963, p. 57; Lord Butler, op. cit., pp. 238–41   10. *Daily Telegraph*, 9 October 1963   11. Anthony Howard, *The Making of the Prime Minister*, Cape, London, 1965, pp. 64–6 12. *Daily Express*, 10 October 1963   13. *Daily Telegraph*, 10 October 1963 14. *Daily Herald, Guardian*, 16 October 1963   15. *Financial Times*, 12 October 1963   16. TV broadcast quoted *Daily Mail*, 19 October 1963 17. *Daily Worker*, 30 October 1963   18. *Birmingham Post*, 28 October 1963 19. *Observer*, 27 October 1963   20. *Scotsman*, 26 October 1963 21. *The Times*, 2 November 1963   22. *Daily Mail*, 15 November 1963 23. *Financial Times*, 13 March 1964   24. *Hansard*, 10 March 1964, 691/255–76, 284–5; *New Statesman*, 13 March 1964   25. BBC-TV, 20 January 1967 26. *Observer*, 16 January 1966   27. *Daily Express*, 25 April 1964 28. Ronald Butt, *The Power of Parliament*, Constable, London, 1967, pp. 262–9   29. *Hansard*, 6 July 1964, 698/32–64; *The Times, Daily Express*, 7 July 1964   30. *Observer*, 23 August 1964   31. *The Economist*, 10 July 1964   32. *Daily Express*, 9 October 1964   33. *Evening News*, 12 October 1964   34. *Daily Telegraph*, 24 October 1964   35. *Sunday Times*, 25 October 1964   36. *Daily Mail*, 30 October 1964   37. *Sunday Times*, 25 October 1964   38. *Guardian, Daily Mail*, 11 November 1964 39. *The Economist*, 18 September 1965   40. *Daily Telegraph*, 2 January 1965 41. *Daily Telegraph*, 5 February 1965   42. *Daily Mail*, 26 May 1965 43. *Daily Telegraph*, 5 January 1965.   44. *Sunday Times*, 7 February 1965   45. *Guardian*, 23 July 1965   46. *Hansard*, 1 March 1965, 707/1037; *Daily Express*, 2 March 1965   47. Andrew Roth, op. cit., ad nauseam, 1970, p. 322   48. *Observer*, 4 April 1965   49. *Hansard*, 6 April 1965, 710/490–519; *The Times, Guardian, Daily Telegraph, Yorkshire Post*, 7 April 1965   50. *Sunday Times*, 18 July 1965   51. *Observer*, 4 April 1965   52. *Guardian*, 21 May 1965   53. *Spectator*, 23 July 1965   54. *Evening Standard*, 24 May 1965   55. *Sunday Telegraph*, 18 July 1965; Kenneth Young, op. cit.,

pp. 230–1   56. Maudling's school was Merchant Taylors'   57. ibid., p. 232
58. *Sunday Times,* 1 August 1965   59. *Evening News,* 23 July 1965
60. *Observer,* 25 July 1965   61. *The Times,* 26 July 1965   62. *Daily Telegraph,* 26 July 1965   63. *Daily Telegraph, Guardian,* 28 July 1965

CHAPTER 13   THE 'SICILIAN VENDETTA'

1. *Sunday Telegraph,* 7 October 1965   2. *Sunday Times,* 15 August 1965   3. *Sunday Times, Observer,* 22 August 1965   4. *Northern Echo,* 15 September 1971   5. *Daily Express,* 30 August 1965   6. *Press and Journal,* 20 September 1965   7. *The Economist,* 25 September 1965 8. ibid.   9. *Daily Express,* 2 October 1965   10. *The Economist,* 9 October 1965   11. *Sunday Telegraph,* 7 November 1965   12. *The Economist,* 9 October 1965   13. Text of speech, p. 56; *Evening News,* 13 October 1965   14. *Spectator,* 22 October 1965; Andrew Roth, op. cit., 1970, pp. 332–5   15. *Sunday Times,* 17 October 1965   16. *Sunday Telegraph,* 7 November 1965   17. ibid.   18. *Hansard,* 9 November 1965, 720/16–27, 532–41; *Evening Standard,* 9 November, *The Times,* 10 November 1965   19. *Westminster Confidential,* 6 January 1965   20. *Spectator,* 22 October 1965   21. *Sunday Telegraph, Observer,* 14 November 1965 22. *Hansard,* 2 December 1965, 721/1431–2, 1438; *Daily Express,* 3 December 1965   23. *Daily Mail,* 4 December 1965   24. *Daily Express,* 21 December 1965   25. *Observer,* 2 January 1966   26. *Daily Telegraph,* 4 January 1966 27. *Daily Express,* 8 January 1966   28. *The Times,* 15 January 1966 29. *Daily Telegraph,* 18 January 1966   30. *Hansard,* 25 January 1966, 723/42–3   31. *Hansard,* 31 January 1966, 723/692–4; *The Times,* 1 February 1966   32. *Punch,* 1 February 1966, cited *Birmingham Post,* 1 February 1966   33. *The Times,* 18, 19, 22 February 1966 34. *Sunday Times,* 6 March 1966   35. *Sunday Times,* 20 March 1966 36. *Daily Mail,* 23 March 1966   37. *The Times,* 16 March 1966 38. *Sunday Times,* 20 March 1966   39. *Guardian,* 29 March 1966 40. *East Anglia Daily Times,* 25 March 1966   41. Andrew Alexander and Alan Watkins, *The Making of the Prime Minister,* Macdonald, London, 1970, p. 82; *Guardian,* 28 March 1966   42. *The Economist,* 9 April 1966 43. *The Times,* 20 April; *Daily Express,* 23 April 1966   44. David Butler and Michael Tinto-Duschinsky, *The British General Election of 1970,* Macdonald, London, 1971, p. 73   45. *Guardian,* 4 June 1966 46. *Observer,* 5 June 1966   47. *Sunday Express,* 12 June 1966 48. *Sunday Telegraph,* 19 June 1966   49. *Daily Express,* 24 June 1966 50. *Hansard,* 28 June 1966, 730/1591–8; *The Times,* 29 June 1966 51. *Hansard,* 3 November 1966, 735/654–9   52. *Sunday Times,* 29 December 1968   53. *Guardian,* 2 May 1968   54. *The Times,* 19 July 1968 55. *The Economist,* 31 January; *Sunday Telegraph,* 1 February 1970 56. *The Times,* 20 April 1970   57. *The Economist,* 16 May 1970 58. Lord Butler, op. cit., p. 136   59. *Sunday Telegraph,* 29 November 1970   60. *Sunday Express,* 19 May 1970   61. *Observer,* 17 May 1970 62. *Sunday Telegraph,* 24 May 1970   63. *The Times,* 28 May 1970 64. 31 May 1970   65. *Daily Telegraph,* 17 June, 4 November 1970

CHAPTER 14   ATTACKING ON THE RIGHT FLANK

1. *Sunday Times,* 21 June 1970   2. *Daily Telegraph,* 17 June 1970 3. *Hansard,* 7 July 1970, 803/503–13; *The Times,* 8 July 1970   4. *Hansard,* 21 July 1970, 804/240–1   5. *The Times,* 2, 9 September 1970 6. Evening Standard, 9 June 1971   7. *The Times,* 10 July 1970 8. *Daily Telegraph,* 31 August 1970   9. *Northern Echo,* 12 October 1970

10. *Sunday Telegraph,* 13 September 1970   11. *Sunday Times,*
29 November 1970   12. *Observer,* 5 July 1970   13. *Fortune,* April 1971
14. *Evening Standard,* 27 October 1961   15. ibid.   16. *Hansard,* 2
July 1970, 803/76–96   17. *Daily Telegraph,* 22 July 1970   18. *Hansard,*
21 July 1970, 804/235–7   19. *Evening Standard,* 21 January 1972
20. *Guardian,* 5, 9 October 1970   21. *Daily Telegraph,* 13 October 1970
22. *Guardian,* 17 October, *The Times,* 17, 19 October, *Sunday Times,* 18 October
1970   23. *Evening Standard,* 7 June 1971   24. *Sunday Times, Sunday
Telegraph, Observer,* 11 October 1970   25. *Fortune,* April 1971
26. *Hansard,* 27 October 1970, 805/37–75; *The Times, Daily Telegraph,*
28 October 1970   27. *The Times,* 10 November 1970   28. *The Times,
Daily Telegraph,* 10 November 1970   29. *The Times,* 17 November 1970
30. *Hansard,* 17 November 1970, 806/1032; *The Times,* 18 November 1970
31. *The Times, Daily Telegraph,* 6 November 1970   32. *The Economist,*
5 December 1970   33. *Observer,* 6 December 1970   34. Text, 5 December
1970   35. *Guardian,* 7 December 1970   36. *New Statesman,* 8 December
1970   37. Gallup Poll, *Daily Telegraph,* 17 December 1970   38. *Evening
Standard,* 14 November 1970   39. *The Times,* 13, 17, 18 December, *Western
Mail,* 21 December 1970   40. *The Times, Guardian, Daily Telegraph,* 19, 20,
21, 22, 23, 25 January 1971; *Observer, Sunday Times, Sunday Telegraph,*
17, 24 January 1971   41. *The Economist,* 13 February 1971   42. *Sunday
Times,* 7 February 1971, *The Times,* 8 February 1971   43. *The Times,*
8 February 1971

CHAPTER 15   TACKING TOWARDS THE TARGET

1. *Sunday Times,* 20 June 1971   2. Conservative Party *Conference Report,*
October 1971, pp. 126–9   3. *Evening Standard,* 15 October 1971, *Sunday
Times,* 17 October 1971   4. *The Times,* 13 July 1971   5. *The Times,
Daily Telegraph,* 12 October 1971, *Sunday Times,* 24 October 1971
6. Gallup Poll, *Daily Telegraph,* 18 October 1971   7. *Hansard,* 28 October
1971, 823/2202–12   8. *The Times,* 29 October 1971, *Daily Telegraph,*
30 October 1971   9. *The Times, Daily Telegraph,* 4 December 1971
10. *Evening Standard,* 26 November 1971   11. *Guardian,* 18 November 1971
12. *Daily Telegraph,* 24 November 1971   13. *Daily Telegraph,* 18 December
1971   14. *Sunday Telegraph,* 19 December 1971   15. *The Times,
Daily Telegraph,* 10 January 1972   16. *The Times, Daily Telegraph,* 1
January 1972   17 *Evening Standard,* 11 January 1972   18. *The Times,*
25 January 1972 (BBC-TV Panorama, 24 January 1972)   19 *Sunday Times,*
23 January 1972   20. 25 January 1972   21. *Hansard,* 24 January 1972
829/1067; *Daily Mail,* 25 January 1972   22. *Sunday Times, Sunday
Telegraph, Observer,* 20 February 1972   23. *The Times,* 21 February 1972
24. *Sunday Times* Insight team, *Ulster,* Penguin, 1972, pp. 249–50
25. *Sunday Times,* 26 March 1972   26. *Hansard,* 22 May 1972, 897/1008–152

INDEX

Aachen, 170
A-bomb, 166
Abyssinian war, 37
Acheson, Dean, 79
Adams, Vyvyan, 58
Adamson, Jennie, 59
Aden, 150
Adenauer, Dr Konrad, 146, 147, 151
Africa, 95, 215
Alanbrooke, Field-Marshal Viscount, 57, 72
Albany, The, 170, 205
Aldington, Lord (ex Toby Low), 3, 7, 111, 134, 174, 208, 209
Algeria, 126, 149
Alenn, Sir Hugh, 30, 40
Allen, Maurice, 32
Alport, Cuthbert (later Lord), 76
American aid, 67
American loan, 81
Amery, Julian, xiii, 90, 91, 111, 129, 194
Amery, Leo, 28
Amory, Derick Heathcoat (later Lord), 130, 139, 143
Anderson, Patrick, 28, 34
Angola, 156
Anglo-Egyptian agreement, 156
Anglo-French nuclear collaboration, 215
Anstruther-Gray, Sir William (later Lord Kilmany), 184, 186
Antwerp, 43, 48, 49
Arab Legion, 102
Arab skyjackers, 214
Ascot, 141
Ashford, 58
Astor, J. J., 110
Aswan Dam, 104
Attlee, Clement (later Lord), 4, 15, 31, 51–2, 60, 63, 68, 77, 79, 82, 99
Australia, 164, 207, 227

Avon, Lord, see Eden, Sir Anthony
Aylestone, Lord, see Bowden, Herbert
Azores meeting, 228

Bagnall, Nicholas, 61–2
Bahrein, 149, 150, 156, 157
Baldwin, Stanley, xiv, 31
Ball, George, 152, 153, 160, 164, 167, 175, 230
Balliol, ix, x, 11, 14, 26, 28, 29, 30, 32, 72, 170; Choir, 30; Concert, 30; Junior Common Room, 40
Bangladesh, 227, 228
Bank of England, 201
Bank Rate 'leak', 120
Barber, Anthony, x, xiii, 180, 181, 195, 208, 209, 210, 212, 216, 217, 226
Barrow, Lt-Col. Richard, 44
Baxter, Beverley, 64
Bay of Pigs, 153
BBC, 89, 109
BEA, 65
Beadle, Sir Hugh, 197
Beaverbrook, Lord, 79, 122
Beaverbrook press, 8, 172, 177, 201
Beckenham, 68, 85
Beevor, Trevor, 61
Belgium, 160
Bell, Ronald, 31
Benn, Anthony Wedgwood, 81, 234
Bennett, D. C., 50
Berchtesgaden, 38
Bermuda, 115, 116
Bevan, Aneurin, 31, 69, 75, 127, 132
Bevanites, 92
Beveridge, William (later Lord), 140
Bevin, Ernest, x, xiii, 66, 79
Bevins, J. R., x
Bexley, 11, 59, 63, 65, 67, 68, 69,

Bexley—*cont.*
  73, 83, 84, 88, 95, 96, 117, 179, 199, 201; Chamber of Commerce, 74, 88; Conservative Association, 15, 56, 60, 63, 64, 66, 139; Young Conservatives, 122
Bexleyheath Observer, 64
Bexley-Sidcup, 234
Bidault, Georges, 170
Biffen, John, 211
Biggs-Davison, John, 107
Bing, Geoffrey, 81
Birch, Nigel (later Lord Rhyl), 122-3
Bird, James, 20
Birrell, Augustine, 140
Black Rod, 203
Blake, George, 171
Blakenham, Viscount, *see* John Hare
Bleak House, 18
Bligh, Sir Timothy, 59, 180
'Bloody Sunday' (Londonderry), 232
'Blue Streak', 143
BOAC, 65
Board of Trade, 174, 175
Body, Richard, 107
Boodles, 3
Boothby, Lord, 36, 110
Borneo, 195, 196
Bottomley, Arthur, 190
Bowden, Herbert (later Lord Aylestone), 108
Boyd-Carpenter, John (later Lord), 200
Boyle, Sir Edward (later Lord), 3, 88, 109, 110, 155, 174, 176, 180, 188, 190, 203, 206
Boy Scouts, 21, 160, 161
Boys' Own Paper, 13
Bracken, Brendan, 59, 64
Braddock, Mrs Bessie, 72
Bramall, Ashley, 30, 33, 55, 57, 59, 65, 67, 68-9, 83
Brandt, Willy, 223
Brittany, 157
Broadstairs, x, 1, 11, 13, 14, 18, 19, 21, 66, 79

Brook, Sir Norman (later Lord Normanbrook), 127
Brown Brothers, Harriman, 82
Brown, Douglas, 128, 133, 138
Brown, Ernest, 140
Brown, George (later Lord George-Brown), 150, 188, 189, 193
Brown, Shipley, 63, 66, 68, 72, 82, 86, 181, 190
Bryan, Paul, 105
Buchan-Hepburn, Patrick (later Lord Hailes), 78, 80, 85, 86, 88, 90, 94, 97, 100
Bulganin, Marshal, 102
Bushe, Rosemary, 73
Butcher, Sir Henry, 88
Butler, R. A. (later Lord), xii, 94, 100, 101, 103, 105, 106, 109, 110, 112, 113, 115, 123, 124, 130, 131, 132, 138, 143, 146, 157, 160, 163, 169, 171, 172, 173, 174, 176, 178, 179, 192
Butler, Samuel, 85
Buzzard, Sir Anthony, 216

Cabinet, 99, 100, 109, 111, 123, 130, 131, 138, 139, 157, 159, 160, 161, 163, 172, 174, 176, 231-2; Committee on Northern Ireland, 233; Emergency Committee, 231
Callaghan, James, xiii, 181, 182, 183
Cambridge Union, 72
Canada, 82, 104, 160, 164
Canterbury, 79, 216
Carlton Club, 36, 101, 128
Carr, Robert, 134, 210, 213, 218, 226, 232
Carrington, Lord, 5, 7, 207, 209, 210, 213, 233
Carron, William (later Lord), xiii
Carson, Hon. 'Ned', 57, 72, 81, 87, 101
Carvel, Robert, 76, 92, 110, 146
Casey, Neil, 95
Castle, Barbara, 153, 219
Castro, Fidel, 153
Cazalet (-Keir), Thelma, 59
Central African Federation, 95
Central Electricity Generating Board, 231

Ceylon, 165
Chadd, George, 44
Chamberlain, Neville, 31, 36, 37, 38, 87, 144, 219, 230
Chambers, Paul, 180
Champagne, 130
Champness, Lt-Col. G. H., 53, 57
Channon, Sir Henry, 73, 74
Charlemagne Prize, 170
Charles, H.R.H. Prince, 65
Chataway, Christopher, 195, 213
Chatham House School, 22, 25, 26
Chequers, 4, 13, 117, 124, 166, 169, 214, 215, 226, 233
Cherwell, Lord, 31
Chetwynd, George, 175
Chichester-Clark, James (later Lord Moyola), 233
China, 149, 224, 226
Chislehurst, 64, 69
Chou En-lai, 227
Church of England, 216
Church Times, 61, 73, 76
Churchill, Lord Randolph, ix
Churchill, Randolph, 59, 101
Churchill, Sir Winston, ix, xi, xii, xv, 4, 5, 15, 18, 31, 36, 44, 52, 72, 78, 80, 85, 86, 87, 88, 90, 91, 92, 94, 97, 99, 111, 115, 123, 140
Churchill II, Winston, 178
CIA, 104, 153
Civil Aviation, Ministry of, 61
Clark, William, 109
Clark, William, MP, xiii, 181, 184
Clifton-Brown, Anthony, 86
Clifton-Brown, Douglas, 71
Coal and Steel Community, 230
Cole, G. D. H., 31
'Comme Chez Soi', 13, 160
Common Market, see EEC
Commonwealth, 160, 163, 164, 165, 220; Prime Ministers' Conferences, 164, 220
Communists, 142, 159
'Concorde', 227
Congo, 160
Coningsby Club, 57, 64
Connally, John, 224
Conservative Central Office, 12, 64
Conservative Party, xiii, xv, 129

Conservative Political Centre, 75, 77, 85, 140, 203
Consultative Assembly, 148
Cook & Sons, Thomas, 218
Corfield, Sir Frederick, 103
Council of Europe, 148
Cousins, Frank, xiii, 190
Covent Garden, 13, 88, 230
Crayford, 19, 20
Cripps, Sir Stafford, 66
Crist, George, 136
'Cross-Bencher', 146
Crossman, R. H. S., 31
Cuba, 5, 153
Curzon, Cecil, 23, 24, 25, 27
Cyprus, 94, 157, 195
Czechoslovakia, 37, 38, 66

Daily Express, 13, 25, 151, 195, 207
Daily Herald, 161
Daily Mail, 153, 185
Daily Mirror, 95, 144
Daily Telegraph, 99, 118, 173, 227
Daily Worker (later Morning Star), 142
Dalton, Hugh (later Lord), 35, 67
Daly, Lawrence, 232
Danzig, 41
Davies, Ivor, 38
Davies, John, 212, 217, 231, 234
Day, Robin, 196
Deedes, William, 58
de Gaulle, Charles, xi, 126, 127, 143, 146, 151, 153, 156, 161, 162, 166, 167, 168, 169, 170, 194, 198, 202, 219
de Grasse, 127
de Havilland, Olivia, 161
Delacourt-Smith, Lord (ex C. P. G. Smith), 35
Dell, Edmund, 234
del Vayo, Alvarez, 37
de Murville, Couve, 157, 163, 164, 166
Denman, Teddy, 3
Devaluation, 66
Devonshire, Duke of, 114, 148
Diamond, John (later Lord), 119
Dickens, Charles, 18
Dillon, Douglas, 148, 160

Dines, Edward, 59–60, 63
Director, 139
Directors, Institute of, 226
Disraeli, Benjamin, xiv–xv, 4, 71
Dixon, Sir Pierson, 158, 159, 162, 163, 167, 170
Dock Workers (Pensions) Bill, 141
Dockers' strike threat, 212
Douglas-Home, Sir Alec (ex Lord Home), xii, 12, 13, 15, 144, 146, 150, 151, 154, 157, 159, 169, 171, 173, 174, 178, 179, 181, 182, 183, 184, 186, 188, 190, 191, 197, 203, 210, 215, 220, 229, 233
Douglas-Home, Lady Elizabeth, 180, 186, 192
Dresden, 41
Drumalbyn, Lord (ex Niall Macpherson), 175
duCann, Edward, 175, 176, 183, 188, 196, 197, 200, 203, 211
Dulles, John Foster, 104, 126
Duncan, James, 59
Dustmen, 213

Ealing South by-election, 125
Economist, The, 82, 103, 108, 110, 111, 139, 144, 148, 151, 184, 185, 189, 191, 200, 207
Ede, Chuter, 74
Edelman, Maurice, 202
Eden, Sir Anthony (later Lord Avon), xi, 15, 28, 36, 90, 91, 94, 96, 97, 100, 101, 102, 103, 104 105, 108, 110, 111, 112, 113, 115, 144
Eden, Guy, 92
Eden, Sir John, 4, 224, 225
Edwards, Robert ('Richard Strong'), 101
EEC, xii, 5, 118, 146, 155, 156, 157, 165, 167, 203, 229–30
EFTA, 147, 157, 160, 165, 167
Egmont Palace, 231
Egypt, 90, 94, 104, 105, 106, 149
Eire, 233
Eisenhower, Dwight, ix, 90, 91, 104, 114, 116, 119, 121, 126, 127, 143
Electricity strike threat, 218

Elizabeth II, H.M. Queen, 93, 112, 113, 174
Elliot, Katherine (later Baroness), 125
Emery, Peter, xiii, 181, 185, 211
Encounter, 196
'English disease', 14
Erroll, Frederick (later Lord), 155, 174, 176
Eton, ix, 35, 71, 72
Euratom, 230
European Payments Union, 119
Evans, Marian Easton, 60, 72, 79, 83, 93
Evening News, 185
Evening Standard, 101, 138
Ezra, Derek, 231

Fairlie, Henry, x, 131, 150
Fascists, British Union of, 25, 205
Faulds, Andrew, 234
Faulkner, Brian, 233
Feather, Victor, 135, 212
Federation of University Conservative Associations, 58
Feisal, King, 104
Finance Bill, 183
Fitt, Gerry, 233
Fleet Street Column Club, 136
Fontaine, Joan, 9, 155
Foot, Sir Dingle, 121
Foot, Michael, x
France, 77, 78, 119, 126, 151, 152, 160, 202, 223
Franco, General, 33, 34
Fraser, Hugh, 28, 33, 42, 129, 211
Fraser, Sir R. Michael, 45, 58, 88, 203
Free Trade Area, 118, 126
Fulbright, Senator, 201
Fulham East, 58
Fulton, John (later Lord), 29, 32, 40
Fyfe, Alan, 35

Gaitskell, Hugh, 104, 105, 106, 108, 109, 111, 121, 127, 130, 132, 144, 165, 199
Gale, George, 178
Gallacher, William, 31

Gallup Poll, 99, 121, 125, 128, 173, 190, 207
Gandhi, Indira, 227
George VI, King, 71
Germany, 66, 77, 78, 79, 119, 152, 160
GKN-Sankey strike, 213
Glubb, Sir John (Glubb Pasha), 102
Glyndebourne, 12, 13, 155
Godkin lecture, 205, 215
Goertz, Dr Hermann, 25
Gonzi, Archbishop, of Malta, 229
Goodman, Lord, 26
Gormley, Joe, 231-2
Gower Report, 142
Grant, Ulysses S., xv
Gravesend Conservative Association, 101
Gray's Inn, 46
Greene, Hugh Carleton, 41
Greenwood, Anthony (later Lord), 124
Greig, Gordon, 198
Griffiths, James, 127
Grimond, Jo, 197
Guardian, 148, 234
Guildhall, 217
Guinness, 73

Hailsham, Lord (Quintin Hogg), ix, 28, 38, 112, 119, 120, 129, 130, 169, 171, 172, 173, 175, 176, 182, 192, 204, 210
Hall, Dr D. H., 89
Hall, John, xiii, 181
Hall, Viscount, 208, 213
Hallstein, Dr Walter, 169
Hampstead Garden Suburb, 12
Hanging, 100
Hare, John (later Viscount Blakenham), 17, 162, 178
Harriman, Averell, 151
Harrington, Major William, 43-53, 87-8
Harris Poll, 207
Harrison, Eric, 60
Harrison, Sir Harwood, 117
Harrod, Roy, 38
Harrow, ix, 72

Hart, Doris, 69
Hartnell, Norman, 140
Harvey, Clare Mayhew, 61
Harvey, Ian, 31, 32, 51, 57, 59, 61, 67, 110, 128-9
Hastings, Sir Patrick, 60
Hayes, Frank, 45
Hayhoe, Barney, 120
H-bomb, 94, 120, 122
Healey, Denis, 29, 31, 159, 202
Heath: family, 2, 56; Mrs Doris, 93; Edith Annie, 10, 18, 19, 20, 26, 27, 67, 79, 83; John, 19, 20, 43-4, 56, 72, 79, 83, 93; Stephen, 19; William, 10, 13, 19, 20, 21, 22, 25, 39, 83, 93
Heavy Anti-Aircraft Regiment, 107th, 11, 43, 87
Heenan, Cardinal, 216
Hinchingbrooke, Viscount (later Victor Montagu), 121
Hitler, Adolf, 7, 33, 38
Hobson, Sir John, 171
Hogg, Quintin, see Lord Hailsham
Holt, Martin, 63, 68
Holy Loch, 143
Home, Lord, see Sir Alec Douglas-Home
Honourable Artillery Company, x, 3, 13, 53, 58, 68, 82, 214
Hornsey by-election, 117
Hornsby-Smith, Dame Patricia, 64, 69-70, 234
Horobin, Sir Ian, 111
Howard, Anthony, 31
Howard, John, 132, 133, 134, 135, 169
Howell, David, 188
Huddersfield Town F.C., 12
Huggins, Sir Godfrey (Lord Malvern), 95
Hughes-Young, Michael, 105
Hull North by-election, 198
Hussein, King, 102
Hutchinson, George, 26
Hyde, James, 50, 51

India, 68, 119, 165, 195, 227
Indonesia, 68, 196
Indo-Pakistan conflict, 227

Industrial Reconstruction Corporation, 218
Industrial Relations Act, 198, 218, 221
Industrial Welfare Society, 141
Industry Bill/Act, 234
Inland Revenue, xiii
Institute of Directors, 218
International Brigade, 40
International Labour Office, 141
Ipswich by-election, 121
IRA, 233–4
Iran, 83
Iraq, 127
Irwin, Jack, 82
Isaacs, George, 140
Isis, 28–40
Israel, 127, 214
Isserlis, David, 213
ITV, 89

James, Robert Rhodes, xiv
Jay, Douglas, 178
Jenkins, Arthur, 38, 52
Jenkins, Roy, 1, 38, 52, 156, 181, 218, 226
Jennings, Arnold, 54
Job, Charles, 69
Johnson, Lyndon B., 201
Jones, Jack, 211
Jordan, 102, 127
Joseph, Sir Keith, 134, 176, 188, 226
'July massacre', 163
Jung, Karl, 10

Kaiser, Philip, 7, 36, 87, 164
Kaunda, Kenneth, 216, 220
Keeler, Christine, 170
Kelvingrove by-election, 125
Kennedy, John, 5, 15, 147, 148, 151, 153, 154, 156, 162, 166
Kennedy, Ludovic, 123
Kenya, 95
Kenya Asians, 204
Kerby, Henry, 102
Kerruish, J. R. J., 38
Kershaw, Anthony, 185
Keynes, Maynard (Lord), xv
Key West, 153, 156

Khaled, Leila, 214
Kilmuir, Lord (ex Sir David Maxwell-Fyfe), 112, 113
'Kim', 50
King Edward VII Hospital for Officers, 129, 173
Kipling, Rudyard, 50
Kirk, Peter, 98, 101, 110, 202
Kisch, Royalton, 26
Kissinger, Dr Henry, 221, 224, 227
Kleinwort, Benson, 180
Knight, Victor, 92
Korea, 78, 79
Krogers, the, 171
Krushchev, Nikita, 102, 143, 144, 150, 153, 159, 171

Ladbrokes, 181
Lambton, Anthony (ex Lord), 150, 185
Laos, 5, 153, 155, 156
Laye, Evelyn, 140
Lebanon, 126
Lee, Sir Frank, 147, 151, 152
Lee, Jennie, 69
Legge-Bourke, Sir Henry, 78, 94
Leipzig, 41
Lennox-Boyd, Alan (later Viscount Boyd), 124
Lever, Harold, 188
Levin, Bernard, 150
Liberal Party, xv
Lincoln, Abraham, xv
Lindsay, A. D. (later Lord), x, 27, 28, 32, 38, 39, 40
Lipton, Marcus, 135
Liverpool, 12
Llandudno conference, 64, 164
Lloyd, Selwyn, 97, 102, 105, 111, 114, 116, 121, 123, 143, 144, 149, 154, 157, 163, 173, 176, 180, 192, 197, 200
Lloyd-George, Gwilym (Viscount Tenby), 114
Local Employment Bill, 135
Locke, Miss Grace, 21
Lockheed 'TriStar', 221
Lockwood, John C., 59
London School of Economics, 15
London Symphony Orchestra, 226

London University General Schools (LUGS), 23
Londonderry, 232
Longden, Gilbert: 76, 86, 134
Lonsdale, Gordon, 171
Lords (cricket ground), 141
Lords, House of, 65
Lothian, Lord, 42
Lovat, Lord, 42
Luns, Dr Joseph, 229
Lympany, Moura, 9, 13, 14, 155
Lynch, James, 233

MacArthur, General, 68
Mackeson, Brigadier Harry, 80, 88
Macleod, Iain, xiii, 58, 76, 77, 95, 123, 130, 133, 134, 135, 140, 169, 171, 172, 173, 174, 180, 181, 188, 198, 204, 206, 209, 210, 212
Macmillan, Lady Dorothy, 166, 213
Macmillan, Harold, xi, xii, xiv, 4, 5, 13, 15, 16, 28, 36, 38, 78, 95, 97, 99, 109, 110, 112–32, 137, 142, 143, 146, 148, 151, 153, 154, 156, 157, 158, 162, 163, 169, 171, 172, 174, 188
Macmillan, Maurice, 28
Maddan, Martin, 105
Maintenance Orders Bill, 124
Maitland, Patrick (Earl Laudersdale), 207
Makarios, Archbishop, 102, 116, 157
Malaysia, 195
Malbert, David, 185
Malta, 228–9
Manorbier, 45
Manston Field, 25
Margach, James, 110
Margaret, H.R.H. Princess, 140, 170
Margate, 44
Marks, Derek, 92
Marlborough, Duke of, ix
Marlowe, Anthony, 60
Marlowe, Mrs Patricia, 60
Marplan, 207
Marples, Ernest, x
Marten, Neil, 184

Martin, Sir Alec, 26
Masefield, Sir Peter, 57
Master Gunner, 82, 95
Mau Mau, 95
Maude, Angus, 76, 77, 110, 196, 211
Maudling, Reginald, 58, 118, 119, 133, 134, 135, 152, 154, 158, 169, 171, 173, 174, 176, 178, 179, 180, 181, 182, 184, 185, 186, 188, 193, 198, 199, 203, 210, 216, 233
Maxwell-Fyfe, Sir David (later Lord Kilmuir), 64
Mayhew, Christopher, x, 33, 38, 57, 61
McAlister, 'Ted', 178
McAlpine family, 18
McGregor, John, 188, 195
Medlicott, Sir Frank, 110
Mellish, Robert, 117
Menuhin, Hepzibah, 170
Menuhin, Yehudi, 155, 170
Merrett-Sykes proposals, 191
Mersey Docks and Harbour Board, 218
Metropole Hotel, Brighton, 225
Metropole Hotel, Brussels, 159, 167, 230
Middle East, 102, 126, 193
Mills, Lord, 117
Minney, R. J., 96
Mintoff, Dom, 228–9
Mitford, Unity, 25
Molotov–Ribbentrop pact, 41
Monckton, Sir Walter (later Lord), xvii, 17, 139, 140
Monday Club, 190
Montgomery, Field-Marshal Lord, xv–xvi, 48, 49, 50, 211, 214
More, Jasper, 225
Morning Cloud, 7, 8, 13, 17
Morning Star, 7
Morris, Charles (later Lord), 29, 32
Morrison, Herbert (later Lord), 82 83
Morrison, John (later Lord Margadale), 171, 173
Moseley, Sir Oswald, 25
Moss Bros, 29
Mozambique, 195, 216

MPs' pay, 93–4
Munich pact, 38
Music, 4, 7, 21, 24, 25, 30, 155, 170, 226
Mussolini, Benito, 33

Nabarro, Sir Gerald, 78, 102, 117, 183
Napoleon, 149
Nasser, Gamal Abdel, 95, 102, 104, 105, 106, 126, 127
National Coal Board, 102, 103, 218
National Joint Advisory Council, 134, 141, 142
National Union of Conservative Associations, 67
National Union of Miners, 230
NATO, 90, 121
Negrin, Dr Juan, 37
News Chronicle, 128, 138
New Zealand, 161, 164
Nicolson, Sir Harold, 107
Nicolson, Nigel, 107, 109, 110
Nijmegen, 49
1922 Committee, 94, 130, 184, 185, 194, 205, 212
Nixon, Richard, 148, 215, 219, 221, 224, 227, 229
Norman, H. C., 22, 27
Normandy, 48
Northern Ireland, 16, 212, 213, 232
Norway, 229
Nuffield Foundation, 142, 182
Nuremberg rally, 34
Nutting, Sir Anthony, 99, 108, 110
Nyerere, Julius, 215, 220

Oakshott, Prof. Michael, 15
Obote, Milton, 220
O'Brien, Sir Leslie, 216
O'Brien, Sir Tom, 134
Observer, 88, 125, 171
Oman, 119
'One Nation Group', 4, 76–7, 86, 134, 180, 211
Ormsby-Gore, David (later Lord Harlech), 153
Osborn, John, 176
Osborne, Sir Cyril, 72, 181

Osborne, Franz, 155
Osborne, June, 155
Oxford Union, ix, 13, 25, 28, 29, 30, 31, 41, 72, 129
Oxford University, 11, 28–42; Conservative Association, 28, 31, 34, 36, 37, 39, 129; Orchestra, 30

Pakistan, 165, 195, 227
Pannell, Charles, 135, 161
'Panorama', 217, 230
Pantony family, 2; 'Old Stump', 18; Mrs, 19; Grandma, 19; William, 24
Paris–Match, 199
Parkin, Ben, 117
Partridge, John, 212
Patrick, Jo, 213
Patton, General, 211
Payment of Wages Bill/Act, 139
Pearce Commission (on Rhodesia), 229
Pearson Report, 212
Persian Gulf, 196, 215
PEST (Pressure for Economic and Social Toryism), 180
Peyton, John, 218
Philby, Harold, 171
Pinay, Antoine, 126
Pittsburgh University, 42
'Polaris', missiles and submarines, 143, 169, 199
Policy Advisory Committee, 179
Pollitt, Harry, 31
Pompidou, Georges, 162, 208, 219, 224, 227–8
Poole, Lord (ex Oliver): 113, 178
Port Said, 109
Portugal, 157
Post Office strike, 16, 220–1
Powell, J. Enoch, 58, 76, 77, 78, 113, 122, 133, 134, 169, 171, 173, 174, 180, 185, 186, 188, 192, 193, 199, 200, 202, 203, 204, 205, 211
Price, David, 98, 110, 175
Prices and Incomes Bill, 203
Prices and Incomes Board, 218
Prior, James, 211, 226
Profumo, John, 129, 147, 170–1

'Putting Britain Right Ahead', 191
Pye, Reginald, 3, 68, 74, 76, 96, 103, 139
Pym, Francis, 225, 226

Queen Mary, 83

Race Relations Bill/Act, 205
Raeburn, Ashley, 57
Rahman, Shaikh Mujibur, 228
Railway strike threat (1960), 138–9; (1972), 17
Ramsgate, 13, 19
Raphael's 'Sistine Madonna', 41
Raven, Kay, 11, 26, 58, 61
Redmayne, Martin (later Lord), 104, 113, 171, 177
Reeve, Captain, 45
Reflation, 223
Renshaw, Keith, 183
Rent Bill/Act, 109, 117, 125
Resale Price Maintenance (RPM), 5, 176, 177
Reuters, 158
Rhodes Scholars, 82
Rhodesia, 95, 190, 191, 192, 193–4, 195, 197, 198, 200, 201, 217, 229
Ricci, Nina, 9
Ridley, Nicholas, 4, 180, 224
Rippon, Geoffrey, x, 103, 134, 200, 210, 220, 230
Robens, Alfred (later Lord), 134
Rochdale by-election, 123
Rodgers, John, 59, 76, 79, 103
Roll, Sir Eric, 158, 159, 167, 170, 188
Rolls-Royce, 16, 218, 221
Rome, Treaty of, 118, 148, 167, 194, 230
Rommel, Field-Marshal, xvi
Rosenberg, Dr Alfred, 34, 52
Rothschild, Lord, 212
Roxburgh by-election, 183
Royal Artillery, 44
RPM, *see* Resale Price Maintenance
Rugby, 34
Russia, *see* USSR

Sackville-West, Victoria, 107

St Helena, 149
St Helen's by-election, 125
St James's Palace, 155
St Peter's, 21
St Stephen's, 157
Salisbury, 207
Salisbury, Lord, 112, 113, 115, 116, 144, 190, 191, 194
Sandys, Duncan, xi, xii, 36, 115, 119, 147, 152, 197, 200
Saunders, Major John, 48
Scamp, Sir Jack, 217
Scanlon, Hugh, xiii
Schuman Plan, 77, 78, 79
Schumann, Maurice, 227
Scotland, 16, 142
SDLP, 233
Seligman, Madron, 1, 7, 9, 34, 35, 39, 41, 58, 68, 106, 119, 158, 188
Selsdown Park conference, 16, 206
SET (Selective Employment Tax), 201
Sevenoaks, 59
Seychelles, 116
Shackleton, Edward (later Lord), 82
Shinwell, Emanuel (later Lord), 83, 162, 203
Shrapnel, Norman, 148
Shrivenham, 44
Silverman, Sydney, 100, 106, 181
Singapore, 150, 220
Ski Club of Great Britain, 35
Skinner, Dennis, 13
'Skybolt', 143, 199
Slater, Lt-Col. Frederick, 45, 47, 48, 51
Smith, Ian, 190, 192, 194, 197, 198, 229
Soames, Christopher, 147, 160, 167, 215
Soref, Harold, 34
South Africa, 16, 143, 207, 215
Southeast Asia, 193, 196, 215
Southern Africa, 229
Soviet Union, *see* USSR
Spanish civil war, 33, 38
Spearman, Sir Alec, 108
Special Branch, 205, 226
Spectator, 196

Spencer-Churchill, Baroness, 9, 178

'Springboks', 207

Sputniks, 121

Stacpole, 'Stackie', 76

Stassen, Harold, 120

Steel, David, 183

Steinway, 170, 214

Stewart, William, 64, 70

Stokes, John, 34

Stonehouse, John, 149, 176

Stormont, 16, 233

Strachey, John, 81

Street, Peter, 42

Strikes, 189

Stuart, James, 100

Stuart, Joan, 11, 26, 46, 61

Studholme, Sir Henry, 92

Sudan, 90

Suez Canal, 89, 90; Company, 104; crisis, 98–117; Zone base, 95

Suez Group/Suez Rebels, 89, 90, 91, 94, 102, 111, 116, 117, 121, 124

Sunday Citizen, 187

Sunday Express, 146, 170, 183, 201

Sunday Telegraph, 196, 227

Sunday Times, 145, 180, 185, 207

'Swan Lake', 12

Swinton, Lord, ix, xii, 5, 80, 88, 178, 189

Swinton College, 15

Taiwan, 149

Tashkent, 195

Tatham, Arthur, 24

Taylor, Edward, 226

Taylor, Mrs, 18

Territorials, 43, 57, 82

Texas Company, 103

Thailand, 153

Thatcher, Mrs Margaret, x, xiii, 206, 213

Thomas, Peter, 133, 135, 140, 211

Thompson, T. F., 130

'Thor' missile, 115, 116

Thorndike, Dame Sybil, 140

Thorneycroft, Peter (later Lord), xiv, 86, 118, 119, 122–3, 147, 152, 158, 181, 185

Times, The, 144, 150, 185, 199, 221, 234

Tixier-Vignancour, M., 202

Todd, Garfield, 229

Tonbridge by-election, 103

Toynbee, Philip, 30, 33

Treasury, xii, xiii, xiv, 109, 142

Treaty of Accession, 229

Trethowan, Ian, 7, 200

Trevisick, John, 61

Trinidad Oil, 103

Trudeau, Pierre, 220

Tshekedi Kama, 82

TUC (Trades Union Congress), 138, 141

Tyne-Tees Television, 187

Tyrrell, Lt-Col. J. G., 53–4

UCS (Upper Clyde Shipbuilders), 16

United Nations, 105

USA, 79–80, 82, 87, 90, 91, 156, 201, 219, 224, 234

USSR, 66, 78, 121, 122, 130, 159, 171, 219, 234

U-2, 143

Vassall, William, 171

Vatican, xiv

Vaughan-Morgan, Sir John (later Lord Reigate), 177

V-bombers, 143

Veeraswamy's, 64

Vestey family, 18

Vickers aircraft factory, 19

Victoria Falls, 95

Vienna, 157

Vietnam, 153, 195, 196, 199, 201, 202, 219

Wales, 16

Walker, Patrick Gordon, 38, 82

Walker, Peter, x, xiii, 185, 200, 210, 218, 226

Walker-Smith, Sir Derek, 69, 71, 109, 110, 119

Wall Street Journal, 82

Ward, Dame Irene, 9

Warsaw, 41
Watkins, Alan, xv
Watson, Tom, 82
Wehrmacht, 43, 49
Weigall, Anthony, 24
Weigall, FitzRoy, 56
Wellstead, Jack, 45
West Indies, 152, 161
Weston-super-Mare   by-election,
    125
WEU, 151
Whips and Whips' Office, 80, 81,
    85, 86, 90, 91, 92, 140–1
Whisky, 130
Whitelaw, William, 7, 8, 15, 182,
    193, 206, 209, 210, 213, 219,
    225, 226, 233
Whittaker, Mrs Gladys, 60
Whittell, Ronald, 25
Wickens, Mrs Emily, 19, 23
Wigg, George (later Lord), 182,
    183
Wilberforce, Lord, 231–2
Williamson, Sir Tom (later Lord),
    134
Wilson, Sir Arnold, 38

Wilson, Harold, xv, 3, 4, 12, 15, 16,
    57, 120, 176, 179, 180, 182, 183,
    187, 188, 190, 191, 192, 194, 195,
    197, 198–9, 201, 208, 219, 230
Winchester, 72
Wood, Alan, 36, 37
Wood, David, xii, 199, 221
Woodcock, George, 135
Woolf, Dr E. A., 27
Woolton, Lord, 57, 64–5, 85
Woolwich Arsenal, 59
Woolwich West, 64, 70
Worsthorne, Peregrine, 150

Yates, William, 106, 149
Yorkshire, 12
Yorkshire Post, 148
Young Conservatives, 15, 122, 144

Zambesi, 95
Zambia, 95, 194
Zeppelin raids, 19
Z-reserves, 81
Zuckerman, Sir Solly (later Lord),
    179
'Zurich, Gnomes of', 189

I₁